RESISTING STRUCTURAL EVIL

LOVE AS ECOLOGICAL-ECONOMIC VOCATION

CYNTHIA D. MOE-LOBEDA

Fortress Press
Minneapolis

RESISTING STRUCTURAL EVIL

Love as Ecological-Economic Vocation

Cover image: Kristen Gilje

Cover design: Justin Korhonen

Library of Congress Cataloging-in-Publication Data is available

Print ISBN 978-1-4514-6267-8

eBook ISBN 978-1-4514-2639-7

The paper used in this publication meets the minimum requirements of American National Standard for Information Sciences—Permanence of Paper for Printed Library Materials, ANSI Z329.48-1984.

Manufactured in the U.S.A.

This book was produced using PressBooks.com, and PDF rendering was done by PrinceXML.

RESISTING STRUCTURAL EVIL

CONTENTS

Endorsements

"This is a grand prophetic book motivated by love and focused on justice—social justice, ecological justice, and dignity for 'the least of these.' Don't miss it!"
—Cornel West

♦

"Cynthia Moe-Lobeda's *Resisting Structural Evil: Love as Ecological and Economic Transformation* takes the form of a powerful contribution to Christian ethics, but in fact it is also a major contribution to anyone in any religious or spiritual tradition who seeks to maintain both a commitment to God and to global healing and transformation. Easily accessible and charming in presentation, deep in its ability to confront difficult issues squarely and in a nuanced way, courageous in insisting that we see reality not only as it is but as it could be if we were willing to be 'unrealistic' for a few moments, manifesting daring of thought combined with a pervasive humility—this is a true classic of spiritual progressive consciousness, packed full of ideas that should be taught in every college and university and religious seminary, every church, synagogue, mosque, and ashram!"
—Rabbi Michael Lerner, editor, *Tikkun Magazine*; chair, The Network of Spiritual Progressives

♦

"Moe-Lobeda provides a powerful resource for those who want to understand and face structural evil by exploring ways to resist and dismantle it. Written in clear and lucid prose, she provides us a compelling and at times moving testament that we matter in the work for justice and sustainable relationships between humans and the earth. This is an invitation to embrace a future in which we live in ways so that abundant life is available for all and the world no longer groans from the violence we visit upon it. Moe-Lobeda's deep and grounded spirituality moves us away from the fresh hell of human and ecological violence to the abiding hope that we can and must make a difference by changing the ways we live in God's good creation."
—Emilie Townes, Andrew W. Mellon Professor of African American Religion and Theology, Yale University

♦

"This book is a gift to all . . . consumers looking for a way out of their addiction. Those of us (myself included) who know our excessive consumption is causing ecological and economic disasters should read Professor Moe-Lobeda's new book. It is the best one-volume analysis of our moral dilemma I know of and, even better, it suggests principles and practices to help deal with it."

—Sallie McFague, E. Rhodes and Leona B. Carpenter Professor of Theology Emerita, Vanderbilt University, and Distinguished Theologian in Residence, Vancouver School of Theology

◆

"The vast majority of the writing and speaking that surrounds us in the newspapers, magazines, books, radio, television, and university classrooms and lecture halls takes for granted the basic structures and practices of the present world order, despite their rendering billions of people destitute and the planet uninhabitable. The best of it, for the most part, tells us how to moderate the evils of the system without redirecting it. A very small part deals with the system as a whole and its unthinkable consequences. Within that part still less combines unflinching realism with a convincing gospel of hope. This book is a shining example of this tiny body of writing that responds wisely and well to what is incomparably the most important need of our time. May it initiate, at least among Christians, the widespread *metanoia* apart from which the world will not survive."

—John Cobb, Ingraham Professor of Theology, Emeritus, Claremont Graduate School

◆

"This book is about the moral oblivion that hides the structural sins that we commit via the built-in economic exploitation of other people and of God's good but finite Creation. Attention is given to the spiritual sources of love, courage, and discernment needed to challenge the overwhelming present force of economistic idolatry. Christians should especially welcome this book, but others will also find it valuable."

—Herman Daly, former senior economist, Environmental Department, World Bank; professor emeritus, University of Maryland, School of Public Policy

◆

"This is great. . . . We badly need new doors into the greatest set of problems humans have ever faced. This prayerful amalgamation of deep concern for social justice and a healthy mystic sense of what might inspire it—it's a blend that could provide great help."

—Bill McKibben, leading American environmentalist, author, journalist, and Schumann Distinguished Scholar-in-Residence at Middlebury College

♦

"With a holy impatience, Cynthia Moe-Lobeda joins Jesus and the prophets of Israel by doing biblically based, analytically tough shock therapy on the corporate powers that are wrecking our earth, exploiting the poor, and blinding our eyes. It is a wake-up call to somnambulant Christians. This book is theopolitical dynamite!"

—Daniel Maguire, professor of ethics, Marquette University

♦

"At a time when religious morality seems narrowly focused on personal behaviors, Cynthia Moe-Lobeda reminds us that the biggest sins of all are those we do not readily see in our daily lives. Through powerful stories of suffering and exploited people around the globe, and a clear analysis of the institutional and economic sources of injustice, she calls our attention to the ways by which our lifestyles, without our seeing it, lead to death and misery far from our shores. She asks us to understand that loving our neighbor requires far more than personal charity and goodwill; in fact, it requires a fundamental change in our hearts and our society. But though it challenges us profoundly as people of faith, this book is no grim jeremiad; it offers profound hope, vision, and ideas for remaking our world in justice while becoming more contented ourselves. It should be required reading for Bible study groups and all who care about the impact of their lives in the wider world."

—John de Graaf, film-maker

♦

"Cynthia Moe-Lobeda's book is one of the strongest statements yet to be made on the intricate connections between ecology and justice. The powerful stories and persuasive arguments lay the groundwork for the necessary transformations ahead. It will be a catalyst for change!"

—Mary Evelyn Tucker, co-director of Forum on Religion and Ecology, Yale University

Foreword

Larry Rasmussen

This signal volume ends with four questions. They test its viability as an ambitious work in Christian ethics:

- Does it speak truth about life on Earth, demystifying what is hidden from view by the blinders of power and privilege?
- Does it seek faithfully to know more fully the God revealed in—but not only in—Jesus Christ?
- Does it move people to align themselves with justice-seeking, Earth-honoring, self-respecting neighbor love?
- Does it wed moral vision with pragmatic steps toward that vision?

Exacting, demanding, far-reaching questions. And the answer is "Yes."

That would seem accomplishment enough. But there is more. The questions are provoked by the greatest collective human challenge posed to date. Namely, how, on a hot, flat, changing, and crowded planet (seven—moving toward nine—billion of us, competing with the rest of the community of life) do we move from industrial-technological civilization to ecological civilization? How do we accomplish a durable future for the children, all the children, human and other-than-human? How do we do so as an unknown geological age, the Anthropocene, intrudes upon the age that has hosted all human civilizations and religions to date, the Holocene? And how do we do so when the global human economy of corporate capitalism collides with the very economy it is wholly dependent upon; namely, the economy of nature? How, to remember Jesus, do we fashion new wineskins (Luke 5:36-39), when all the forces say "The old is good" (Luke 5:39) and seek to get the very economy back on track that generates climate change and inaugurates the Anthropocene, the same economy that buries power and privilege so subtly in a way of life that it seems not only routine but the way things ought to be?

This is the world, and the necessary civilizational transition, that Cynthia Moe-Lobeda interrogates with relentless honesty and unflinching compassion; yes, with love. Fortunately, the result goes well beyond most treatises of our dilemmas and dead-ends. Hers is neither a jeremiad nor a facile program of voluntary individual lifestyle changes and upgrades (all of us driving Toyota

Priuses to Home Depot or Lowe's). Rather, she leads the reader to see the systemic evil of colossal structures that will only be changed as we are also changed. Transformation by another name, of both ourselves and the systems we live by.

And how is that done? Only by forces with the tenacity and strength of genuine faith in the possibility of a different way of life, this one attuned to all life and its parental, generative elements—earth (soil), air, fire (energy), and water. In short, attuned to creation and its claims upon our lives.

My response to the author and the book is gratitude. The times ahead will be neither comfortable nor easy. They are not for the faint of heart. Yet gratitude is the fitting response for a work in which the right questions and the right analysis are brought to the challenge we and future generations face: creating new wineskins for the new wine of a tough, new planet.

Larry Rasmussen
Reinhold Niebuhr Professor Emeritus of Social Ethics
Union Theological Seminary, New York City

Acknowledgments

One does nothing alone.

I acknowledge first the beauty and healing power of the Earth and especially the sensation of breezes on my flesh during my morning jogs and the glorious colors that welcome me to the new day. They feed my spirit. Secondly, I thank my ancestors for passing on to me the gift of life and the knowledge that comes from them to me and to my children in ways that I do not fully comprehend.

This book would not exist were it not for the many people who have shared with me their stories of life on the "underside" of advanced global capitalism—that is, the exploitation they have experienced and the courageous tenacious struggles for life that they have maintained. To them I am accountable. May this book be one small way of honoring their lives, integrity, and struggles.

I am immeasurably grateful to many friends and colleagues who make life worth living, and who nourish my energy and Spirit. Their support, encouragement, reality checks, and trust—especially when my spirit flagged—were a godsend. So too has been their forgiveness for my spending far too much time on this book and far too little with them. Among these people are dear friends and colleagues at Seattle University who bring joy to my daily work life, my marvelous sisters in the circle of Lutheran Women in Theological Studies, and the splendid "tribe" of friends/colleagues associated with Union Theological Seminary as alumnae or fiends of alumnae.

Ideas and critical consciousness change lives and societies. My gratitude goes to people who have stimulated, in particular, my thinking about the workings of white privilege and white racism in important ways that contributed to this book. They include Tracie West, Mary Hobgood, Emilie Townes, and Jennifer Harvey.

I thank the people and organizations who invited me to participate in colloquia or to give presentations that prompted crafting or refining various parts of this volume, particularly Allen Boesak for the invitation to present a paper at a consultation of the World Alliance of Reformed Churches in South Africa; Karen Bloomquist and the Lutheran World Federation for bringing me into a number of projects that she initiated; the World Council of Churches for inviting me into its work on globalization; and Professor Gordon Lathrop and his invitation to address the *Societas Liturgica* in Sicily.

The ingredients of a book are many, one of the most precious being time. I thank the Association of Theological Schools and the Lilly Foundation for the Lilly Theological Research Grant, Faculty Fellowship 2010–2011, which allowed me to take a full-year sabbatical for work on this project. Deep appreciation goes also to the Wabash Center for Teaching and Learning in Theology and Religious Studies for a summer grant that enabled significant progress on the book.

For the last year of work on this volume, I thank the Seattle University community and, in particular, the office of the provost for awarding me the Wismer Professorship in Gender and Diversity Studies that provided course release time for scholarship. I am grateful to Provost Isiaah Crawford and Associate Provost Jacquelyn Miller for structuring that professorship to be dedicated primarily to scholarship and to Jacquelyn Miller for guiding me in wise use of that time. I am grateful also to Seattle University's College of Arts and Sciences and its dean, David Powers, for two grants to fund research assistants and for a summer research grant.

One cannot write without a place to do so. I am indebted to Ron Young and Carol Jenson, and to my dear sister, Suzan Stegemeoller, and Phil Stegemoeller, for giving me precious work time in their lovely cabins. I thank a number of Seattle area coffee shops for providing a welcoming environment away from home or office in which to work, sometimes for hours on end, and for their endless flow of exquisite decaf. A few baristas even put on a fresh cup of decaf as I walked in the door or offered the occasional cup on the house. How kind you were!

I will be grateful forever to Larry Rasmussen and Bev Harrison for shaping me as a Christian ethicist and for shaping my sense of critical consciousness in the service of justice-making love.

I thank the amazing artist Kristen Gilje for graciously allowing her painting "Tree of Life" to lend its spirit to the book's cover. To Michael West, formerly of Fortress Press, I offer my gratitude for believing in this book when it was but an idea and for getting it off to a good start. Will Bergkamp and Lisa Gruenisen carried it forward with patience and wisdom. I thank them both as well as the skilled team with which they work. My thanks go also to Barbara Boardman who stepped in with her skilled editor's eye when I needed it most. Red and Suzan Birchfield, Carol Jenson, Ron Young, Mary DeMange, Robbie Rohr, Ron Moe-Lobeda, and Leif Moe-Lobeda graciously read chapters and offered helpful input. I deeply appreciate three excellent research assistants—Maiana Curran for work during the book's early stages, and Eva Jacobson and Gabe Moe-Lobeda in its later.

I am particularly indebted to two people for their direct contributions to this book. Pam Brubaker and George Zachariah read the entire manuscript (parts of it more than once) and provided invaluable formative feedback at a number of stages. I am humbled and inspired by their exemplary intellectual generosity. The book is far better because of them.

To George Zachariah, I am additionally grateful for inviting me to India and arranging an incredible month of meeting and working with people's movements and graduate schools in that country around issues of eco-justice. I thank also the colleagues in India who—as a result of Dr. Zachariah's meticulous planning and generosity—shared wisdom and experience with me. They include Vijayan M. J. and Anil T. Varghese of the Delhi Forum; the Rev. Dr. J. David Rajendran, Rev. Dr. M. Gnanavaram, and Rev. Dr. Solomon Victus of Tamilnadu Theological Seminary; Dr. David Selvaraj and Mercy Kappen of Visthar; Dr. John Chelladuria of the India Peace Centre; Rev. Dr. Monica Melanchthon and Rev. Dr. Prakash George Achin and Alice, Rohan and Ramya Achin of Gurukul Lutheran Theological College and Research Institute; Rev. Christopher Rajkumar of the National Council of Churches of India; and Dr. Wati Longchar of Serampore College.

And then there are Larry Rasmussen and Frederica (Freddie) Helmiere! To them I owe the most. Larry not only read the entire manuscript and provided invaluable feedback but also was present with support and wisdom from the book's beginning to its end. He is the mentor par excellence, and I can hope to repay him only by serving others as he has served me.

For nearly two years, Freddie worked with me as research associate. She brought each of the vignettes in this book from being a small seed of an idea to a carefully researched, artfully written, nuanced window into complex links between people in this world who have too much and people from whom too much has been taken. Her intelligence, creativity, verbal agility, adventuresome mind, integrity, commitment to justice and to the Earth, and ready laughter rendered these stories far more vivid and compelling than they would have been had she not been their primary creator. Working with her was pure pleasure, and I must thank also Mary Evelyn Tucker for putting me in touch with Frederica Helmiere.

Lastly and perhaps most importantly, I thank my precious family for their unfailing love and support. My parents—Richard Moe, Marcia Moe, and Lila Moe—and my sister, Suzan Stegemoeller, are a wellspring of empowering love. And my wonderful-beyond-words sons and new daughter-in-law—Gabriel,

Leif, and Emily Moe-Lobeda—bring me joy beyond description. Ron, to you, my love, what can I say but that life and love with you are an unfolding and beautiful gift?

Opening Words

Life arising from death and destruction is Earth's song of hope and God's song of love. Hope and love are the food of life. In these pages we feast on both. First, however, we spend time with evil. We dare to recognize it, ferret out a few of its hiding places, and expose it.

This is not the evil of intentional or willful cruelty. Rather, it is evil that inhabits our lives by virtue of the economic policies, practices, institutions, and assumptions that shape how we live. The "we" in this inquiry are the world's small minority of extravagantly consuming people, especially those of us in the United States. Many of the movements and rhythms, the practices and products of our daily lives have destructive, even deadly impacts on countless impoverished people. Although we do not intend harm, our ways of life are killing people through climate change and through enslaving them in mines or plantations, poisoning their water or selling it on the global market, taking their land and homes, obliterating their fish supplies, and more. Moreover, through myriad forms of ecological degradation we are disrupting a fundamental quality of God's garden—its life-generating capacity. We are *uncreating*.

To repent of structural evil, we must recognize it. Morality and faith in God require recognizing haunting realities such as these named above and acknowledging our finely honed propensity to deny them.

Yet the truth of our participation in structural evil is only a partial truth. Moral vision that recognizes structural evil has a second lens that sees signs of hope breaking through the volcanic wasteland of economic and ecological violence. Hope springs forth from the courage, tenacity, and creativity of people and movements in our own land, in India and Nigeria, in Mexico and the Maldives, and around the globe who are generating alternative practices, policies, institutions, and worldviews. This book will take the reader from the terrain of "what is" to this terrain of "what could be." We will poke around in it, and find that "what could be" is, in fact, becoming. We will witness ordinary people from all walks of life forging paths toward sustainable Earth-human relations marked by justice.

Moral vision has yet a third lens. It sees that human creatures are not alone in the move toward more just and sustainable ways of living. The sacred life-giving and life-saving Source of the cosmos is with and within Earth's creatures and elements—human included—luring creation toward God's intent that all may "have life and have it abundantly" (John 10:10).

In the world's monotheistic traditions, that power is known as YHWH, God, or Allah. This sacred mystery, as understood through a Christian lens, dwells in, with, among, and beyond us. This presence brings seeds of hope, including two promises. Despite evidence to the contrary, God's will for all of creation to have life with abundance and joy ultimately will be fulfilled. And even in the depths of human brokenness—including entanglement in structural sin—the loving, liberating, and forgiving God is present.

This three-eyed vision of seeing what is, what could be, and the presence of the Sacred will be called "critical mystical vision." It offers a framework in which to acknowledge structural evil, name it, and counter it with its opposite: justice-making love. As such, critical mystical vision opens the door to moral-spiritual power for challenging and undoing structural evil manifest as unjust social structures.

Love that seeks justice is the counterpoint of structural evil. The magnificent call to love is heard in many tongues through many faith traditions and other schools of wisdom. From a theological perspective, all of creation is beloved by a love that will not cease and is more powerful than any force on Earth or beyond. Although embedded in systemic evil, we humans are nevertheless charged with seeking the widespread good, abundant life for all, through ways of justice-making love. For fulfilling this calling, we are bearers of that divine and indomitable love.

I suggest that we will fulfill this calling not as the people we thought we were, but as an integral and utterly dependent species in a planetary communion of creatures and elements who share origins, body matter, and—in some way beyond human ken—ultimate salvation. The provoking question remains: What does it mean for the "uncreators" to "love"? Christianity, along with other religious and wisdom traditions, must enter the question anew for each time and place, learning from the wisdom and the mistakes of the past. We must step cautiously into this mystery, moving with the humility of knowing that the question defies conclusive answers.

This volume will tease out what is entailed in loving for a particular people in a particular context. It is a context of economic and ecological violence that shapes our moral relationships with self, neighbor around the globe, and Earth itself. For the material beneficiaries of that violence, *love becomes not only an interpersonal vocation but also an economic-ecological vocation*. That the two—economic and ecological—are inseparable will become apparent.

Unraveling all the implications and gifts of loving neighbor as self in an economic and ecological sense is impossible in a single volume. We will explore one constellation of implications. It is to reconfigure the economic dimension of life, to reorient it toward building ecologically sustainable and socially just ways of living on planet Earth. The role of religion in the twenty-first century includes offering the gifts of religious traditions to this pan-human and interfaith task.

The global economy will change. Corporate- and-finance-driven global capitalism is not an impenetrable fortress. It will change, if for no other reason than that Earth's atmosphere and "services" cannot support it. The question is: In what direction and how will it change? The call to love as an economic and ecological vocation is a partial response. This book, then, is one tiny part of a much larger human endeavor, the seeming impossibility of which should dissuade no one from joining it. It is the reorienting of human life to render it both sustainable on this planet home and characterized by increasing degrees of social justice. In this reorientation we are called by God and by life itself to celebrate, relish, and stand in awe of Earth's beauty, unfolding complexity, and life-generating goodness.

1

Introduction

"We are now faced with the fact that tomorrow is today. We are confronted with the fierce urgency of now. In this unfolding conundrum of life and history there is such a thing as being too late. . . . Over the bleached bones and jumbled residue of numerous civilizations are written the pathetic words: 'too late.' . . . Now let us begin. Now let us rededicate ourselves to the long and bitter—but beautiful—struggle for a new world."

Martin Luther King Jr.[1]

♦

"If we don't do the impossible, we shall be faced with the unthinkable."

Petra Kelly[2]

****

Some years ago, while working on a project for the Lutheran World Federation, I met a church leader from India who was assisting tribal people in the state of Orissa in their struggles to halt bauxite mining on their lands. Southern Orissa, one of the poorest regions of India, is home to rich bauxite deposits. The mining operations are forcing tribal people off the lands that have sustained them for centuries and into urban destitution. People by the thousands are losing their homes, villages, sacred lands, community, livelihood, and means of maintaining culture. For many, these losses are worse than death. Some have been killed by the repression that met their efforts to organize opposition to the mining operations.[3]

As this leader spoke of his people's courage and years of perseverance in seeking to save their homes and culture, I could imagine the many products in my home made with aluminum that could come from Orissa—aluminum cans containing beverages and food, construction materials, electronic products, car parts. Which of India's urban poor were forced into the city by mines that provide the aluminum in my life?

I learned too of people in the Global North "swimming upstream" to counter this injustice, guided by their contacts among the Indian tribal people. The Indian church leader worked for a rural development project sponsored by the United Evangelical Church in India. He and this organization, together with many other NGOs, were assisting the people in their appeals to churches in the mining companies' host countries. The hope was that the churches would urge the companies to cease the mining operations, and urge their governments to divest from those companies. The church of Norway and the Norwegian government were the first to respond. Following an extensive study by its ethics council, Norway's pension fund (the world's second-largest sovereign wealth fund), sold 13.2 million U.S.-dollars' worth of shares in Vedanta Resources, a British mining company working in Orissa, due to the "systematic" environmental and human rights failures including "forced relocation" of indigenous tribes.

★★★★★★★★★★★★★★★★★★★★★★★★★★★★★★★★★★★★

Awareness that all was not well between people like me and many of the world's impoverished people dawned in me through a film. It was shown to a Lutheran youth group, Luther League, when I was fourteen years old. I watched, aghast, as the film depicted the harsh exploitation of sugar cane workers in the Dominican Republic and their ensuing suffering. Lines were sharply portrayed between these workers' nearly insufferable reality and the vast profits made by corporate owners of the sugar industry located in my country. Equally clear and even more troubling to me was the connection between those workers' suffering and what we North Americans eat. I soon learned, to my horror, that this was but one instance in the complex webs of exploitation enabling our extravagant acquisition and consumption.

Years of activism followed. I believed that if the people of my country simply knew what was on the other end of their material wealth, their consumption patterns would change. But merely knowing, I learned, was not enough to enable radical social change toward justice. The chains that bind us into systemic exploitation of others and of the Earth are intricate and cleverly hidden. These chains, however, can be broken and transformed. The world is full of people doing just that. In these pages, we examine these chains as "structural evil," forces that bind our power to live in ways that "love neighbor as self" and to protect Earth's well-being. These forces include intricate webs of interrelated power arrangements, ideologies, values, practices, policies, and ways of perceiving reality that span generations and have unintended snowballing consequences.

The language of evil, especially structural or systemic evil, may be misinterpreted in a sense that would severely undermine central points of this book. By structural evil, I do *not* refer to metaphysical forces beyond human agency. To the contrary, while structural evil may be beyond the power of individuals to counter, it is composed of power arrangements and other factors that are humanly constructed and therefore may be dismantled by other human decisions and collective actions.

Facing the structural evil in which one is implicated is dangerous and defeating unless one also explores ways to resist it and dismantle it. Herein, therefore, we also uncover pathways for gaining freedom from "structural evil." They are paths toward a world more oriented around justice and sustainable Earth-human relations.

I write, then, to confront a contradiction and a question of morality that have haunted me since I was fourteen: This land is replete with profoundly caring human beings, motivated not only by self-interest but also by infinite wellsprings of compassion and by desire for justice and goodness. And yet everyday life, a "good life" in the United States, entails consumption, production, and acquisition patterns that threaten Earth's capacity to sustain life as we know it, and exploit vast numbers of people worldwide, some even unto death. Our ways of life and the economic policies that make them possible contribute to severe, even deadly, poverty and ecological degradation on massive scales. This assertion may seem untenable or outrageous to readers not familiar with it. I ask only that you allow it to unfold in the pages of this book, and especially in the life stories spread throughout. This link between our relative affluence and the poverty of many, I refer to as "economic violence." The ecological aspects of it—introduced below—constitute "ecological violence."

With climate change, economic and ecological violence fuse. Law Professor Amy Sinden writes regarding climate change: "The haves of the world are responsible for the vast majority of the greenhouse gases that have already accumulated, and yet it is the have-nots who are likely to bear the brunt of its effects . . . this crisis divides us both in terms of culpability and vulnerability."[4]

The devastating hand of economic violence is not limited to other lands. It strikes incessantly in the U.S. as well, and has been all the more virulent with the rise of neoliberal economic globalization in the late 1970s through today.

Of the "new financial wealth created by the [U.S.] American economy" from 1983 through 2004, 94 percent went to the richest 20 percent of the nation's people. It should come as no surprise then that the most recent census shows nearly half (48 percent) of [U.S.] Americans are either poor or low-income.[5]

The "sinking abyss of poverty" now traps all kinds of Americans.[6] However, the poor in this country are disproportionately women and people of color.[7] That racial wealth gap is the "largest since the government began publishing such data a quarter century ago."[8] Poverty today in the United States is devastating; it renders countless children malnourished and without homes or healthcare. I recall the sinking feeling when I learned that many of the homeless people in my city, Seattle, are children whose parents or parent work but are not paid enough to cover the rent.

Ecocide and economic violence, moreover, are not the most brazen manifestations of systemic evil in our day.[9] Greater still are their seductive guise as "good" to many who "benefit" materially from them. People of economic privilege live and breathe as players in a great "masquerade of evil." Most of us do so unintentionally and unwittingly. As a whole, we do not fully recognize the vast wealth discrepancy, poverty, and ecological degradation that haunt our country and our world. United States society—the society most linked with controlling political-economic powers—generally promotes the excessive consumption and wealth accumulation enabled by prevailing economic arrangements as a good life. In general, we demonstrate effective allegiance to this way of life and the political-economic alignments that enable it.

Said differently, the prevailing social order morally legitimates our exploitative ways of life by failing to effectively recognize them as such. Structures of exploitation persist and grow when people who benefit from them fail to recognize and resist them. This moral oblivion and the ensuing abdication of moral power are pernicious forms of sin pervading our society, and must therefore be faced practically and theologically. In this book, I seek to do so.

Assumed powerlessness in the face of systemic evil is a fundamental problem of contemporary United States society. It is a society rich with compassionate and well-intentioned people who, nevertheless, live in ways that spell death for many of Earth's most impoverished human beings and for the planetary web of life. I write for these dangerous people, and as one of them. What does it mean for us, killers, to claim moral lives? Morality and Christian ethics in the context of systemic evil that parades as good is the focus of this book.

The ensuing decades between the film and this book have taken me through worlds of action and inertia, guilt and forgiveness, hopelessness and hope, the stifling pain of powerlessness and moral power. Some of these experiences appear in the pages of this volume. What I have learned creates this project's purpose and starting points.

PURPOSE AND STARTING POINTS

My purpose is not to instill guilt in the "overconsuming class." Experience convinces me that guilt about my participation in exploitative social structures does not engender moral power to seek justice. Rather, guilt can breed a sense of subtle or overt powerlessness; moral paralysis ensues.

My purpose, rather, is to nourish moral-spiritual power for imagining, recognizing, forging, and adopting ways of life that build equity among human beings and a sustainable relationship between the human species and our planetary home. (By "ways of life," I mean overarching principles, policies, and practices applied on household, corporate, institutional, and government levels.) Moving in that direction requires recognizing truths about society that most people strive to avoid.

I believe that vast numbers of "us," the "overconsumers," would refuse to comply with economic and ecological exploitation if we truly recognized the pain, suffering, and damage caused by the ways that we live *and* if we could envision viable alternatives. This simple statement belies an extraordinarily complex claim. My intent in this book is to play it out by enabling moral vision. Moral vision is clearer vision of (1) the consequences of economic and ecological injustice woven into our lives; (2) more just and sustainable alternatives; and (3) moral-spiritual power for embracing these alternatives. For me, that moral-spiritual power lies in a trust that the sacred forces of life, known in Jewish, Christian, and Muslim traditions as God, is coursing through all of creation, and is bringing about healing and liberation despite all evidence to the contrary. This threefold moral perception breaks through moral oblivion and is a central theme of this book.

The next three chapters focus on the first of these fields of vision. They may be difficult to read because the realities they expose are fiercely painful. Later chapters move on to view alternatives and moral spiritual power for living into them. This is crucial. As an educator committed to the moral task of opening eyes to social injustice, I am convinced of this: it is unwise to face the realities of structural injustice and one's complicity with it without also viewing paths out of that injustice and sources of moral power for treading them. Herein, we do so.

Finally, I am not asking you to take on another cause—be it poverty, environmental degradation, economic exploitation, or other. Rather I am inviting you and myself to perceive more fully:

- the profound necessity of radical change in foundational aspects of the way "we" live,
- the shape of that change and paths toward it, and
- sacred power at work in the world to bring abundant life for all.

It is my fervent hope that you and I will experience a growing sense of power and hope for living into those paths and that sacred power. Without awareness of this purpose it would be difficult to understand the chapters to come.

Knowing my theological starting point is equally important. I start with the conviction that all of creation is embraced by a Love that "will not cease in all the endless ages to come."[10] It is a Love both intimately personal—for every one of us without exception, embracing our very being—and expanding vastly beyond the person to envelop creation as a whole.[11] This Love is more magnificent than we can imagine. It is luring us and the entire creation toward a world in which justice and compassion are lived in their fullness by all. Our primary calling in life is to receive and trust this justice-making and compassionate Love, and to live it into the world.

I believe that this Love remains fully with and for us all, regardless of whatever we do or are. Neither our participation in structural evil nor whatever evil deeds we do as individuals can diminish it. Of this conviction, I became fully aware when my mother was brutally murdered by three young men. It was clear to me from the first that these men remained embraced by the Love of God regardless of what they had done. God's love for them and hunger for their wholeness and well-being was not diminished. This deep-seated knowing led me to advocate against the death penalty for these men. That nothing in this world or beyond it can separate us individually or collectively from this Love, and that we have it as pure gift, is known theologically as grace.[12] Trust in the steadfastness of this Love enables me to face the horror of my own participation in systemic evil, and thus to repent.

To begin with faith claims is dangerous. It could imply that this book is not relevant for people outside of these claims. *Be assured that it is not important for the reader to share this faith perspective, only to be aware of it in order to understand the grounding of the work to come.*

Two other motivations beyond the aforementioned theological claims motivated this project. One is outrage that a small portion of the world's people are disproportionally responsible for severe ecological degradation, yet others, who bear far less responsibility for the ecological disasters at hand, suffer first and foremost from them. Equally important as a motivating force is the beauty and sacredness of creation. The extravagant beauty surrounding and imbuing this planet's living beings and the life-force pulsing within creation feed my spirit. The feast of sensuous delight in the forms of wind caressing skin, shimmering colors flooding eyesight, the song of birds and of music, human touch, and infinitely more are glimpses of the Divine. They bring joy and strength. The mysteries of material reality unfolding in scientific exploration are yet another revelation of God. For the exquisite beauty and sacred pulse of this world I am profoundly grateful. They propel and sustain my work.

LANGUAGE OF THEOLOGY FOR THE SAKE OF THE WORLD

The reader will find herself or himself moving between the discourse of theology and of social theory. That interdisciplinary dialogue is essential to the task at hand, and produces deeper understanding of systemic injustice/evil and far more paths for dismantling it than does either theology or social theory alone.

Theology is the age-old effort to make sense of our many stories in light of God's presence and power in, with, and for this good creation. Theology is the quest to hold the stories of one's life and kin, of societies and cultures, of humankind, of otherkind, of the Earth, and of the cosmos in one breath with the mystery that some call God.

While I employ theology and write as a person situated within Christianity, I do not write only for people who identify with it or with any religious tradition. I believe that all of Earth's great spiritual traditions are called upon to plumb their depths for the wisdom to meet the moral challenges of our day. Moreover, the wisdom from any religious tradition is richer and fuller when placed in dialogue with others.

Yet, I am fully convinced that neither religious wisdom nor secular wisdom (found in the natural sciences, social sciences, mathematics, philosophy, and other fields) *without the other* will enable movement toward a more just and sustainable future. For many centuries in the Western world, religious knowledge was recognized as the supreme and unassailable "truth." With the enlightenment, scientific knowledge dethroned religion as the reigning form of valid knowledge. Neither, separated from the other, has proven adequate to meet the moral and technological challenges of humankind. In the twenty-first century, the ecological century, religious, and secular wisdom will join forces for the sake of equitable and sustainable life on Earth.

This claim, while vital, harbors arrogance. As a person situated within these two forms of knowledge, how easy it is for me to attribute their inadequacy to their failure to work together. A closer look, informed by subaltern communities, cries out, "and what of our wisdom?" Is it not possible that religious wisdom and modern secular wisdom together remain sorely unequipped to meet the unprecedented challenges of ecocide and rampant economic injustice precisely because these bodies of knowledge have summarily ignored voices from the underside of history? Yes, meeting the moral challenges at hand will require religious inquiry and scientific inquiry to include and privilege the perspectives of communities heretofore marginalized by the epistemological arrogance of the Euro-Western world.[13]

I make no claim that Christianity holds moral wisdom superior to that of other religions or spiritual traditions. However, it bears a unique burden. Christianity, inseparably wound up in the philosophical, ideological, and cosmological assumptions of modernity, has contributed immeasurably to the Earth crisis. Scholars and activists have analyzed those contributions endlessly. Doing so is essential; for only by recognizing them can we rethink and reconstruct. Rehashing that story is not my project here. I assume the damage done by Christian beliefs and practices undergirding human dominion and oppression. I assume also that, having played this historic role, Christianity bears a tremendous responsibility to offer its resources to the pan-human task of rebuilding Earth's health. Yet I write out of a sister assumption, a conviction that the damage wrought by Christianity is matched and surpassed by the potential within Christianity for helping to build new ways of being human marked by equity among people and mutually enhancing Earth-human relations.

This potential exists, I believe, in all of Earth's great faith traditions. As a result, all bear a tremendous moral responsibility: if the people faithful to particular religious traditions do not uncover and draw upon the resources offered by their tradition, then those life-saving and life-sustaining resources remain dormant. Tremendous gifts of power for life and for the good are left untapped.

To those who suggest that religious wisdom ought to stay separate from issues of public life in a secular religiously pluralistic society, I would say, there are many good reasons to hold this claim. However, each of those reasons has a counter, which, I believe, is stronger.[14] That is, the reasons *for* religion's role in public life outweigh the reasons against.[15] That religion, as well as philosophy and the arts, ought to play a role in deliberation of public issues depends in part upon one's understanding of religion. If religion were understood primarily as doctrinal teaching about God, then it would be an inappropriate resource for use beyond the sphere of the particular religion considered. However, that is a highly truncated understanding of religion, so much so as to be false. Religion in a broader sense refers to the systems of beliefs, moral vision and norms, ethical behaviors, rituals, symbols, institutional arrangements, and historical legacy that "are premised on the understanding of human beings as other than or more than simply their purely social or physical identities"[16] and that link humans to the "matrix of mystery from which life arises and unfolds."[17] As such, religious wisdom is essential to debates about what will enable human and planetary flourishing. To exclude it from discussions of how to shape society would be to rip the heart and purpose out of the deliberations that shape how we will live together.

In reality however, the question of whether religion should play a role in matters of public morality is moot. Because so much of Earth's human population derives its moral bearing from religious grounds, religion is inherently at play in public morality. The question is not *whether* but *how*; by what criteria is religion's role appropriate and valid? I assume two. Not valid is any claim to know the will of God or God's truth with absolute certainty. And the aim of religiously grounded public engagement is not to convert people but rather to offer religious wisdom to the work of building justice, compassion, and ecological well-being.

A tragedy of human history is the all-too-frequent Christian falsification of its own truth claims in such a way that the hope and power they offer pertain only to people who accept certain theological propositions as true. That is, the church often has claimed that, if you do not believe certain truths then you are condemned.[18] However, *such exclusive truth claims and the necessity of believing them are not true to the heart of Christianity.* The heart of the tradition is this: the God who called this world into being loves it with a love beyond human imagining that will never die, is liberating this good creation, and is calling and sustaining human creatures to share in that life-saving work. This "heart of Christian faith" does not depend upon professing belief in any particular dogmas. Thus I draw upon Christianity, not to "Christianize" the social order, but rather because I expect it to yield life-saving wisdom and courage for facing the moral test now confronting us.

In that effort theology has three tools. One is critique. People of faith within the tradition are called to search out and name the ways in which Christian symbols, convictions, commitments, images of God, and practices have obscured or betrayed the good news of God's love for this creation and presence in, with, and for it/us. The second move is retrieval (or reclamation).

We rediscover and reclaim the many seeds of Earth-care that inhabit the tradition but have been overlooked, suppressed, or domesticated throughout the centuries. Those seeds are in the Bible, in teachings throughout two millennia, in liturgical practice, in little heard voices, and more. Third is the move of reconstruction (or reinterpretation). We imaginatively reconstruct core concepts, perceptions, teachings, images, practices, and commitments, allowing them to speak the saving Word and be the saving presence in the midst of today's stark realities.

These moves are not chronological but rather weave together, informing each other. They are integral to faith. They permeate this volume, for all three are necessary in bringing Christianity fully to the cause of ecological healing and justice-making.

I pretend no comprehensive response to the questions of moral complicity and moral power in the face of systemic evil raised in this book. That must be the work of multiple disciplines and areas of human inquiry and endeavor, for the roots of moral complacency in the face of systemic evil span many dimensions of human life. I probe just one small piece of a response, drawing upon tools of Christian ethics. May my efforts be useful to other people of goodwill who embrace that aim, whether they identify as religious or not.

WE: THE "ECONOMICALLY PRIVILEGED" . . . THE "OVERCONSUMING CLASS"

Clearly, not all human beings are the culprits in economic and ecological injustice. Nor are we *all* responsible for the global wealth gap. Of just what "we" do I speak? At times in this book, "we" signifies humankind. At other times, "we" refers to those who have benefited materially from more than five hundred years of globalization: the descendants of the tribes of Europe who colonized four continents and ravaged their peoples. More specifically, I speak of and as a subset of that group. The subset consists of those of us whose wealth has been gained through what people the world over now refer to as contemporary "empire" or "neocolonialism" and who have, a least theoretically, the political agency to challenge it: White, United States citizens who also are relatively secure economically.[19] These are the "we" of whom I speak. I am one of them.

I recognize that the boundaries of this "we" are ambiguous. In some senses, all U.S. citizens participate in economic exploitation, yet many are exploited through inadequate wages, nonexistent or sparse benefits, poor working conditions, wage theft, regressive taxation, conversion of affordable housing, exorbitant healthcare costs, and more. As a result, many live in poverty that may even have life-threatening consequences, or maintain a constant struggle to avoid poverty. These people are not my primary audience, but more important they are not the "we" of whom I speak. This is crucial. Ethical obligations are particular. God's call to love neighbor as self takes divergent forms depending on just who that "self" is. An ethic for people who systematically have been denied access to the necessities for life would begin with the right to have those goods, not with the call to relinquish them.[20]

I speak of, as, and to U.S. citizens whose economic situation is "privileged." By this I connote people whose economic lives might be described in the following terms: Their income is not totally dependent upon wages or salaries. They have back-up resources (that is, family support, possibility of buying a less expensive home, investments, and so on). A severe recession, such as that of 2009, probably would not place them in a position of having no home; inadequate food; or no access to healthcare, transportation, or other necessities. Perhaps more significant to this project, the economically privileged have enough economic resources that, without jeopardizing the basic ingredients of life with dignity for themselves and their dependents, they *could* make economic choices (pertaining to consumption, investment, employment, etc.) that would serve the cause of economic justice and ecological health, *even if those choices were to diminish their own financial bottom line.* They could choose, for example, to buy local, shun Walmart or other companies with exploitative practices, invest in socially and ecologically responsible investment funds, purchase a hybrid car or commuter bike, boycott products even if they are less expensive than the alternative, take time away from income-earning work, and dedicate that time to efforts for social change. I am not suggesting that the economically privileged are likely to make these choices; the point is that they *could* do so without endangering themselves or their dependents.

This category of "economically privileged" is porous. "Basic necessities for life with dignity," "adequate food," and "poverty," for example, have many meanings. And the people fitting this description of economic privilege occupy widely ranging economic strata. Nevertheless, the intent is to signify the large body of U.S. citizens whose economic status bears these characteristics. I will use "economically privileged" interchangeably with "overconsuming class."

These terms and my emphasis on economic oppression may mislead. I am not using the designation, "overconsuming class" or "economically privileged," in the sense that reifies economic oppression as more significant than racism or gender-based oppression. To the contrary, I see these three forms of oppression as inextricably intertwined, with none taking priority over the others as the taproot of oppressive relationships. Rather, I emphasize economic violence (together with ecological violence) because at this point in history, I see it as the most unchallenged and unrecognized form of systemic oppression.

The claim that "economic exploitation is woven into our lives" may seem odd to readers not yet acquainted with it. The term does not refer primarily to direct acts of exploitation. It may well be that I do not underpay my employees, own or manage a sweatshop, engage in "wage theft," relocate my company to skirt environmental standards or labor protection laws, and so on. Nevertheless, my life benefits materially from these and other exploitative practices or the policies and principles that enable them. These practices, policies, and principles are systemic and they are historical. (Herein "systemic" and "structural" are used interchangeably.)

By "structured" or "systemic" I mean that structures of society (be they political, economic, cultural, military, or other) are arranged in ways that enable some people to have vastly more access than other people to material goods and other resources, tools for acquiring them, and power for determining the terms of life in common. Said differently, institutional arrangements, economic theories, marketing practices, tax laws, international trade agreements, mortgage and other finance practices, and other economic processes and policies favor people with money over people without. The same structures that privilege people with more wealth deprive many people who have none. They enable excessive consumption by some *at the cost of* impoverishing others and Earth. That these structures and patterns have developed historically is crucial; it means that human agency, having constructed them, also can change them. The stories woven throughout the book illustrate more fully how the structured and historic nature of oppression plays out in life.

The vital points are two: (1) Social systems or structures are created by people over time. What is constructed by human decisions and actions is subject to human agency. That is, *it can be changed or dismantled by other decisions and actions.* (2) Dismantling systemic oppression or systemic evil *requires recognizing it as systemic,* rather than merely a function of individuals. These may be two of this book's most important points.

A Map of the Inquiry

Meeting the moral and practical challenge of ecological sustainability wed to social justice requires exposing and countering the structural violence that is woven into the fabric of our lives. What shifts in how morality and ethics are practiced will cultivate moral-spiritual power for that work and for forging alternatives more consistent with God's love for this world? A response begins by noting, in understandings of morality and Christian ethics as they have developed in North America, fault lines that truncate the moral-spiritual power for renouncing structural violence. These fault lines include inadequate attention to the structural nature of sin, to moral vision, and to the economic and ecological dimensions of love that are the central Christian moral norm.[21] This book elaborates upon these three problems, but its main focus is to counter them with corresponding shifts in morality and ethical method. Consider now a brief sketch of what is to unfold in the book.

LIFE STORIES

People's lives express the complexity and intimacy of the connections between our wealth on the one hand and others' impoverishment and Earth's devastation on the other. Stories or vignettes from people's lives weave throughout this book, helping to explain both the damage wrought by our consumptive ways of life and viable alternatives. While many of the stories portray people I have known, others engage constructed "characters" and situations. Where the stories are written in the first person, that person often is not actually I, but rather is a constructed "I."

As you encounter each "life story," it is crucial to bear in mind that each is revisited later in the chapter or in a subsequent chapter. These second "episodes" or "counter-narratives" illustrate how the injustice seen in the first can be undone, and more just and sustainable alternatives developed. In the second episodes we return to the people in the stories, and take steps with them to resist structural violence and to build alternatives. The reader will encounter people and their undertakings actively engaged in changing policies and practices of life on four levels: the individual or household, corporate, other institutions, and government.

THE MORAL CRISIS

Chapter 2 introduces the twofold moral crisis addressed in this book: the ways in which our lives perpetuate ecological devastation and economic injustice. It explores the inseparability of economic and ecological violence, and views links connecting our excessive consumption to others' severe poverty and Earth's devastation. Finally, this chapter introduces four overarching principles for the life-giving alternatives possible if human communities generate the moral-spiritual power to imagine and adopt them.

STRUCTURAL SIN: SOCIAL AND ECOLOGICAL

Chapter 3 explores structural injustice, complicity with it, and moral-spiritual power for challenging it through theological lenses. It unearths theological problems presented by economic and ecological injustice and then translates structural injustice into the two theological concepts most aligned with it: structural sin and structural evil. Christian traditions hold that freedom from bondage to sin begins with confession and repentance but where sin is not acknowledged, it cannot be confessed. I assert, therefore, the necessity in ethics and morality of honing skills in *seeing* structural sin, especially where it masquerades as good. Examining structural injustice as structural evil divulges its propensity to hide and its devious means of doing so. Finally, the insights into structural sin and evil dialogue with a body of social theory aptly suited for demystifying structural injustice: structural violence theory.

CRITICAL MYSTICAL VISION

Chapter 4 takes up the challenge to "see" presented in the previous chapter. We cannot change what we do not see. Therein lies the grave danger in the "hiddenness of evil." This chapter identifies specific factors contributing to moral oblivion.

The focus of chapter 5 is enabling moral vision. It introduces the idea of "critical mystical vision," and proposes that it entails a profound shift in moral consciousness. The shift is to a less anthropocentric and a less privatized sense of morality. This sense of morality sees the human species as a part of rather than outside of Earth's web of life, and accounts for the moral impact of our *collective* actions, not only our individual ones. Furthermore, this moral consciousness seeks to prioritize perceptions of reality as expressed by those on the underside of power and privilege, including voices of the Earth, reversing history's pervasive allegiance to the perceptions of the winners.

The sixth chapter explores yet another key to moral vision: the mystical dimension of critical mystical vision. This chapter faces head-on the paralyzing forces of hopelessness and denial that so easily thwart the desire to confront social injustice and work for a more just and ecologically healthy world. We examine seeds of hope and moral vision for contemporary life that are found in ancient theological claims.

LOVE AS AN ECONOMIC AND ECOLOGICAL VOCATION

In Christian traditions, "vocation" refers to a calling, something to which a person or group is called by God. (The word comes from the Latin *vocare*, meaning "to call out.") Neighbor-love is understood as a vocation. Humans are called by God to love neighbor as self. This is the central moral norm of Christian life.

If sin is structural as well as individual, then love, the force that redeems from sin, must also have both social structural and individual relevance. Neighbor-love, however, commonly is seen as pertaining to interpersonal relationships alone. That is, love is a matter of private or individual life. Little attention is paid to the structural dimensions of neighbor-love, and especially the economic and ecological dimensions. This inattention invites a privatized sense of morality. Far too readily, deep and heartfelt concern about poverty and hunger, for example, is channeled primarily into the private or interpersonal arenas of charitable service and giving, while efforts to challenge the systemic causes of poverty drift to the wayside.

For people wrapped up in the structural sins of ecological and economic exploitation, neighbor-love becomes an "economic-ecological vocation." These are the concerns of chapters 7 and 8. Chapter 7 explores the mystery and reality of neighbor-love as a biblical and theological norm. Chapter 8 examines how these characteristics of neighbor-love play out in our context of complicity with economic and ecological injustice. Along the way it develops the four overall principles for a moral economy introduced in chapter 2.

A MORAL FRAMEWORK FOR JUSTICE-MAKING EARTH-KEEPING LIFE

Chapter 9 develops a moral framework for love as an economic and ecological vocation. The framework brings together and summarizes the approach to ethical inquiry used and theorized throughout the book. This chapter specifies goals for realizing the principles developed in chapter 8. In the process we unfold a theology and ethic of neighbor-love for the "uncreators."

Chapter 10 illustrates a portion of that framework in utterly practical terms. It focuses on one of the proposed goals that often seem impossible, and illustrates policies and practices already underway that aim at reaching it. It is the goal of reducing the power of global corporations relative to citizen power.

THROUGHOUT THE CHAPTERS

A note about my subject positions in this text is in order. As has become common in much theological and social theoretical work, I write intentionally from a particular social location. That is, I speak as the particular "I" and "we" discussed earlier in this chapter. I speak not only *from* that position but *about* it and *to* it. However, the notion of a situated subject position, as I use it, has another wrinkle. The position is not only social but also ecological.[22] I assume that our locations in ecosystems shape us. I must admit, I am only beginning to grapple with the bemusing implications of this assumption. These factors of location invite a bit of hopping around between first and third person discourse, with an occasional second person address—to you, the reader—tossed in. May your patience hold, and may my indicators of where "I" am in the text be adequate. My location within a Lutheran form of Christianity will become evident, as will my conviction that to be true to a religious tradition one must be critical of it.

The language shifts between a more and a less academic voice. This may be uncomfortable for people who prefer one or the other, and especially vexing for readers who tend to either resent or dismiss one of the two. I believe, however, that the purpose outweighs the problems. Academic work at its best, I believe, is translated into easily accessible language. Yet as Patricia Hill Collins notes, academic discourses have not only their limitations but also their strengths and "in some cases express ideas not easily translatable into everyday speech."[23] Where important ideas are more clearly expressed in academic language, I invoke it.

Unlikely conversation partners frequent these pages. That is intentional. Injustice is known most fully and described most clearly by those who suffer from it. Ethics, therefore, is to draw upon the wisdom, knowledge, and experience of people and places on the underside of power and privilege. Moreover, the paths toward a more just and sustainable future are often best known by people already forging those paths. Ethics, thus, must draw upon activists engaged in the issues at hand. I have tried to put in conversation activists, scholars, activist/scholars, people whose lives are threatened or have been taken by ecological and economic violence, ancient voices and contemporary. Because I am convinced that the problems faced herein will be solved only if varied fields of human endeavor bring their wisdom into constructive exchange, the reader will encounter in these pages the theories and methods not only of Christian ethics, but also other fields of theological studies, political theory, economics, critical race theory, feminist theory, and the natural sciences.

This book is a constructive work in Christian ethics in the context of complicity with structural evil, especially as it appears in ways of living that threaten ecological well-being and enable a few to thrive at the expense of death or degradation for many. The inquiry seeks to take seriously both the depth of that evil, and the healing, liberating, life-transforming power of love, especially as revealed by the God whom Jesus loved. How, I ask, are we to do ethics and live morally as a people called to love yet deeply engaged in systemic evil that masquerades as normal, natural, inevitable, or even God's will?

CHRISTIAN ETHICS

The terms *morality* and *ethics* commonly are used interchangeably. In the discipline of ethics and in this volume, they are not. *Morality* refers to the lived dimension of life pertaining to doing and being—for individuals and groups (small and large)—in ways that are good, right, and fitting. *Ethics*, on the other hand, is "second order discourse" reflecting on that dimension of life; ethics is disciplined inquiry into or study of morality. This book is, in the first place, about morality, about living a moral life for people whose everyday ways of life have decidedly immoral consequences on others and on the Earth.

Secondarily this book is about ethics. Within Christianity, Christian ethics is the theological discipline charged with enabling people to draw upon their faith heritage to meet the moral challenges of each particular time and place in a way that reflects the love of God for all of creation. The aim of Christian ethics is, in the words of Christian ethicist Miguel de la Torre, to enable "relationships where all people can live full abundant lives, able to become all that God has called them to be,"[24] to "have life and have it abundantly" (John 10:10). By definition, then, ethics seeks to dismantle dehumanizing and destructive forces such as racism, colonialism, classism, sexism, and ecological degradation, and seeks to cultivate conditions that enable right relationships within Earth's web of life and with God.

However, Christian ethics in the North Atlantic world has not significantly enabled church or broader society to craft ways of life that counter both the ecological destruction and the economic violence that mark our day. The problem in Christian ethics has roots in fundamental presuppositions about neighbor-love as a biblical and theological norm, about sin, and about moral vision. Equally significant, ethical norms and processes in any society are established by dominant sectors to reflect their sense of morality and to uphold the power arrangements that maintain their dominance. Thus, the established moral code rationalizes itself and cannot assess itself. That is, socially constructed moral values and norms perpetuate, through moral sanctioning, a prevailing order that might be considered unjust according to another moral vision. As de la Torre points out, conscience, and even interpretations of "what Jesus would do," are socially constructed within this moral code and therefore are ill-equipped to counter it. The focus of ethics becomes determining what is ethical according to the prevailing moral code, rather than challenging the rightness of that moral framework itself.[25] Christian ethics, therefore, must reveal the presupposed assumptions regarding what is morally good that sanction "the way things are." My efforts to counter these inadequacies in ethics unfold in this book.

Here, I summarize four ways of understanding Christian ethics that I have developed and that shape this book. The four are consistent, yet each emphasizes a different dimension of ethics. According to one understanding, Christian ethics is the disciplined art of coming to know ever more fully the mystery that is God and the realities of life on Earth, and holding these two together, so that we may shape ways of living consistent with and empowered by God being with, in, among, and for creation. "Knowing" here refers not merely to "knowledge of," but to "being in relationship with." Where vision and knowledge of God and of life's realities (what is going on and the historical roots and consequences of what is going on) are obscured or distorted, a task of Christian ethics is *to know and see differently*, so that we might *live* differently.

In another and complementary sense, the "meaning of ethics" is, as Paul Tillich writes, "to express the ways in which love embodies itself and life is maintained and saved."[26] The boundless implications of ethics thus understood depend upon the meaning of "love" as a biblical and theological norm. Herein lies the import of our effort to see love as inherently justice-making and Earth-honoring, and as an ecological-economic vocation.

Third, Christian ethics may be seen as disciplined inquiry into morality. It is the art-science bringing self-consciousness, method, critical vision, and faith to the tasks of (1) discerning what is good and right for any given situation and context, (2) finding the moral-spiritual power to act on that discernment, and (3) discovering what forms individuals and society toward and away from the good.

Finally, Christian ethics is the theological art-science enabling Christian communities to draw critically upon their traditions and read "the signs of the times," in order to shape ways of living consistent with faith in the God whom Jesus loved. That God is revealed in Jesus Christ and through the Spirit and may be revealed in scripture and in God's first book of revelation, the creation itself. Critical mystical vision is key to "reading the signs of the times" in ways that disclose and counter structural injustice. In all four of these understandings, the overall question of Christian ethics becomes: "How are we to perceive our world, and how are we to live in it *because of God's boundless love for creation and presence with and in it?*"

These varied yet complementary ways of understanding Christian ethics signal the great challenge inherent in Christian ethical inquiry. It is to perceive and "tell the truth" about the human capacity to render and rationalize brutality while *never subordinating that reality to the bigger one: the goodness, beauty, joy, and laughter in life and the inherent goodness of being created in the image of God.* To "tell the truth" about the former without also celebrating the latter, in the long run, is to harbor a lie.

Clearly, my approach to ethics assumes an overlap of the mystical and the moral aspects of life. That is, the human longing for the sacred relates in some vital ways to the longing for more compassionate, just, and Earth-honoring ways of being human. That connection is central to a moral framework capable of meeting the challenge of systemic evil in our day.

The moral framework emerging herein has four fundamental markers. The first is its focus on moral agency. The inadequacies in ethical method addressed in this work contribute to (and, to a certain extent, derive from) a basic flaw in Christian ethics. It is the reduction of ethics to questions of moral deliberation and formation, largely bypassing questions of moral agency. The "deliberative dimension" of ethics refers to processes of moral decision making, responding to the question of "what are we to do and be?" "Moral agency" on the other hand, refers to moral-spiritual power to "do and be" what we discern we ought. Ethics as response to the question of "what we are to do and be" is dangerously inadequate, especially in the contemporary context, because far too readily we *do* know what we ought to do in response to economic and ecological violence, but fail to find the moral agency to act on that knowledge. Ethics in the context of structural sin must go beyond moral deliberation and formation; ethics must be concerned with the moral agency to move toward more equitable, compassionate, and sustainable social orders. The basic moves in ethics and morality developed herein foster moral agency.

The second central marker is the de-privatization of sin, love, morality, and spirituality in constructions of Christian faith and ethics. Ethics for the uncreators, as proposed in this book, reveals the dangers of privatization and argues for a more structural sense of sin and of love, and more relational and collective notions of moral being and doing. The next marker is the commitment to hold the quest for social justice and the quest for ecological sustainability as inseparable. Finally, the proposed ethical framework centers in critical mystical vision—enhanced capacity to see "what is," "what could be," and God's presence within creation working toward the latter.

The book, then, constructs Earth-honoring justice-seeking Christian ethics. The *how* of ethical reflection determines its outcome, and thereby may have life-and-death consequences. For this reason, my intent is to propose and employ substantive shifts in *how* ethics is done in response to the context of structural evil. I propose and employ an approach to morality and ethics that could help communities of faith and other concerned people of the Global North respond morally to the reality of our historic and contemporary participation in structural evil, especially as it is manifest in economic and ecological violence.

This effort responds constructively to calls issued by the World Council of Churches, the Lutheran World Federation, and the World Alliance of Reformed Churches to engage in transforming the reigning paradigm of economic globalization because of its dire impacts on the world's impoverished people and ecosystems. "The churches and the ecumenical family [are] called to move beyond critique of neoliberal globalization to stating how God's grace can transform this paradigm. The call [is] for an ecumenical vision of life in just and loving relationships, through a search for alternatives to the present economic structure," declares the World Council of Churches in its "Alternative Globalization Addressing Peoples and Earth (AGAPE)."[27]

Finally, this work is drawn out of me by the Spirit. The Evangelical Lutheran Church in America (ELCA), in its rituals of baptism and confirmation, makes an utterly astounding (but often not recognized as such) affirmation. The people gathered in worship affirm that, at baptism, God makes a covenant with the baptized person that she or he *will* "strive for justice and peace in all the earth." The Spirit is breathed into us, and into all of creation, as moral-spiritual power for this lifework.

Notes

1. "Beyond Vietnam: A Time to Break Silence," speech delivered on April 4, 1967 at Riverside Church in New York City.

2. Petra Kelly (1947–1992) was a founder of the Green Party in Germany.

3. One project alone, for example, would "directly affect 9000 people and displace 3500 people from their habitat in 40 villages." William Stanley, "Land Does Not Belong to Us—We Belong to the Land: Mining in Orissa, India," *Echoes* 21 (2002), a publication of the Lutheran World Federation.

4. Amy Sinden, "Climate Change and Human Rights," *Journal of Land, Resources, and Environmental Law* 27 (2007): 255.

5. Hope Yen, "Census Shows 1 in 2 people are poor or low-income," Associated Press, December 15, 2011. http://finance.yahoo.com/news/census-shows-1-2-people-103940568.html. See also www.census.gov.

6. Cornel West, luncheon presentation at Queen Anne United Methodist Church, Seattle, April 2012.

7. For analysis of the racial economic divide in the U.S., see annual *State of the Dream* report by United for a Fair Economy.

8. The median wealth of white households is twenty times that of black households and eighteen times that of Hispanic households, according to a Pew Research Center analysis of newly

available government data from 2009. Pew Research Center, "Wealth Gaps Rise to Record Highs Between Whites, Blacks and Hispanics," Washington, D.C., 2011, 1.

9. "Ecocide" was used in theology as early as 1993 by Elizabeth Johnson in *Women, Earth, and Creator Spirit* (New York: Paulist, 1993).

10. Hadewijch of Brabant, thirteenth-century mystic and poet. Columba Hart, ed. *The Complete Works of Hadewijch*, (New York: Paulist, 1980).

11. "Personal" does not mean "private."

12. Romans 8:38-9.

13. George Zachariah, *Alternatives Unincorporated: Earth Ethics from the Grassroots* (London: Equinox, 2011).

14. Roger Gottlieb in *A Greener Faith: Religious Environmentalism and Our Planet's Future* (Oxford: Oxford University Press, 2006) summarizes five prominent, cogent arguments against religion in public life and then counters them.

15. The separation of church and state does not mean a separation of religion and public life.

16. Roger Gottlieb, *This Sacred Earth: Religion, Nature, Environment* (New York: Routledge, 1996).

17. Mary Evelyn Tucker, lecture delivered at "Renewing Hope: Pathways of Religious Environmentalism," conference at Yale, 2008.

18. What those "truth claims" are has varied depending upon the bent of any particular Christian group. The examples are endless: "Jesus is the son of God." "Jesus is my Lord and Savior." "Jesus was born of a virgin." "The world was created in seven days."

19. Clearly, "overconsumers" are not limited to the U.S.; they also populate all continents. However, the U.S. and U.S.-based corporations have been disproportionately powerful in structuring the currently prevailing form of world economy and its "free" trade regimes that privilege the wealthier nations.

20. Paraphrase of a statement by womanist Christian ethicist and clergyperson, Melanie Harris.

21. They are not the only disciplinary factors that have impeded critical moral vision. Another is the location of the discipline's main voices (until the emergence of womanist, feminist, and other liberationist ethics) on the "winning side" of white supremacy, male supremacy, colonialism, and capitalism's ascendance.

22. As far as I know, the term "ecological location" was coined by ecological ethicist Dan Spencer.

23. Patricia Hill Collins, *Fighting Words: Black Women and the Search for Justice* (Minneapolis: University of Minnesota Press, 1998), xx–xxi.

24. Miguel de la Torre, *Doing Ethics from the Margins* (Maryknoll, NY: Orbis, 2004), 6.

25. De la Torre, *Doing Ethics*.

26. Paul Tillich, *The Protestant Era* (Chicago: University of Chicago Press, 1948).

27. Justice, Peace, and Creation Team of the WCC, "Alternative Globalization Addressing Peoples and Earth (AGAPE)" (Geneva: WCC, 2005), foreword.

2

Moral Crisis, Context, Call

"Before you finish eating your breakfast this morning, you've depended on more than half the world. This is the way our universe is structured . . . We aren't going to have peace on earth until we recognize this basic fact of the interrelated structure of reality."

Martin Luther King Jr.[1]

The following accounts depict people whose lives have intersected with mine. Their stories may be hard to hear; they were for me. These people have changed my life, causing torment and hope, defining my sense of what it means to be a person of God.

****

A small World Council of Churches (WCC) team at a United Nations project gathered around a table to introduce ourselves to one another. When his turn arrived, one man uttered a single sentence in a voice of quiet power: "I am Bishop Bernardino Mandlate, Methodist bishop of Mozambique, and I am a debt warrior." Later that week, when asked to address the United Nations Prep-Com meeting concerning the causes of poverty in Africa, Bishop Mandlate identified the external debt as a primary cause. The debt, he declared, is "covered with the blood of African children. African children die so that North American children may overeat."[2]

"African children die so that North American children may overeat?" What can this man mean? How can this be? The bishop was speaking of the millions of dollars in capital and interest transferred

yearly from the world's poorest nations to foreign banks, governments, and international finance institutions controlled largely by the world's leading industrialized nations.

A child who wakes up in Mozambique did not borrow any money, but she pays the price for her country's heavy debt burden. Her country received loans packaged with the promise of development and immediate poverty alleviation but with conditions (established by lenders) that did not serve her people well. Often the loans were secured by corrupt leaders who pocketed or wasted much of the principal, but who are no longer around to be held responsible. Yet this child's creditors still demanded payment.

In Mozambique, as in many other "heavily indebted poor countries," the loans crippled real development rather than fostering it.[3] Julius Nyerere, while President of Tanzania, asked, "Should we really let our children starve so that we can pay our debts?" The debt repayments, while stunting the growth of many highly indebted poor nations, contributed to the wealth of already-wealthy countries. Bishop Mandlate's words ring a note of horror in the heart for those of us whose economies benefit from the capital and interest paid by the world's poorest nations.

"Frances," a church leader from another African nation, was a part of the same WCC team. She spoke with quiet outrage of clothing donated by people in the United States and England to people in Africa whose livelihoods had been devastated when their small-scale local textile production was destroyed by U.S. trade practices. Under the name of "free trade," very inexpensive textiles produced in the United States were "dumped" (sold at very low prices) in her nation. They undercut the Kenyan small-scale textile businesses, driving their owners—largely women—from self-sustaining livelihoods into poverty.

We move now to Mexico. While leading a delegation of local elected officials from the United States to Central America and Mexico, I came to know a Mexican woman who struggled to make a living picking strawberries. Her voice rings in my ears. "Our children," she said, "die of hunger because our land which ought grow food for them, is used by international companies to produce strawberries for your tables." Soon thereafter the Jesuit priest, Jon Sobrino, meeting with our group in his small office at the University of Central America in San Salvador, declared that for many people in El Salvador, "poverty means death. Our people are *not poor due to their own fault or to bad luck. They are poor because the economic systems that create your wealth, make them poor."*

And what of the United States? Not long ago, I came to know a woman who lives in a shelter for homeless people in Seattle. Sharon (false name) works full time. Her job pays too little for her to afford even the least expensive available housing in the city. Probing further I learned that of Seattle's 6,000 to 10,000 homeless people, many work at full-time or near full-time jobs. They are providing services to those of us who enjoy the low-cost goods that their cheap labor enables.

****

The Moral Problem: Affluence and Poverty Linked

Our concern here is the moral implications of these and similar narratives. This book would not be necessary if we who are economically privileged did not care about the well-being of others. If self-interest were all that motivated our decisions and actions, then exploitation of others and of the Earth would not be so hard to explain.

This, however, is not the case. Most of us do care about others' well-being; we don't want them to suffer. Were someone to say to me, "Cynthia, shove the tribal people off of their lands in the Orissa province of India and kill the protesters because we need to mine bauxite from that land," I would refuse. "Cynthia, your next task is to evict this woman from her tiny apartment. Her wages don't cover the rent, and we will keep her at minimum wage in order to hold down the cost of your clothing and household goods."

Were you, my reader, or I, asked to commit these deeds, we would exclaim "no," crying out that such acts would betray our values, our sense of what it means to be a decent human being. Yet, we continue living according to economic practices and policies that effectively, albeit indirectly, follow these unacknowledged commands. This book asks, Why? What gives rise to acquiescence? What has prevented us from refusing such brutality over the years and today? What would enable us to live the opposite?

Nor would this book be necessary if the abject poverty of many were not connected to our overconsumption and to the public and corporate policies and practices that enable it. If that link did not exist, then charitable relief and assistance would be adequate responses to extreme poverty. The point is crucial. If, for example, factors leading to poverty in the Global South were internal to those nations or regions, then our moral obligation would be far different than it is, given our structured implication in others' poverty and Earth's distress. We would be called to generosity—to invest in health and education, infrastructure, technology, agricultural productivity, food and water supplies, and micro-business.[4] The moral question would be relatively simple: "How and how much ought we—who have more than enough—share our resources with people who live in abject poverty and hunger?"[5]

However, *this question is an utterly inadequate and deceptive moral lens if we play a causal role in others' impoverishment or benefit from it.* Three questions reveal troubling moral connections: (1) Do we, relatively economically privileged U.S. citizens, play an indirect role—through public policy or U.S.-based corporate activity—in causing or perpetuating others' poverty here in the U.S. or in other lands? (2) Do we benefit from that poverty or the factors that cause it? (3) Do we have tools and capacity for contributing to a changed situation? In large part, the response to these queries is yes.

Many factors lead to extreme poverty in the world's most low-income countries. To be sure, in some cases, they are factors in which we play no causal role. However, in many circumstances underlying poverty in the poorest nations, we do play a significant role, one that often brings material wealth to some people in the United States. The questions apply likewise to poverty in the United States. The wealth of some is bought by policies and practices (low pay, lack of benefits, regressive taxation, access to ownership and education, and much more) that privilege people with wealth over those without.

With these realities, the moral pendulum swings away from the adequacy of charity. As expressed by Thomas Pogge, "If affluent and powerful societies impose a skewed global economic order that . . . makes it exceedingly hard for the weaker and poorer populations to secure a proportional share of global economic growth . . . such imposition is not made right by" assistance from the former.[6] If more affluent sectors within a society benefit from an economic order that makes it difficult for impoverished sectors in that society to secure a proportional share of wealth, charitable assistance does not make that injustice right. If affluent societies are disproportionately responsible for climate change, then "assistance" to the millions of climate refugees, while a moral imperative, is not a morally adequate response.

These connections hurl our moral world into tormenting tumult. Life lived in ways that cost other people their lives, *where alternatives exist or are in the making and where political action toward them is possible,* is not a moral life. To claim a moral life without seeking to challenge the systemic evil of which I am a part seems to me an absurdity.[7] The truth is that the structural violence depicted in these stories will not change unless some of us who benefit materially from it decide to recognize the problem and act on it.

Most of us do not play that causal role as individuals, but rather as parts of ongoing historical processes and social structures—economic, political, military, and other social systems. Three historical dynamics link our relative affluence and the severe poverty of others. The five-hundred-year legacy of colonialism is one. Another is ecological injustice.

The third dynamic is the currently reigning form of economic globalization, which gained ascendency in the early 1980s under the Thatcher and Reagan administrations. It is widely known as neoliberalism. Neoliberalism currently shapes life and death for millions. At its heart are "free trade," financialization of economies, and the external debt of many impoverished nations. "Financialization" refers to the "increasing role of financial motives, financial markets, financial actors, and financial institutions in the operations of the domestic and international economies."[8] Various forms of speculative investment are the core of financialization. Financialization redirects capital toward achieving short-range high profits for its owners despite the terrible costs to many others.[9] The recent global financial crisis was one result.

Two of these links—ecological injustice and neoliberal globalization—are *maintained currently through policies and practices established by human beings.* As humanly constructed, they can be challenged and changed. That is, perhaps, the most important point in this glimpse of the links between affluence and poverty.

Held together, these dynamics make possible the world as we know it and determine the life chances for millions of people worldwide. They may determine also the life chances of our children and grandchildren. Understanding these connections is a powerful tool for dismantling them. *The Supplement to chapter 2 on this book's webpage elaborates these historical dynamics linking affluence to poverty.*

★★★★★★★★★★★★★★★★★★★★★★★★★★★★★★★★★

A LIFE STORY

INTERNATIONAL HAZARDOUS WASTE

Alma Bandalan and her three children, Justina, Elmer, and Dabie, used to live in a simple two-room nipa hut near the shore of Mactan Island in the central island region of the Philippines. Alma's husband, Irwin, would head out well before dawn each day on a small wooden outrigger boat to catch fish for his family and to sell in the local mirkado. They were not wealthy but the sea usually provided food, and Alma was usually able to sell the fish along with some simple fruits and vegetables grown near their home.

And then—it seemed to almost occur overnight—resorts began to crop up left and right. And with the resorts came tourists. The stretch of beach on the east coast of Mactan Island had become prime real estate for tourism, with its clear waters and views out into the ocean, away from smoggy Cebu city. The Bandalans, their extended family, and all their neighbors were forcibly displaced to make room for a row of shiny beachfront resorts: the Maribago Bluewater Resort, the Hilton Cebu, and the Shangri-La.

Irwin Bandalan took a job as a jeepney fare-collector in Cebu city, hanging off the back of the brightly painted open-air buses in the exhaust-filled streets to make sure that passengers paid their seven pesos for each ride. Alma took the children into Cebu, but without the ocean to provide fish, the small plot of land to grow vegetables, or a roof under which to sleep, they became economically desperate. Finally, Alma found a position in a "recycling" center on the outskirts of the city. Justina, Elmer, and Dabie canvassed the massive piles of scrap metal during the day, looking for valuable parts. Alma worked inside, stripping down appliances that someone else far away had used. Her work required burning plastics and dipping materials in vats of acid. Within weeks, she began to experience skin and respiratory problems.

The children seemed worse off. All day they sifted through deconstructed machines, cords, plugs, wires, chips, metal, and plastic parts, inhaling toxic fumes and exposing themselves to lead, mercury, chromated copper arsenate, methylmercury, PCBs, and hundreds of other chemicals, the effects of which can be severe. Exposure to neurological toxins such as lead is poison to the developing brains of infants and children, even in tiny concentrations. Lead can paralyze the moving neurons within the growing brain of a child, limiting the child's later learning and development. Lead exposure is associated with lower IQ, aggressive behavior, distractibility, and lower language skills. Alma's children and several other children who lived and worked in this metal scrapyard began to display evidence of neurodevelopmental disorders: difficulties listening, speaking, memorizing, calculating, understanding. Levels of autism and mental retardation rose in this population, as well as ADD, ADHD, and dyslexia. Asthma was almost universal, and as carcinogens settled into these young bodies the seeds of later cancers were sown.

Alma's choice was between destitution and poison. She chose the poison, and still ended up with a fair bit of destitution. The recycling center paid its workers less than a dollar per day to dismantle toxic scrap waste that came over from America on a ship. Some of the supposedly innocuous materials that arrived in shipping containers were in fact hazardous waste, often mislabeled as "scrap metal" and "material for recycling." Officials at the nearby port in Mactan were too busy to inspect all containers, or sometimes accepted bribes to turn a blind eye to the hazardous materials entering the country. Often, they were simply deceived by the false labeling.

Jason and his college housemates inherited a blender from the apartment's previous residents, but it had been acting up recently. On top of that, the scroll feature on Jason's iPod stopped working. The blender, which was four years old and no longer covered by warranty, emitted a vaguely smoky smell, and the motor was weak. The iPod issue seemed isolated to one small area, but it was frustrating since the device was only a year old. Annoyed and eager to fix both, Jason began looking into repair options. He searched online for electronics repair shops but they were either too expensive or unable to fix the problem. His roommates all gave the same advice: "Just buy a new one." "They're getting cheaper—and you can upgrade while you're at it."

Jason's mom agreed that he should just buy a new blender and iPod. She was in the process of remodeling her kitchen and was looking forward to upgrading all the appliances and installing a flatscreen TV on the kitchen wall. "Don't we already have two TVs in the house?" Jason asked his mother. "Well yes," she replied, "but this is so I can watch while I'm cooking dinner." Jason didn't push the issue, although he wondered what would happen to the old kitchen appliances that were probably still perfectly useful. That got him wondering just how many appliances now occupied his childhood home: stereo systems, electric toothbrushes, power tools, video game consoles, lamps, refrigerators, chargers for mobile devices, printers, air conditioners, a laundry machine, etc. His parents even had a charcoal broiler in the backyard that plugged in to an outdoor outlet.

Jason followed the advice of his friends and his mom, and soon life was back to normal, but with some shiny new electronics. He threw the blender in the trash, and added the iPod to the recycling, hoping that it would count as scrap metal.

This story continues in chapter 10.

BACKGROUND TO LIFE STORY

"Transboundary dumping" refers to the export of waste products across national borders. On average, the residents of the richest countries throw away 1,763 pounds of trash each year, and much of that ends up in landfills in the Global South. As incinerators close in the North, incinerator developers often reopen the facilities in impoverished countries, where the municipal, medical, and hazardous waste of industrialized nations is burned. This constitutes a massive legal transfer of hazardous waste products from North to South, a process that harms public health as well as water, soil, and air quality.[10]

One form of "transboundary dumping is electronic waste, or "e-waste." This refers to discarded laptops, cell phones, refrigerators, washers, dryers, air-conditioner units, fluorescent light bulbs, stereos—essentially any gadget or appliance that runs off electricity. Personal computers are the most visible and harmful component of electronic waste. These and other electronic goods discarded by consumers in the Global North are often shipped to Asia or Africa where residents disassemble them for sale in new manufacturing processes or where they are dumped as waste. Most electronics contain high levels of toxic materials. Computer monitors alone house cathode ray tubes with four to eight pounds of lead, not to mention numerous other toxins. When these monitors end up in landfills, they are crushed and the lead releases into the soil and atmosphere. Toxins don't impact only the environment and those who live in it, but the workers who transport, load, unload, and manage the waste.

Some critics argue that the United States is not a major contributor to international trade in hazardous waste, because the U.S. only exports a small fraction of all hazardous waste produced domestically. This claim is misleading, because most toxic waste exported out of the U.S. is designated as recycling or scrap metal.

****

A TWOFOLD MORAL CRISIS: ECONOMIC AND ECOLOGICAL

The moral crisis screams. Its ecological and economic dimensions are inextricably intertwined, and are unprecedented in the history of humankind.

ECOLOGICAL

One young and dangerous species now threatens Earth's capacity to regenerate life as we know it. *Homo sapiens* are using and degrading the planet's natural goods at a rate that Earth's ecosystems cannot sustain. We have generated an unsustainable relationship with our planetary home. The credible scientific community is of one accord about this basic reality and hundreds of its widely respected voices have been for over two decades.[11]

The 2005 Millennium Ecosystem Assessment—the most comprehensive sustainability assessment ever undertaken—proclaimed that "human activity is putting such a strain on the natural functions of the Earth that the ability of the planet's ecosystems to sustain future generations can no longer be taken for granted."[12] In the midst of unprecedented "spending" of Earth's natural bounty—food, fresh water, wood, climate and air, and so on—it is now "time to check the accounts . . . and it is a sobering statement with much more red than black on the balance sheet."[13]

Now seven years past this study, the signs are yet more ominous. The *IPCC's Fourth Assessment Report* of 2007, based on scientific analysis and data of over 3800 scientists from more than 150 countries, reveals that global warming is accelerating far more rapidly that projected in earlier reports.[14] The polar ice caps are melting far more rapidly than predicted at that time. The loss of ice, in turn, hastens global warming; as the cooling impact of the protective ice layer diminishes, earth absorbs more sunlight. The litany of perils is now familiar. Rise in sea levels "threaten[s] low-lying areas around the globe with beach erosion, coastal flooding, and contamination of freshwater supplies. . . . Even major cities like Shanghai and Lagos would face similar problems, as they also lie just six feet above present water levels."[15] The Maldives, a low-lying island nation, is threatened with loss of its entire land. The nation could be forced to relocate.

Catastrophic impacts on food production have begun and will increase for already-impoverished people. "Even slight warming decreases yields [of major cereal crops: wheat, corn, barley, rice] in seasonally dry and low-latitude regions. . . . Smallholder and subsistence farmers, pastoralists and artisanal fisherfolk will suffer complex, localized impacts of climate change . . .

[including] spread in prevalence of human diseases affecting agricultural labor supply."[16]

The United States too will experience rising seas. "Scientists project as much as a 3-foot sea-level rise by 2100. According to a 2001 U.S. Environmental Protection Agency study, this increase would inundate some 22,400 square miles of land along the Atlantic and Gulf coasts of the United States, primarily in Louisiana, Texas, Florida and North Carolina." Loss of Arctic ice will affect weather and with it food production in the U.S. "Loss of Arctic ice would affect wheat farming in Kansas, for example. Warmer winters are bad news for wheat farmers, who need freezing temperatures to grow winter wheat. And in summer, warmer days would rob Kansas soil of 10% of its moisture, drying out valuable cropland."[17]

In a word, humankind has become a menace to life on Earth. Gus Speth, former Dean of the School of Forestry and Environmental Studies at Yale University, speaking of the factors behind environmental deterioration, avers:

> The much larger and more threatening impacts stem from the economic activity of those of us participating in the modern, increasingly prosperous world economy. This activity is consuming vast quantities of resources from the environment and returning to the environment vast quantities of waste products. The damages are already huge and are on a path to be ruinous in the future. So, a fundamental question facing societies today—perhaps *the* fundamental question—is how can the operating instructions for the modern world economy be changed so that economic activity both protects and restores the natural world?[18]

ECONOMIC

The ecological dimension of the crisis is accompanied by an economic justice dimension, produced by many of the same political-economic dynamics. We have created and are deepening a morally reprehensible gap between those who "have too much" and those who have not enough for life or for life with dignity. "Global inequalities in income increased in the twentieth century by orders of magnitude out of proportion to anything experienced before. The distance between the incomes of the richest and poorest country was about 3 to 1 in 1820, 35 to 1 in 1950, 44 to 1 in 1973 and 72 to 1 in 1992."[19] Recent reports indicate the distance to be nearing 100 to 1. The diagram of wealth distribution on the next page tells part of the story.

The facts are numbing. A comprehensive study of wealth distribution released in December 2006 by the United Nations University World Institute for Development Economics Research reports that the richest tenth of the world's adults owned 85 percent of global assets in the year 2000. The poorest half, in contrast, owned barely 1 percent.[20] A previously issued United Nations report showed similar findings: 225 people now possess wealth equal to nearly half of the human family.[21] The number of children under age five who die each day, mostly of poverty-related causes, equals roughly 26,000.[22] Pause for a moment, to resist letting these numbers drift by unconsidered.

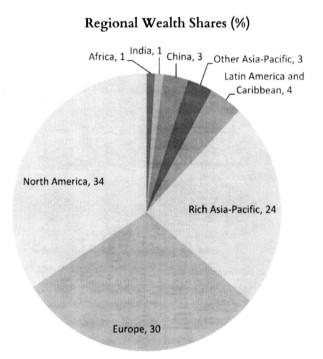

Regional Wealth Shares (%)

Africa, 1 | India, 1 | China, 3 | Other Asia-Pacific, 3 | Latin America and Caribbean, 4 | North America, 34 | Rich Asia-Pacific, 24 | Europe, 30

"Metrics 2.0 Business and Market Intelligence" using data from World Institute for Development Economics Research of the United Nations University (UNU-WIDER), The World Distribution of Household Wealth, December 2006.

This diagram misses a crucial part of the story. On it, North America appears as one section. Regional wealth figures, however, hide vast inequities in wealth and income distribution. Wealth in the United States is highly concentrated, with income disparity rising dramatically since the late 1970s (the beginning of neoliberal economic globalization) and reaching its highest recorded level in 2007.[23] The wealthiest 1 percent now owns nearly 43 percent of financial wealth (defined as net worth excluding the value of one's house), while the bottom 80 percent owns only 7 percent.[24] Imagine, then, an accompanying chart revealing a United States of ten people in which one of them owns close to half the wealth and eight of the people have a mere 7 percent.

Our imaginary chart of wealth and income distribution in the U.S. would reveal more if coded for gender and race. As Christian ethicist Pamela Brubaker demonstrates, "single female-headed families [in the United States] have the lowest median family income . . . and the biggest drop in income of any group between 2007–10."[25] Drawing upon the Institute for Women's Policy Research, she reports that, "'Black and Hispanic workers of both sexes earn considerably less than white males, but the gap in earnings is particularly marked for women in these groups. The median income of Latinas is 54.5% of white men's."[26] In the recent economic downturn, Hispanic and black families lost far more in net worth than did white families. "From 2005 to 2009, inflation-adjusted median wealth fell by 66% among Hispanic households and 53% among black households, compared with just 16% among white households."[27] While a few Americans became much richer, far more—disproportionately people of color and women—were thrust more deeply into poverty.[28]

Most unsettling of all from a moral perspective is this: poverty on a global and domestic basis is directly related to what Pope John Paul II called "inadmissible overdevelopment." By this he means an economic order that enables a few of us to consume a vast proportion of Earth's life-enabling gifts, while many others die or suffer for want of "enough," and in which the poverty of many is linked to the wealth of others.[29] Vigorously avoided in common knowledge, for example, is the reality that famine often is not the result of insufficient food supplies. It is the result of maldistribution of land and income.[30] And the distribution of the world's food supplies is determined by the decisions, policies, and actions of the world's powerful nations and people.[31]

The global wealth gap, like wealth inequity in the U.S., is shaped around color lines. Worldwide, people of colors other than white are overwhelmingly among the economically impoverished. "Massive poverty and obscene inequality are such terrible scourges of our times," declared Nelson Mandela in 2005, "that they have to rank alongside slavery and apartheid as social evils."[32]

Median Net Worth of Households, 2005 and 2009

in 2009 dollars

2009

Whites $113,149

Hispanics $6,325

Blacks $5,677

2005

Whites $134,992

Hispanics $18,359

Blacks $12,124

Source: Pew Research Center tabulations of Survey of Income and Program Participation data.

CLIMATE INJUSTICE AND ENVIRONMENTAL RACISM

Ecological and social justice dimensions of the "Earth crisis" are inseparable. The connections are not hard to see. They take many forms, two of which are climate injustice and environmental racism.

United States citizens, to illustrate the former, daily produce roughly forty times the greenhouse gases per capita as do our counterparts in some lands,[33] while the world's more impoverished people and peoples suffer most and first from the more life-threatening consequences of global warming.[34] White privilege also marks the climate crisis. The over six hundred million environmental refugees whose lands will be lost to rising seas if Antarctica or Greenland melt significantly will be disproportionately people of color, as are the twenty-five million environmental refugees already suffering the consequences of global warming. So too will be the people who starve as global warming diminishes crop yields of the world's three staples—corn, rice, and wheat. The 40 percent of the world's population whose lives depend upon water from the seven rivers fed by rapidly diminishing Himalayan glaciers are largely not white people.

Moreover, impoverished countries are less able to implement adapting strategies than are we of the industrialized world. The United Nations *Human Development Report 2007* explains: "While the world's poor walk the Earth with a light carbon footprint they are bearing the brunt of unsustainable management of our ecological interdependence. . . . Cities like London and Los Angeles may face flooding risks as sea levels rise, but their inhabitants are protected by elaborate flood defense systems. By contrast, when global warming changes weather patterns in the Horn of Africa, it means that crops fail and people go hungry."[35] These are examples of what many voices from the Global South refer to as "climate injustice" or "climate imperialism."

The social inequity and ecological degradation nexus takes a second form—"environmental racism." The term was coined in 1987 by Benjamin Chavez, an African American civil rights leader, in the groundbreaking study, "Toxic Wastes and Race," commissioned by the United Church of Christ Commission for Racial Justice. "Environmental racism" refers to governmental or corporate policies and decisions that "target certain communities for least desirable land uses, resulting in the disproportionate exposure of toxic and hazardous waste on communities based upon certain prescribed biological characteristics." It is the "unequal protection against toxic and hazardous waste exposure and systematic exclusion of people of color from environmental decisions affecting their communities."[36]

Illustrations of environmental racism are countless. The aforementioned study documented the disproportionate location of facilities for treatment, storage, and disposal of toxic waste materials in or near racial and ethnic minority communities in the United States. And it found that the disproportionate number of racial and ethnic minorities living in communities with commercial hazardous waste facilities was not a random occurrence but rather a consistent pattern. More recent studies bear similar findings.[37] The term, while initially referring to environmental discrimination based on race alone, has also come to denote the disproportionate distribution of environmental dangers in communities of economically marginalized people.

****

Sitting in the sparsely furnished basement office of a social movement organization in Dehli, I looked up to see a small dark-skinned woman enter the room. Obviously ill at ease, yet bearing a simple dignity, she spoke very little. Hers was a tribal language accompanied by the subtle nodding of the head typical of many Indian tribal peoples. A thin quiet child clung to her hand, enabled to breathe by a tube situated in his throat. He and his mother were to spend the night in the office, having come a long distance by bus to receive medical care for the child. His mother's exposure to toxic gas leaked by the Indian subsidiary of Union Carbide in Bhopal caused his birth defect. The leak killed thousands of people and caused long-term grave injury in tens of thousands.

That leak would not have happened in a wealthy neighborhood of the United States.

****

The ongoing grind of "hidden" environmental racism is ubiquitous. Our food, clothing, transportation, housing, and consumption are built on it. "The production chain of textiles is a sequence of poisons: cotton fields are sprayed with chemical cocktails to which the workers are also exposed without protection and which subsequently contaminate the soil. In spinning and weaving factories, workers are exposed to dust as the dyers later are to fumes from the dye." The razing of rainforests for cattle strips livelihood and home from many of the world's 350 million forest dwellers. The beneficiaries are the corporations responsible and "we," the consumers. Neither bear the environmental and human costs. The victims are disproportionately not white.

The transfer of ecologically dangerous production plants and toxic waste in mass quantities to countries of the Global South are two further manifestations of environmental racism on a global level. In the former, U.S.-based corporations close plants in the United States and move them to Mexico, Guatemala, India, Indonesia, and elsewhere in order to avoid environmental and labor regulations and taxes. Lawrence Summers, President Emeritus of Harvard University and former Secretary of the Treasury (1999–2001) "is infamous for writing a 12 December 1991 memo as a chief economist at the World Bank that argued that 'the economic logic behind dumping a load of toxic waste in the lowest wage country is impeccable,' and that the Bank should be 'encouraging more migration of the dirty industries to the LDCs [less developed countries].'"[38]

Thus we see two broad dimensions of the link between social injustice and ecological degradation: climate injustice and environmental racism. Together on the global stage, they are known by some as "ecological imperialism." The term is gaining currency in both secular and theological discourse as a means of expressing the social justice–ecology link on a global scale. Julian Agyeman, Robert Bullard, and Bob Evans summarize it well:

> While the rich can ensure [at least for the time being] that their children breathe cleaner air . . . and that they do not suffer from polluted water supplies, those at the bottom of the socio-economic ladder are less able to avoid the consequences of motor vehicle exhausts, polluting industry and power generation or the poor distribution of essential facilities. This unequal distribution of environmental 'bads' is, of course, compounded by the fact that globally and nationally the poor are not the major polluters. Most environmental pollution and degradation is caused by the actions of those in the rich high-consumption nations, especially by the more affluent groups within those societies . . . [yet] affluent countries in the North are avoiding or delaying any real reduction in their greenhouse gas emissions.[39]

Religious and secular voices concerned with social justice caution that efforts to address climate change and other aspects of the earth crisis will either exacerbate or reduce existing injustice based in race/ethnicity, gender, and class. This concern demands holding social justice and ecological well-being as inseparable in the quest for a sustainable relationship between the human species and the planet. Eco-justice is a term for that linkage.

****

Amidst a cacophony of bleating car horns, a tiny cab maneuvered through darting motorbikes and weaving rickshaws packed with young women in flowing saris, zipped past hungry beggars, and veered into a calmer, greener space. It was the modest headquarters of the National Council of Churches of India. Simple, dormitory-like dwellings with screened porches joined a larger building surrounded by trailing plants. From it slowly emerged fifteen or twenty smiling men and women conversing, I soon realized, in at least two or three languages. They converged around a banner and, with rather tired but spirited smiles, stood together for a snapshot recording their shared work. High-level leaders of Christian denominations and networks throughout India, they had been gathered by the National Council of Churches of India to design an "eco-justice Sunday School curriculum" to be used throughout the nation.

The next day would begin a second consultation, in which I had been invited to participate as a co-planner and a presenter. It convened thirty-some professors of theology from throughout India and Sri Lanka who taught or were preparing to teach green theology and eco-justice as a required component of graduate-level education in theology and ministry. They were people of courage and commitment. They were teaching eco-justice because the lives of their people depended upon it and because they understood it as integral to faith in God.

Eco-justice ministries had many faces for the people that I came to know in this brief consultation. One young woman pastor who helped to facilitate the consultation, had been assigned to ministry in the state of Orissa. Her work was with tribal people who for years had been organizing and risking their lives to resist the international Bauxite mines that were destroying their lands and driving them from their communities. She had once walked with other village women for two days in rough and dangerous terrain bearing the body of a person killed in the movement of resistance to the mines.

Two others were faculty at a seminary near Sir Lanka's Negombo Lagoon. The lagoon had been a means of life for the area's people for centuries. That source of food, employment, culture, community, and homes was falling prey to the foreign-owned tourist industry and a nearby Free Trade Zone. The once life-giving lagoon was being converted to a landing strip for sea planes serving tourists. Production plants in the Free Trade Zone were poisoning the water with chemicals and garbage. Seafood supplies were fast diminishing, and the shores from which fisherpeople had once launched boats and nets now boasted high-end hotels and restaurants. Simple homes were being replaced by tourist facilities, and the longtime dwellers displaced into urban poverty. Eco-justice ministry was, for the professors from this area, a matter of life and death for their people.

****

ECO-JUSTICE

Countless individuals, groups, and networks around the globe strive persistently toward eco-justice. This movement has at least two streams. One is the environmental justice movement, and the other is the climate justice movement.[40] These two overlapping movements respond to environmental racism and climate injustice respectively. The two streams are rapidly converging as the links between climate injustice and environmental racism become clearer and more insidious.

Eco-justice calls forth the morally and politically charged questions of "ecological debt" and "environmental space" elaborated in chapter 8.[41] The former holds that overconsuming countries of the Global North owe an "ecological debt" to those who suffer most from ecological degradation but contribute least to it. Ecological debt theorists suggest also that we owe an ecological debt to future generations for what we have taken from them through climate change, ocean acidification, loss of biodiversity, endocrine-disrupting chemicals, and more. "Environmental space" is a rights-based and equity-based approach to eco-justice. It suggests that all people have rights to a fair share in the goods and services that Earth provides to humankind.

A dangerous intellectual and moral fault line of the environmental movement in the United States has been the seductive temptation to disassociate Earth's degradation from the pernicious forms of social injustice madly eating away at our lives (yet largely unseen by people of the upperside of power and privilege). The eco-justice movement counters this problem.

A Shift in the Discourse: Theft Acknowledged

Earlier we noted three historical trends that have produced relative wealth for some people while impoverishing and at times brutalizing multitudes (colonialism, the reigning form of economic globalization known as neoliberalism, and ecological injustice). Frequently in these dynamics, economic and ecological violence have worked in concert, in the past and today. The result is collective theft, historical and ongoing. That the theft is, for most of us, unintentional makes it no less deadly. It is a central moral transgression of our lives. It is a form of systemic sin in which we take part.

The pathos of our situation stuns. We may desire to make this world a better place and strive earnestly to do so. Yet, our lives have become deadly to the very life-systems that enable life on earth—air, water, soil, biodiversity—and to countless people who have died and continue to die in the wake of European conquest of Africa, the Americas, and parts of Asia, and the economic colonialism and ecological degradation that have followed.

As Thomas Pogge writes, given these dynamics, our failure to address them and to reduce poverty "may constitute not merely a lack of beneficence, but our active impoverishing, starving, and killing millions of innocent people by economic means. To be sure we do not intend these harms. . . . We may not even have foreseen these harms when we constructed the new global economic architecture in the late 1980s. . . . So perhaps we made an innocent and blameless mistake. . . . But it is *our* mistake nonetheless, and we must not allow it to kill yet further tens of millions in the developing world."[42] The issue is accepting active responsibility for our participation in structural evil.

OUR MOMENT IN HISTORY

SOMETHING NEW REQUIRED OF HUMANKIND

Our moment in history is breathtaking. The generations of people now living will decide whether or not life continues on this planet in ways recognizably human and verdant. In this context, something new is required of humankind: to forge ways of being human that do not threaten Earth's life-sustaining capacity, and that vastly diminish inequity in access to the necessities for life with dignity. We are beckoned toward the fourth great revolution in the brief history of our species (following the agricultural, industrial, and informational revolutions), an ecological revolution that is simultaneously an unrelenting commitment to social equity.[43] All fields of human inquiry are called upon to contribute to this pan-human interfaith "great work" of our day.

For humankind to achieve a sustainable relationship with our planetary home, the economic order that we assume as a given—*advanced global capitalism and ways of life in accord with it—is not an option.* This is not an ideological statement or a political or moral opinion. It is a statement about physical reality. *Earth as a biophysical system cannot continue to operate according to the defining features of capitalism as we know it.* Capitalism as it has developed from classical economic theory, through neoclassical theory and on to neoliberalism, aims at and presupposes what Earth can no longer provide or provide for:

- Unlimited growth in production of goods and services.
- Unlimited "services" (required for unlimited growth) provided by Earth. Those services include "soil formation and erosion control, pollination, climate and atmosphere regulation, biological control of pests and diseases," and more.[44]
- Unlimited "resources" (required for unlimited growth) provided by Earth, such as oil, coal, timber, minerals, breathable air, cultivable soil, air with a CO_2 concentration of somewhere between 275 and 350 parts per million,[45] oceans with a balanced pH factor, the ocean's food chain, potable water, etc.
- An unregulated market in which the most powerful players are economic entities having:
    - a mandate to maximize profit

- the legal and civil rights of a person
- limited liability
- the legal right and resources to achieve size larger than many nations
- no accountability to bodies politic, be they cities, states, nations, or other
- the right to privatize, own, and sell goods long considered public.

• Freedom of individuals to do as they please with economic assets (including unlimited carbon emissions and speculative investment that may result in the economies of nations crashing).

The Earth can no longer provide or support these requirements of unregulated corporate- and finance-driven fossil-fueled global capitalism. Hence, carrying on indefinitely with advanced global capitalism—economic life as we know it—is not an option.[46] The option is something different. (Clearly that "something different" is not state socialism, which is yet another form of centralized economic power dedicated to growth and unaccountable to a democratic public.)

This is not a stand against business. It is a stand *for* business that is not dominated by mega-corporations, business that is not entitled to the rights of a citizen and compelled by a mandate to maximize profit. And it is an appeal for business to become an active force of ecological sustainability and restoration. Moreover, it is a firm appeal to resituating the market as one instrument of society, rather than the determining actor in society.

While we have no choice in *whether* or not economic life will change dramatically, we have tremendous choice about the *nature* of that change. Enter here ethics and morality. Humankind understands itself to be a moral species. We determine (or seek to determine) how to live together based not only on brute force, bare necessity, or survival of the fittest, but on what whatever we deem to be right, true, and good.

What are the options for the economic order following corporate and finance-driven, fossil-fueled global capitalism? The default option is to try to carry on with the economy largely as it is while establishing a few regulations related to carbon emissions and pollution. The consequence—relatively unchecked climate change—is horrific.

Another possibility would be serious concerted efforts to mitigate climate change, *without* also questioning some basic market norms, such as the assumption that certain rights (the right to potable water, protein sources, nontoxic food, clean air, and so on) are based on ability to pay. This option would continue to grant a few people of the Global North disproportionate use of the atmosphere and oceans for absorbing carbon emissions. This group also would continue to have relatively greater protection from floods, hurricanes, and other climate-related "natural" disasters. As crops and water supplies diminish, this group would consume an increasingly disproportionate share of them. Where this option would lead, we do not know. We do know that it would produce millions of environmentally caused deaths in Asia and Africa.

Or we could choose to move toward economic orders shaped by other norms. This book will propose four. They are ecological sustainability, environmental equity, economic equity, and distributed accountable power. Said differently, we would aim toward economies that:

- operate within, rather than outside of, Earth's great economy.
- move toward more equitable "environmental space" use.
- move toward an ever-decreasing gap between the world's "enriched" and "impoverished" people and peoples, and prioritize need over wealth accumulation.
- are accountable to bodies politic (be they of localities, states, nations, or other), and favor distributed power over concentrated power.

At first glance, these aims may seem far beyond the realm of the possible. I will argue the opposite.

Let us assume, for a moment, adequate moral courage and political will to move toward economies shaped by the four aforementioned norms. A flock of birds flying gracefully through the sky presses forward in one direction. Then, in a flash and as a whole, a great swoop occurs and they are off in an utterly different direction. The radical change to which we are called is that dramatic: an "utterly different direction." The birds have an ingrained mechanism that enables them to redirect themselves radically as a whole and with tremendous grace and apparent ease. We don't. We must forge an unknown path, step by step, piece by piece. The only way to get there is to go there. We will end up in the direction that we head. Needed is an ethic for this move toward more sustainable, equitable, and democratic economic orders. This book is one small contribution to that ethic.

Something New Required of Religion and Religious Ethics

When something new is required of humankind, something new is required of Earth's longstanding faith traditions, primary sources of moral wisdom and moral courage. They are called to plumb their depths for relevant moral-spiritual wisdom, and to offer those gifts to the table of public discourse and decision making. Herein we consider one constellation of these faith traditions: Christian traditions. Christian theology and practice are replete with invaluable contributions to offer. People located within Christian traditions are responsible to wrestle with them, demanding and trusting that they will yield guidance for movement into ecologically sound and socially just societies. This means engaging Christian sources—biblical narratives, the lives and writings of faith forebears, church teachings, liturgical practices, moral norms—insistent on seeing both where they have led us astray (contributed to the ecological-economic crisis) and where they offer sound counsel and resources. Where Christian beliefs and practices have contributed to the Earth crisis, we are called to critique and "re-formation." Where the resources of Christian traditions reflect God's boundless love for creation and offer moral power for the good, we must grasp their depths, and tender them to the broader community. Similar opportunity and responsibility sits on the shoulders of people within the other religious traditions.

Moving On

In this chapter we faced the moral challenge of affluence linked to poverty and ecological devastation, and examined eco-justice—a wedding of ecological well-being and economic justice. Finally, we posited the inevitability of dramatic economic change imposed by Earth's limitations, and previewed the four norms that guide movement toward more life-giving alternatives.

The reality that "we" (the overconsuming classes) are inextricably connected with neighbors far and near by virtue of our food, clothing, shelter, transportation, recreation, and more is a given. So too is the fact that our lives have monumental impacts on Earth's life-systems. These connections will grow more significant as water, fish, and oil become more scarce and climate change more pronounced. However, and this is the crucial point, *the terms of our relationships* with other human beings and with the other-than-human parts of creation *are not given. They are constantly determined by human decision and actions*—based in part upon what we choose to see and what we choose to ignore. Determining the extent to which those relationships continue to breed death and destruction or nurture the opposite is the core moral and theological challenge of the twenty-first century.

Notes

1. Martin Luther King Jr., "A Christmas Sermon on Peace," sermon preached at Ebenezer Baptist Church, December 24, 1967.

2. Bernardino Mandlate, in presentation to the United Nations PrepCom for the World Summit on Social Development Plus Ten, New York, February 1999.

3. In Haiti and other countries, for example, dams were built that benefited relatively few people while displacing far more people (usually impoverished people).

4. These are core investments needed to reach seven of the eight Millennium Development Goals.

5. The question is not in actuality "simple," only relatively so. The question is complexified by multiple factors: finite resources versus infinite needs, how to share across international boundaries, determining how much of what I have I need and how much I to ought share, and so on.

6. Thomas Pogge, "Priorities of Global Justice," *Metaphilosophy* 32, no. 1/2 (January 2001): 16–17.

7. This stance presupposes the situation of "economically privileged" citizens in a nation with constitutionally "guaranteed"—albeit not universally upheld—civil and political rights.

8. The term "financialization" in fact has varied definitions. For an accounting of them, see Gerald Epstein, "Introduction: Financialization and the World Economy," in Gerald Epstein, ed., *Financialization and the World Economy* (Cheltenham, UK: Edward Elgar, 2005), 3.

9. Financialization was enabled, in part, by redesigning regulatory regimes established in the New Deal era. They—most notably the Glass-Steagall Act of 1933—had been established to prevent banks from risking depositors' money in stock markets, and to prevent single financial institutions from dominating financial markets. For the shift of financial flow from goods/services to speculative investment, see L. Randall Wray, "Monetary Theory and Policy for the Twenty-first Century," in Charles Whalen, ed., *Political Economy for the Twenty-First Century* (New York: Sharpe, 1996).

10. David Naguib Pellow, *Resisting Global Toxins: Transnational Movements for Environmental Justice* (Cambridge, MA: MIT Press, 2007), 186.

11. See "Warning to Humanity," issued in 1992 by 1600 of the world's senior scientists, including a majority of all living Nobel Laureates in the sciences.

12. *Millennium Ecosystem Assessment*, 2005, was written by nearly one thousand of the world's leading scientists in biological fields. *Millennium Ecosystem Assessment*, 2005. "Ecosystems and Human Wellbeing: Biodiversity Synthesis." World Resources Institute, Washington, DC. http://www.maweb.org/en/index.aspx.

13. *Millennium Ecosystem Assessment*, 2005, "Natural Assets and Human Well-Being," 5.

14. M. L. Parry, O. F. Canziani, J. P. Palutikof, P. J. van der Linden, and C. E. Hanson, eds., *Contribution of Working Group II to the Fourth Assessment Report of the Intergovernmental Panel on Climate Change, 2007* (Cambridge: Cambridge University Press, 2007).

15. National Resources Defense Council at www.nrdc.org/globalwarming/qthinice.asp.

16. Parry et al., *Contribution of Working Group II.*

17. National Resources Defense Council at www.nrdc.org/globalwarming/qthinice.asp.

18. James Gustave Speth, *The Bridge at the End of the World* (New Haven: Yale University Press, 2008).

19. United Nations Development Programme, *Human Development Report, 2000* (New York and Oxford: Oxford University Press, 2000), 6.

20. James Davies, Susanna Sandstrom, Anthony Shorrocks, Edward Wolff, *The World Distribution of Household Wealth* (UNU-WIDER, 2006). "Wealth" in the study means "net worth."

21. United Nations Development Programme, *Human Development Report, 1998* (New York and Oxford: Oxford University Press, 1999), 29–30.

22. "State of the World's Children Report 2008," UNICEF, 6. For additional figures on global poverty, see "Fast Facts: The Faces of Poverty," at www.unmilleniumproject.org/resources.

23. Timothy Noah, "The United States of Inequity: The Great Divergence," *Slate*, September 2010.

24. UCSC professor, William Domhoff in www2.ucsc.edu/whorulesamerica/power/wealth.html.

25. $29,220 median and 2.8 percent drop. Pamela Brubaker, "Class and Power," unpublished paper.

26. Pamela Brubaker, "Class and Power," ibid., citing Ariane Hegewisch and Claudia Williams, "Gender Wage Gap 2010," Institute for Women's Policy Research. September 2011.

27. Pew Research Center, "Wealth Gaps Rise to Record Highs Between Whites, Blacks and Hispanics," Washington, D.C., 2011, 1. It goes on: "As a result of these declines, the typical black household had just $5,677 in wealth (assets minus debts) in 2009; the typical Hispanic household had $6,325 in wealth; and the typical white household had $113,149."

28. For analysis of racial economic divide in the U.S., see annual *State of the Dream* report by United for a Fair Economy.

29. John Paul II, *Solicitudo Rei Sociales*, Encyclical Letter on the Concern of the Church for the Social Order, Vatican Website, December 30, 1987.

30. The U.N. Food and Agricultural Association reports that "[t]he world produces enough food to feed everyone. World agriculture produces 17 percent more calories per person today than it did thirty years ago, despite a 70 percent population increase. This is enough to provide everyone in the world with at least 2,720 kilocalories (kcal) per person per day (FAO 2002, 9). The principal problem is that many people in the world do not have sufficient land to grow, or income to purchase, enough food."

31. See Mike Davis, *Late Victorian Holocausts: El Niño Famines and the Making of the Third World* (London: Verso, 2001).

32. Cited in United Nations Development Programme, *Human Development Report, 2000* (New York and Oxford: Oxford University Press, 2005), 4.

33. From the Union of Concerned Scientists, citing 2008 data from the Energy Information Agency (Department of Energy). http://www.ucsusa.org/global_warming/science_and_impacts/science/each-countrys-share-of-co2.html.

34. While China has risen to be one of the highest greenhouse gas producing nations, with a carbon footprint surpassing that of the U.S., it remains far behind in terms of carbon footprint per capita. Nor does it have the U.S. and Europe's two-hundred-year history of emissions.

35. United Nations Development Program, *Human Development Report 2007: Fighting Climate Change: Human Solidarity in a Divided World* (Oxford: Oxford University Press, 2007), 3.

36. United Church of Christ Commission for Racial Justice, "Toxic Wastes and Race: A National Report on the Racial and Socio-Economic Characteristics of Communities with Hazardous Waste Sites," 1987.

37. A 2009 study tracking toxic pollutants from American industry and companies found that communities composed largely of people of color or economically poor people suffer disproportionally from industrially generated air pollution having both cancerous and noncancerous health impacts. Produced by Political Economy Research Institute and the Program for Environmental and Regional Equity at University of Southern California. "Justice in the Air: Tracking Toxic Pollution from America's Industries and Companies to Our States, Cities, and Neighborhoods."

38. Daniel Fabor and Deborah McCarthy, "Neoliberalism, Globalization, and the Struggle for Ecological Democracy: Linking Sustainability and Environmental Justice," in Julian Agyeman, Robert Bullard, and Bob Evans, eds., *Just Sustainabilities: Development in an Unequal World* (Cambridge, MA: MIT Press, 2003), 54.

39. Ibid., 1–2.

40. For overview of the environmental justice movement in the United States, see Robert Bullard, ed., *Quest for Environmental Justice: Human Rights and the Politics of Pollution* (Sierra Club, 2005). For an introduction to environmental justice on the global level, see Agyeman et al., *Just Sustainabilities: Development in an Unequal World.*

41. See chapter 8. See also Duncan McLaren, "Environmental Space, Equity, and the Ecological Debt," in Agyeman et al., 19–37.

42. Pogge, "Priorities of Global Justice," 15.

43. Larry Rasmussen, *Earth Community Earth Ethics* (Maryknoll, NY: Orbis, 1996).

44. Janet Abramowitz, "Putting a Value on Nature's 'Free' Services," *World Watch Magazine* 11 (Jan./Feb. 1998): 1, 14–15.

45. "Parts per million" refers to the ratio of carbon dioxide molecules to all molecules in the atmosphere.

46. Historically, the question has been: Can capitalism as we know it change substantively? The question no longer pertains, because capitalism as we know it cannot *not* change. The question has become, "In what direction? And by whose directions?"

3

Structural Violence as Structural Evil

"The great masquerade of evil has played havoc with all our ethical concepts. For evil to appear disguised as light, charity, historical necessity, or social justice is quite bewildering to anyone brought up on our traditional ethical concepts."

Dietrich Bonhoeffer[1]

◆

"Evil exists as an interstructural web of oppressive relationships."

Mary Hobgood[2]

◆

"Evil is as long as evil has the last say."

Dwight Hopkins and Linda E. Thomas[3]

How does our participation in ecological and economic injustice look when held in light of the God revealed in Jesus Christ? What might we learn about moral-spiritual power for seeing and undoing economic and ecological injustice by examining them through a theological lens? We begin this chapter by identifying theological problems emerging from climate change and economic oppression, and then proceed down two paths. They translate structural injustice into the theological categories best suited to examine it: structural sin and structural evil. Examining structural evil reveals its propensity to remain invisible and its devious mechanisms for doing so. Finally, the paths converge as we hold these insights into sin and evil in the light of structural violence theory.

This delving into sin, evil, and structural violence is based on the premise that by understanding them better, we become more equipped to recognize them, and thereby more equipped to undo them. The theological concepts of sin and evil and the sociological concept of structural violence enable deeper understanding of ecological and economic injustice, acquiescence with it, and paths for resisting and transforming it. Understanding lays groundwork for what Ivone Gebara terms "an epistemology of evil, a way of telling it, knowing it, trying to denounce it, and also fighting it."[4]

****

A LIFE STORY

FREDDIE'S OILY MORNING

In the first thirty waking seconds of my day—between pulling back the sheets on my bed, placing my feet on the carpet, and reaching for my glasses—oil has already played an indispensible role. My sheets are a cotton polyester blend; the cotton was grown in fields dependent upon petroleum-based fertilizers, pesticides, and fungicides, as well as the irrigation systems and machinery to grow and harvest the crop. Afterwards, this cotton was mechanically picked, separated in a mechanical gin, blended with polyester (petroleum-derived) fibers and treated with polystyrene (also derived from crude oil). Finally, it was dyed with petroleum-based chemicals, wrapped in plastic, and transported in an oil-fueled vehicle to a distribution center and then a store. An oil-burning furnace in the basement of my home heats my bedroom. The carpeting on my floor is polypropylene-based with synthetic latex backing, all derived from petroleum. The lenses in glasses that I sleepily don contain ore-based strontium and barium oxide, coated in graphite made from petroleum. Circling the lenses are frames made of petroleum-based plastics and covered with a petroleum-based varnish.

My morning continues as I pull on a polyester-cotton blend shirt, which started out as a few ounces of petroleum.[5] The 1930s saw the introduction of nylon, a petroleum-derived synthetic polymer, into the textile industry. I slip nylon stockings on my legs, followed by shoes with rubber soles made of styrene-butadiene, synthesized from Saudi petroleum and benzene. Breakfast consists of Cheerios, the grains of which were grown, irrigated, and transported with the help of petroleum. Nearly all plastics are derived from oil. After consuming my Cheerios, I reach into my freezer and pull out a plastic drawer containing bags of frozen fruit—enclosed in plastic wrapping made of polyethylene terephthalate, kept from expiring by petroleum-derived preservatives. While eating, I peruse information on my laptop about my upcoming flight across the country to see my family for Thanksgiving. Little do I know that the round-trip flight will consume about 30,000 gallons of fuel and produce a total of about 0.68 metric tons / 650,000 pounds of greenhouse gases.[6] Divided by some 200 passengers, my share is about 3,250 pounds.

As I step outside, my first inhalation sends traces of traffic-produced petroleum fumes and microscopic particulate matter into my lungs. My car pulls out of the driveway and onto pavement: twelve inches of asphalt from Texas petroleum poured over a graded roadbed. Petroleum fuels my car and about 87 percent of the cars I see on the road, as well as the airplanes flying over my head.[7] The rubber tires of my car came from oil, and the petroleum-based engine lubricant and antifreeze trace my path with a drip line that will end up in the water system after the next rain. The voices on my radio include politicians who are heavily influenced by oil lobbies, reporters announcing a catastrophic oil spill, and guests commenting on a war that depends upon and is arguably fought over, oil.

Living on the outskirts of a city and commuting by car is made possible by the powerful automobile industry's influence on developers.[8] Transportation is the primary use of oil in the U.S. The estimated cost of financial aid given directly or indirectly to the auto and oil industry by each American every year is $2700.[9]

In short, I am a petroleum addict. Facing the moral implications of this addiction means asking, how do we acquire that oil? What happens to people and the earth in the extraction and refining process?

The story continues in chapter 5.

BACKGROUND TO LIFE STORY

CLIMATE CHANGE

"Please ladies and gentlemen, we did not do any of these things [lead high carbon-emission lifestyles] but if things go business as usual, we will not live. We will die. Our country will not exist."

President of Maldives, Mohammed Nasheed[10]

The Maldives is a country composed of 1200 islands and atolls in the Indian Ocean, covering about 115 square miles. Its highest point is only eight feet above sea level, making it one of the countries most vulnerable to sea level rise. In addition to loss of land, the impacts of climate change threaten the Maldives with more powerful tropical storms and higher storm surges, beach erosion, biodiversity loss, and a blow to the fishing industry upon which many livelihoods depend.[11] The Maldives has become a leading nation in calling for serious action around climate change. In 2009 the president and his advisors staged an underwater cabinet meeting in scuba gear, to draw attention to the plight of this nation and other countries that may be first and hardest hit by the effects of unchecked climate change. Sea level rise is just one impact of climate change.

Ocean acidification, caused by dissolved CO_2 from the atmosphere, threatens the bottom rung of the marine food chain by lowering the pH of the entire ocean. Algae and other tiny sea creatures are strongly affected by this phenomenon.[12] Pteropods, for example, have translucent shells that are literally dissolving from the levels of acid in the ocean. As they die off, so do the small fish that feed on them, and the larger fish that in turn feed on the smaller fish. A significant part of humankind's food chain is in a state of invisible jeopardy.

MISSISSIPPI RIVER CHEMICAL CORRIDOR

The Louisiana industrial corridor, aka "Cancer Alley," is a stretch of the Mississippi River lined with petrochemical companies and oil refineries. The ground, air, and water along this corridor are so infused with carcinogens and mutagens that the area has been called a "massive human experiment."[13] Louisiana ranks number one in per capita toxic releases into the environment.[14] The polluting facilities are clustered predominantly in areas with high concentrations of African Americans. Eighty percent of the total African American community in this industrial corridor lives within three miles of a polluting facility. The petrochemical industry denies any responsibility for the noxious odors and ill health effects on the area residents, despite contradictory scientific evidence.

Petrochemical corporations wield tremendous power in the state of Louisiana. The industry's lobby shamelessly uses its power to ensure that the state legislature represents its interests, such as offering tax incentives and loopholes that privilege the industry. In 2000, the Louisiana Shell Corporation had an income of 26 billion dollars and ranked fourth in the state in receipt of tax exemptions.

During a tour of Cancer Alley by the Deep South Center for Environmental Justice, a Nigerian man said, "I cannot believe that this is happening in the U.S. I know that the oil companies exploit my people and degrade and devastate the environment, but I had no idea that this was being done in the U.S."[15]

NIGER RIVER DELTA

Nigeria exported 962,000 barrels of oil per day to the U.S. in 2010.[16]

Oil and violence travel hand in hand in Nigeria, Africa's leading petroleum producer. The Ogoni are a minority ethnic group that have lived in the Niger River Delta for centuries. Today they live daily with oil spills, gas flares, seepage from drilling, soot spewing from the methane gas flares, and constant noise and flickering lights. Their aquatic life is decimated, their waterways are infused with oil, and their mangrove forests are destroyed. They suffer from elevated rates of asthma, bronchitis, pneumonia, skin diseases, and emphysema. Food shortages and limited health services and educational opportunities are their reality.[17] In the industrial city of Port Harcourt, natural gas flares dot the land, acid rain rusts the galvanized iron roofs within two years, and miles of pipeline often burst, sending sticky black oil into the fields. Meanwhile, since 1958, 30 billion dollars' worth in petroleum has been extracted from the four hundred square miles that the Ogoni people occupy. They have seen none of the money but experience all of the devastation. The development of oil resources in Nigeria is undertaken by several multinational oil companies (the biggest of which is Shell), the federal government of Nigeria, and a small handful of local elites.

Opposing the oil production on the land has proven dangerous—even deadly—to the Ogoni people. In May 1994, four prominent Ogoni chiefs were brutally murdered in a clash between federal government soldiers and Ogoni activists. Nine environmental activists, members of the Movement for the Survival of the Ogoni People, were framed and tried by a federal military tribunal that sentenced the innocent men to death by hanging. Prosecution witnesses in the trial later confessed to accepting bribes and job offers at Shell from the Nigerian government. The incident provoked international outrage and talk of sanctions against Nigeria, but Shell Oil proceeded with its drilling and extraction and admitted no responsibility for *the events. In response to lawsuits, in 2009 Shell paid $15.5 million to the victims' families in an out-of-court settlement.*[18]

If drilling were to be done in a manner that did not damage the life and land of the Ogoni people, we would most likely pay a steep price per gallon and buy less gas.

PERSIAN GULF

Concerns over the United States' control of oil supplies have prompted American military action throughout the world, but especially in the Persian Gulf, and at great cost. Amory and Hunter Lovins point out the finances associated with maintaining military forces abroad in order to protect our supply lines and trade. In 1985 alone, the United States "spent $47 billion projecting power into the Persian Gulf: $468 per barrel imported from the Gulf in that year, or eighteen times the $27 or so that we paid for the oil itself. . . . In fact if we spent as much to make buildings heat-tight as we spent in one year on the military forces meant to protect the Middle Eastern oil fields, we could eliminate the need to import oil from the Middle East" *(emphasis mine).*[19]

When Iraq nationalized its oil production in 1972, major oil importers like the United States, UK, and France were no longer able to control and profit from Iraq's oil. A report by policy analyst Gregory Muttitt explores the involvement of foreign oil companies, U.S. and British governments, and a small group of powerful Iraqi politicians in pushing for a system of contracts that would hand over control of 64 percent of Iraq's oil reserves to multinational oil companies. These "production sharing agreements" (PSAs) would cost Iraq hundreds of billions of dollars in revenue and offer rates of return to oil companies as high as 162 percent.[20] *The U.S. State Department heavily promoted these private contracts, and arguably the American invasion of Iraq in 2003 was undertaken to secure these agreements.*[21]

****

MORAL CRISIS AS THEOLOGICAL PROBLEMS

Climate change presents new theological problems for our young and dangerous species. The monotheistic traditions hold in common the claim that God's creation is fruitful. It spawns and supports life with a complexity and generosity beyond human ken. Fundamental to Christian faith is the claim that creation is "good," *tov* (Genesis 1). The Hebrew *tov*, while often translated as "good," also implies "life-furthering." Indeed as recent scientific inquiry probes ever further into the mystery of life, it confirms more fully the awe-inspiring, mind-boggling, unfathomably fecund nature of this planet. Its essential quality seems to be its life-furthering capacity. Earth is the only body in our solar system and the only body of which we are aware in the universe that generates the capacity to produce and further life itself.

The great Mystery that we call God must have a voracious, insatiable hunger for life. This God uses even death and destruction to produce *life*. The signature moment of the God revealed in Jesus was to raise up life from a brutal death, execution on a stake. Resurrection is the song of Earth.

The song resounds throughout the earth. After Mount Saint Helens erupted over thirty years ago in Washington State, it was thought that life could never return to the barren volcanic wasteland that once was a mountaintop. To the surprise of all, within a year plants began, as if by miracle, to emerge. Walking in the Olympic rainforest, one occasionally is struck by an absolutely straight line of five or six young hemlocks. Again, death itself spawns life; this string of trees has emerged from the decay of a magnificent cedar fallen to the ground. These logs, known as nurse logs, are a voice in the forest's song of resurrection.

So thirsty for the *tov* (the life-furthering goodness) was this Originating Force that from cold lifeless cosmic space and from cosmic infernos it caused a rocky muddy watery planet capable of generating life to spring forth. But no, not merely life—what came into being was more. It was *life capable of furthering life in ever more complex and life-generating forms.* It was creative and life-creating life. This is the mystery of *tov.* And God says it over and over, seven times: "God saw that it was *tov.*"

Out of nothingness, some fourteen billion years past, spewed forth all the matter and energy that ever would exist. Some four hundred thousand years after the "big bang," as this wildly expanding universe began to cool, free electrons and other subatomic particles combined with nuclei to form neutral atoms. Hydrogen, helium, and traces of lithium were made. By the time of Earth's birth some 4.6 billion years ago, the creative energy and cosmic elements of the universe had formed carbon, nitrogen, oxygen, and all the other elements in the periodic table. Earth thus had all the ingredients to form rocks and water, and to generate life. Yet, lifeless it was.

The creating urge toward life and toward greater complexity forged on. Organic molecules composed of oxygen, hydrogen, nitrogen, and carbon (with traces of sulfur and phosphorus) came into being. As they combined variously to form cells of proteins, carbohydrates, lipids, and nucleic acid, a creative process—beyond human full comprehension—gave birth to life itself. Possibly as "soon" as a billion years after earth formed, single-celled life emerged. This lone planet had become life-generating, Planet Home.

From there the complexity explodes. Cells came together to form organisms. Organisms generated sea creatures. These ancestors emerged from the waters making ever more complex life forms: fish, amphibians, reptiles, . . . and finally birds and mammals. On one lone branch of that family, emerged the brainy mammal, *homo sapiens*. Science today suggests yet another depth of life-generating capacity. Amino acids, the building blocks of living cells, may have the capacity not only to encode and transmit the instructions and patterns that shape life but to alter them based upon learning.[22]

With the evolution of the human animal, the complexity gravitated to the human mind. The creature called human had the ability and fierce urge for something new. It was the impulse for self-reflection and conscious pursuit of the good. Morality was born. With time, the scope of that morality expanded, both temporally and spatially, from tribe to nation to global community, and from things of the present and past to include things of the future.

In the last century, yet another unprecedented human ability emerged. Humankind today possesses the knowledge and resources to *abad* and *shamar* (Genesis 2:15)—"tend and protect"[23]—Earth's life-web on a global scale. That is, we comprehend that actions in one location on Earth have impacts around the globe (deforestation in the Amazon affects the North Pole and North Dakota), and we have the resources to take actions that either "tend and protect" or degrade the planetary garden.

We arrive at the first and haunting theological problem. The primal, first, and most characteristic act of the God proclaimed in Judaism and then in Christianity is not merely to create a magnificent world but a magnificently *life-furthering* world that mirrors and embodies the Life-Creating Energy who brought it into being. The scandalous point is this. We are *undoing* that very *tov*, life-generating capacity. We, or rather some of us, are "uncreating."[24]

A second theological problem concerns the ancient faith claim, present in multiple streams of Christian traditions, that God dwells within creation. If Christ fills Earth's creatures and elements, then the Earth now being "crucified" by human ignorance, greed, and arrogance is, in some sense, also the body of Christ. Are those of us most responsible for global warming, poisoned rivers, the extinction of tens of thousands of species per year, and ocean acidification crucifying Christ?

A third theological problem concerns revelation. Christian traditions hold that God not only creates the Earth and sees it as good, but also reveals Godself in that creation. It is the "first book" of revelation. If to do and be as God would have us, we must receive God's self-revelation, then God's self-revelation is necessary for the life of faith. Yet, humankind is pelting headlong down a trajectory of destroying essential features of God's "first book" of revelation. What do we make of endangering the first and enduring "book" of revelation?

Fourth, Christians claim that human beings are created "in the image of God." Yet, if global warming continues unchecked, we may be, in the words of Catholic moral theologian Daniel Maguire, "an endangered species." How do we make sense of a human trajectory now aimed at destroying the creatures crafted "in the image of God"?

These four unprecedented theological problems are accompanied by a *fifth* that is more familiar. Two millennia of Christians and the Hebrew people before them claimed that God calls Her people to receive Her love and then "to love the Lord your God with all your heart, with all your soul, and with all your strength (Deut. 6:5)," and "to love your neighbor as yourself" (Lev. 19:18). This is our lifework, to receive God's love, and to live that justice-making mysterious and marvelous love into the world. This, according to a widespread understanding of the Christian story, is the human vocation. Love implies active commitment to the well-being of whom or what is loved. Where people suffer under systemic injustice, seeking their well-being entails seeking to undo that injustice.

The implication is shaking: If we fail to recognize the injustice that is damaging neighbor, and hence fail to address it, are we not defying the call to love? If I am professing love for neighbor by feeding the poor and sheltering the homeless, and yet am ignoring the systemic factors that have made them hungry and homeless, am I loving neighbor? Peter Pero, in discussing the global economy puts it starkly: "In ecclesiological terms," he writes, "if the church is the one universal body of Christ, this body of Christ is divided among active thieves, passive profiteers, and deprived victims."[25] What does it mean for the former two to claim "love" for the "deprived victim"?

We have considered five theological problems posed for people of the Global North by the contemporary reality of ecological degradation and economic injustice from which we reap immense material wealth. All five are manifestations of structural sin. We can ignore structural sin and our participation in it or we can face it and repent. To repent is to turn the other way, both in actions and in consciousness. Probing the reality of structural sin—

seeing how it works in human life and how it hides—will provide valuable tools for repentance.

STRUCTURAL INJUSTICE AS STRUCTURAL SIN

Sin manifest in societal structures that have social and ecological impact is our concern in this inquiry. The salient point, however, is not *that* sin may take structural form. As we will see, this point is well established in contemporary theology. Rather, *the crucial point is that social structural sin makes monumental demands on the practice of faith and of morality, and many of those demands remain largely unacknowledged.* Consequently, in many faith communities, response to sin is aimed at the individual's sin, rather than at social structural sin in which the individual participates simply by living as we do. *To the extent that structural sin is not taken seriously, so too, are central aspects of Christian life ignored.*

Sin has been understood variously throughout Christian history. A common misunderstanding is sin as individual wrongdoings (including thoughts, words, feelings, acts, etc.). Biblical faith holds a far more complex and far-reaching notion of sin. Sin in its fullest sense refers to disorientation from right relationship with God, which then leads to disorientation from right relationship with self, others, and all of creation. That disorientation results in wrongdoings. Sin is dislocating God from the center of reality.

Sin as disorientation may be manifest in serving one's own uncensored desires and perceived interests regardless of the cost to self, others, and Earth, and regardless of what would "displease" God. Paradoxically, sin may be quite the opposite of this "self-centeredness" for people whose full self and center have been denied them. For those who have been socialized or coerced into self-sacrifice, self-denial, or self-hatred, sin may take the form of *not* attending to one's own well-being. The former is sin as defined by patriarchy and the experience of men in positions of domination, while the latter reflects womanist and feminist theologies. Both are valid and powerful expressions of human reality. In either case, sin counters the call to love God with "heart, soul, mind, and strength," and to love neighbor as self.

Martin Luther provides a useful image of sin in the former and more recognized form. Drawing upon Augustine, he taught that human beings tend toward serving their own self-interest above all other considerations and deceive themselves into believing that they are not. He insisted on the pervasive presence of sin, the humanly insurmountable reality of "selves curved in on self" (*se incurvatus in se*).[26]

This idea that sin denotes both the individual's wrongdoings (sins) and the individual's state of profound disorientation (sin) overcomes the problem of reducing sin to wrongdoings. Yet this expanded notion remains inadequate and misleading. The remaining problem is the reduction of sin to a condition of *individuals*. To the contrary, sin exists not only in the individual, but also in the social structural relationships that shape societies and their impact on ecosystems. That is, groups and societies as well as individuals may be agents of sin. Racism, classism, sexism, and imperialism are examples of social structural sin. The increasing destructive power of humankind, seen most blatantly in the buildup of nuclear weaponry and in destructive climate change, calls for probing structural sin and its power more deeply.

The image of many human beings "curved in on" their imagined self-interest speaks directly to the heart of life for people positioned in relative privilege in the global community today. Collectively, we are selves curved in on ourselves. We may long to live according to justice-making, self-honoring love for Earth and neighbor, to live without exploiting neighbor or Earth. But look at us. A species destroying the very life-support systems upon which life depends. A society so addicted to our consumption-oriented ways that we close our hearts and minds to the death and destruction required to sustain them.

Advanced global capitalism gorges on "selves turned in on self." For the global market to continue in its purpose of maximizing growth and accumulating wealth, it must convince people to consume as much as possible. Advanced global capitalism is an engine of "selves turned in on self." It stokes the compulsion to consume, quietly coiling chains of bondage around its unwitting objects.

This understanding that sin exists in both individual and social structural spheres of life is widely accepted in many trajectories of Christian theology, especially since the development of theoretical frameworks for conceptualizing human life in social-systemic terms. Correspondingly, salvation is conceptualized in social or systemic terms as well as individual terms. Such has been the move of liberation theology and other political theologies, in which salvation refers, in part, to liberation from systemically imposed oppression. Given my concerns in this book, however, I expand the understanding of salvation to include not only liberation from oppression but also liberation from *committing or perpetrating* it. Ultimately, salvation entails the restoration of the entire created world to one in which none flourish by degrading others or otherkind.

The church's entry into struggles for ecological well-being has expanded the notion of sin to include degradation of the earth. This move—first made on an ecclesial level by His Holiness Patriarch Bartholomew, leader of Orthodox Christianity—is now affirmed by many Catholic, mainstream Protestant, and evangelical voices. With this move, sin as "selves curved in on self" expands to include not only individuals and societies but humankind in relationship to the rest of creation. We became a species "turned in on itself," oriented around humankind and human desire as the centerpiece of earthly reality to the detriment of all else. Sin as disoriented relationship with God, self, others, and "the rest of creation" takes on fuller meaning.

Grappling with the meaning of "sin" is no mere intellectual entertainment. The nature of a problem shapes its remedy. How we define sin determines what constitutes salvation, freedom, or liberation from it, and the path toward that freedom. A reduced understanding of sin means a truncated vision of salvation. Moreover, considering sin *per se* may give us insight into a focal point of this inquiry: how particular manifestations of systemic sin—such as economic and ecological violence—so easily hide from their perpetrators, how it is that we so readily acquiesce, and how these forms of structural sin might be exposed and resisted.

IMPLICATIONS FOR MORALITY

Taking seriously the structural nature of sin in social and ecological forms creates daunting demands on morality. This book seeks to shift Christian moral practice and theory in light of them. Structural sin presents four oft-ignored moral challenges. Each arises from a characteristic of structural injustice. Viewing four defining features of structural injustice as structural sin reveals more about their implications for the moral life. These features are:

1. the relative invisibility of structural injustice to those who do not suffer directly from it,
2. the fact that structural injustice continues regardless of the virtue or vice of people involved,
3. its transmission from generation to generation unless exposed and confronted, and
4. its expansion as a result of concentrated power.

Viewing these features of structural injustice theologically as structural sin renders daunting challenges for morality. We examine each in turn.

IF UNSEEN, THEN UNRENOUNCED

The first challenge pertains to renouncing sin. Fundamental to virtually all forms of Christianity is the claim that Christians are called to eschew sin, and that freedom from sin begins with repentance. Repentance means ceasing the way of sin and "turning the other direction." *Teshuvah*, the Hebrew word often translated as repentance, suggests turning from sinful ways and toward the good by means of turning back to God. It is a powerful act of changing direction that can redirect one's life. The Greek *metanoia* means to think and perceive differently, to have a new mind and consciousness. Repentance then involves a distinct turning away from sin, in both consciousness and action.

Repentance and confession are possible only where sin is acknowledged. One insidious characteristic of structural injustice (structural sin), however, is its tendency to remain invisible to those not suffering from it. If we do not see the structural injustice in which we live, we cannot repent of it. Failing to renounce it, we remain captive to it. Failure to see structural sin breeds complicity with it, and passes it on to the next generation. The call to renounce sin contains a call to "see" the structural sin of which we are a part, in order that we might repent of it, renounce it, and resist it.[27]

Moral vision, therefore, does not simply see the impoverished child of Mozambique or the family displaced by global warming. Moral vision sees also our functional relationship to that child and sees, in particular, whether or not our "way of life" and the public policies and corporate actions that make it possible are contributing to her poverty. Moral vision must extend beyond interpersonal relationships to social structural and ecological relationships.

Herein is a call by Christian faith to develop a structural (or systemic) view of the world. This means that when we imagine who we are in the world and the relationships that shape our lives, we will perceive the threads that bind us to people and ecosystems we never see and whom we may not know exist: the children who do not eat because their lands grow our strawberries, the mothers whose low wages produce our inexpensive consumer goods, the young people whose lives are lost fighting the invasion of their homelands by the oil companies that supply our homes with heat. This is an impossible calling for individuals alone; it is, instead, the work of communities.

THE PARADOX OF PRIVILEGE

The first challenge thickens with the second. It is the paradox of privilege.[28] Even when a person does recognize and repent of structural sin, it is not possible to divest oneself from the impact of the social structures into which our lives are woven. Not by will or intent, I am involved in the sins of economic and ecological exploitation even where I seek to resist them. Regardless of personal repentance through radical changes in how I live, I continue to reap the "benefits" of economic and ecological violence. My life continues to depend, for example, upon products containing petroleum extracted by destroying the homelands and livelihoods of people in the Niger Delta, Chad, the Gulf Coast of the United States, or elsewhere, or by waging war in Iraq. I cannot refuse all use of petroleum-based roads, fabrics, plastics, fire trucks, public utilities, and medical care, and more that, in today's world especially, depend on petroleum. Social sin transcends *individual* moral agency.

Aida Hurtado, speaking of white privilege, cuts to the heart of the paradox of privilege: "[I]t does not matter how good you are, as a person, if the political structures provide privilege to you individually based on the group oppression of others; in fact, individuals belonging to dominant groups can be infinitely good because they never are required to be personally bad. That is the irony of structural privilege: the more you have, the less you have to fight for it."[29] As a citizen of this nation, I belong to a group that "has an oppressive relationship with" other groups without being "an oppressive person who behaves in oppressive ways."[30] This paradox helps to hide oppression. But that is not the end of the story.

The fact that individual actions are relatively powerless in the face of structural sin does *not* mean that personal efforts to counter it are immaterial, ineffectual, or unnecessary. *To the contrary, the individual's response is essential and effectual.* I cannot overstate the importance of recognizing this paradox: Structural sin, while it cannot be dismantled by individual actions, cannot be dismantled without them. As James Poling notes: Every "system of evil requires personal actions to make it work."[31] Thus every system of evil also requires people to resist their own and others' participation in it, even while acknowledging that their acts of resistance in themselves appear relatively ineffectual. While individual acts will not in themselves change the course of social structures, they are necessary for that change to be achieved. This is powerful knowledge. It makes individuals' actions infinitely important. Living responsibly within this paradox is central to the work of loving neighbor as self in the context of structural sin.

While structural sin transcends *individual* moral agency, it does not transcend collective agency. The imperviousness of structural sin to individual actions "forces us to look beyond individual agency."[32] Social movements demonstrate that people, working together, can indeed counter structural sin. Again, a systemic view of the world is called to the fore as a vital ingredient of moral vision.

FROM GENERATION TO GENERATION UNLESS CHALLENGED

The structural sin of socio-ecological injustice is transmitted from generation to generation. Because human beings are inherently social, we establish patterns of interaction. Sociologists refer to these patterns, power arrangements within them, and belief systems by rationalizing them as "institutions" or "social structures." They may be as small as families and as large as economic systems. Members of a society are socialized toward assuming unconsciously that its social structures and attendant values and worldviews are normal, natural, inevitable, and even divinely ordained. In this process of socialization cultural, political, economic, and ideological structures that perpetuate injustice tend to be uncritically accepted and passed on to the next generations as though they were just "the way things are," maintained by a force akin to nature, rather than products of human decisions and actions.

In Christian ethical terms, this process of socialization is considered a process of moral formation and malformation. To illustrate: parents in our society today commonly teach children to make money and make it grow in order to be "successful." Children strive for the material comforts sought by parents and paraded by public idols. Tacit communications teach that poverty or apparent poverty signifies failure. A life of voluntary "downward mobility" in terms of material consumption, if even imagined, would bear the hue of failure in the eyes of society. Thus are we morally malformed away from such a choice.

This dynamic is "crucial in understanding how we become inheritors of previous acts and how our collective acts influence and shape the coming generations."[33] Over time, inherited patterns of human interaction and perceptions become what Marcus Borg refers to as "common wisdom," and Stephen Brookfield as "culturally produced assumptions." Where these patterns are exploitative or oppressive, this structural injustice is passed on.

However, we may choose to intervene and halt that passage. Doing so requires *recognizing* the injustice as such. The call to "see" through a social structural lens echoes a third time.

In this sense the idea of original sin assumes meaning distinct from the ontologically or genetically inherited phenomena postulated by Augustine and later theologians. Original sin may signify the socially transmitted state of being entangled in structural injustice from birth by virtue of participation in a society built on social injustice and ecological violence. That entanglement deepens as one serves as a conduit for transmitting uncritically accepted injustice to future generations, simply by living the life prescribed by society.

CONCENTRATED POWER

Another challenge posed by structural sin faces citizens of the most powerful nation the world has known. We have referred to sin as the human tendency to be "selves curved in on self." Where power collects, so too does power for human beings to serve self-interest and mask the damage entailed.

Reinhold Niebuhr is perhaps the most notable modern theologian to theorize sin as it is manifest in social structures. His conclusions are found wanting from feminist perspectives—including my own—in his separating the public from the private spheres of life and limiting the norm of love to the latter. Yet, his deep and serious theology of sin is invaluable. All human agency, he avers, is subject to the sin of elevating self-interest over all else. Political agency is most vulnerable because it wields power to shift social groups toward injustice in service of self-interest, a societal version of Luther's "self curved in on self."

Perhaps more than any other nation in history, the United States has held power to pursue its perceived interests regardless of the harm to others or to Earth's ecosystems, and to distort that state of affairs into the appearance of a moral "good." Accordingly, we, the nation's citizens, participate in that unprecedented power for committing structural sin. The call to renounce sin entails a hermeneutic of suspicion regarding moves to concentrate power. The movement against the reigning form of economic globalization is in large part a movement against the concentration of economic power (and hence political power). Neoliberal globalization, by concentrating wealth into the hands of a few enormous global corporations, also has concentrated their power for structural sin.

Structural injustice, when it is viewed as structural sin, unearths these four moral challenges. Facing them requires acknowledging the reality of structural or collective sin. Jesus' call to repent entails a call to see the social and ecological systems and collective actions in which our lives are entangled. This notion of a "systemic" moral vision will emerge as central in our quest for moral–spiritual power to counter systemic injustice.

STRUCTURAL INJUSTICE AS STRUCTURAL EVIL

Throughout history, some theologians have distinguished between sin and evil.[34] Others use the two terms "almost interchangeably (to) . . . mean nearly the same thing."[35] While I could argue either perspective, contributing to that debate is not my intention. I use structural sin and structural evil to signify theologically the same reality: structural injustice. That decision is significant;

I draw upon both because each yields distinct insight into structural injustice, and hence into resources for resisting it.

"Evil" has been defined diversely by different theologians. For some, "evil" is shorthand for "moral evil." Others use "evil" as an umbrella category including "moral evil," "natural evil," and "metaphysical evil" (referring to the condition of finitude and limitation). The realities commonly referred to as natural evil and metaphysical evil, I do not consider to be evil. Thus my use of "evil" denotes what some label "moral evil." Beyond that I will not define evil except to make two distinctions. First, my understanding of "evil" differentiates it from "suffering." Christianity has distinguished between the two; suffering is not necessarily evil.[36] Nor does suffering necessarily stem from evil. Secondly, I do not use the term "evil" to denote structural sin *in contrast to* private sin. Rather I hold that both sin and evil can be manifest both in private relationships and in social structures. My concern in this volume is sin and evil as manifest in social structures.

I intend neither a systematic inquiry into evil nor a comprehensive survey of what evil has "meant" at various times in Christian traditions. Nor will I be asking which ways of being and doing are evil and which are not; I am not developing criteria for what is evil. Rather my intent in using the term "structural evil" is a functional one. "Structural evil" is a theological category for what social theory calls "structural injustice" or "structural violence." My inquiry into structural evil then, like inquiry into structural sin, is for the purpose of better understanding structural injustice in the forms of economic and ecological violence, and understanding our ready complicity with it.

What, then, can theological inquiry into systemic evil reveal about what makes it so difficult for people of privilege to recognize structural injustice and our participation in it? What does theological insight into systemic evil teach about seeing and resisting it? Four authors who work with concrete realities of structural evil are useful here. Their intent is enabling resistance to structural evil, as is mine.

Emilie Townes explores how structures of evil are produced and reproduced by the cultural force of racist images that become historical and contemporary "truth." Observing that most analysis of evil focuses on "rational mechanisms that hold oppression and misery in place," she moves instead to examine the power of the "fantastic hegemonic imagination" for producing evil.[37] She exposes the production of stereotypes and caricatures that shape our understanding of the world, ourselves, and others, and that direct our actions toward brutal forms of oppression (evil) lived out in our everyday lives. More insidious, these culturally produced images and assumptions manage to hide that oppression from the awareness of its perpetrators. Her understanding of hope for resisting these forces will inform later parts of this book.

Eleazar Fernandez develops a theological anthropology responsive to the systemic evils of racism, classism, sexism, and what he calls "naturism."[38] He, like I, uses "evil" and "sin" interchangeably and treats both theologically. James Poling asks what enables some people to resist and survive evil. His interdisciplinary work draws on history, psychology, and theology to examine historical communities who have resisted the power of evil. Poling works in particular with racial and gender oppression, identifying them as evil and suggesting theological resources for resisting them. All three of these authors pay special attention to the institutional and systemic nature of evil, and to its hiddenness from its perpetrators.

Ivone Gebara's concern is how the interpretation of evil has been gendered, and the impact that male perceptions of evil have had on women's lives. She addresses evil "in gender relations, evil in the construction of gender, and, especially, evil as lived and performed by women."[39] Her work is particularly relevant to me in its focus on how evil is woven into the fabric of society through social constructions, and her attention to the role of habit in perpetuating evil.

These authors turn to faith as a source of protection from evil or resistance to it (despite religion's profound participation in perpetuating evil).[40] I join with them and learn from them.

Yet I have a hunch that, beyond their work, there is still more to know about structural evil and about renouncing it if we: (1) include ecological devastation as an ever-present companion of social oppression, (2) put theological inquiry into sin and evil in dialogue with structural violence theory, (3) use both "sin" and "evil" as theological categories, and 4) consider evil through the lens of Dietrich Bonhoeffer's letters from prison. In taking these steps, our primary aim is *insight into how evil manages to hide itself from the consciousness of its perpetrators, or to become acceptable.*

Bonhoeffer, reflecting from prison on the widespread complicity with fascism in Hitler's Germany, provides striking insight into the hiddenness of evil. "The great masquerade of evil has played havoc with all our ethical concepts," he writes. "For evil to appear *disguised as light, charity, historical necessity, or social justice* is quite bewildering to anyone brought up on our traditional ethical concepts, while for the Christian who bases his [*sic*] life on the Bible, it merely confirms the fundamental wickedness of evil."[41] *Its ability to "appear disguised"—to hide—confirms its wickedness.* That is, the cloaked nature of structural evil is at its very heart. Bonhoeffer's words reveal more. They name four masks behind which evil hides: "light, charity, historical necessity, [and] social justice."[42]

As a Lutheran theologian, Bonhoeffer is steeped in the longstanding theological recognition that, in all things human, evil and good are intertwined. That is, though we strive for the good, the human condition of finitude and fallibility means that never is the good, as a human doing, completely free from evil. This insight draws attention to the ambiguity of what is just and unjust, what is consistent with the ways and will of God and what is not. The call to resist evil is fraught with vexing ambiguity in a world in which all alternatives to an unjust situation may themselves be tainted with injustice and in which what brings well-being to some vulnerable people may bring damage to others. For example, if public advocacy closes down a shale-fracking operation in Pennsylvania because of the many dangers it poses, what becomes of the families whose bread-earners are left unemployed?

Such ambiguity, together with the pernicious presence of sin invading human good, make knowing what is morally good a vexing task. Evil and good intermingle and may seem confoundingly indistinguishable. This ambiguity itself is a fierce draw, pulling the eyes of our hearts and minds away from recognizing injustice where it is so entangled with good. Learning the arts of moral discernment may be a key to critical moral vision.

Recognizing the intertwining of good and evil and the latter's ubiquitous presence in human life yields a point that, while not vital to the argument here, is crucial to the later work of challenging evil. Neither pure evil nor pure good may be attributed to any one person, group, or "side" in a conflict. That is, no one and no group is outside the possibilities of good. Nor can any person or group be treated as less than human based on a claim that she or he is singularly evil.

James Poling, half a century after Bonhoeffer, comes to conclusions strikingly similar to his. Poling too finds evil hiding by "masking itself as good," "claiming necessity," or "remaining intertwined with the good."[43] And like Bonhoeffer, he sees evil's "double character—its existence and its hiddenness."[44] People perpetrating structural evil enable it to hide either by denying its existence or allowing it to remain in the unconscious.[45]

To what extent are these "hiding places" at play in our dangerous overconsumption of oil in spite of the death and devastation it brings forth? Yes, my daily drive to the university "intertwined evil with good." It spewed unacceptable amounts of greenhouse gases into the air. Yet it got me to work quickly, enabling me to be with my children before they set off for school in the morning and to visit my aging aunt after work, while still being on campus for long hours to meet with students who truly needed attention and to keep the irregular schedule demanded by my campus responsibilities. This set of "goods" may not have been possible had I bused, biked, or carpooled to work. These goods do not justify the evil entailed in my daily drive; rather they illustrate the intermingling of good and evil, and the extent to which that mixing may serve to cloak evil.

Ivone Gebara describes eloquently the hiddenness of evil and adds insight into how "evil present in institutions and social structures . . . is sometimes beyond recognition. One lives with it daily." Evil, she notes, is "so mixed up in our existence that we can live in it without even taking account of it as evil."[46] While Gebara illustrates her point with soldiers fighting in war, I would suggest locating the systemic evil in this case less with the soldiers than with the multitude of people and processes that *place* soldiers in the war and that enable it to continue. Those processes include the economic policies that force many low-income young women and men into the military because it is the only viable way to earn a living or gain an education, society's insatiable demand for oil, citizens funding the war with tax dollars, etc.

Gebara suggests three avenues for evil's slippery escape into obscurity: it may be "accepted as fate, as God's design, or as punishment for hidden sins." Moreover, like Bonhoeffer and Poling, she notes that evil slips into obscurity by intermingling with good: It is "not easy to spot evil's presence" when it is "intermingled in our culture, education, and religion—events or behaviours regarded as normal, common, even good."[47]

Let us see what further help may be gained by placing theological insights in dialogue with social theory, in particular structural violence theory. First, we consider structural violence as it appears in a "life story."

****

A Life Story

"Free" Trade and Sweatshops

For generations, the Chantico family of Oaxaca, Mexico grew maize on their three-hectare plot, just as their Zapotec Indian ancestors did for centuries before Columbus landed. This corn fed the family, providing 70 percent of their caloric intake, with some left over to sell in the local market.[48] The Chanticos and their ancestors developed this particular corn cultivar, criollo, over centuries to suit the area's climate and soil, to resist pests, and to provide essential proteins and vitamins. This lifestyle staved off poverty and allowed the Chanticos to provide for themselves and their community.

In 1993 President Bill Clinton signed into law an international trade agreement between American neighbors Mexico, Canada, and the United States called the North American Free Trade Agreement (NAFTA). As the name suggests, this trilateral agreement reduced tariffs on trade between these countries in an effort to foster economic growth for all three nations and reduce protectionist policies on certain types of goods or industries. But in practice several measures required by NAFTA prevent the agreement from being fair, beneficial, or effective.

In 1994, the Mexican government enacted a series of "reforms" called for by NAFTA. These included signing away its right to protect its own corn industry. Inexpensive U.S. corn flooded the Mexican market, priced around 20 percent less than Mexican corn. Although the U.S. corn was intended for animal feed, it nevertheless depressed the entire Mexican corn market. American agribusinesses, highly subsidized by its own federal government, bankrupted Mexican farmers like the Chantico family, who were forced off their land—land that had grown indigenous corn for centuries. Their land was bought for a pittance by foreign direct investors who streamlined operations and planted mass monoculture acres of genetically modified, chemical-dependent crops for export—all in order to meet the American demand for off-season fruits and vegetables, and cheap beef. The profits of these exports pad the coffers of foreign-based corporations.

The displaced Chantico family migrated north to the town of Nogales at the border, where rumor spoke of $0.85 per hour factory shifts in the maquiladoras.[49] Many factories in Nogales had formerly operated out of small towns in the United States, but the managers knew costs would now be lower in Mexico. No labor unions, no worker benefits, longer hours, lower wages, no disability benefits, and the possibility of child labor all made the shift an enticing one. Maria Chantico began mind-numbing work in a factory, hunched over for fifteen hours a day and ending her shift at 4:00 am. The youngest children scavenged food and clothing from the nearby trash dump. They lived in a cramped shack made of cast-off materials from the factory, next to a dry riverbed (dry due to the factory's overpumping) that now served as a dumpsite for *industrial waste: copper tailings, unregulated dumped toxic chemicals, and untreated sewage.*[50] *The people of Nogales experience unusually high rates of cancer, neurological disease, miscarriages, and birth defects. Maria's children scavenge a 55-gallon drum from the factory to contain the potable water brought in on trucks—a drum that used to hold toxic chemicals. In addition to the injuries that Maria and her fellow workers experience due to the elimination of safety devices, many of the women are victims of sexual exploitation and physical abuse.*

Meanwhile, Colleen, a young woman living in New Hampshire, shops at her local Old Navy where tank tops are on sale for $5.99. In the clearance section she can buy two and get the third for free. The "Made in Mexico" label was tiny, hard to see. Holding the clean, fresh-smelling shirt in her hands, surrounded by immaculate tile floors, fluorescent lighting, and pleasant music, it's difficult to imagine the series of events that led to the production of this shirt. Colleen knows none of this backstory as she compares the sky-blue racerback tank to the surfboard yellow jersey tee. She has a limited budget and appreciates a good deal. Cheap Mexican labor allows Old Navy's prices to stay low.

Colleen's mutual fund includes companies that invest in maquiladoras, but she is unaware of this. Her parents' income over the years has included dividends from funds invested in the agribusiness now flourishing through attaining new corn markets in Mexico and farmlands formerly owned by Mexican farmers. Many forces conspire to obscure the reality of Maria Chantico, sweating in 104-degree heat, surrounded by loud machines, handling toxic chemicals with her bare hands, only to leave the factory with blurred vision, an aching back, skin sores, and not enough pesos in her pocket to buy food for her family.

As Maria left work, the finished tank top left the factory. It was packaged and transported via truck to a regional transportation center, and then onto a bigger truck that passed through customs and into the United States. Two weeks later it arrived at the Old Navy in New Hampshire.

The transportation process contributed to releasing greenhouse gases into the atmosphere, but this is merely a fraction of the total carbon footprint for one tank top. Two thousand gallons of water produced the pound of conventional cotton in a field in China, not to mention a third of a pound of chemical pesticides and fertilizers.[51] *The cotton was then shipped to the gin and pressed mechanically into bales, then shipped to another factory for spinning into yarn, and then to yet another location where mechanical looms wove it into rough gray sheets of cotton. Heat and chemicals then transformed the sheet into its final look and feel, producing wastewater that was dumped into the local water system. The finished cloth was then placed on a container ship and sent to Mexico where Maria served as one member of an assembly line, shaping it into a women's aqua lace-trim rib-knit tank.*[52]

Not merely clothing but appliances, vehicles, household goods, and electronics are produced in maquiladoras in Mexico just south of the U.S. border. In fact, much of Colleen's food comes from Mexico and carries chemicals from pesticides and fertilizers that are outlawed in the U.S. but permitted in Mexico. Ground transportation of goods is an enormous industry in the U.S.

The Chantico family is one of countless families driven north by NAFTA into sweatshop labor. Some were small farmers like the Chanticos. Others owned small businesses that were forced out of business by clauses in NAFTA that allowed large foreign corporate business to come in and undercut the local small businesses.

This story continues in chapter 5.

****

STRUCTURAL VIOLENCE

STRUCTURAL VIOLENCE THEORY

The term "structural injustice" is effective and vital for describing the dynamics at play in the Chanticos' life situation and countless others like it. The term could serve the purposes of this book well, as it has up to this point. However, I have chosen, henceforth, to use the term "structural *violence*" and evolving structural violence theory rather than "structural *injustice*" and theory related to it. My reasons are three. "Structural injustice" is as variously understood and theorized as is "justice." Using it with integrity would entail untangling a body of theory, which would distract from my central purposes. Secondly, structural violence theory has been used to denote economic inequity and the poverty it causes, and is well suited for expansion to include ecological damage.[53] But most importantly, the concept "structural violence" and the associated body of theory are sharp tools for demystifying moral oblivion, moral passivity, moral vision, and moral agency in the contemporary context of economic and ecological injustice.

"Structural violence," as a concept, emerged out of peace studies and the work of Norwegian professor of peace and conflict research, Johann Galtung, who also founded the International Peace Institute in Oslo in 1969.[54] In recent decades, the term has figured in political discourse, medical anthropology, clinical medicine, and mental health studies. One prominent theorist is medical anthropologist and physician Paul Farmer. Probing the concept unearths invaluable clues to complicity with systemic evil and to building empowering moral vision.

"Social structure" is a very broad term used to denote the ordering of human relationships on multiple levels from macro (that is, a national economy or social classes) to institutional (that is, an educational system), to micro (that is, a family), to ideological (that is, a value system). A structural perspective assumes that social structures shape human identities, interests, and interactions, providing, to an extent, "both the possibilities and limits for human action."[55]

"Structural violence" refers to the physical, psychological, and spiritual harm that certain groups of people experience as a result of unequal distribution of power and privilege. James Gilligan, Harvard Medical School professor, defines structural violence as "the increased rates of death and disability suffered by those who occupy the bottom rungs of society."[56] Astrophysicist and sustainability leader Robert Gilman describes structural violence as "physical and psychological harm that results from exploitive and unjust social, political and economic systems. . . . Hunger and poverty are two prime examples of what is described as 'structural violence.'"[57] He cites others who estimate structural violence on an international level by asking, "[H]ow many extra deaths occur each year due to the unequal distribution of wealth between countries?"[58] In short, structural violence degrades, dehumanizes, damages, and kills people by limiting or preventing their access to the necessities for life or for its flourishing.

I suggest a second aspect of structural violence: the complicity or silent acquiescence of those who fail to take responsibility for it and challenge it. Herein structural violence refers to these two dimensions—the harm that is done and silent acquiescence to it. Racism, classism, sexism, and heterosexism are common forms.

Paul Farmer vividly illustrates the ways in which structural violence causes extreme poverty and ill health in Haiti. He emphasizes that structural violence is the result of power disparities.[59] This power disparity generally runs along the lines of class, race, and gender. "Structural violence" is his shorthand for "inegalitarian social structures."[60] Power asymmetries determine who is most at risk for devastation by disease, weather-related disasters, unjust imprisonment, economic downturns, poverty, and other afflictions, including incidents often labeled natural disasters. "These afflictions," Farmer insists, "are not the result of accident . . . they are consequences, direct or indirect of human agency." This agency is not primarily the acts of individuals but of historically developed and often economically driven social processes. The importance of these final points cannot be overstated: *That which is the result of human agency can be challenged by it!* My use of "structural violence" shares Farmer's emphasis.

STRUCTURAL VIOLENCE, DIRECT VIOLENCE, AND CULTURAL VIOLENCE

The presence and nature of structural violence become clearer in contrast to what Galtung refers to as "personal violence" or "direct violence."[61] Whereas in direct violence the perpetrator (person or group) can be identified, in structural (or "indirect") violence, "there may not be any person who directly harms another person in the structure. The violence is built into the structure and shows up as unequal power and consequently unequal life chances."[62] "In both cases individuals may be killed or mutilated. . . . But whereas in the [case of direct violence] these consequences may be traced back to concrete persons or actors, in the [case of structural violence] this is no longer meaningful. . . . The important point here is that if people are starving when this is objectively avoidable, then violence is committed, regardless of whether there is a clear subject-action-object relation."[63] Galtung illustrates, "[I]n a society where life expectancy is twice as high in the upper as in the lower classes, violence is exercised even if there are not concrete actors one can point to directly attacking others, as when one person kills another."[64] "Direct violence is an *event*; structural violence is a *process*."[65]

This distinction helps illuminate how easily structural violence remains unrecognized. Recall the story of Colleen and Maria just above. Maria lost her home, and the sense of personhood that accompanies maintaining a family's livelihood. Her unborn child may be born disfigured by toxins released into her new environment by the factories that employ her and others. Her human rights are transgressed and she has no recourse. The same systems that displaced Maria and keep her in inhumane conditions produce for Colleen inexpensive clothing and a growing mutual fund.

And yet Maria's misery is not Colleen's fault. No specific person may be held responsible for what has been done to Maria. No single person was responsible for the NAFTA treaty that destroyed her corn-based livelihood and forced her to move north to the border. No one "forced" her to hire on with the *maquiladora*; she technically is "free" to leave if she wants to avoid the toxic dangers and sexual overtures of supervisors. The wage structure was set by corporate policy and is not traceable to any one person. Plant managers are simply carrying out their orders and obeying policy; they may even be paying a slight bit more than neighboring plants. The constellation of violence against Maria and countless like her is a process, not a direct act by identifiable individuals.[66] Many people involved in that process and benefiting from it remain oblivious to the impact on Maria.

Structural violence generally is not criminalized. Direct violence is far more likely to be perceived by society as a crime, punishable by legal systems. This status of legality helps to maintain the relative "invisibility" of structural violence.

Galtung's assertion that structural violence is a "process" involving many people over time yields further insight into society's astounding capacity to ignore it. The people involved generally are disconnected from each other and are kept relatively unaware of each other's actions and of other stages in the process. More importantly, many actions required to maintain structural violence are taken by people who may not be responsible for the decisions that mandate those actions. To illustrate: the middle-level manager at Walmart did not make the policy that denies some employees benefits and wages adequate to maintain their health. The gas station employee did not decide to pay militias to kill Ogoni people who protested Shell Oil's desecration of their lands in the Niger Delta.

The insidious nature of structural violence has yet another face. Those who perpetrate one form of structural violence may themselves be victims of another form that precludes their taking opposing actions *without the support of a broader community*. The Walmart middle manager may risk losing her job if she fails to fire the employee who has been unable to work due to illness. The gas station employee may have lost his previous job to downsizing by a corporation whose CEO earned 450 times what this worker earned. Resistance to structural violence calls for change not only in individuals' lives but also in the structures of society—public policy, corporate rights, and institutions. The call to neighbor-love pertains not only to private life but also to the ecological and economic dimensions of life.

Structural violence at any given time stands on a vast array of decisions and actions that began decades, sometimes centuries, ago. Without structural moral vision—vision that enables seeing that history—we march on in moral oblivion.

When structural violence begins to break into public awareness, those responsible for it briskly and effectively deflect that dawning awareness onto more sensational and easily understood acts of *direct* violence. When torture at

Abu Graib prison in Iraq was publicly exposed, the high-ranking people who had decided to make torture an "acceptable" means of interrogation and to socialize young soldiers into accepting it as normal, quickly hid by blaming the individual soldiers at Abu Graib. The powerful people and processes responsible for implanting brutality into the hearts and minds of the young soldiers were off the hook. Blaming direct violence obscures the more dangerous structural violence.

Structural violence theory offers yet another tool for explaining complicity with structural evil. It is the concept of "cultural violence." The term was coined by John Galtung to denote "those aspects of culture . . . that can be used to justify or legitimize direct or structural violence. . . . Cultural violence makes direct and structural violence look, even feel, right—or at least not wrong."[67] Direct, structural, and cultural violence form what Galtung calls a tri-fold paradigm of violence. "[A]t the bottom is the steady flow through time of cultural violence, a substratum from which the other two can derive their nutrients. In the next stratum the rhythms of structural violence are located. Patterns of exploitation are building up, wearing out, or torn down. . . . And at the top, visible to the naked eye . . . is the stratum of direct violence with the whole record of direct cruelty perpetrated by human beings against each other and against other forms of life and nature in general."[68] Dismantling structural violence thus calls for identifying the cultural violence that nourishes it.

What is the cultural violence that enables U.S. society to normalize and accept the practice of paying CEOs 450 times the earnings of their lowest-paid workers, especially when that wage does not meet the bare-bone needs of food and shelter? What mesmerizing forces of cultural violence make it desirable for Seattleites to build huge luxurious houses while ignoring the city's six to ten thousand homeless people and lobbying against the movement to effect an income tax on the wealthiest citizens of Washington State? Tom Shadyac in his film, "I Am," calls such cultural violence into question with a brief story: "Here's a story, a true story," he begins, "to show just who we've become."

> Once there was a native tribe that lived in peace and harmony for thousands of years, and every day the routine was the same: the hunters would go out from the tribe, and when they returned, the bounty from the hunt was shared equally by all members of the tribe. No one went hungry when food was available, not even the weak, the sick or the elderly. One day the most skilled hunter said, 'I'm the best hunter. I kill more than my share of deer. Why should I share the bounty of my hunt?' And from that day forward he began storing his

meat in a high mountain cave. And then other skilled hunters said, 'we kill more than our share of deer too. Shouldn't we have the right to keep the bounty of our hunt?' And they too began to store their meat in high mountain caves. And then something began to happen in the tribe that had never happened before. Some people, especially the old, the weak, and the sick began to be hungry while others were well fed. In fact it became so commonplace that no one even thought it unusual that some were starving while others had more than they needed. And what's even more strange, the tribal elders began teaching their young to emulate the hoarding habits of these few. Now that story isn't true because it happened. It's true because it's *happening*.

The concept of cultural violence is invaluable for unlocking the puzzle of complicity with economic and ecological exploitation. The coming chapter unearths faces of cultural violence in our context.

STRUCTURAL VIOLENCE: WHAT IT DOES

Another key to understanding structural violence is its consequences, what it *does*. Where structural violence is at play, it is likely to:

- sharply influence who will be at risk for imprisonment, death in childbirth, poverty, devastation in the face of ill health or weather-related disasters, etc. In Farmer's words, structural violence "influences the nature and distribution of extreme suffering."[69]
- lead to direct violence in the forms of revolutionary violence, riots, "terrorism," domestic violence, hate crimes, war, and more.
- contribute to (as well as grow out of) power imbalance that disadvantages those who hold little power.
- put those who challenge it at risk.
- lead to internalized oppression.
- in its most potent forms, determine who will have the necessities for life with dignity and who will not.
- enable a few people to benefit far more than many others from interactions. In structural violence, "the topdogs get much more . . . out of the interaction . . . than the other, the underdogs. . . . The underdogs may in fact be so disadvantaged that they die (starve, waste away from diseases) from it. . . . Or they may be left in a permanent, unwanted state of misery, usually including malnutrition and illness."

STRUCTURAL VIOLENCE: DEFINING FEATURES

Identifying defining characteristics of structural violence yields still keener insight into how it functions, how it hides, and how we might dismantle it. Not surprisingly, the previously noted features of structural injustice and structural sin turn up again here as the first four features of structural violence noted below. Structural violence:

- is generally invisible to or ignored by those who perpetrate it and or benefit from it.
- cannot happen without the actions of individuals, yet operates independently of the goodness or wickedness of the people perpetrating it.
- is passed on from generation to generation unless challenged.
- becomes more devastating with concentration of power in fewer hands.
- consists of interlocking rather than isolated forms of oppression. Hence one may "benefit" from structural violence along one "axis of oppression" while being victimized by it along another.[70]
- may trap perpetrators by victimizing them in the very structural violence they perpetrate.
- entails ideologies or worldviews, institutional policies, and practices so embedded in society that they *appear* natural, normal, inevitable, or divinely mandated.

These consequences and features of structural violence will provide vital insights as we work toward seeing and dismantling the particular structural violence of concern in this project: economic and ecological violence. These features and impacts of structural violence are manifest in the "life stories" throughout.

STRUCTURAL VIOLENCE CALLS FOR STRUCTURAL MORAL VISION

Severe poverty, extreme asymmetry of wealth, and the compromised life chances they engender are manifestations of structural violence grounded in inequality of power. So too is ecological degradation. Thus, challenging them requires different means than if they were primarily the result of wealthy individuals' greed, insensitivity, acts of direct violence, or lack of generosity, or the result of impoverished people's misfortune, misdeeds, or inadequacies. Trying to solve the problems of structural violence with *individualized* responses not only fails to solve the problem, but also reinforces its invisibility. To counter structural violence, moral vision must, itself, be structural.

In Sum

We noted five theological problems stemming from our complicity in structural injustice, and identified them as structural sin. Viewing structural injustice as structural sin revealed obstacles to overcoming it:

- Where we remain unaware of structural sin/injustice, we cannot repent of it.
- Where awareness leads to repentance, we are faced with the paradox of privilege.
- Structural sin/injustice is passed on from generation to generation unless recognized and challenged.
- Concentrated power renders structural sin/injustice more potent.

Next, seeing structural injustice as structural evil illumined how it is woven into our daily lives and how it hides under the guise of good, inevitability, divine mandate, or social necessity. The lens of structural violence theory confirmed power disparity as a cause of structural injustice, and pointed out the ominous role of cultural violence in breeding and perpetuating structural violence.

These dynamics cry out: A core aspect of Christian faith, renouncing sin, requires a moral consciousness that accounts for the impact of people's collective actions. The structural nature of sin and evil calls forth also a structural understanding of neighbor-love. We will call it love as an ecological-economic vocation.

Notes

1. Dietrich Bonhoeffer and Eberhard Bethge, *Letters and Papers from Prison* (London: SCM, 1967).

2. Mary E. Hobgood, *Dismantling Privilege: An Ethics of Accountability* (Cleveland: Pilgrim, 2000).

3. Preface to Emilie Townes, *Womanist Ethics and the Cultural Production of Evil* (New York: Palgrave Macmillan, 2006), xii.

4. Ivone Gebara, *Out of the Depths: Womens' Experience of Suffering and Evil* (Minneapolis: Fortress Press, 2002), 71.

5. Alan Durning and John C. Ryan, *Stuff: The Secret Lives of Everyday Things* (Seattle: Northwest Environment Watch, 1997), 20–22.

6. The Energy Information Association of the United States provides the emission coefficient of greenhouse gases for certain types of fuel. A 747 jet releases 30.638 kilograms per kilometer of flight.

7. "Energy: Alternative Fuel: Alternative Vehicles," from Project America website: http://www.project.org/info.php?recordID=237; also: Melissa Hinca-Ownby, "Predicting Sales of

Alternative Fuel Vehicles," *Mother Nature Network*, March 8, 2010. http://www.mnn.com/transportation/cars/stories/predicting-sales-of-alternative-fuel-vehicles.

8. The automobile industry and related industries have exercised considerable control over transportation policies in America over the past century. The 1920s and 30s saw auto and oil companies (specifically GM, Standard Oil, and Goodyear Tire) purchase and disassemble public transportation and light rail systems in several major American cities in order to eliminate competition for the car.

9. Terry Tamminen, *Lives Per Gallon: The True Cost of Our Oil Addiction* (Washington, DC: Island, 2006), 54.

10. Unpublished address presented at UN Summit on Climate Change, September 22, 2009.

11. Justin Hoffman, "The Maldives and Rising Sea Level," ICE Case Studies, Number 206, May 2007. http://www1.american.edu/ted/ice/maldives.htm.

12. *A Sea Change,* directed by Barbara Ettinger (Hudson, NY: Niijii Films, 2009). DVD.

13. Beverly Wright, "Race, Politics, and Pollution: Environmental Justice in the Mississippi River Chemical Corridor," in Agyeman et al., *Just Sustainabilities*, 129.

14. Ibid.

15. Ibid., 135–36.

16. U.S. Energy Information Administration, Country Analysis Brief on Nigeria. http://www.eia.doe.gov/cabs/Nigeria/Oil.html.

17. Wright, "Race, Politics, Pollution," 137.

18. Tunde Agbola and Moruf Alabi, "Political Economy of Petroleum Resources Development, Environmental Injustice and Selective Victimization: A Case Study of the Niger Delta Region of Nigeria," in Agyeman et al., *Just Sustainabilities*, 269, 283.

19. Lovins and Lovins, cited by Herman Daly and John Cobb, *For the Common Good: Redirecting the Economy toward Community, the Environment, and a Sustainable Future* (Boston: Beacon, 1989), 344.

20. Greg Muttitt, "Crude Designs: The Rip-Off of Iraq's Oil Wealth," Report for Platform and Global Policy Forum, November 2005, p. 4.

21. Greg Muttitt, "Production Sharing Agreements—Mortgaging Iraq's Oil Wealth," *Arab Studies Quarterly* 28, no. 3 (2006): 1.

22. *Journey of the Universe*, directed by Brian Swimme and Mary Evelyn Tucker, 2011. DVD.

23. Other translations include "dress and keep," "work it and care for it," "cultivate and watch over it."

24. Later in the text we encounter the "terminator seed," developed by Monsanto. The terminator is designed to be incapable of reseeding itself. Subsistence farmers who have been sold the terminator must rebuy seed each year. Monsanto profits. The terminator seed is the quintessence of "uncreating" the life-furthering capacity of life.

25. Albert Pero Jr., "The Church and Racism," in *Between Vision and Reality: Lutheran Churches in Transition,* ed. Wolfgang Greive (Geneva: Lutheran World Federation, 2001), 262.

26. Luther is drawing upon Augustine's image of sin as the "heart curved in on itself."

27. I am not raising sin as a problem related to personal "salvation" for life after death. That issue is of no concern to me. I believe that we are forgiven and are assured eternal life after death regardless of the magnitude of sin. Hence we are free from striving toward the good *for the purpose of gaining "heaven" after we die;* we are free to seek the good as a matter of loving God, self, neighbor, and Earth.

28. The phrase comes from Allen Johnson, *Power, Privilege, and Difference.* He uses it with a different meaning than do I.

29. Aida Hurtado, *The Color of Privilege: Three Blasphemies on Race and Feminism* (Ann Arbor: University of Michigan Press, 1996), 34.

30. Johnson, *Power, Privilege, and Difference*, 39.

31. James Poling, *Deliver Us from Evil: Resisting Racial and Gender Oppression* (Minneapolis: Fortress Press, 1996), 121.

32. Eleazar Fernandez, *Reimagining the Human: Theological Anthropology in Response to Systemic Evil* (Saint Louis: Chalice, 2004), 68.

33. Fernandez, *Reimagining the Human*, 65.

34. Christopher Morse defines evil as "whatever stands in the way of life taking place" [according to the revelation of God in Jesus' "Incarnation unto the Cross," his "Resurrection," and the "Parousia"], and the word "sin" denotes our complicity in this evil. Christopher Morse, *Not Every Spirit: A Dogmatics of Christian Disbelief* (Valley Forge, PA: Trinity Press International, 1994), 239.

35. Ted Peters, *Sin: Radical Evil in Soul and Society* (Grand Rapids: Eerdmans, 1994), 8–9. Edward Farley uses the two more or less interchangeably (see note 36 below, especially 120) using theological inquiry into sin as inquiry into evil. So too does Eleazar Fernandez in his *Reimagining the Human: Theological Anthropology in Response to Systemic Evil.*

36. "Differentiating sin from the tragic [and suffering] is a seminal insight of the Hebraic tradition." Edward Farley, *Good and Evil* (Minneapolis: Fortress Press, 1990), 125.

37. Emilie Townes, *Womanist Ethics and the Cultural Production of Evil* (New York: Palgrave Macmillan, 2006), 18.

38. Fernandez, *Reimagining the Human.*

39. Gebara, *Out of the Depths*, 3.

40. "Although religious faith and practice have been used to perpetuate evil, true faith is our only protection against it," writes Poling in *Deliver Us*, 134. "[S]omewhere deep inside each of us we know that perhaps the simplest, yet most difficult, answer . . . is *live your life faithfully*," Townes declares in *Cultural Production of Evil*, 164.

41. Bonhoeffer, *Letters and Papers.*

42. James Poling's account of evil's hiddenness resonates with Bonhoeffer's. Poling notes that "evil hides under claims to goodness or necessity" (119).

43. Poling, *Deliver Us*, 119.

44. Ibid., 119.

45. Ibid., 113.

46. Gebara, *Depths*, 2.

47. Ibid., 2–3, and 58.

48. Peter Canby, "Retreat to Subsistence," *The Nation* (July 5, 2010).

49. This is at low end of the range of hourly wages for maquiladora workers.

50. Giovanna di Chiro, "Living Is for Everyone: Border Crossings for Community, Environment, and Health," *Osiris* 19 (2000): 116.

51. National Resources Defense Council, "From Field to Store: Your T-shirt's Life Story."

52. Ibid.

53. Johan Galtung began to do so in "Cultural Violence," *Journal of Peace Research* (August 1990): 291–305.

54. Johan Galtung, "Violence, Peace, and Peace Research," *Journal of Peace Research* 6, no. 3 (1969): 167–91.

55. Todd Landman, *Studying Human Rights* (New York: Routledge, 2006), 45. The extent to which structures constrain individual agency is contested. See Kathleen Ho, "Structural Violence as a Human Rights Violation," *Essex Human Rights Review* 4, no. 2 (September 2007) and Todd Landman, *Studying Human Rights*, 36–55.

56. James Gilligan, *Violence: Reflections on a National Epidemic* (New York: Vintage, 1997).

57. Robert Gilman, "Structural Violence: Can We Find Genuine Peace in a World with Inequitable Distribution of Wealth among Nations?," *Foundations of Peace* (Autumn 1983): 8.

58. Gernot Kohler and Norman Alcock, *Journal of Peace Research* 13 (1976): 343–56.

59. Paul Farmer, *Pathologies of Power: Health, Human Rights, and the New War on the Poor* (Berkeley and Los Angeles: University of California Press, 2004).

60. Ibid., 230.

61. These two categories are not always mutually exclusive.

62. Galtung, "Violence, Peace, and Peace Research," 171.

63. Ibid., 170–71.

64. Ibid., 171.

65. John Galtung, "Cultural Violence," 294.

66. Direct acts of violence may also be committed against Maria and others in her situation.

67. Ibid., 291.

68. Ibid., 294–95.

69. Farmer, *Pathologies of Power*, xiii.

70. To illustrate: A homeless white man in Seattle who lost his affordable apartment to high-end condo conversion is the victim of economic injustice. Yet at the same time, he will stand a better chance in court than a homeless black man if the two are picked up as suspects in the rape of a white woman.

4

Unmasking Evil That Parades as Good

"Through clever and constant application of propaganda, people can be made to see paradise as hell, and also the other way round."

Adolf Hitler[1]

****

A LIFE STORY

BLOOD MINERALS

My sleep is broken at 7:00 a.m. by a gentle tone pulsating from the cell phone on my night table. This cell phone increasingly functions as my alarm clock, and in my groggy morning stupor I glance at icons on the screen to find out today's weather forecast. Breakfast is spent scrolling through a series of texts that arrived overnight, and as I race out the door with coffee in one hand and my smartphone in the other, its screen reveals Google map directions to a morning meeting.

Over the course of the day, I will receive somewhere around two hundred emails, texts, and calls on my smartphone. It has become an indispensable part of my day. It guides me to my next location, tells me when the bus is coming, plays songs, takes pictures, connects me to hundreds of people, channels news headlines, sports scores, and the stock market, even tracks my pace when I'm jogging. In addition to my cell phone, I also own a camera, an iPod, a DVD player, a television, and a laptop.

The small device that causes my cell phone to vibrate is called a pinhead capacitor. About the size of my pinky nail, it also regulates voltage and stores energy. These capacitors are found in essentially all the electronic devices in my home. They're made from a mineral I've never heard of called coltan, which is found in large quantities in the Congo.

To mine coltan, men, women, and children dig large craters in streambeds or chip away chunks of rock, scraping away the dirt from the surface and then sloshing the dirt around in washtubs, which allows the heavy coltan to settle at the bottom. Workers use magnetic tweezers to extract the mineral, which makes its way to trading posts in neighboring countries for export to the global market. International mineral trading companies in Europe, Asia, and the U.S. import coltan, which then passes through the hands of processing companies and capacitor manufacturers. Once processed, the refined metals are bought by electronics manufacturing companies such as Nokia, Compaq, Dell, HP, Ericson, and Sony, who turn it into usable components for electronic devices.

Working conditions for coltan miners are severe, and at times deadly. Militiamen armed with AK-47s force laborers, including children as young as eleven, to work long hours each day, and collectors often cheat the miners out of their profits. Coltan is extracted in a 'craft' manner, using small tools available locally, such as spades, hoes, and iron bars. "In some circumstances, the use of explosives is common," according to a report, "resulting often in a high death toll among the diggers, soldiers, and the local community" either from the explosives themselves or associated respiratory problems.[2] Add to this the danger of landslides and collapsing mines, and the picture is bleak. But the working conditions of coltan miners are not the only problem.

The global demand for coltan fuels a bloody civil war in central Africa, one that has claimed six million lives to date. A UN report claims that all parties involved in the Congolese civil war have been involved in the mining and sale of coltan.[3] The multimillion-dollar trade of Congolese coltan and other natural resources by foreign armies, rebels, and militias fuels the conflict by motivating armed groups to wage war, and by providing them with the cash to do so. "There's no question that the minerals fund armed groups in the largely lawless region," writes a CNN reporter. The Enough Project, Global Witness, UN reports, and others have documented extraordinary human rights abuses associated with the incredibly lucrative mining industry. "The general use of violence against communities includes forced labor, torture, recruitment of child soldiers, extortion, and killings by armed groups to oppress and control civilians," reports the Enough Project. In the context of a Congolese war in which warlords use terror as an essential weapon to ensure control of regions where international companies mine for valuable metals, sexual violence is especially horrendous. "Competing militias rape in order either to drive communities out of contested areas or else as a means of controlling or subjugating those living in the areas they control."[4]

The impact of coltan mining on biodiversity and soil and water quality is devastating. Much coltan is mined near national parks, and some workers rely on poaching to eat. Kahuzi Biega National Park, home of the mountain gorilla, has suffered particularly from coltan mining. Widespread hunting has driven lowland gorillas and elephants to the brink of extinction, and massive deforestation from mines and airstrips, as well as water pollution from mine tailings, has killed off all edible wildlife in the park. The ecosystem has been effectively plundered, according to a UNEP report.[5]

When I upgrade my cell phone using Verizon's "new every two" plan, or replace my old TV with a plasma screen, or make the leap to an iPad, the new devices will not come with a label that reads "Warning! This device was made with raw materials from Central Africa that are nonrenewable, were mined in inhumane conditions, and then sold to fund a bloody war of occupation. Moreover, the device has caused massive soil and water contamination and the virtual elimination of endangered species. Enjoy."

Even with such a label, would I think twice about where my electronics come from? Would I speak up to influence public policy around coltan imports? Would I consider sharing electronics with neighbors, or forgo owning some of them at all? Would I contact Apple, Microsoft, or other companies that produce electronics?

The story continues in chapter 9.

BACKGROUND TO LIFE STORY

Coltan is a shorthand term for columbium-tantalum. Many devices beyond cell phones contain this mineral: cameras, mp3 players, computer chips, pagers, DVD players, video game systems, missiles, and airplanes all depend on coltan. Americans use and discard cell phones at a faster rate than any other nation and tend to own far more household electronics than do other people. The United States is the largest consumer of coltan in the world, accounting for 40 percent of global demand.[6]

****

One factor leading to moral inertia in the face of systemic injustice on the part of people privileged by it is their failure to "see" it, and to acknowledge their implication in it. This is a failure to recognize the structural links between the privilege of a few and the suffering of the many. We do not notice how the "patterned behaviors we engage in daily . . . exploit, silence, disable, or marginalize some as they confer status, profits, and other benefits on elites." We may enjoy the spotless interior of a well-cleaned business building, but "are socialized not to see the [janitors] whose work maintains our lifestyle" and not to "grasp the economic system that gives us access to better jobs" and underpays the janitors.[7]

A crucial initial step in challenging social structural mechanisms that build material wealth for some at the expense of others and of Earth's ecosystems is realizing that they exist. If indeed morality requires challenging and seeking to undo those structures, then a task of morality is to *see* them in order to dismantle them. This is one role of moral vision.

How is it that white, economically secure adults did not see the racial and economic injustice shaping life for thousands of black and poor white residents of New Orleans for decades *preceding* Hurricane Katrina? The matter is not one of private or personal choice alone. Power arrangements, economic power in particular, play a role in obscuring from the "haves" the reality of the "have nots." Public sociologist, Gary Perry, describes how freeways were designed in New Orleans to enable tourists and other airline travelers to move from the airport to tourist havens and other relatively wealthy parts of town *without seeing* the impoverished areas and the people who inhabit them.[8] They are hidden from view of wealthier people. People who live, work, and play in non–poor neighborhoods are drawn into moral oblivion by "powers that be" who have a strong vested interest in hiding the horrors of abject poverty.

Indeed, crucial moral weight lies in perceptions of "what *is*." *What* we see and refuse to see, and *how* we see are morally loaded, bearing on whether we foster or thwart life-saving change. A primary function of Christian ethics is developing tools for morally responsible vision, especially vision of the power dynamics that determine who has the necessities for life and determine humans' impact on planet Earth.

This chapter and the next two respond to the moral imperative of honing skills in *seeing* structures of injustice cleverly hidden behind the blinders of social privilege, and in particular economic privilege. I seek tools for "unmasking social evil where it parades as good." I refer to that unmasking process as critical vision.

It has been fascinating to encounter other voices alluding to "seeing" as an integral dimension of morality and ethics. Hear just a few:

> Hebrew Bible scholar Walter Brueggemann: "The ones who minister to the imagination, who enable people to see the world differently and to live now in the world they see are fatally dangerous to the establishment."[9] "Poets and artists are silenced because they reveal too much of what must remain hidden."[10]

> Christian ethicist Daniel Maguire: The "bane of ethics" is to ignore or "inadequately see reality."[11]

> Jesus: "Are your hearts hardened? Do you have eyes, and fail to see?" (Mark 8:17–18)

A first step in enabling critical vision is unearthing the dynamics that impede it. We begin there, probing for factors that cloak structural injustice "to the point of invisibility."[12] The focus here, then, is less on the power dynamics that cause injustice, and more on the dynamics that cause us *not to recognize* it.

The task is not merely to unmask the mechanisms of moral oblivion. The challenge is to do so in ways that evoke and sustain moral agency for the long haul toward forms of economic life that do not accumulate massive wealth for a few at great cost to the many and that do not endanger Earth's regenerative capacities.

SOCIALLY CONSTRUCTED MORAL OBLIVION: THEORETICAL OVERVIEW

For people or social sectors who are invested consciously or unconsciously in preserving "the way things are," moral vision is socialized or culturally constructed to affirm "the way things are" as good, as "the way things ought to be." Or if "the way things are" is not perceived as good, it is accepted as the way things simply must be. More specifically, vision is constructed to normalize and rationalize existing social and ecological conditions (the way things are) that may be evil, allowing them to parade as good, inevitable, or normal. This entails *not* seeing (or seeing but disregarding) evidence to the contrary.

To understand the social construction of vision, we turn to a sister concept with a more developed body of theory: hegemonic knowledge or vision. We first examine the concept and then, to concretize and contextualize it, we isolate and analyze eight factors contributing to hegemonic vision in the current context. Each factor lends concrete form to the previous chapter's discoveries regarding evil's capacity to disguise itself as good, social necessity, normal, or simply inevitable.

For years I have taught my students to keep in mind what I call a "boilerplate question"—an overall query to bear in mind while walking through the events of daily life: "What in any given circumstance is uncritically presupposed to be natural, normal, inevitable, or divinely ordained, that in fact may be none of these, but rather a social construct?" The purpose of this "boilerplate question" is to expose and examine the "knowing" and social vision that shapes our unconscious and semi-conscious assumptions about what is natural, normal, inevitable, or divinely ordained and about what power we have or do not have to build a more just world.

The students are exposing "hegemonic vision." The term refers to the constellation of socially constructed perceptions and assumptions about "what is," "what could be," and "what ought to be" that maintain the power or privilege of some people over others, and "blind" the former to that privilege. We are working here with a basic insight of the postmodern turn: that ideas have the power to shape social reality and to do so in ways that may not be recognized by those who benefit most from that constructed reality.

The grave danger of hegemonic vision is its deadening impact on social change. What is natural, inevitable, or divinely mandated is not subject to human decisions and actions. With hegemony, notes Stephen Brookfield, "there seems to be no chance of opposition, no way to develop alternative possibilities."[13]

To probe the forces that hide injustice from the eyes of those who "benefit" from it, but could resist it, may seem to be a breeding ground for hopelessness itself. To the contrary, it is an excursion of hope and into hope. For this quest is born of the firm conviction that human beings—enlivened by the breath of God—bear vast moral power. It is the power to see and resist what betrays God's boundless, unquenchable yearning toward abundant life for all. That power requires stark honesty. Uncovering hegemonic vision is an act of stark, subversive honesty.

The theorist most associated with the term "hegemony" is Italian political theorist and cultural critic Antonio Gramsci. Gramsci used "hegemony" to denote the social control exercised by dominant sectors through ideological means. Neither state nor military domination is required to elicit the general population's consent to the overall direction imposed on life by dominant sectors or culture. Rather, consent is garnered through worldview, values, and ideas, even where that societal direction is exploitative or oppressive to the very people who consent to it. For Gramsci and many other theorists, hegemony refers in particular to the processes that convince people to accept rather than to resist cultural norms and practices that betray their own best interests while appearing to support them.[14] A hegemonic culture, notes Cornel West, is "a culture successful in persuading people to consent to their oppression and exploitation."[15]

Hegemony elicits consent in part by convincing people that existing social arrangements are normal or necessary. Hegemony is, in West's words, "the set of formal ideas and beliefs and informal modes of behaviors, habits, manners, sensibilities, and outlooks *that support and sanction the existing order.*"[16] Particularly relevant to the contemporary reality of unintentional yet brutal economic and ecological exploitation woven into our lives is the insight that hegemony "constitutes a sense of reality . . . beyond which it is very difficult for most members of the society to move, in most areas of their lives."[17]

In opposition to hegemonic vision stands critical vision. To accept as reality the world as it appears to be through lenses constructed by dominant social forces is, in Gramsci's words, to live without "a critical awareness."[18] It is to adopt "the uncritical and largely unconscious way of perceiving and understanding the world that has become 'common' in any given epoch" regardless of its detrimental impact on the very people who hold it.[19]

My intent is not to adopt precisely Gramsci's use of "hegemony." Rather, I draw critically upon his insights and the insights of others who have adapted the term and Gramsci's basic premises about it to other contexts, and who have done so in order to pursue questions similar to mine. These scholar/activists are valuable not only for their astute insight into hegemony, but also for their firm conviction that it can be overcome and transformed into socially responsible action for change.

Hegemony may be seen as a process. Brookfield defines it as "the process by which we *learn* to embrace enthusiastically a system of beliefs and practices that end up harming us and working to support the interest of others who have power over us."[20] Hegemony, he writes elsewhere, is "the process by which people *learn* to live and love the dominant system of beliefs and practices," a process "not imposed on them so much as it is *learned* by them. If anything can be described as lifelong learning, it is this."[21] I aim to isolate and analyze elements of those processes, to untangle their elusive strands.

Below we unravel the forces of collective deception not for the sake of intellectual curiosity or some perverse desire to uncover the ills of American society. The purpose is singularly constructive. It is to understand processes that build collective moral oblivion so that we may dismantle them, and enable moral vision.

Socially Constructed Moral Oblivion: Eight Ingredients

With socially constructed vision—and more specifically, hegemonic vision—as the illuminating concepts, and hegemony the informing theory, what are concrete factors that produce hegemonic vision in the given context? What processes garner consent to the dominant mode of economic life despite its dangerous consequences? What convinces us that there is "no chance of opposition, no way to develop alternative possibilities"?[22]

The factors behind moral oblivion may be values, ideas, practices, symbols, social trends, norms, emotions, presuppositions, or other influences. They may be conscious or not. Here we focus sequentially on eight. Consider these as ingredients in a soup, ingredients that tend to be mutually reinforcing, that draw out each other's flavor so to speak.

This list of dynamics is not comprehensive. An all-inclusive survey of the processes by which we learn to ignore our complicity in structural evil would be a multidisciplinary task, involving the social sciences, philosophy, learning theory, neuroscience, and more. Rather, my account here illustrates the function and power of a few potent factors. I have described others elsewhere.[23]

Ingredient #1: Privatized Morality and the Blinders of Charity

Impervious adherence to economically and ecologically exploitative lifeways stems in part from a historical penchant for misperceiving social problems as individuals' problems. This leaning sports manifold faces. The most obvious is the tendency to locate the causes of social suffering—particularly poverty—in individual failings or misfortune rather than in the historical and current political, economic, and cultural forces that produce it. We sever the link, for example, between a certain homeless woman on the street and the real estate development that replaced her low-cost apartment complex with luxury condos.

Another common avenue for avoiding structural causes of poverty is locating them in the inadequacy or historical misfortune of *groups*. What do Euro-Americans in areas of significant indigenous American populations do to rationalize the vast economic disparity between white people and the indigenous of their locales? A mere 150 years ago, native peoples thrived on land now covered by cities in northwest Washington. Today, the native population suffers from shockingly high rates of death from diabetes, alcoholism, tuberculosis, suicide, and unintentional injuries compared to all other Americans.[24] On some deep unconscious level, do we rationalize the disparity by assuming historical necessity or tribal peoples' inadequacy in the face of modernity?

In like manner, if hunger in Africa or India is understood to be caused by the tragic misfortune of drought or by people's inability to develop adequate farming techniques, then foreign aid and development assistance are in themselves adequate responses. If, however, hunger is the result of colonial policy that destroyed African economies, trade policies that shift market advantage to wealthier nations, corporate takeover of coastal fishing areas, lakes dried up by global warming, or water supplies privatized and sold on the global market, then the moral response called for is quite different. Our turn to foreign aid and development assistance may distract us from the trade policies, corporate exploitation, climate change, and other connections between our overconsumption and others' hunger.

Even where social structural causes of suffering are recognized, solutions often are seen in personalized terms of charitable giving or service. Far too readily, deep and heartfelt concern about poverty and hunger is channeled primarily into the interpersonal or private arenas of charitable service and giving, and concern for the morality of society itself drifts to the wayside. Impeded then are sustained efforts to counter injustice in public policies, social systems, institutions, economic policies and theories, corporate practice, public budgets, cultural norms, and other dimensions of public life. While in many circles—ecclesial, academic, activist—"social justice" is common parlance, it often is used to signify a commitment to service in society or to helping the needy rather than to uprooting structures of unjust power and privilege.

Enter here the gnarled dilemma of individualized and charitable response to human suffering rooted in systemic arrangements. Human beings have immense capacity to feel compassion for others who are suffering, and to act on that compassion. Christianity maintains that to serve the needy other is integral to faith. In my city, Seattle, countless people work diligently to feed and shelter the city's homeless people. A front-page newspaper article about a young child severely injured by the United States' bombing of Iraq produced an outpouring of money to bring the child to the United States for reparative surgery. Hurricane Katrina's devastation elicited a wealth of time, money, energy, and creativity on behalf of the victims.

Such charity is a strong and necessary response to God's call to love neighbor as self. However, alone, it is NOT a turn away from—a renunciation of—structural sin. I may respond in charity to a homeless woman and continue to support and benefit materially from public policies and corporate actions that rendered her homeless. I may help pay for the injured child's surgery while still enjoying cheaper oil enabled by the Revenue Sharing Agreements with Iraq obtained in part through the American war on that country. I may rebuild houses in New Orleans and remain a beneficiary of the white privilege that made Katrina's victims disproportionately black.

My point here is *not* the long-touted and mistaken idea that charity must be replaced by work toward social justice. I do not believe this simplistic formula. The two overlap and are both mandates of Christian faith. To affirm work for systemic change while devaluing charitable response to suffering would be naïve and cruel. Rather, my point is this: Where suffering is caused, at least in part, by societal or systemic factors, rather than singularly individual factors, charitable service aimed at meeting the needs of individuals and groups without *also* challenging those systemic factors may build social consent that perpetuates the suffering's powerful systemic roots. It is crucial, therefore, to excavate the dangers of channeling compassion for suffering *singularly* through the individualized lens of charitable service and giving.

Charity may become a blinder, obfuscating the systemic roots of suffering. A problem that is addressed by helping individual people may be seen as a problem rooted in individual misfortune, inadequacy, loss, or lack of knowledge or opportunity. In Lee Artz's terms, charitable service throws a "cloak of invisibility" over structured oppressions and may lead inadvertently to constructing the oppressor as good.[25] Charitable service may individualize or privatize the causes of social problems, obscuring their systemic roots.

A second danger is that a turn to charity suggests its adequacy. An old adage notes that it is better to teach a person how to fish than to give her or him a fish. And yet the charitable act of teaching someone to fish will not provide food if the fish supply is rapidly drained by a large dam built upstream to benefit elite interests, overfishing by global corporations, global warming, or toxic waste. The individualized response of charitable service and giving may reinforce a dominant worldview that "a thousand points of light" is alone the answer to social suffering.

Privitizing systemic problems helps us ignore and accept unjust systems. In the words of Margaret Miles, the "effort to remain altogether private [beings] is to become "morally insensible." Bonhoeffer's warning that evil can "masquerade as . . . charity" echoes here.

INGREDIENT #2: BLESSINGS VEILING STOLEN GOODS

"The rich are in possession of the goods of the poor even if they have acquired them honestly or inherited them legally. . . . [If they do not share,] the wealthy are a species of bandit."

John Chrysostom, fourth-century church "father"

Gratitude is widely accepted as a moral good. I firmly agree. Christians affirm that material goods and the life-enhancing opportunities they provide are fundamentally a blessing, a gift from God for which we give thanks. According to this idea, we ought to live in gratitude for these gifts and generously share them with others. The liturgical life and prayer life of the church, as well as Christian education, teach this understanding. It is the basis of the stewardship practices that have enabled the church worldwide (in its various ecclesial communions) to provide hospitals, schools, housing, and other vital life services. Gratitude is what we teach our children in forming them into people who always will give away at least a tithe to people in need. Listen in:

> "We have been given so much," a father teaches his child. "God has blessed us greatly. So, we share it with those less fortunate. When you get your dollar allowance, you will put a dime in the jar to give away to those less fortunate.

> "God, we give thanks for the food that we are about to eat" a mother recites sincerely before dinner.
> "We were able to get the loan for the house in spite of the difficulties," a young couple shares. "God has been so good to us."

These prayers are good. *I remain convinced that gratitude is a bedrock disposition of Christian faith.* One of my spiritual practices is to give thanks upon arising each morning. Yet, I have begun to realize a haunting paradox. Many of the material goods for which I give thanks became mine because they were "taken" from others through complex economic, political, cultural, and military systems. For those others, as illustrated in the stories throughout this book, that loss may have been devastating, even deadly.

Is it possible that our prayers and attitudes of gratitude for our many blessings subtly rationalize and normalize the ways of life that produced my material blessings while also generating global warming and toxic dumping?[26] Do those prayers conceal the enormous extent to which those blessings are stolen goods, stolen primarily from the world's peoples of color? To conceal that theft is to perpetuate it.

Here, therefore, we dare to look. Recall the people of Orissa in India, where aluminum companies mining rich deposits of Bauxite pushed the tribal people off the lands and into urban destitution. When I give thanks for a meal, am I thanking God for food that came in aluminum cans containing Bauxite from India? Vacations are a blessing. How many of us vacation in beach hotels on land stolen from its longstanding residents by global corporate business? Was the computer on which I write this book less costly because it was produced in a "free trade zone" in which the company producing it was "freed" from environmental protections as well as labor productions? These "freedoms" from regulations increased the efficiency of production and lowered my computer's price, enabling me the blessing of owning it at low cost, and enabling the corporate CEO his lucrative income. He well may give thanks to God for that "blessing."

How many relatively well-off American families fund their children's education and remodeled house with investment returns from lucrative companies that do not pay all employees a living wage? Were the diamonds in my wedding ring mined by what is essentially slave labor in South Africa? How many white middle-strata churchgoers in Seattle own homes because black people were prevented from buying them by redlining laws or were forced out of them by gentrification?

My husband is a pastor and I a professor. I give thanks for truly wonderful material blessings enabled by our modest salaries—basic camping equipment, funding for travel to visit family and dear friends, books, healthy food. To what extent were the monies that pay our salaries produced by companies that supply the weapons and airplanes used to bomb Iraq? The money that produces my salary probably passed through a bank that profited from debt repayments paid by Mozambique, the money that should have produced healthcare and food accessibility for the people of that country. When I donate money to an agency working in Mozambique, dare I consider a gift what is frankly "stolen goods"?

These are the material blessings for which we give thanks. God, forgive them, for they know not what they do, cried the crucified one.

St. Ambrose, a fourth-century theologian, cried out: "How far, oh rich, do you extend your senseless avarice? Do you intend to be the sole inhabitants of the earth? Why do you drive out the fellow sharers of nature, and claim it all for yourselves? The earth was made for all, rich and poor, in common. Why do you rich claim it as your exclusive right? The soil was given to the rich and poor in common—wherefore, oh, ye rich, do you unjustly claim it for yourselves alone? Nature gave all things in common for the use of all." Ambrose speaks to us.

The questions raised are these: Does giving thanks for our material benefits help us not "see how the suffering and unearned disadvantages of subordinate groups are the foundation for [our material] privileges?"[27] If so, how could our practices of gratitude spur us to the work of creating more equitable and ecologically healthy economic relationships?

Chapter 3 suggested that the intermingling of evil and good and the ensuing moral ambiguity bred by that mix is one reason that we so easily fail to see evil. Here that claim has taken concrete form.

INGREDIENT #3: DENIAL, GUILT, GRIEF

For people who care deeply about others and who seek to live in ways that enhance life and ameliorate suffering, denial is a seductive ingredient of moral oblivion, the bouillon in the soup, perhaps. Denial is rarely conscious and comes in many versions. It could simply deny that our actions are causing others to suffer or are endangering Earth's life-regenerating capacities. Or it might simply state that "there is nothing that I can do about these problems," and I cannot acknowledge what is both horrible and unchangeable. Or denial might whisper that these claims about injustice and ecological disaster are claims of leftists or of a fanatic few.

I will never forget the honesty of a woman who had listened to a talk I gave years ago, after returning from Central America where I led a delegation of U.S. elected officials. She was a person whom I had come to know as having an unusually deep sense of compassion for others and their suffering. "Cindy," she said, "I honestly can hardly bear to listen to what you are saying. It is too painful." Her honesty was clear and I respect her for it.

Many of us do not see because seeing would be too terrible. We are like the mourner, distracting himself or herself from engaging the grief of a loss because the emotions are simply too raw, too sad. It would be too painful to recognize our implication in profound and widespread suffering, and in what threatens the life of the world today. Our overconsumption is "covered with the blood of African children," declared the Methodist Bishop from Mozambique. Over 500,000 children under the age of five died in Iraq between 1991 and 1998 from diseases connected to the United States bombing (devastation of water systems, electrical system, and land contamination), and U.S.-invoked sanctions that prohibited medicines from entering Iraq. How could we live with realities like this, if we truly took them in? How could we face the piercing, life-shattering anguish endured by the parents of those children? While human life depends upon the health of Earth's life-support systems (air, soil, water, biosphere), "every natural system on the planet is disintegrating"[28] due in significant part to massive consumption of petroleum products in the last fifty years. How can we think the unthinkable, acknowledge the utterly unacceptable?

We run from awareness of our implication in structural brutality. We run with body, heart, and clever mental manipulations. The reality would be too horrible, my guilt and grief too great. On a level too deep for words, I fear being shattered by them. Denial or its companions, defensiveness and self-justification, race in to shield us from a vision too appalling to face.

A sense of entitlement produces another form of denial. Denial and entitlement are mutually reinforcing. I feel entitled to the lifestyle that I lead because I worked hard, even sacrificed to achieve it. Many years of education, thousands of tuition dollars and loans, and years of living on a restricted budget should entitle me to a few niceties. Conventional wisdom declares that if I have inherited some wealth, it is because my parents sacrificed tremendously to provide me with this gift and their deep desire was that I enjoy it. Where people understand themselves to be entitled to the material wealth and wealth of opportunity that they possess, they are likely to deny that having it required exploiting other people. Denial then protects us from seeing injustice inherent in the reigning order of things and, thereby, seduces us into accepting it.

Yet another source of denial is the claim to "necessity." Its soothing and deceptive voice infiltrates the public consciousness, insisting that the Highly Indebted Poor Countries repay their debt. Free trade agreements are necessary for goods to circulate and economies to grow. Climate change may be a problem but allowing industries freedom from environmental constraints is necessary for a healthy economy, this voice purrs.

One rarely acknowledged face of denial stems from "othering," the process—often unconscious—by which people exclude others and render them less than "us." The "others" may be less important, less worthy, less real, or weaker. The environmental refugees of Asia and Africa, for instance, are so very "other" and distant from me. They are a dense mass of people, crowded together, scantily clad, and speaking strange sounds. Somehow their deaths do not count as much as ours.

Denial in its varied forms is made easier by the geographic locations of privilege. Most of us do not experience directly the damaging effects of our actions on people and climates across the globe. If we are aware of climate refugees, we know them as facts but not through actual experience or relationships. Not encountering the victims is an open door to denial.

Thus is constructed the seductive lure of denial. We "distance ourselves from the horror and terror that inhabit" the products and activities of our daily lives.[29] To see would be nearly unbearable.

INGREDIENT #4: DESPAIR OR HOPELESSNESS AND . . . PERCEIVED POWERLESSNESS

Where denial fails or numbness thaws, despair or hopelessness knocks. Seeing the "data of despair" invites it. Recognizing the complexity of systemic injustice, we may feel powerless to make a difference in the face of the massive suffering it causes. We may retreat into overwhelmed exhaustion or slip back into the safety of denial.

Hopelessness and perceived powerlessness are not necessarily conscious. People do not walk around admitting that they are resigned to lives of economic and ecological exploitation. Erich Fromm, a theorist in Germany's Frankfurt school of critical theory, explains: "most people do not admit to themselves feelings of . . . hopelessness—that is to say, they are *unconscious* of these feelings."

"What are you writing about?" asked a man sitting down at the table next to mine in the coffee shop.

"Oh . . . you don't want to know," I responded with a sigh. "I'm trying to deal with what it means to live a moral life given that we are killing people all over the world—through climate change, and by taking their land to grow our snowpeas, destroying their fishing communities to build resorts, poisoning their water supplies to make Coca-Cola, . . .

"I know, I know," he interrupted. "Listen, I totally agree with you."

"You do?"

"Look, any sentient middle-class person in America knows," he went on. "There's a gnawing sense of guilt. We know we're destroying the planet. We also know we're the ones who can fix it . . . we have the money, the science, the power."

"So, what do you do about it," I asked, typing his words as he spoke.

"What do I do about it? What does anyone do about it? Nothing. I buy another latte, or a toy for my car. Listen, I drive a big gas-eating car. Hey, I'm a total socialist but it doesn't change anything I do," he confessed, holding up his latte in a paper cup with a plastic lid. "What's there to do? I don't see much changing."

A sense of powerlessness is understandable given the structural roots of the suffering described in this book. The structural injustice will continue despite my actions to the contrary. Even my fervent commitment and actions will not force Monsanto to stop patenting seeds and promoting chemically based farming.

Precisely here we see the vital importance of recalling and even embracing "the paradox of privilege" discussed in the previous chapter: While individuals' actions will not alone dismantle systems of evil, *those systems will only be dismantled if individuals do act.* Our actions toward justice are vital, even while they may seem inconsequential.

Grave moral danger accompanies the subtle but debilitating sense of powerlessness and despair that lurk when one recognizes the magnitude of suffering connected to how we live. Where we experience no hope for change and no power to move toward it, "the way things are" becomes "the way things simply must be." If I see no hope for different forms of global economic relationships and no power to move toward them—even in small ways—then currently prevailing economic policies, practices, and structures become, according to my reality, inevitable. I am lulled into accepting the existing order of things and satisfying my compassionate urges by helping individuals or small groups escape from poverty. Drained away are the will and capacity to enter into movements aimed at uprooting its causes; lost is the impetus for seeking more just and sustainable forms of economic life. Herein lies the peril of this poisonous ingredient: lost hope and perceived powerlessness.

INGREDIENT #5: UNCONSCIOUS CONFORMITY

Erich Fromm dedicated himself to understanding how and why people collectively conform to ways of thinking and living that reinscribe existing power structures and belief systems, even where they are socially destructive. He worked in the context of rising fascism in mid-century Europe and sought to unravel the tangled roots of what he called "automaton conformity," a social character prone to conform to and adopt ideas and practices that reinforce existing structures of power and privilege, all the while under the impression that they are "following their own will."

Conformity may be driven by the hunger for approval. Socialization into attitudes and habits geared toward gaining social approval is also socialization into patterns of extraordinary consumption. Normalizing degrees of consumption previously unheard of in human history proceeds without people's full awareness. Through "a complicated process of indoctrination, rewards, punishments, and fitting ideology," Fromm writes, "most people believe they are following their own will and are unaware that their will itself is conditioned and manipulated."[30]

The sources of social manipulation in our context are not coercive but seductively persuasive. They are a complex array of anonymous influences, the persuasive power of which remains largely below the consciousness of the public. They include public opinion, conventional wisdom, political spin, ideological manipulation, the normative "scripts" of one's family and subculture, the availability of consumer goods, and perhaps more powerful than all else, advertising in its many forms.

One key factor in producing widespread conformity, in Fromm's analysis, is modern capitalism and its need for people who "cooperate in large numbers, consume more and more, [and] have standardized tastes, to a degree unknown in most cultures." Capitalism, he argued, needs people who are "malleable consumers . . . [who] equate living with consuming, gain identity from brand names," and can be persuaded to conform to the market's aim of maximized profit.[31] The directives to consume are (using Brookfield's term) inscribed in the cultural DNA.

The values and practices of capitalism in its neoliberal form infiltrate all areas of life and are universalized as the only normative way to live. We conform to these norms unwittingly, assuming their universal normativity. The result is a "fog" of moral oblivion that wipes away awareness of the dramatic amputation of alternatives.

Not only the consumer norms demanded by market-driven society but the color lines it draws around economic and ecological violence demand our conformity. White people, unless shocked out of compliance, etch those lines ever more deeply into the fabric of societies. As American citizens conform to the tacit but fierce mantras—"buy more electronic toys!" "Drink more bottled water!"—people of color in India or the Philippines see more and more toxic waste and plastic bottles piling over their lands, and people of the Congo die in the coltan mines or the wars fueled by them. As we admire flaunted wealth and consumption on television, as we invite the "free speech" of corporate America to convince our children that "stuff" will make them happy and successful, as we unwittingly conform to these standards—people of color in Africa, Asia, and the Pacific Islands lose their communities and livelihoods to the consequential climate change. We white people do not tend to see these color lines.

A defining feature of structural violence noted in chapter 3 was its lineage from generation to generation through socialization processes. Here that feature has come into full view.

Conscience, Fromm points out, is a casualty of automaton conformity. "[H]ow," he asks, "can conscience develop when the principle of life is conformity? Conscience, by its very nature, is non-conforming; it must be able say no, when everybody else says yes. . . . To the degree to which a person conforms, he cannot hear the voice of his conscience, much less act upon it."[32]

Likewise, critical thinking shrivels under the pressure to conform. Disabled conscience and critical thinking curtail the questioning of existing structures of injustice that are not readily visible to people who are advantaged by them. "Automaton conformity," then, is a potent and vital ingredient of the moral oblivion that invites evil to parade as good.

INGREDIENT #6: CORPORATE INVESTMENT IN MAINTAINING PUBLIC MORAL OBLIVION

Edward Bernays (1981-1995), a nephew of Sigmund Freud, drew upon Freud's ideas to develop promotional campaigns for products ranging from bacon to cigarettes. Bernays is considered a father of the public relations industry. He helped convince the American public that Dixie Cups were the only sanitary form of drinking cup. Resolving "to transform America's eating habits" on behalf of Beechnut Packing Company, a huge bacon producer, he convinced Americans that bacon with eggs was the ideal breakfast. Serving the United Fruit Company (which paid him enormous amounts of money yearly) and the American government, he promoted the idea, in the American media and in Guatemala, that Guatemala's then president, Jacobo Arbenz, was a communist threat—in order to justify his overthrow orchestrated by the CIA in 1953–54.[33] Bernays was master at using propaganda to shape public policy to favor large corporate business. "[I]t remains a fact," Bernays opined, "that in almost every act of our daily lives, whether in the sphere of politics or business, in our social conduct or our ethical thinking, we are dominated by the relatively small number of persons—a trifling fraction of our hundred and twenty million—who understand the mental processes and social patterns of the masses. It is they who pull the wires which control the public mind, who harness old social forces and contrive new ways to bind and guide the world. . . . As civilization has become more complex . . . the technical means have been invented and developed by which opinion may be regimented."[34]

Corporate public relations and advertising conspire to manipulate our perceptions of what we ought to value and strive for and of how we should behave. They attempt, often with great success, to define our self-worth, and our sense of what constitutes a successful life, what makes us worthy of others' esteem, what renders us lovable, what is necessary for happiness, and, simply, what is *true*. The "reality" defined by much corporate advertising is a reality in which many global businesses that enslave children, destroy water supplies, and disgorge massive quantities of greenhouse gases are represented as good, vibrant producers of happiness and well-being. It is a reality in which we will be more worthy, more successful, more respected, more attractive, and happier if we buy and consume.

Public relations is a powerful industry worldwide, with billions of dollars spent each year on reshaping reality, altering perception, and "manufacturing consent."[35] Corporate clients engage marketing firms to mobilize private detectives, attorneys, satellite feeds, sophisticated information systems, social media—all with the intention of shaping the image of the corporation or business or government industry that they represent, and controlling public perception of this business or industry.[36]

For example, "video news releases" written and filmed by marketing firms frequently air as story segments on news shows without any attribution to their source in the marketing industry. One day the evening news might show a short segment about proposed drilling in the Alaskan National Wildlife Refuge, featuring a news reporter interviewing an actor posing as a "man on the street" about his views on drilling (they are, of course, positive). Pre-selected "experts" are interviewed to give their professional opinion. Even product demonstrations or corporate logos may make their way into the segment. The end result is a short, evocative "news story" about the benefits of drilling in ANWR, produced by a marketing firm.

Marketing firms engineer groups such as the "Coalition for Vehicle Choice," the "National Smokers Alliance," and "Americans for Prosperity." These names give the impression of genuine grassroots organizations, when they are in fact front groups for corporate interests. The National Smokers Alliance has been alive and well for almost twenty years. Founded by the Phillip Morris Tobacco Company, this group was intended to appear as a grassroots movement of people opposed to smoke-free laws, unaffiliated with the tobacco industry. The group's sophisticated, hi-tech campaigns target unemployed college students in bars and bowling alleys, exhorting them to "stand up for their rights" and offering stickers to place in stores and restaurants that say, "I am a smoker and have spent $_____ in your establishment."

Marketing firms frequently target populations that are young, vulnerable, less educated, and susceptible to peer pressure.[37] The explosion in recent decades of marketing to young children, even infants, exemplifies the power of these covert persuaders. The sinister world of marketing to women, and specifically the creation and exploitation of insecurities around women's body image, sexuality, and self-esteem, demonstrates the power of psychological manipulation in marketing. Betty Friedan's *The Feminine Mystique* traces some of the origins of advertising to American housewives in the 1950s that began manipulating insecurities into dollars. A marketing service report at that time instructed advertisers to capitalize on "guilt over hidden dirt" and stress the "therapeutic value of baking." Identify your products with "spiritual rewards," almost a "religious belief," the report advised.[38] Today the focus has shifted from household goods to clothes, cosmetics, and the body itself. Weight-loss, clothing, and cosmetics industries are well aware of the lucrative market at their fingertips provided that the cultivation of body dissatisfaction continues. "Advertising aimed at women works by lowering our self-esteem," writes Naomi Wolf, author of *The Beauty Myth*. Media images of female beauty are simply unattainable for all but a very small number of women, but the cultivation of body dissatisfaction is so lucrative that the misguidance continues.

INGREDIENT #7: UNCRITICAL BELIEF IN "GROWTH" AS GOOD

The next ingredient of moral oblivion is the assumption that economic growth is inherently good and ought to continue regardless of the unintended consequences. This idea is central to the idealization of material wealth in our nation and the world today. Mainstream economics and common wisdom equate economic growth with economic well-being. This assumption shapes American domestic and foreign public policies that determine wealth or poverty, even life or death, for many. The growth myth blinds its adherents to the dangers of economic life as we know it.

As the theory goes, growth in a nation's Gross Domestic Product (GDP) increases and is *necessary* to increase prosperity, employment, and living standards for most people. An economy must grow in order to maintain jobs and prevent recession and inflation. During the economic breakdown at the turn of this decade, for example, we were encouraged to buy things in order to help the U.S. economy to grow. Growth has no fixed limits, and boundless economic growth will bring all people to a state of prosperity as defined by Western middle-class standards.[39] This theory is the bedrock of economic policy today. It is an ideological foundation of the global economy in its current form.[40]

FAULTLINES

Without a doubt, economic growth has reaped incredible bounty for a good many, and has enabled many others to escape poverty. However, the theory that economic growth is an accurate and adequate indicator of economic well-being for all or that more economic activity necessarily means a healthier economy is invalid, today, for many reasons. Here we note four and then focus on a fifth.

First, growth figures do not account for the consequences of economic or financial activity beyond the period to which the figures pertain. Thus, for example, the speculative activity that caused the recent financial crisis was given free rein. Faulty investments that created growth in the short-term proved treacherous in the long-term.

Second, growth theory does not account for distribution of wealth and income. Thus growth, in terms of GDP or average household income or wealth, frequently obscures an accompanying increase in poverty. India illustrates this.

Third, growth as measured by GDP does not distinguish between destructive and beneficial economic activity. Socially and environmentally destructive economic activity counts as a gain for humanity. Ten-year-olds purchasing cigarettes, alcoholics feeding their addiction, sale of pornography, oil spills, rising cancer rates, and electrocutions all contribute to growth. The GDP, for example, treats the extraction of natural resources as income rather than as depletion of an asset.

Fourth, growth as measured by GDP is an inadequate measure of economic well-being because GDP attributes to a host country profits that actually are repatriated. Thus while Coca-Cola's operations in India register as growth in GDP for India, the vast portion of the wealth produced does not stay in India.

Fifth, and most relevant to our current purposes: Growth figures fail to account for Earth's economy. That economy includes goods and essential services that Earth provides as well as costs. The theory that growth has no limits fails to recognize that the planet *does*. This problem is multifaceted.

Growth theory assumes that natural goods such as air, water, soil, fossil fuels are unlimited. Yet, as many economists, scientists, environmentalists, and ethicists now point out, the human economy is part of a much larger planetary economy of life whose limits in both renewable and nonrenewable goods have been so pushed that unchecked growth now further impedes Earth's regenerative capacities.[41]

Likewise, growth theory does not recognize the limitations in Earth's capacity to provide essential services. Nor does the theory account for the economic value of the services provided by Earth without which we would not survive. Earth's services—better known as "ecosystem services"—include purification of air and water, generation and renewal of soil and soil fertility, pollination of crops and natural vegetation, detoxification and decomposition of wastes, nontoxic control of the vast majority of potential agricultural pests, and protection from the sun's ultraviolet rays.

Yet another facet of this problem concerns externalized *costs,* the unacknowledged price tag of economic growth. Growth figures fail to factor into the bottom line and the price of goods the environmental costs of production and commerce. Rather, the harmful ecological impacts are considered "externalities" to be paid by society at large or by future generations. Thus, for example, China's economic growth figures for the last decade do not include the eventual cost of massive environmental degradation due to coal burning, and water and soil depletion.

A NECESSARY SHIFT

I am not arguing against economic growth per se. Some forms of economic growth are necessary—especially for the underconsuming world and impoverished people of affluent nations. I am arguing vehemently against the assumption that growth *unqualified* is necessarily a good and that growth is an adequate and accurate indicator of economic well-being. The myth of growth's inherent goodness is integral to the worldview shaping the society and lives of high-consuming United States citizens.

Four changes regarding growth theory are required for more just and sustainable economic ways:

> 1. Growth, as a good, will be qualified; growth is a good if it is "pro-poor, pro jobs, and pro environment."[42]
> 2. Growth will be dethroned as the *only* or the *central* measure of economic well-being, while remaining a supplemental measure. Other measures are being proposed and tested.[43]
> 3. The assumption that growth is the necessary savior of economies and hence of life as we know it will be discarded.
> 4. Environmental and social costs will be factored into financial "bottom lines" rather than externalized, and will be factored into calculations regarding growth.

These changes in how we view economic growth would dramatically reconstitute our economic lives. They would change how we produce goods; transport, house, and feed ourselves; use energy; and meet the material needs of everyday life.

For the moment, the salient point here is this: The assumption that growth is inherently good obscures the economic and ecological violence rendered when growth is pursued at all costs, and obscures alternative economic ways. Allegiance to unqualified growth as the aim of the economy is yet another factor in moral oblivion; it clouds moral vision.

This discussion of growth theory illustrates *theory functioning as truth*. The theory that "economic growth benefits all" became an assumed truth, rationalizing and justifying the prioritizing of economic growth despite the costs. Evidence to the contrary can then be ignored or discredited because it does not cohere with the "truth." Theory functioning as truth can cement into place "how things are," and obscure "how things could be."

INGREDIENT #8: MORAL OBLIVION EMBEDDED IN PRACTICE

These ingredients of moral oblivion are reinforced by practicing them. We learn them and reinscribe their normality through performing them in daily habits, behaviors, and rituals. Stephen Brookfield says it well: "[H]egemony is lived out a thousand times a day in our intimate behaviors, glances, body postures, in the fleeting calculations we make on how to look at and speak to each other, and in the continuous microdecisions that coalesce into a life."[44] Moral oblivion—and with it our pervasive acquiescence to exploitative economic norms—is learned in part through what we habitually do.

Breaking that pattern of reinforcement requires seeing how it works. How do economically privileged United States citizens ritualize these dynamics in our roles as citizen, parent, spouse, friend, daughter, provider of material goods, creature with need for food and water, etc.? In what senses do our activities of everyday life embody the ingredients of moral oblivion described herein and, more importantly, reinscribe them? Let us imagine.

"Your sweater is beautiful. I love the color." "Thanks! Believe it or not, I got it on sale for only ten dollars." (This is said with a sense of accomplishment and of absolution.) This ubiquitous exchange betokens much. It is okay that I bought another sweater (that I do not need) because it cost so little. No, it is more than okay; it is virtuous to have purchased the sweater so inexpensively.

This is *practiced* denial and powerlessness. I have denied the sweater's hidden price tag. The low monetary price came at high cost to others. The sweater, like other products, may have been made in a sweatshop in which women like Maria Chantico were sexually and economically exploited. The discount store that sold it paid its workers so little that some are homeless and ill. Ignored too is the petroleum component of the sweater's synthetic fabric, and the greenhouse gasses emitted in producing, packaging, and shipping it. I have affirmed my powerlessness to clothe myself without damaging and degrading others. Exploitation has become consumer virtue.

A trip to the grocery store to purchase a pound of hamburger quietly convinces the everyday consumer that the amount of water consumed and greenhouse gases released in producing that meat is acceptable.[45] In putting inexpensive strawberries on my table and sprinkling them with inexpensive sugar, do I deny the reality of the strawberry pickers' children, and of the former employees of the Kenyan sugar industry that was crippled by the dumping of U.S. sugar? Do I filter from my consciousness their ensuing abject poverty, and the lives that may be destroyed by it? Or do I see them, but remain hopeless that my family may eat in ways that do not deprive others? Or perhaps I convince myself that I can "make up for" the destroyed sugar industry by buying chickens or goats for impoverished people in Kenya? When my family sits down to eat, we give thanks for the food. We are blessed.

"I see here that when I buy this bottled water, Starbucks will give a percentage of the proceeds to help provide water to villagers in Africa. What a great idea," muses the woman in line for coffee at Starbucks while gazing at a lovely ad showing a smiling African boy. "And with the economy in such bad shape, spending money helps it to grow." Denied are the people whose water supply was sold on the global market to fill that bottle, and the people whose land will become its dumping ground.

The ingredients of moral oblivion are ingested by "practicing" them. The routine behaviors, thoughts, decisions, and social interactions of daily life protect us from seeing the consequences of our lives on people and ecosystems imperiled by them. Our everyday actions ritualize the acceptability of how we eat, transport ourselves, communicate, recreate, invest our money, and the other aspects of life as we know it. What we do persuades us that "the way things are" is "the way things will remain." Practicing moral oblivion forges it.

In the following story, look for the ingredients of moral oblivion at play.

****

A LIFE STORY

EXPLOITATION OF WORKERS IN THE UNITED STATES

I step off the number 7 bus in downtown Seattle and zip up my fleece against the chilly drizzle. My destination is only a few blocks away but I'm already craving the warm and sheltered interior of a building. As I trudge up Union Street, I pass a middle-aged woman in several bundled layers, smelling slightly stale.

She is squatting in a doorway, rattling a Wendy's paper cup with a few coins in it. Her jacket looks several sizes too big and her pants look like they haven't been washed in a while. I hesitate for a moment, feeling guilty. I'd rather not rustle around in my backpack on this busy street and I'm already late. What's she going to buy with this money anyway? My eyes meet hers for a second, and I hastily make my decision. Swinging my bag around, I reach into the outermost pocket and find a few coins at the bottom. Sensing my intentions, she tilts the cup toward me. I walk over and drop the coins in her cup, slightly embarrassed when I realize that I had unconsciously been holding my breath while near her. But I feel pretty good about supporting someone in need, and by the time I arrive at my destination I've forgotten all about her.

This woman has a name: Robin Martin. I passed her on the street today, but I didn't see her in Renton last month, working the register full-time at a Walmart. I was in the adjacent checkout aisle, buying an mp3 player for my brother's birthday, as well as a bunch of running socks and a closet organizer. Robin's cheap labor, among other things, makes it possible for Walmart to sell items at extremely low prices. She worked a nine-hour shift at the store that day and stayed in a shelter that night, because she had lost her apartment. Walmart didn't pay her enough to keep up with rent, even at her cheap apartment that she shared with a few others. Even if she could have kept up with rent, all tenants had received notice that the apartment complex had been bought up by developers who planned to convert it into condos in response to rising land values as that particular neighborhood gentrified.

Robin worked the register for as long as she could, but she caught something in the shelters that exacerbated a preexisting medical condition, and before long wasn't able to handle the nine-hour shifts on her feet. After several occasions of showing up late due to illness or leaving early for a doctor's appointment, Robin was laid off.

Later that day a friend told me about an opportunity to attend a fundraiser for a local homeless shelter. Thinking of the woman I saw that morning, I made a $20/month online donation to the cause. The thought never crossed my mind that my contribution—significant as it is—does not address the roots of the problem, or that charity generally doesn't solve the problems of poverty.

Today Robin sat on that same stoop for most of the day. When it began raining more heavily she thought about making her way to the local library, one of the few places that allow homeless people inside during the day. But in the end she decided to wait it out under the doorway. She

*checked the time on the parking meters periodically, because at 5:55 pm she
needed be in line at a shelter nearby. If she were to line up any earlier than
that she would be chased away by local establishments who loathe loiterers.
If she were to show up even a few minutes later, she might not get one of
the thirty-five beds in the shelter.*

*My friends at dinner were impressed by how little I had spent earlier
on my socks, mp3 player, and closet organizer, and I felt pretty good about
it too. Frankly, I always try to get a good deal when I'm shopping. I don't
want to get ripped off or ever pay more than I really need to for something.
That's why I like Walmart.*

*At home I signed onto my computer and noticed that my mutual fund
finally went up in value again. Phew! Walmart is one of the companies
in which my fund is invested; the company's commitment to maximizing
profit is working. I whispered a little prayer of gratitude. Little did I know
that low wages contributed to that profit, or that Robin and I were connected
through this company and this mutual fund: her poverty increases and my
"wealth" increases. I didn't know where Robin was and I didn't think much
about it. Powerful blinders kept me from seeing and powerful structures
kept me from knowing the reality of her existence.*

The story continues in chapter 6.

****

In Sum

We have uncovered dynamics that prevent economically privileged people
from recognizing the dire impact of our lives on many of the world's
impoverished people and on Earth's web of life. I have argued that moral
vision is socially constructed to reinforce and rationalize "the way things are"
for those who are invested (consciously or not) in keeping it that way. We
examined eight dynamics at work in luring us to accept "the way things are"
in the contemporary context of economic and ecological injustice. These eight
mutually reinforcing factors are mainstays in the edifice of moral oblivion that
enables systemic evil to remain invisible to its material beneficiaries. Hard-won
insight into socially constructed moral oblivion has been for the sake of moral
vision that enables societal transformation toward social justice and ecological
well-being. Toward that vision we now turn.

Notes

1. Adolf Hitler, *Mein Kampf,* cited in Diane Halpern, *Thought and Knowledge: An Introduction to Critical Thinking* (Hillsdale, NJ: Lawrence Erlbaum, 1984), 36.

2. Celine Moyroud and John Katunga, "Coltan Exploration in Eastern Democratic Republic of the Congo (DRC)," in Jeremy Lind and Kathryn Sturman, eds., *Scarcity and Surfeit: The Ecology of Africa's Conflicts* (Pretoria: Institute for Security Studies, 2002).

3. United Nations Press Release SC/7057, "Security Council Condemns Illegal Exploitation of Democratic Republic of Congo's Natural Resources," United Nations, March 5, 2001, cited in: "Coltan, Gorillas, and Cell Phones," *Cellular-News.*

4. John Prendergast, "Can You Hear Congo Now? Cell Phones, Conflict Minerals, and the Worst Sexual Violence in the World," *Enough Project Press Release,* April 1, 2009.

5. "Kahuzi-Biega National Park: Democratic Republic of the Congo," United Nations Environmental Programme, World Conservation Monitoring Centre.

6. Kristi Essick, "Guns, Money, and Cell Phones," *Industry Standard Magazine* (June 11, 2001).

7. Mary E. Hobgood, *Dismantling Privilege: An Ethics of Accountability* (Cleveland: Pilgrim, 2000), 5–6.

8. Gary Perry, in conversation at Seattle University, 2010.

9. Walter Brueggemann, cited by Loretta Whalen, "Dear Colleague" letter from Church World Service Office on Global Education, 31 October 1998.

10. Walter Brueggemann, unpublished address at Fund for Theological Education's Conference on Excellence in Ministry, housed at Vanderbilt University, Summer 2001.

11. Daniel Maguire, *Death by Choice* (Garden City, NY: Image, 1984), 65–66.

12. Gloria Albrecht, *The Character of Our Communities: An Ethic of Liberation for the Church* (Nashville: Abingdon, 1995), 63.

13. Brookfield, *Power of Critical Theory,* 102.

14. "Hegemony" in Gramsci's use had two connotations. The connotation most commonly associated with Gramsci is the one used here. For discussion of a second use of the term see Antonio Gramsci, *Selections from Prison Notebooks* (New York: International, 1971), xiv.

15. Cornel West, *Prophecy Deliverance: An African American Revolutionary Christianity* (Philadelphia: Westminster, 1982), 119.

16. Ibid.

17. Brookfield, *Power of Critical Theory,* 96–97, citing Raymond Williams, *Marxism and Literature* (New York: Oxford University Press, 1977), 110.

18. Antonio Gramsci, Quintin Hoare, and Geoffrey Nowell-Smith, *Selections from the Prison Notebooks of Antonio Gramsci* (New York: International, 1971), 323.

19. Ibid.

20. Brookfield, *Power of Critical Theory,* 93.

21. Ibid., 97.

22. Ibid., 102.

23. Moe-Lobeda, *Healing a Broken World: Globalization and God* (Minneapolis: Fortress Press, 2009), ch. 3 for discussion of our cultural misconstrual of "freedom as market freedom," and the power of that myth in disabling moral vision and agency.

24. U.S. Commission on Civil Rights, "Broken Promises: Evaluating the Native American Health Care System," September 2004, 2. The Centers for Disease Control (CDC) report that the prevalence of diabetes in Native Americans is twice that of all U.S. adults, the mortality rate from liver disease is three times that of all Americans, the infant mortality rate is 1.7 times higher (9.2/ 1000), and the incidence of SIDS is more than double that of the white population. CDC publication, "Health Disparities Affecting Minorities: American Indians and Alaska Natives," Office of Minority Health and Health Disparities.

25. Lee Artz and Bren Adair Ortega Murphy, *Cultural Hegemony in the United States* (Thousand Oaks, CA: Sage, 2000).

26. This idea was seeded partly by Traci West in *Disruptive Christian Ethics: When Racism and Women's Lives Matter* (Louisville: Westminster John Knox, 2006). She writes: "prayers of thankfulness for what 'God has given us' can undergird a sense of entitlement to material 'blessings'" (119).

27. Hobgood, *Dismantling Privilege*, 16.

28. Paul Hawken, *The Ecology of Commerce* (San Francisco: Harper, 1993), 22.

29. Larry Rasmussen, "The Brothers Bonhoeffer on Science, Morality, and New Theology," presented at Bethlehem Evangelical Lutheran Church, Los Alamos, NM, April 2008, 10.

30. Erich Fromm, *To Have or to Be?* (New York: Harper, 1976), 83.

31. Ibid.

32. Erich Fromm, *The Sane Society* (New York: Holt, 1955), 173.

33. See *The Century of the Self*, award-winning 2002 documentary by Adam Curtis, and Larry Tye, *The Father of Spin: Edward L. Bernays and the Birth of Public Relations* (New York: Crown, 1998), 59, 51, 165–78.

34. Edward Bernays, *Propaganda* (Brooklyn: IG, 1928), 37–40.

35. For a detailed account of corporate PR's strategies to undermine environmentalism, see Sharon Beder, *Corporate Spin: The Corporate Assault on Environmentalism* (White River Junction, VT: Chelsea, 2002).

36. John C. Stauber and Sheldon Rampton, *Toxic Sludge Is Good for You: Lies, Damn Lies, and the Public Relations Industry* (Monroe, ME: Common Courage , 1995).

37. Stauber and Rampton, *Toxic Sludge Is Good for You*, 17–24.

38. Friedan as cited in Naomi Wolf, *The Beauty Myth: How Images of Beauty Are Used against Women* (New York: Morrow, 1991), 66–67.

39. Then U.S. Secretary of the Treasury, Henry Morgenthau, at the opening session of Bretton Woods called for embracing the "elementary economic axiom . . . that prosperity has no fixed limits." Cited in David Korten, "The Failures of Bretton Woods," in *The Case against the Global Economy: And a Turn for the Local*, ed. Jerry Mander and Edward Goldsmith (San Francisco: Sierra Club, 1996), 21.

40. See Organization for Economic Cooperation and Development in *Open Markets Matter: The Benefits of Trade and Investment Liberalization* (Paris: OECD, 1998). For voices articulating this theory from the private sector, academic economics, and Christian ethics respectively, see the International Chamber of Commerce, at http://www.iccwbo.org, and the United States Council for International Business at http:/www.uscib.org; R. Dornbusch and F. Helmers, eds., *The Open Economy: Tools for Policymakers in Developing Countries* (New York: Oxford University Press for the World Bank, 1995); Michael Novak, *Cultivating Liberty* (Lanham, MD: Rowan & Littlefield, 1999).

41. The idea of biophysical limits to the planet was suggested by three seminal thinkers: John Kenneth Galbraith in 1956; Kenneth Boulding in *The Economics of the Coming Spaceship Earth* in 1966; and Herman Daly in *The Stationary-State Economy*, Distinguished Lecture series, University of Alabama in 1971 and in *Toward a Steady State Economy* in 1973. (Daly credits Georgescu-Roegen, one of his teachers at Vanderbilt, with having pointed out that the principle of entropy is incompatible with endless economic growth.) The idea of planetary limits to growth became more publicly recognized with *The Limits of Growth* in 1972 and Daly's *Steady State Economics* in 1977. Notre Dame philosopher Kenneth Sayre details the history and theory rationalizing economic growth and an economic approach that does not require continuing growth. See *Unearthed: The Economic Roots of Our Environmental Crisis* (Notre Dame: University of Notre Dame Press, 2010), 166–220.

42. Kennedy Mbekeani, "Macroeconomic Policy Issues in South Africa," paper commissioned by Ecumenical Service for Socio-Economic Transformation (Johannesburg: ESSET, 1997).

43. Alternatives include the Genuine Progress Indicator (GPI), the Capabilities Approach, and the Human Development Index (HDI).

44. Brookfield, *Power of Critical Theory*, 96–97.

45. Beef production is responsible for about 9 percent of total anthropogenic carbon dioxide emissions, 37 percent of methane emissions, and 65 percent of nitrous oxide emissions according to H. Steinfeld et al., *Livestock's Long Shadow: Environmental Issues and Options* (Rome: Livestock, Environment, and Development, 2006), 391.

5

Countering Moral Oblivion

"How, indeed, is a mind to become conscious of its own bias when that bias springs from a communal flight from understanding and is supported by the whole texture of a civilization?. . . No problem is at once more delicate and more profound, more practical and perhaps more pressing."

Bernard Lonergan[1]

The quest is for moral vision potent for forging societies in which the economic well-being of some is not bought by the blood of others, and in which humankind is not toxic to its planetary home. By what paths may we learn to see how our patterns of consumption, production, and investment—and the public policies that govern them—are linked to others' poverty and to ecological devastation? What would kindle and sustain our capacity to recognize systemic evil, and to live toward the greater good, even when so doing may be costly?

The challenge is not merely unmasking systemic injustice, but doing so in ways that evoke moral action. Moral vision without action is not *moral* vision. What conditions of seeing will lead from awareness of exploitation to actions that dismantle it?

Enabling moral vision in this sense is the focus of this chapter. It proceeds in three parts. The first introduces "critical mystical vision." The next dwells on one dimension of critical mystical vision, perception of "what *could* be." The chapter's third section argues that critical mystical vision entails a tectonic shift in the moral consciousness undergirding economic life as we know it.

CRITICAL MYSTICAL VISION INTRODUCED

Recognizing causal links between our wealth on the one hand and Earth's demise and profound human suffering on the other, can be devastating and hence dangerous *unless* simultaneously we see something else. *Seeing "what is," when the view is of systemic evil, is morally empowering if accompanied by a second and a third form of vision.*

The second kind of vision is seeing "what could be"—that is, more just and ecologically sound alternatives. "People can be morally and emotionally disgusted with what the system is doing but still cooperate because they see no alternative."[2] Seeing alternative modes of economic life and movements that are living into them is vital to critical vision. A Chinese proverb cautions, "Unless we change direction, we will get where we are going." Changing direction begs first recognizing, even dimly, alternative viable destinations. These two together—vision of "what is" and of "what could be"—I call critical seeing.

The third mode of vision, I refer to as "mystical vision." By this I mean acknowledgment of sacred powers at work in the cosmos enabling life and love ultimately to reign over death and destruction. Mystical vision confirms what eco-theologian Sallie McFague refers to as "our hope against hope that our efforts on behalf of our planet are not ours alone but that the source and power of life in the universe is working *in and through us* for the well-being of all creation, including our tiny part in it."[3]

"Critical mystical vision," then, is a phrase to signify the union of vision in these three forms:

- seeing "what is going on" in whatever situation is at hand, and especially unmasking systemic evil that masquerades as good.
- seeing "what could be," that is, alternatives. These two together I call "critical seeing."
- seeing ever more fully the sacred Spirit of life coursing throughout creation and leading it—despite all evidence to the contrary—into abundant life for all.

Christian ethics, the art-science of Christian morality, has at its heart the crucial task of holding these three in one lens. Vision of this sort is subversive because "it keeps the present provisional and refuses to absolutize it."[4] Critical mystical vision reveals a future in the making and breeds hope for moving into it.

Why "critical"? "Critical" in this volume does not refer to its common meanings. Rather, it refers to a stream of social theorizing that may be seen as stemming from the Frankfurt school of social theory. The Frankfurt school emerged in Germany in part to counter the rise of fascism. "Critical" connotes an approach to understanding social reality that exposes and demystifies oppression and the power alignments and truth claims that rationalize it, rather than presupposing and thus reinscribing them. A critical approach exposes social structures as historically contingent and thus, at least theoretically, subject to human agency, rather than being natural and inevitable and thereby nontranscendable. Critical theory seeks to empower people for structural social change. In short, a critical approach seeks to reveal that "the way things are" is not "the way things must be."

"What Could Be"—Alternative Futures in the Making

We cannot go where we cannot envision. Recognizing "what could be" comes from unearthing a phenomenon barely recognized in the dominant public discourse. It is the visionary and practical organizing of little-known groups throughout the world aimed at surviving, resisting, and transforming neoliberal global economic arrangements and the social and ecological destruction wrought by them. *These people are constructing viable and vibrant alternatives.*

Nothing imperils a more just future more than our tacit and often unacknowledged belief that such a future is not possible. "What are you writing?" queried a woman who saw me writing this manuscript in a coffee shop. I explained that I was trying to understand why we agree to live in ways that damage so many people worldwide through the injustice embedded in the global economy and through environmental destruction. Thinking she would not "get it," I was humbled by her instant response: "I think," she said, "people don't want to see those things, because we *don't know any way out.*"

However, as we will see here and in subsequent chapters, vast numbers of people and groups around the world are creating ways of life that earth can sustain and that do not impoverish some to the benefit of others. They are forging lives, institutions, and bodies politic in which huge transnational unaccountable corporations do not determine the distribution of water, seeds, and jobs. They are reshaping households, businesses, schools, and cities to live in harmony with Earth's economy of life. They are building communities in which the well-being of humankind and otherkind trumps wealth accumulation. Public policies, practices of daily life, and re-constituted principles of economic life are the building blocks of this movement.

Paul Hawken and the Wise Earth Network that he founded conclude that "over one—and maybe even two—million organizations currently are working toward ecological sustainability and social justice." "I believe this movement will prevail," he writes. "It will change a sufficient number of people so as to begin the reversal of centuries of frenzied self-destructive behavior."[5] Peasants and other farmers, scientists, economists, factory workers, educators, elected officials, students, heathcare professionals, homemakers, educators, journalists, and more comprise this social force. Some are from communities of oppressed people. Others emerge from communities of conscience among highly privileged people. Profoundly needed is *knowledge that they exist and recognition of the connections between them.*

The following story illustrates a few small pieces of this pan-human movement. The remaining chapters and the vignettes spread throughout dig further. These stories are merely droplets in this fertile and growing river. They reveal the interplay of principles, policies, and practices. Note them at play in household life, institutional life, corporate and other business life, and government. Note too the rich variety in forms of action toward justice and sustainability.

If the public was aware, on a regular basis, of these movements and the rapidly growing number of people they represent, we would be far more likely to believe that alternatives are possible and are worth joining. That knowledge whittles away at the doors of denial and allows recognizing the economic and ecological violence embedded in our lives. Seeing "what could be" opens windows to seeing "what is." Moreover, seeing "what could be" breeds the joy and freedom of moving in that direction. Indeed, seeing alternative paths is a crucial ingredient of moral power.

****

A Life Story Revisited

Revisiting "Free" Trade and Sweatshops

The story of Free Trade and Sweatshops, begun in chapter 3, closed with Colleen pleased with her "good buy" on tank tops made in Mexico, and Maria Chantico in a sweatshop on Mexico's northern border having been driven north by the impact of NAFTA.

Imagine that Colleen, the contented new owner of a sky-blue racerback tank top from an Old Navy store in New Hampshire, learns about the backstory to her purchase. She learns about Maria Chantico and her family, the reality of maquiladora life, and the consequences of NAFTA's "free trade" doctrine. Once knowing, what can she do about the connection that she now knows exists between her and people like Maria Chantico and her family? How will her behaviors change?

Perhaps Colleen starts with some basic changes. She starts frequenting used clothing stores, and tries to curb her impetuous consumption of goods. But Colleen also knows that lifestyle changes are only one tool for dismantling immoral trade regimes and worker exploitation. In itself, it will not stop corporate abuses. She wants to act on another level and acquire more powerful tools. Colleen might learn from countless individuals, households, and communities that are taking concrete steps of resistance and rebuilding.

Some people put their economic weight into ending sweatshops and unfair trade through boycotts and investments in socially responsible companies and mutual funds, as well as selective buying. These people make a habit of knowing about supply chains and refusing to purchase items that are produced under oppressive conditions. In this they are aided by sources like Green America's Guide to Ending Sweatshop Labor and The Better World Shopping Guide.[6] In stores, they fill out customer comment cards asking the company to work with its suppliers to make sure that workers are treated fairly. They buy coffee, tea, chocolate, produce, and crafts from companies that belong to the Fair Trade Federation. They ask questions before buying a product and let company management know that they're asking. If they own stock, they vote by proxy to support shareholder resolutions that require improved labor policies. They ask companies to provide annual reports that account for a "triple bottom line": not only financial, but also social and ecological. "We will only do business," they are saying in myriad ways, "with companies that pay a living wage, provide safe working conditions, allow union organizing, and eliminate environmental degradation including waste for export." By making these actions into regular "habits," and teaching them to their children, they are creating a culture that expects just and sustainable business.

Since the 2010 Supreme Court decision to overturn limits on corporate spending, the movement to rein in corporate power at its roots is rapidly growing. More and more people are calling for a constitutional amendment that rescinds the rights of personhood granted to corporations by another Supreme Court decision in 1886. Colleen might join a national group—such as the Network of Spiritual Progressives or Move to Amend—that is organizing for such an amendment.

THE ANTI-SWEATSHOP MOVEMENT

The student organization United Students against Sweatshops (USAS) formed in 1997 when college students, skeptical of NAFTA and free trade regimes, decided to act in solidarity with the struggles of working *people around the world. These young people recognized that colleges and universities were licensing their logos and names to clothing companies such as Nike and Champion, and could therefore demand that these companies produce college apparel in factories that pay workers a living wage and respect workers' rights to unionize. A procurement standard emerged called the "Designated Suppliers Program." It is enforced by an independent monitoring agency called the Worker Rights Consortium, which assesses worker conditions and reports back to universities.*

With chapters in 250 schools, the USAS is now the largest anti-sweatshop community in America. It did not come about easily. Early on, students from the University of Michigan, University of Wisconsin at Madison, Georgetown, and Duke occupied presidents' offices to draw attention to the issue, and students at Purdue completed an eleven-day hunger strike in order to persuade their school's administration to adopt the Designated Suppliers Program. In March 2011, USAS launched a cross-country "Truth Tour" with U.S. students and workers from the Dominican Republic to highlight labor abuses by Sodexo, a global outsourcing giant.

THE FAIR TRADE MOVEMENT

Some actions are emerging at the town and city level. Norman, Oklahoma is situated on the edge of America's prairielands. The town responded to a campaign by Green America, an organization that harnesses the economic power of consumers, investors, businesses, and the marketplace to promote a sustainable and just society. One way that Green America does this is by urging towns to join the international Fair Trade Town community. Norman was intrigued. An action group formed called Norman Fair Trade, which collaborated with local businesses, farmers, city council members, student organizations, faith-based organizations, and environmental groups to increase the availability and demand for Fair Trade products. Ajit Bhand, organizer with Norman Fair Trade, commented on the town's motives for taking on this project: "Not only does it help local and small businesses, it also positively affects the lives of thousands of farmers and workers in other parts of the world."[7]

In Florida, Claremont's Community of Faith United Methodist Church has, like many churches in America, switched to Fair Trade coffee at their Sunday-morning fellowship hour. Fair trade coffee, chocolate, tea, rice, sugar, honey, wine, fresh fruit, and olive oil are increasingly accessible in stores throughout the U.S., as more shoppers keep asking for it. Efforts at responsible buying are complemented by larger initiatives such as Oxfam's "Make Trade Fair" campaign.

With participation and donations from thousands of supporters, Oxfam influences corporate practices. Regarding coffee, for example, Oxfam urged large coffee companies to introduce a portion of Fair Trade Certified coffee to their product lines, which resulted in twice the annual U.S. Fair Trade coffee imports. Oxfam would not be able to exert leverage if it were not for supporters from around the world who back their actions. Twenty million people signed Oxfam's international petition urging Congress to make trade fair.

★★★★★★★★★★★★★★★★★★★★★★★★★★★★★★★★★★★★

"Seeing" undertakings such as these and stepping into their current throws a bucket of cold water on the face of moral oblivion. It counters many of the factors identified in the previous chapter.

Recognizing systemic violence and the possibilities for a more equitable and Earth-honoring future is impeded by the privatized, victor-oriented, and anthropocentric moral consciousness that shapes the Western world. Developing "critical mystical vision" calls for profound shifts in moral consciousness. To that challenge we now turn.

A Profound Shift in Moral Consciousness

A Revealing Contradiction

Contradictions often illumine a way through murky problems. Here, the contradiction between the *public or collective* moral impact of our lives on the one hand, and pervasive perceptions of the moral life as a *private* matter on the other, is revealing. *Collective* human activity is shaping the material and cultural conditions of life. Yet, moral consciousness enacted in our society is, generally speaking, increasingly *privatized*. We practice the privatization of morality and deny our moral responsibility for collective morality, even while that collective activity has enormous moral consequences.[8]

For instance, the culture of the automobile—generated through many forms of corporate persuasion including legislative lobbies, campaign financing, and consumer persuasion—is a central feature of public life in the United States. The ecological consequences of the automobile obsession are infinitely *public* and costly. Yet we hold the absurd assumption that driving a large vehicle that produces enormous quantities of greenhouse gases is a matter of *individual* freedom, and that the move not to do so must depend upon individual conscience rather than on a move of public policy aimed at limiting global warming. Moral consciousness must confront the contradiction between the collective shaping of public life on the one hand, and our privatized sense of moral response on the other.

Here, we call for and sketch a shift to moral consciousness that: (1) perceives the world as interconnected; (2) seeks persistently and humbly to perceive reality through the narratives and experiences of subjugated people and peoples; and (3) locates human life and morality within Earth's matrix of life, rather than outside of it.

While others have called for similar shifts in worldview, I relate these shifts specifically to moral consciousness. And I aver that they are required if we are to see more clearly the roots and consequences of ecological and economic violence. Moreover, I insist that such shifts have vast implications for the meaning of neighbor-love.

MORAL CONSCIOUSNESS: SEISMIC SHIFTS

This contradiction between privatized moral consciousness and the inherently public moral impact of our lives presents a clue to morally responsible vision. It prescribes a shift in moral consciousness that would be an antidote to many ingredients of moral oblivion identified in the previous chapter. We consider three facets of that shift and then suggest a way of putting them into practice.

MORAL CONSCIOUSNESS: INTERCONNECTED

In the first place, the shift is away from the privatized sense of morality created by modernity's "turn to the individual" as the primary unit of existence and neoliberalism's fetishizing of it. The modern individualized moral consciousness allows us to assume that because I am not *individually* culpable in another's suffering, I am innocent. An interconnected sense of morality, in contrast, recognizes that while I am I, I am *not only* I, but also am "we" and "us." What I do as part of a larger body of people has moral consequences for which I am, to some extent, accountable. What I eat, how I heat my home, what I purchase, where I vacation, how I speak *as part of a society in which these ways are common practice* has moral impact even if my individual piece, isolated, does not. By "interconnected," therefore, I mean not only awareness of the structural connections between me and others the world over, but also awareness of the moral weight of those connections.

A privatized moral consciousness has another related consequence. It is the subtle but engulfing persuasion to serve the well-being of self, family, and "tribe," to the extent that the well-being of distant "others" becomes functionally irrelevant. This is nothing new. However, it is far more dangerous than ever before in human history because of the vastly expanded freedom and power of the world's ultra rich to do just that.

The recent global financial meltdown demonstrates this expanded danger of freedom to pursue self-interest regardless of the cost to others or the Earth. That financial disaster was rooted in a global financial architecture (neoliberalism) structured to prioritize wealth accumulation by the ultra-wealthy above all else. And its taproot was a privatized moral consciousness that affirms "freedom" to accumulate personal wealth with little regard for the costs to others and to the Earth. Millions of people worldwide suffered and many died as a result.

MORAL CONSCIOUSNESS: FROM THE UNDERSIDE

Another crucial transformation in how we, the world's over consumers, perceive morality is the ongoing attempt to recognize "the eyes through which we see" and to glimpse the world as it is known by people who are denied life's basic necessities by the systems that deliver our material wealth. Societies paint reality from perspectives of those with power, the victors. Critical vision to meet the ecological-economic crisis of our day will open the doors of perception to reality as experienced by those whom we plunder or even destroy (within this society and beyond it), and to their authority in describing "what is going on."

Feminist, womanist, and postcolonial social theorists have paved the way. They insist that social analysis produced by people in positions of privilege is limited by their failure to recognize that their ideas are shaped by those positions of privilege. A responsible moral consciousness must seek to stand "outside dominant thought patterns and to know something we could not have known without the tools of the outsider's point of view."[9] That is, we are to learn about what is and what could be from people whose lives are damaged or threatened by ours, and who are proposing alternatives. There is revealed the deeply disturbing truth from which we run. "If the perpetrators of injustice want to step into the truth of their lives," writes Jürgen Moltmann, "they must learn to see themselves through the eyes of their victims."[10] Perhaps the most unsavory revelation of a structural view of the world informed by voices from the underside of history is awareness that "privilege and oppression do not simply coexist side by side. Rather, the suffering and unearned disadvantage of subordinate groups are the foundation for the privileges of the dominant group."[11]

In short, humanity and the planet now need wisdom born on the underbelly of power and privilege. Moral wisdom for a humane future will be learned by listening to people and places who suffer from the ecological and social exploitation of our day, and by putting their wisdom into conversation with other moral sources.

This valid and vital claim also is complex and messy. Feminist philosopher of science Donna Haraway says it well. "To see from below is neither easily learned nor unproblematic."[12] The problems are countless. Who has the right to determine what is "below" or what are the "margins"? How are we to locate and see from social sites that we never have imagined and that we may not even know exist? One cannot "be" a colonized indigenous person, a poisoned river, a displaced *campesino* if one is not. Furthermore, the standpoints of the subjugated are infinitely multiform and conflicting, and they are not "innocent positions."[13]

The intention to see and learn from standpoints on the underside of one's own privilege, though crucial, is also audacious and presumptuous unless accompanied by admitting the inherent dangers. How am I to "learn from" without repeating colonializing assumptions of my right to possess what "they" have, in this case knowledge or wisdom? And what of the dangers of patronizing and silencing when I try to communicate another's story? The effort to see from the margins demands accountability.

Yet another problem lies in the tendency to learn "about" rather than "from." The difference is the difference between the verbs *saber* and *conocer* in the Spanish language. The former means to "know about." The latter is to "know" as being in relationship. The former is safer, less risky, less demanding than the latter. And often to know *about* a people or situation is far easier than actually to "know" that people or situation. The former is passed through a third party—be the medium a person, website, or book. It then bears the inherent danger of intending to represent the other while unknowingly misrepresenting. All in all, "from below" or "from the margins" is not an uncomplicated visual lens.

Nevertheless, it is imperative because the magnitude of evil is known most fully by those who experience it, and by their stories that reveal my participation in it. Beyond this, a surefire antidote to hopelessness is to encounter and act with people who are indeed impoverished or otherwise hurt by our economic or ecological violence and who are going forward in hope to resist it and build alternatives. Becoming an "ally" ignites hope and with it, moral agency.[14]

MORAL CONSCIOUSNESS: ECOCENTRIC

Finally, the requisite shift in moral consciousness includes moving from our anthropocentric to an emerging ecocentric perception of the world and of morality. By ecocentric I do *not* mean necessarily prioritizing the well-being of Earth over that of humans. Such prioritizing by a person of the Global North is morally questionable, given that so many of Earth's human beings still are denied the basic necessities for human life. The shift from anthropocentric to ecocentric consciousness does not refer to a shift *in what gets priority*. It means a shift in how we fundamentally see the human in relationship to the rest of creation. It is a move from assuming that all of life centers around the human, to recognizing that this is biologically not true. And it is a move to expand the moral universe beyond the human.

Moving from anthropocentric to ecocentric perceptions of reality is not, in itself, adequate. Alone, it would not address the power asymmetries within and between human societies. Indian Christian ethicist George Zachariah says it well: "Environmental ethics that locates the earth crisis in *anthropocentrism that can be rectified by interconnectedness, relationships, community and the like*" is sorely mistaken. The crisis of earth is also a *"crisis of prevailing social relations,"* by which he means in particular relations of *domination.*[15]

Ecocentric moral consciousness will perceive the "exquisite interconnectivity of all life" and its implications for morality.[16] That interconnectedness renders humankind first and foremost *a part of* nature and its economy, rather than *apart from* these. Moral obligation and even moral agency extend beyond the human to the greater community of life. The purpose of economic life is not only production and distribution, but also the well-being of Earth's ecosystems.[17]

Such a sense of morality recognizes that "I" and "we" do not act apart from our literally countless relationships with other species and elements. They enable every breath we take. Not even a twitch of my muscle is possible without the aid of other creatures and the elements that give them life. And all that I do has impact on the other-than-human conglomerates of organic and inorganic molecules making home on this planet. D. John Chelladurai, Director of the India Peace Center in Nagpur, expresses eloquently this ecocentric dimension of the shift in moral consciousness. He writes:

The five elements . . . make us shareholders of the same body. The oxygen we consumed ten minutes before is now part of our body. We can no more distinguish it as oxygen. It has gone into the remotest interior of our body and merged with it to become an integral part of the body. . . . The oxygen we consumed just now was released a while before by a plant close to us. Before it was released, that oxygen was part of the plant's body. That which was the body of a plant is now the body of me.

Blood is our lifeline, an integral part of our being. The blood cells in our body have a life span of forty to one hundred and twenty days. Then they are eliminated from our body through excretion and urination. The epithelial cells constantly are eroded and washed out of our body. Every day when we bathe, we remove a thin layer of our body that is flushed out down the gutter. The cell that was 'I' travels through the gutter and reaches a canal or a pond in the outskirts, settles in the tank bed, disintegrates into amino acids and sucrose, glucose etc. Now 'I' am absorbed by the grass that grows on the banks, and the grass is now eaten by a cow, now the milk of that cow is sold in our neighbourhood, the man across the road consumes that milk. . . . This way there is a definite passage of our individual body into different bodies around us. . . . Don't we hold common body? What is true is we do not know how much of our body parts are exchanged with our neighbor with whom we are ill at ease.[18]

Wherein lies the necessity of this shift from anthropocentric to ecocentric moral consciousness? In the most pragmatic terms, self-interest as a species warrants the change. We, the human ones, are dependent, in every moment on millions of other species without which we would die. Our lives depend on thousands of unseen organisms living on and in our bodies, thousands more in a foot of soil, the trees of the Amazon rainforest. Yet our numbers, consumption levels, and disregard for the other-than-human are destroying species and life-support systems crucial to human health and survival. To continue in this disregard may be to write our death sentence as a species.

Not only self-interest but also social justice, and hence morality itself, demand the move to reinstate the human world into Earth's world (in particular, to resituate human economies into Earth's economy). As we have seen, social degradation and ecological degradation are inextricably linked. Ecological degradation produces social inequity in the forms of climate injustice and environmental racism. If, therefore, an expanded sense of morality is requisite for arresting the Earth crisis, then justice itself demands that expansion.

Theological integrity too prompts this move to a non-anthropocentric moral framework. In the creation stories in Genesis, God declares that creation is "good" long before human creatures appear in the story. And an ancient Christian eschatological assumption claims that the "already and not yet" reign of God includes the other-than-human parts of creation.

The shift to an ecocentric understanding of reality goes further. The lifeweb of which we are a part is not merely a system of connectedness and interdependence, but also, in a sense, a system of ontological sameness. We, as every other thing, living and nonliving, are offspring of the same parent that flared forth some 13.7 billion years ago in the cosmic event known as the "big bang." We are "distant cousins" to the stars and "close relatives" of myriad species extant, extinct, and yet to come.[19]

This would be startling enough were it to stop here, with humans sharing molecular composition, interdependence, intrinsic worth, and ultimate salvation with the other-than-human, while retaining sole status as the species with political agency. Yet the ecoshift in morality extends even further. Eco-theology and ecological ethics are uncovering or recovering the *agency* of the other-than-human.[20] The Hebrew scriptures indicate the powerful agency of the wind, mountains, water, and more. They too are called upon by God to undertake the crucial task of witnessing to the power and presence of God.

Moral consciousness expanded to include the other-than-human is fraught with complexity. To illustrate: How are we to understand moral subjectivity in the other-than-human? On what grounds do specific moral values and obligations apply differently to humans than to other-than-humans? What moral constraints ought be placed on human beings in light of our sameness with and dependence upon otherkind? These and related conundrums illustrate crucial work to be done in Christian ethics and other fields if we are to develop a sense of morality that extends beyond the human.

The call for privileging perspectives from the margins of power discussed in the previous section alters dramatically from an ecocentric moral perspective. The Earth crisis has moved the "margins" and the "underside." If moral wisdom is to be found on the underside of dominant power structures, then the other-than-human has wisdom to communicate. (I am *not* suggesting that nature is a model of morality. Such a claim would have to ignore many processes that are natural but certainly not normative for human morality—predation, unchecked disease, and so on.)

How will we hear, from voices not human, wisdom for living in sync with Earth's needs? How can we conceptualize perceiving and learning from other-than-human perspectives? Conversion to Earth-honoring lifeways beckons the church to explore more fully and bring to public use the biblical testimony that God calls upon the creatures and elements of Earth to "testify," "witness," "minister" (Ps. 104:4); convey God's message (Ps. 104:4); and praise God (Ps. 148).

Critical vision for a just and sustainable future will venture into this uncharted terrain of asking how human creatures may hear moral wisdom spoken in "languages" of otherkind. Practices and theory shaped by this principle are foreign beyond imagining for people who have assumed that the knowledge of dominant sectors mediated by rational discourse is the most valid knowledge. The path toward just and sustainable living will make provocative leaps in ways of knowing. The foremost may be to recognize the profound "otherness" of moral knowing marked by the contours of the Earth rather than of the human. Learning to negotiate this terrain in an Earth community is a fascinating and formidable challenge for the "uncreators."

This move in moral consciousness is a requisite for seeing more clearly the roots and consequences of the economic and ecological violence that binds our lives. Equally important, are the implications of this move for neighbor-love. *Such a shift in moral consciousness calls for rethinking neighbor-love*, to be explored in the final four chapters.

HISTORICAL PRECEDENTS AND THEIR FLAWS

Such a way of seeing the world has precedents in valiant historical efforts against oppressive social arrangements. The shift in moral consciousness that I suggest has its early stages in the second half of the twentieth century, if not before. The 1950s found German social theorist Erich Fromm seeking to unearth the roots of widespread complicity with the rise of fascism and totalitarianism. His findings attribute that acquiescence in part to an "individualized view" of life, an inability to perceive the broader societal dimensions of personal life. He called for "a structuralized picture of the world" as a necessary ingredient in action for social change toward "a social order governed by the principles of equality, justice and love."[21] A structuralized view of the world "interprets individual experience in terms of broader social and economic forces," analyzing "private problems and personal dilemmas as structurally produced."[22] Fromm held that the lack of "structuralized picture of the world ... [paralyzes] the ability to think critically."

In 1959 the American sociologist C. Wright Mills coined the term "sociological imagination" for the capacity to connect the experiences of individual life with broader social and historical forces. He recognized the trauma of ordinary people attributing their difficulties to personal circumstances while, in fact, their lives were tossed about by circumstances of social history such as wars, industrialization, and macroeconomic developments. By recognizing that seemingly private troubles are manifestations of larger societal circumstances, people would see that change in personal life required political action and could seek to become politically engaged.

Subsequently, political theologies arising in Germany and liberation theologies beginning in Latin America insisted that work for justice requires social analysis, analysis of the historical and structural roots of poverty and oppression. The early decades of liberation theologies paid special attention to uncovering the players and power arrangements that enabled wealthy and powerful—yet relatively small—social sectors to accumulate enormous wealth by exploiting and subduing the majority of people who were forced into abject poverty.

Liberation theologians were not the first theologians to insist that Christian moral responsibility demands close and critical attention to the structural dynamics that determine the distribution of economic resources. "The lack of thinking in economic terms is fatal to a sense of reality, and every Christian is under orders to learn how to think in these terms." The voice is Vida Scudder, a late nineteenth-century/early twentieth-century Episcopalian churchwoman and professor of literature at Wellesley College. Scudder was an economically privileged United States citizen. Having spent much time in the burgeoning Settlement House movement, seeking to help people in poverty, Scudder decried Christians' tendency to see poverty as a malady affecting individuals that could be addressed primarily through helping those individuals. Christian faith, she insisted, calls people to see the social structural roots of poverty, and to engage actively in advocacy for systemic change. Scudder insisted on action for structural change as a *necessary* and *integral* dimension of Christian faith.

Fromm's "structuralized picture of the world," Mills's "sociological imagination," liberation theology's "social analysis," and Scudder's insistence on "thinking in economic terms" all demystify social systems that accumulate wealth for some at the expense of poverty and oppression for others. These movements have been invaluable. Efforts to dismantle social justice in its many insidious forms are indebted to them.

These early- and mid-century admonitions to a structural sense of morality, important as they are, bear two lethal flaws. First, they prescribed and described a structural worldview that was not a view of the *world*, but rather a view of the *human world*. The rest of creation was a kind of stage on which the "real" drama, the story of humankind, unfolded. Clearer perception of the economic and ecological violence infecting our lives requires a view of reality that encompasses the earth as well as its human societies.

The other faultline is epistemological and stems from socio-ecological location.[23] With the exception of many liberation theologians, the aforementioned theorists occupied the world of privileged European-Americans and Europeans. They assumed a worldview constructed by the experience of people at the centers of power or privilege. Perspectives from the underside of history went unacknowledged.

A SHIFT IN MORAL CONSCIOUSNESS PRACTICED

The contradiction between collective moral impact and individualized moral consciousness suggests a key to seeing the connections between "those who have too much" and "those who have not enough." The key is a move to picturing life and morality through a lens that situates human social systems within Earth's larger systems, recognizes the impact of our collective actions, and favors perspectives from the margins of power. This moral consciousness transgresses how we have been trained to understand the world: with human beings as the centerpiece of life and with history's winners as the determiners of what is normal, socially respectable, good, and true.

Enough of abstractions. What does such a moral consciousness imply in practical terms? Here we illustrate with the practice of "ecological-economic justice literacy."

People in American society tend to hold in mind a fundamental economic query that in varied articulations pervades virtually all aspects of life: "Am I getting a good buy on this purchase? Can I get a 'better deal' elsewhere?" These questions influence what we buy and what we do.

"Ecological-economic justice literacy" means that another set of questions will play an equally determinative role: "What is the ecological impact of this article of clothing, hotel, or food? And to what extent and how does its production, transport, use, or consumption exploit marginalized people who have little power to counter that oppressive impact?"[24] In simple terms, what does this "cost," including the cost of greenhouse gas production, other ecological costs, and the costs to people exploited to keep the monetary price low? Such questions enable recognizing what is masked by structural evil—ways in which our collective lives unwittingly bring death and destruction to others, and ways in which our lives could bring well-being to ourselves, the earth, and others.

Someone once asked the Dalai Lama, "What is the most important meditation for us now?" He replied, "critical thinking followed by action."[25] "Ecological-economic justice literacy" is a mighty form of critical thinking. It means gaining the tools to find out whether or not specific aspects and activities of our lives indirectly exploit or oppress other people, or damage Earth's regenerative capacities, and how. Moreover, given the magnified collective impact that we have, it means learning to recognize that collective impact. That is, the question broadens from, "Does *my* eating this hamburger damage other people's life chances?" to "Does *our societal practice* of regularly eating beef damage other people's life chances?"

This step into "ecological-economic justice literacy" produces jolting results.

****

Beef production plays a significant role in the emission of three of the four global warming gases: carbon dioxide, nitrous oxide, and methane.[26] *From "field to fork," the long production chain of beef releases greenhouse gases through the burning of forests for cattle pasture, the incineration of agricultural waste from feed crops, the mechanized agricultural production and petrochemical-based fertilization of feed crops for cattle, and the significant methane release from fermenting manure, flatulence, and belching of approximately two billion cows across the surface of the earth.*[27] *Methane and nitrous oxide trap more solar heat than carbon dioxide; the former has 23 times the global warming potential (GWP) of carbon dioxide and the latter has 296 times the GWP of CO_2.*[28] *A single dairy cow produces about 75 kilograms of methane per year—the equivalent of about 1.5 metric tons of CO_2.*[29] *The UN Food and Agriculture Organization reported that livestock is responsible for 18 percent of global warming emissions.*[30] *Furthermore, a great deal of protein goes into producing beef. According to a Cornell report, every year "an estimated 41 million tons of plant protein is fed to U.S. livestock to produce an estimated 7 million tons of animal protein for human consumption."*[31]

****

Making ecological-economic justice literacy integral to daily life seems at first glance overwhelming. Indeed it would be if undertaken alone. However, uncovering the ecological and social justice consequences of our lifeways and building that knowledge into common consciousness is not the work of individuals alone. It is collective work, people collaboratively generating the wisdom they need to live responsibly. This means incorporating such inquiry into church life, healthcare, childrearing, educational systems, and dinner conversations. It means weaving these questions into the body of "tips for living" that we commonly pass from friend to friend. "Ecological-economic justice literacy" implies making questions about the consequences of our individual and collective economic practices and policies a fundamental frame of reference while treading the hallways of everyday life.

Ecological-economic justice literacy calls for shifting the information-gathering habits of daily life—frequenting websites and journals that provide information about the justice implications of products and activities. And it implies a shift in public discourse on individual and institutional levels and in the discourse of faith. In teaching this shift to my students, I have instituted a set of "reality-revealing questions" for them to weave into daily life. The first is this: Who benefits and who loses from "the way things are"? "The way things are" could refer to a purchase, a public policy, a power structure, or more.

The *economic* side of "ecological-economic justice literacy" is arguably integral to Christian faith; it is a tool for responding to God's love and God's call to "love neighbor." This tool enables unmasking structural evil; it enables discerning where our lives serve to "love neighbor" and where they do quite the opposite. For this reason, economic justice literacy ought to be integral to Christian education. In Vida Scudder's words, "[T]he lack of thinking in economic terms is fatal to a sense of reality, and every Christian is under orders to learn how to think in these terms."

"*Ecological* literacy," the ability to "read" the language and realities of Earth's life-systems and how they interact with human factors, is equally key to the life of faith. If God loves this world, found it essentially good, and calls upon it to witness, testify, and praise God's self, then how wildly absurd that many of us have assumed no need to understand how it works (with the exception of the scientists among us), or to interpret its languages.

Until my recent incipient efforts to the contrary, I have journeyed through life ecologically illiterate and have perpetrated that illiteracy in my students. I have not known that my body is nearly 60 percent water and that the salt content of my blood mirrors that of Earth's seas. I did not realize that a single gram of forest soil contains about ten billion individual organisms—and only four thousand or so are known to scientists. Never did I imagine that the cells in my body contain atoms that were once part of stars.

More elusive than learning *about* the Earth and its life-systems is the question of learning *from* them. What—in practical terms—does it mean to "learn" moral wisdom, and how to live from voices that are not human? Of this, modern humans know very little. We will forge new (or reclaim ancient) epistemological pathways. This will mean learning and teaching our children (or learning from them) to decipher Earth's other-than-human languages no less than we teach them to understand the humanly created languages of ATM machines, computers, and college entrance exams. As we will see in the following chapter, hope and moral wisdom lie not only in the human but also in the other-than-human parts of creation. How great, then, will be our gain in learning to access that hope and wisdom.

The move to ecological literacy is underway. Ethicist Dan Spencer initiated ecological autobiography exercises for his students, and he identifies "ecological location" along with social location. Elementary school children in Seattle work with salmon and their life-cycles vis-à-vis the city's waterways. The Earth Bible series explores scripture from perspectives of the Earth. "Green Sisters" (Catholic sisters dedicated to hearing the cry of the earth, healing the earth, and developing religious culture that enables both) offer "earth-literacy training."[32]

Biomimicry, the art and science of imitating nature's designs for human use, has gained traction in recent years. Airplane designers are inspired by the tiny bumps on the edge of a whale fin called tubicles, which could increase airplane efficiency by 32 percent and save significant fossil fuels. Peacocks emit color in their feathers not with pigment, but through carefully designed shapes that emit a certain hue when light passes through—potentially reducing our use of harmful dyes.

In short, if our economic policies and practices mean life and death for people thousands of miles across the globe, and threaten Earth's life-systems, then we must develop tools to understand the impact of what we are doing and the possibility of alternatives. From a theological perspective, if repentance calls for seeing structural sin that is craftily hidden, then repentance also calls for literacy in the fields of that sin, including ecological and economic violence. Literacy of this kind is a way to practice a transformed moral consciousness.

COUNTERING MORAL OBLIVION: A RE-VIEW

The individualized, anthropocentric, and victor-oriented moral consciousness shaping the modern world obscures critical vision—our sense of "what is" and "what could be."

A transformation in moral consciousness is called for. It will be less privatized and anthropocentric, and will seek persistently to know reality as it is experienced on the losing side of power and privilege. Such a consciousness will acknowledge the moral consequences of *collective* human actions as well as individual actions.

If critical mystical vision entails three forms of seeing—"what is," "what could be," and "the sacred powers of life at work in the world to bring wholeness for all"—then it remains to consider the third of these, what I call the "mystical vision" dimension of critical mystical vision. Like seeing "what could be," seeing sacred healing power at play is an antidote to the denial, hopelessness, and the powerlessness that may ensue with daring to see "what is." "Mystical vision" and the hope it brings claim our attention in the next chapter. Before going there, we return to a life story begun in chapter 3. In hearing it, be alert for the shifts in moral consciousness traced in the current chapter.

****

A Life Story Revisited

Freddie's Oily Morning Revisited

This story in chapter 3 revealed Freddie's "petroleum addiction" and her unawareness of it. It revealed also the impact of the oil industry on people of low-lying coastal lands, Mississippi's Cancer Ally, and the Niger Delta, and those impacted by U.S. military action in the Persian Gulf.

The bicycle—that 150-year-old, human-powered, pollution-free, efficient mode of transport—is rising as a worthy and increasingly popular antidote to our societal obsession with automobiles and our petroleum addiction. Cyclists and bike commuters are challenging the idea that cars are necessary, that they are a human right, and that they control the streets of our cities and towns. They challenge the idea that there is "no other way" to get around.

The Pedal People Cooperative in Northampton, Massachusetts is a human-powered hauling and delivery service. This small business hauls up to three hundred pounds of residential and municipal trash, recycling, and compost on trailers hitched to the back of bicycles, and also runs a grocery and diaper delivery service. The business is growing, and many *customers prefer the bike-trash haulers to the loud, polluting garbage trucks. Watching people pedal away with huge trailers full of trash has also served as a deterrent to producing large amounts of waste. "We try to help people reduce the amount of trash they make," explains one Pedal People employee. "[We] encourage reusing and reducing what people think they need to live on."*33

Individual lifestyle choices alone cannot bring about communities that consume far less oil. For that to happen, public policy is needed. The movement to reduce automobile use through biking is a good example. One gray morning as I biked from home to work, a white van backing out of a driveway collided with my bike, sending me sprawling onto the road. Fortunately I was fine, and my bike was undamaged, but the collision stunned me. I spent the rest of the day thinking about how much worse it could have been, and how the accident might have been different. We could live in a city with no bike lanes, no helmet laws, and no driver (and biker) education around sharing the roads. The driver of the van could have argued that I was at fault, that bikes shouldn't be on the roads, and the law might have been on her side. But instead, our city values bike commuters and creates public policies that encourage them. We have bike lanes, road signs, rails-to-trails programs, driver education, bike-sharing programs, bike rack installations by the city, bike racks on public buses, and bicycle advocacy organizations. As a result, we increasingly see parents with young children in buggies or bike seats, kids biking alongside their parents, and panniers full of groceries as a shopper returns home via bicycle. Without public policies in place, biking would be much riskier—so risky that most citizens might decide it's not worth it, and stick to their cars.

*Bicycles are only one manner in which communities are addressing our oil addiction, and contributing to a shifting moral consciousness. Alternative energy movements are gaining traction in cities and countries across the world. NativeSUN is a solar project of the Hopi Foundation, an organization by and for Hopi people.*34 *The Foundation makes photovoltaic cell panels affordable to the low-income reservation community through a revolving loan fund. Over three hundred homes now have solar panels on the roof. The project reflected the assessment of the Hopi community regarding its needs. Author and activist Winona LaDuke summarized the guiding mentality as: "Use less, produce what you can on your own, and be* cognizant of the implications of each decision on others."[35] *In these few words, LaDuke eloquently voices the call to ecological-economic justice literacy.*

And what of the places far from home where oil is extracted and refined? How can we practice a collective moral consciousness that attunes itself to the lives of the workers and residents in the Niger River Delta? Rehabilitating our oil addiction in our own homes is certainly necessary. There are also ways to influence the inhumane living and working conditions for communities in Nigeria, the Mississippi River Delta, and other places on earth where oil is extracted or refined.

Amnesty International, for example, runs a campaign that would force the Nigerian government to hold oil companies accountable for the oil spills and gas flares that kill the fish, pollute the water and air, and endanger the people of the Niger River Delta.[36] According to Amnesty International, multinational oil companies such as Shell, Total, and Chevron, as well as the Nigerian government are jointly responsible for gas flaring, but no one is held accountable. Amnesty International teams have now collected over ten years' worth of satellite imaging, and mapping data revealing the close proximity of gas flares to waters where people drink, bathe, fish, and wash their clothes. When representatives meet with government officials and oil company officials to urge an end to gas flaring, they do so armed not only with collected data but the names of thousands of citizens in the U.S. and across the world who have signed a petition indicating that they know and care about what is happening there. Without that participation of individual citizens, these initiatives would not work.

Some people choose to organize around public policy change and corporate change. 350.org is a global, decentralized, volunteer-led, grassroots movement of campaigns, organizing, and mass public actions to solve the climate crisis. The movement is active in 188 countries and at one point initiated a campaign to address the problem with the U.S. Chamber of Commerce. The Chamber is notoriously supportive of a gas-guzzling America. It fought to weaken clean air standards,[37] lobbied against the Kyoto Protocol, and opposed a hazardous waste dumping ban. The Chamber petitioned the EPA to do nothing about climate change, arguing that "populations can acclimatize to warmer climates via a range of behavioral, physiological, and technological adaptations."[38]

Recognizing that the Chamber of Commerce no longer represents many businesses in America, especially small businesses, 350.org is committed to organizing small businesses to weaken the Chamber's grip on political life. "Maybe," the organizers write, "we can finally get rid of the huge subsidies to our fossil fuel industries. Maybe we can finally get a law passed to start dealing with the worst crisis our planet has ever faced."

****

Notes

1. Bernard Lonergan, *Insight: A Study of Human Understanding* (New York: Philosophical Library, 1958).

2. Mary Hobgood, *Dismantling Privilege: An Ethics of Accountability* (Cleveland: Pilgrim, 2000), 151.

3. Sallie McFague, *The Body of God: An Ecological Theology* (Minneapolis: Fortress Press, 1993).

4. Walter Brueggemann, *Prophetic Imagination* (Philadelphia: Fortress Press, 1978), 119, 44.

5. Paul Hawken, *Blessed Unrest* (New York: Viking, 2007), 2, 186, 189.

6. *The Better World Shopping Guide* collects data from a wide range of public, private, and nonprofit sources that track information on one or more of the five issue areas (human rights, the environment, animal protection, community involvement, and social justice). The data are organized into a massive database that calculates an overall responsibility score.

7. Gene Perry, "Normal Becomes Oklahoma's First Fair Trade Town," *Voices of Oklahoma*, May 14, 2010.

8. Catholic ethicist David Hollenbach documents the movement in American society toward privatizing virtually all aspects of life. Hollenbach, *The Common Good and Christian Ethics* (Cambridge: Cambridge University Press, 2002).

9. Hobgood, *Dismantling Privilege*, 16–17.

10. Jürgen Moltmann, in a presentation delivered at Seattle University, October 23, 2007, as part of the Great Theologians lecture series.

11. Hobgood, *Dismantling Privilege*, 16.

12. Donna Haraway, *Simians, Cyborgs, and Women* (London: Free Association Books, 1996), 192.

13. Ibid., 191.

14. For analysis of this dynamic, see Mark R. Warren, *Fire in the Heart: How White Activists Embrace Racial Justice* (New York: Oxford University Press, 2010).

15. George Zachariah, *Alternatives Unincorporated: Earth Ethics from the Grassroots* (London: Equinox, 2011), 101, 104.

16. David Suzuki, *Sacred Balance: Rediscovering Our Place in Nature* (Mountaineers, 2002), 3. Other theologians and theorists have proposed some form of ecocentric shift in worldview. They include Teilhard de Chardin, Thomas Berry, Mary Evelyn Tucker, Brian Swimme, and Larry Rasmussen.

17. This threefold purpose of economic life is articulated by Larry Rasmussen, in "Green Discipleship," *Reflections* (Spring 2007).

18. D. John Chelladurai, "Symbiotic Life: Organism Earth," unpublished paper presented for *Greening Young Minds*, an NCCI conference, October 2008, Nagpur, India.

19. The terms are Larry Rasmussen's.

20. In ecological ethics, outstanding work in this area is Nancy Erhard's *Moral Habitat: Ethos and Agency for the Sake of Earth* (Albany: State University of New York Press, 2007).

21. Erich Fromm, *The Art of Loving* (New York: Harper, 1956), 125.

22. Stephen Brookfield, *The Power of Critical Theory: Liberating Adult Learning and Teaching* (San Francisco: Jossey-Bass, 2005), 352.

23. The term "socio-ecological location" was coined by environmental ethicist Daniel Spencer.

24. This proposal applies to the intended audience of this book: people of "economic privilege." For a single parent with low income trying to feed and house three children, from a moral perspective, the priority question might be, "Will this economic decision help me to provide a healthy life for my children?" rather than "How will it indirectly impact others?"

25. Cited from the film *I Am* by Tom Shadyac.

26. Fred Pearce, "Methane: The Hidden Greenhouse Gas," *New Scientist* (May 6, 1989); Alan Durning and Holly Brough, *Taking Stock: Animal Farming and the Environment* (Washington, DC: Worldwatch Institute, 1991), 17; World Resources Institute, World Resources 1990–91, 355.

27. Biopact, "UN Climate Chief: Less meat = Less heat," September 7, 2008.

28. Ibid.

29. According to Pete Hodgson, New Zealand Minister for Energy, Science, and Fisheries. Cited in "Meat: Now It's Not Personal, But Like It or Not, Meat Eating Is Becoming a Problem for Everyone on the Planet" by Worldwatch editors, 2004.

30. Tracy Fernandez Rysavy, "Eat Less Meat, Cool the Planet," *Green American* website, October 2007.

31. Cornell University Science News, "U.S. Could Feed 800 Million People with Grain That Livestock Eat," August 7, 1997.

32. Sarah McFarland Taylor, *Green Sisters: A Spiritual Ecology* (Cambridge, MA: Harvard University Press, 2007).

33. See *Yes! Magazine*'s "Food for Everyone," Spring 2009 issue and Pedal People website.

34. Winona LaDuke, *All Our Relations: Native Struggles for Land and Life* (Cambridge, MA: South End, 1999), 187.

35. Ibid., 189.

36. See "Nigeria: Petroleum, Pollution, and Poverty in the Niger Delta," a 2009 report by Amnesty International. The report included recommendations to countries in which the companies are located, such as the United States. These are, in effect, recommendations for citizen action.

37. Brad Johnson, "Chamber of Commerce Continues Decades-Long Assault against Clean Economy," *Think Progress* (February 1, 2011).

38. Kate Shepherd, "Chamber: Global Warming Is Good for You," *Mother Jones* (October 2, 2009).

6

Theological Seeds of Hope and Power

We must sleep with eyes open,
we must dream with our hands,
we must dream the dreams of a river seeking its course,
of the sun dreaming its worlds. . . .
We must dream backward, toward the source. . . .
    Octavio Paz

Danger lurks. The expansive moral consciousness called for in the previous chapter easily aggravates denial and powerlessness. This enhanced moral vision exposes the devastating impact of economic life as we know it, on the Earth and on neighbors who are dispossessed by our possessions. To acknowledge the widespread suffering that may be linked to my material abundance would be tormenting. How could I live with the knowledge if I truly took it in? And if I dare to see, then I view also the power and complexity of structural violence and the relative insignificance of individual efforts at change. Where would I find the moral-spiritual power to transgress tidal waves of cultural, political, economic, and military force pushing to maintain the way things are? A sense of inevitability has almost magnetic power for depleting hope. What is inevitable, I cannot change. Hope for economic and ecological relations may fade before ever it sees full bloom, and with it moral vision and power.

I know this insidious descent into hopelessness well. It has been part of my life. I began this book relating an experience of my early teen years. It was a documentary film depicting the extraordinary suffering of sugar cane workers in the Dominican Republic at the hands of the Gulf + Western Corporation. My world was changed forever. I was shocked beyond words to think that my breakfast cereal and other sugar-bearing foods came at the expense of brutal exploitation and suffering. Soon thereafter, I attended a six-week "immersion experience" in Oakland, organized by a Lutheran youth organization. The immersion was designed to expose participants to people exploited by the economic systems upon which our lives are based. As a result, I became an activist during my high school years, working with Welfare Rights mothers, migrant workers, anti-hunger organizations, anti-imperialism campaigns, and the church. As time went on I became ever more troubled by what seemed to me the absurd lack of concern or even interest on the part of so many people. I was young, idealistic, passionate, and raised to believe that people would do the right thing. The combination was dangerous. I became filled with anger and hopelessness, and felt lost in the confusion of despising my own people—white middle-class Americans—for what we were doing to people of (what was then called) the "Third World," and to many people of color and impoverished people here in the United States. We return to this part of my life presently.

As Patricia Hill Collins insists, the litmus test of critical social theory is the extent to which it *overturns* powerlessness and moves people to struggle toward justice. Such too is a litmus test of theology. All of our theorizing and theologizing to uncover the roots of complicity with structural evil is worth little if it does not engender a sense of hope and moral power for the struggle toward justice and sustainable Earth-human relations. Yet a theology must do more. It must cultivate not only compassion for others but compassion for self. A theology must bring a sense that I and all others are beloved creatures of God regardless of all circumstances, including my entanglement in systemic evil.

WHY RELIGION FOR READERS NOT AFFILIATED WITH RELIGION

Chapter 4 identified hopelessness and denial as potent forces clouding our vision of the structural violence running throughout our lives. They also drain our power to see alternatives and to work toward them. It is time to face head-on the morally devastating and virulent forces of hopelessness and denial.

It may be here that the role of religion is most crucial. It provides a sense of hope that the powers of greed, exploitation, and brokenness are not the final word, and that the sacred Source of all is flowing through creation, is healing and liberating, and ultimately will reign. We are not alone in our quest for just and Earth-honoring ways of living.

In order here is a word about the relevance of this turn to religion and spirituality, and particularly Christianity, for readers who may not be affiliated with it or with any other religious tradition. The book's Introduction addressed this turn more fully. Here we note in particular its implications for hope and moral power. Since the beginning of recorded time, many religious traditions have engendered hope, moral vision, and moral courage in the face of the impossible.

At times secular voices have called upon religious traditions to provide moral leadership and strength in the face of moral crisis. The Earth crisis has made this era such a time. Voices from outside of religion increasingly are calling upon religion to play its role in the pan-human quest for sustainable Earth-human relations. These requests come from the scientific community, the secular NGO community, the public policy community, the United Nations, and more. The Earth Charter illustrates this recognition that the world's religions and spiritual perspectives can catalyze the human community toward a sustainable future.

Internationally renowned scientists are beckoning religious leaders to address the environmental crisis. In 1992, the Union of Concerned Scientists released their "Warning to Humanity," stating that "we require the help of the world's religious leaders" for evoking a "new ethic . . . for caring for ourselves and for the earth."[1] In 1990 thirty-four internationally recognized scientists wrote an Open Letter to the Religious Community, arguing that "Problems of such magnitude and solutions demanding so broad a perspective must be recognized from the outset as having a religious as well as a scientific dimension" and that "efforts to safeguard and cherish the environment need to be infused with a vision of the sacred."[2] Hundreds of religious leaders from multiple faith traditions responded, forming the Joint Appeal in Religion and Science, and eventually, the Forum on Religion and Ecology. In such appeals, religion is seen as offering moral norms, values, networks, a sense of obligation beyond the self and "tribe," hope, vision, and courage. These foment moral power.

Here, we consider a set of theological resources within Christianity that may counteract a sense of hopelessness and denial. While I articulate these resources in terms of Christian theology, I believe that closely related resources are offered by other faith traditions. All of Earth's religions must bring their resources to the table of human endeavor at this point in history. My task, as a theologian and ethicist within Christianity, is to probe it, and then to offer its resources to the human family. People of other religious traditions are called to do the same. Within Christianity this endeavor is wildly complexified and enriched by the multiplicity of "Christianities." Theologies, faith claims, and practices within Christianity throughout the centuries, continents, cultures, and subcultures contain more differences than exist between some forms of Christianity and other faith traditions.

From the many wellsprings of hope within Christianity, I highlight the following few because I believe that they may be relevant both to Christians and to people who do not identify with Christianity but are interested in its moral and spiritual resources. Moreover, these aspects of the tradition—quite frankly—are all too often ignored or domesticated.

MYSTICISM AND MORAL-SPIRITUAL POWER

The call to love neighbor as self is one thing. The moral–spiritual power to do so is another. I have long sensed that mysticism is a boundless source of moral–spiritual power for human beings to receive divine love and then live it into the world. Where morality and the mystery of God's presence are held in one breath—moral life understood as mystical life—moral agency may be found for forging paths toward more just, compassionate, and sustainable ways of living.

One aspect of Christianity (and of some other religions) that breeds hope is the claim that we are called toward some form of union with the great power of life, the source of all, what many call God. We are destined to be with or fully a part of the Holy Source, and that union begins this side of death. In Christian traditions, union with God is also union with the force that we call love. Our destiny is union with divine love. It is not a task to be achieved as much as a gift to be received and then shared, in the present.

Irenaeus of Lyon, leader of a persecuted second-century community of Christians, is one of the first to flesh theologically the conviction that human destiny is union and communion with God. According to Irenaeus, not only human beings but the entirety of creation is destined for that end. The role of human creatures is to be "educated" or "matured" by the Spirit. Irenaeus's imagery is compelling. The "dew of the Holy Spirit [is] dispersed throughout all the earth."[3] We are to remain moist by that Spirit so that Word and Wisdom may mold us like moist clay toward our destiny of union and communion with God.

Throughout the ages, many have referred to this union, experience of it, trust in it, and movement toward it as "mysticism." The term has multiple connotations and ambiguity surrounds them. Our intent is not to argue a definition of mysticism or to map its range of meanings, but rather to unlock its boundless possibilities for hope and other ingredients of moral agency. For our purposes here, "mysticism" refers to the experience of or faith in the presence and power of God with, in, and among human beings and the other creatures and elements of Earth, even when God *seems absent*.

In this sense, mysticism does not refer to an esoteric experience to be had by only the few who are dedicated to and privileged by visions or periods of extraordinary consciousness. Nor does it refer singularly to moments of heightened experience of God's presence. Mysticism, as used herein, is accessible to all. Here we consider five related aspects of mysticism in this sense. They are the food of hope and, as such, of moral power for resistance to ecological and economic violence and other forms of systemic evil.

SEEING SELF THROUGH THE EYES OF GOD

"You will love your neighbor as yourself," may also be translated accurately as "You will love your neighbor as God loves you." To love neighbor as God loves oneself implies viewing oneself through the eyes of God's love.

Here we take a clue from the Beguines, a heterogeneous movement of Northern European women religious that rose, flourished, and was suppressed from the late twelfth through mid-fourteenth centuries. Medieval convention bound religious life to specific rules and church-recognized orders that remained detached from secular life. Beguine communities, in contrast, lived dedicated religious lives while remaining engaged in worldly life and relatively unaccountable to male authority figures.

Many Beguines professed to be authorized by God, trusted the truth of their own experience, and engaged in public theological discourse. They were, therefore, seen as challenging the exclusive authority of the church hierarchy in its roles as singular medium of redemption, exclusive source of theological truth, and regulator of discourse. The strength of Beguine moral-spiritual power cast fear into the heart of hegemonic power. While some were burned at the stake, others were forbidden to spread their teachings, speak publicly, travel, or become Beguines before the age of forty. The words of Beguines' persecutors reveal the power of their agency in spite of efforts to repress it. The "way of life" of the Beguines, wrote the General Council of Vienne in 1312, "is to be permanently forbidden and altogether excluded from the Church of God. Because they . . . promise no obedience to anyone and do not profess an approved Rule."

These women did not perceive themselves as "moral agents" or as undermining hegemonic power structures of their day. (Such assertions would be anachronistic.) Yet, many of them were both.[4] Wherein lay their moral-spiritual power to exercise such agency despite the threat of death, even death by fire?

It had many roots. Their power derived in part from the lens through which they perceived themselves. The Beguines, at least as we know them through their surviving literary works, saw themselves as they believed that God saw them—as beloved by God. The extraordinary extent to which these women were moral agents and subjects of their lives seems to lie in a perception of self and each other derived directly from knowing themselves as *in* God, *beloved* by God, and *lovers* of God. Hadewijch of Brabant, a thirteenth-century Beguine poet and mystic, declares: "I entreat you . . . open the eyes of your heart (Eph. 1:18) to see clearly and contemplate yourself in God."[5] This way of knowing self issued in a way of doing and being, a form of moral life characterized by nearly irrepressible agency. They understood themselves to be "subject to no one save Love alone doing service and performing the works of Love . . . day and night in all liberty, without delay of fear and without counting the cost."[6]

We note an incredible wealth of what moderns call moral subjectivity and agency—awareness of self, strength of self-expression, and power to act with a purpose based on conviction. It was grounded in seeing God as Love itself and seeing self as primarily God's beloved, in whose veins Godself coursed and was poured out to others. This vision found self to be good and able to act because of who they understood themselves to be in the eyes of God: ". . . and then you will be Love, as I am love . . . go forth and live what I am," declared God's voice to Hadewijch.[7]

To see oneself through the eyes of God, to see what God sees, is to see a human creature loved beyond all comprehension. Our socially constructed identities and our "need" to maintain them give way to a primary and primal identity—the beloved. Seeing self through the eyes of God—seeing self as beloved by God before all else—engenders the compassion and deep love for self that flows into love for others. To see others through the eyes of God is to see them first and foremost as precious beloved creatures of God. The others that we construct—the others that we must impress, or be better than, or use, or dominate—give way to the neighbors who are, before all else, beloved.

The power of receiving God's love is beyond full human knowing. We do know that it draws one away from serving the needs of self alone, and evokes deep compassion for the pain and needs of others. And, if the witness of the Beguines holds truth, it engenders the moral-spiritual power to serve God and to love self and others regardless of the risks entailed. In this sense, seeing through the eyes of God evokes hope that we might live love into the world, hope as enduring as is that love, infinitely so.

GOD "FLOWING AND POURING THROUGH ALL THINGS"

Multiple streams of Christianity, from its earliest centuries, have affirmed the *mysterium tremendum* that God, the source of life itself, the One who is saving and has saved, abides within human beings and is at work within us. Early Christians came to know this indwelling presence as the Holy Spirit and as Christ dwelling within. Less common, yet present in many Christian traditions throughout the centuries, is the affirmation that God dwells not only within human beings, but within the entirety of creation.

This latter incarnational claim is particularly striking in voices not widely recognized for it. One of those is Martin Luther. ". . . the power of God," he declares, ". . . must be essentially present in all places even in the tiniest leaf."[8] "Christ . . . fills all things. . . . Christ is around us and in us in all places . . . he is present in all creatures, and I might find him in stone, in fire, in water."[9] The assertion that God indwells all created being has been present in Christian theology for two millennia. It is far more present in Orthodox theology than Western, which tended to submerge or sideline it until the last half of the twentieth century.

In Western theology of the late twentieth century, the idea of God's presence within creation is well developed in Sallie McFague's argument that the world is God's body and in Leonardo Boff's understanding of cosmogenesis in which God is the very energy of the cosmos unfolding, yet is beyond the cosmos as its the creative force. For Boff, "All is not God. But God is in all and all is in God."[10] More recently, Mark Wallace and John Hart elaborate distinct yet complementary visions of the creation as bearer of the immanent Spirit of God.[11] Wallace unfolds a theology of the Spirit as "an agent of social transformation who empowers persons and groups to challenge the structures of domination and oppression."[12] Hart holds that "the Spirit permeates creation," "making all space sacred space."[13]

The understanding that God dwells within creation has at times been misinterpreted as pantheism, and hence denounced as antithetical to Christian notions of God. Such is a gross misconception. God's indwelling presence is rightly understood not as pantheism but as pan*en*theism, meaning God's presence within creation as well as above and beyond it (*pan* = all; *en* = in; *theos* = God). God can be neither conflated with the created world nor separated from it.

The term *panentheism* is far from precise and panentheistic theologies come in multiple versions, especially with increased attention to God's immanence in the twentieth century. So prevalent is one form or another of panentheism in recent decades that Philip Clayton refers to a "panentheistic turn" in modern theology.[14] Broadly speaking, panentheism refers to the idea that the world is "not merely a product of God's willing or doing, but also a part of God's very being."[15] The world is in God and God is in the world. Panentheism is a radical declaration of God's immanent presence.

Panentheism affirms God's immanence within creation while simultaneously affirming God's transcendence beyond it and beyond human understanding. Immanence comes from the Latin "*immanere*"—to remain within. Christian tradition is marked by this radical claim of both immanence and transcendence. Different schools of Christian theology have emphasized God's immanence, transcendence, or a balance between the two.[16]

At times in Christian history the two are placed in a contradictory relationship whereby more of one means less of the other. However, a deeper understanding holds transcendence and immanence as inseparable and as mutually magnifying. The holy Mystery is far more fully transcendent than we can imagine, vastly beyond the transcendent God figure of classical theism. God is the essence of being and becoming, the force of life itself. Yet, this reality is at the same time more fully immanent than we can know. The transcendent Energy of the cosmos is also immanent, incarnate in the material world. The immanent divine—while intimately present within the core of our being—is also infinitely beyond all material reality.

If the creating, saving God is present within the trees, waters, and creatures, what are the implications for human hope and moral power to confront and transform systemic evil? How could this God presence dwelling within the Earth and its biotic community be teaching, guiding, empowering, and equipping us to fashion ways of living that serve God's healing, liberating work toward abundant life for all?

One implication of God's presence within the Earth is christological. If indeed Christ fills Earth's creatures and elements, then the Earth now being "crucified" by human ignorance, greed, and arrogance is, in some sense, also the body of Christ. Followers of Jesus the Christ in every age are charged with asking Bonhoeffer's question: Who is Christ for us today? Where is the cross today? Where are we lured into denying Christ crucified today? If Earth, as habitation of God, as body of Christ, is cruciform, and if believers took seriously this christological claim, might we be moved to treat this Earth differently?

Another implication stems from the affirmation that the creating God is also the saving liberating God. The power that is creating the universe is at play within creation and beyond, healing and liberating it, including human society. The idea that God as justice-making liberating love is present in Earth's creatures and elements heralds startling and hope-giving possibilities. *Other-than-human creatures and elements then embody divine agency toward creation's flourishing.* Earth embodies God, that is, not only as creative and revelatory presence, but also as teaching, saving, sustaining, empowering presence . . . as agency to serve the widespread good. The Earth becomes, in ways that most of us have not yet glimpsed, a *subject* with divine energy.

The inhabitants of a modern Western worldview do not customarily think of moral agency in creatures other than human. We commonly assume that a distinguishing characteristic of humankind is our capacity for moral doing and being. A theology of God's immanence together with a re-read of the biblical texts suggests otherwise. New life-giving possibilities for understanding the roles of the other-than-human emerge as we attempt to relinquish the anthropocentric (which often means Eurocentric) blinders shaping received interpretations.

Christian ethicist Nancy Erhard argues convincingly that other-than-humankind may play a role in moral agency. Her work on Genesis 1–3 and 6–9 finds these texts attributing moral being and doing to creatures and elements. Waters and earth collaborate with God in the acts of creating. "In Genesis 1-2:4a, the waters and Earth respond to God. They fulfill God's command by action of their own, becoming collaborators if not co-creators."[17] And what they do in response to God's bidding, God deems as "good," *tov*, connoting not only aesthetic goodness but also moral goodness of a life-generating nature. The story of the flood reveals that "all flesh,"—a category including birds and animals as well as humans—had a role in the destruction resulting in the flood. Their capacity for knowing and acting for good (or refusing) is confirmed in the covenant that God makes with them along with Noah (Gen. 9:10). Moreover, Erhard reminds, "A tree confers 'knowledge of good and evil.'"[18]

Erhard's point is that the biotic community plays a role in shaping the moral values, assumptions, norms, and imagination that comprise the morality of a given context. These "moral habitats" influence moral agency. They may, she concludes, "transform . . . human agency on behalf of the flourishing of the whole earth community."[19]

Other biblical texts also suggest roles that otherkind may play in nurturing the moral power of human creatures to serve God's ways. For example:

- Job 12:7-10 portrays animals and plants as teachers of humans who are admonished to learn from the plants and animals what God does on Earth. "But ask the animals, and they will teach you; the birds of the air, and they will tell you; ask the plants of the earth, and they will teach you; and the fish of the sea will declare to you. Who among all these does not know that the hand of the Lord has done this?"
- Psalm 19:1 shows the cosmos itself revealing to humans some of the nature of God. "The heavens are telling the glory of God; and the firmament proclaims [God's] handiwork."
- In Psalm 148 God enjoins even fire, frost, cedars, and "creeping things" to praise God. "Praise [the Lord], sun and moon; praise [the Lord], you highest heavens, and you waters above the heavens! . . . Praise the Lord from the earth, you sea monsters and all deeps, fire and hail, snow and frost . . . Mountains and all hills, fruit trees and all

cedars! Wild animals and all cattle, creeping things and flying birds!" (vv. 3-4, 7-10). Praising God has moral implications.

- According to the Deuteronomistic historian, the Earth is called upon as witness in one of the most crucial choices faced by the ancient Hebrews and by people of all times who read life through the lens of faith in God: to choose life or to reject life in accord with God (Deut. 30:19-20).
- In Job 38:1, as in numerous texts, God works through winds, waters, and creatures: "The Lord answered Job out of the whirlwind."

God's Spirit—the Spirit of boundless love—at play in and with otherkind may nurture humans' power to heed God's call to love neighbor as God loves. We are well advised to learn from and heed the other-than-human languages of this Earth. It is uncharted terrain—creation as abode and servant of divine and indefatigable love.

Nature does not "model" morality. One predator taking down the mother or offspring of another, the agonized faces of tsunami survivors, the fierce onslaught of disease, or slow and agonizing death dispel that notion. What is natural is not necessarily moral. The point is not to hold up nature as a blueprint for morality. Rather, the point is to cultivate receptivity to hearing the voice of God in the other-than-human parts of nature, learning from them about how to live rightly, and being nourished for the work of Earth-keeping and justice-making by God's Spirit at play in creation.

We have considered the ancient faith claim that God's love is "flowing and pouring through all things" and there offers creating, saving, and sustaining power for the healing of a broken world.[20] Two notions stemming from this claim—of Christ crucified in a crucified Earth and of God's saving presence at work within creation—indeed may render hope and moral agency for the long and uncharted journey toward a world in which humankind is not toxic to our planetary home and in which none amass wealth at the cost of others' impoverishment.

HUMAN CREATURES: ABODE OF INDOMITABLE LOVE

God's presence within human creatures and human communities makes sense in light of the profound human goodness that shines in history. But what of human brutality? What of history's wreckage in the last century alone? Two world wars, genocide, and ecocide do not witness to a Spirit of divine love indwelling human beings.

A widely accepted Christian understanding is that we live in a paradoxical moral reality, corresponding to the "already and not yet" reign of God on Earth.

This "already and not yet" condition has been expressed diversely throughout Christian history. In sweeping terms: We are alienated from God and as a consequence of this alienation (sin), we will betray (to some extent) the ways and will of God. Instead of living according to God's commandments to love God, self, and others, and we will live as "selves curved in on self," captive to self-interest. The profound paradox is that simultaneously, we are saved by God.[21] Salvation frees us from living as "selves curved in on self," and saves us for loving God, self, others, and this good Earth. God renders us living abodes of God's justice-making love.

This paradox reverberates with power for the good. It means that regardless of our implication in cruel forms of oppression, human beings also are capable of and called to lives of justice-making love. We are the body of God on Earth, bearers of Christic love. We are, that is, filled with moral agency for healing and liberating.

Dietrich Bonhoeffer probed the ethical implications of God's love embodied in human communities. He was adamant that the love of Christ, revealed most fully in the cross, abides in the Christian community. After experiencing non-Christians courageously resisting fascism and the failure of much of the institutional church to do so, he determined that the God-bearing community includes non-Christians who are serving God's purposes. In Bonhoeffer's terms, Christ dwelling in the community of people who embody God's love "conforms" them to "the form of Jesus Christ." That is the form of God's overflowing love embodied as community that acts responsibly in the world on behalf of abundant life for all, especially on behalf of those who are persecuted or marginalized.[22] This action requires recognizing structural evil, naming it, and "putting a spoke in the wheel" of earthly powers that demand disobedience to God. The power to resist structural evil, even when so doing is terribly costly, is the actual love of Christ taking form in human community.[23] As revealed in the cross and resurrection, this love is indomitable, even when it appears to be defeated.

The God of Christian tradition—and Jewish tradition before it—works with and within extraordinarily fallible human beings and communities. Divine love does not come to people because they deserve it or are particularly noble, good, or courageous. All inhabit the paradoxical state of being both "in bondage to sin" and an "abode of God's active love."

This paradoxical moral anthropology harbors profound implications for moral agency in the current context. It frees us from the fatalism that may accompany honest acknowledgment of one's inability to love fully or to seek justice fully. That failure does not prevent God's presence in and among us as justice-making, self-honoring neighbor-love. As a dwelling place of the God revealed in Jesus Christ, human beings become not only objects but also *subjects* of a love that cannot be stopped in its quest to bring fullness of life to all. The church today is called to rekindle this ancient claim, to live in the promise that indeed this God is incarnate within us and, there, is hungering and hastening toward the restoration of this precious world. This vision may enable us to open our hearts and minds to the "data of despair"—including our implication in ecological and economic violence—and not drown in it, but rather enter into it on behalf of life in its fullness.

SPIRIT AWAKENS HEALING LIBERATING POWER

Since shortly after Jesus' execution, Christians have claimed that God's Spirit works within and on believers. Pneumatology from the first century to the twenty-first affirms that the Spirit enables people to act as God would have them act. In the words of Catholic theologian Yves Congar: "The Spirit-Breath is first and foremost what causes [humans] to act so that God's plan in history may be fulfilled."[24] To the extent that living as God would have us live includes challenging structural evil, the Spirit enables that challenge.

But what *is* that morally empowering role of the Spirit? In what sense does the Spirit enable moral agency for serving God's will? With and through whom does the Spirit act to engender humans' healing and liberating power?

Myriad responses have found their way into church history and into the biblical texts. Responses in Western Christianity reflect its tendency—until recent decades—to prioritize the first and second persons of the Trinity over the third. The Holy Spirit, until recently, was underexamined in Christian ethics. This was unfortunate, for the Spirit is the person of the Trinity most closely aligned with moral agency, at least where moral agency is understood as the capacity to heed the ways and will of God.

Here we focus on the biblical witness rather than on later Christian understandings. Seeking insight into how God's Spirit within humans might engender hope and moral-spiritual power for the healing of the world, we look first at the Hebrew Bible (Old Testament) and then at the Second Testament (New Testament). In both, ambiguity and diversity abound.

HEBREW SCRIPTURES

"Spirit," where it refers to the Spirit of Yahweh translates the Hebrew, *ruach*.[25] According to the Hebrew scriptures, the ancient Hebrews experienced a power of the One whom they called YHWH reaching into their lives and into the entire created world, making things happen according to the will of that One. They called this power *ruach*.[26]

Ruach (like *pneuma*, *espiritu*, and *spirit*, its most frequent renditions in Greek, Latin, and English respectively) has multiple denotations and connotations in the biblical texts. Its meanings shift over the centuries of the Old Testament and among different cultures within it. Those meanings range from a forceful movement of air to the fundamental energy of God. While our concern here is the last of these, a sense of it requires insight into what the word means and implies in its other usages.

The word's root significance "probably had to do with the movement of air,"[27] or more specifically with a "gale,"[28] but over time took on varied meanings. At times, *ruach* is a tempestuous or raging wind coming forth from God or sent by God to move things dramatically, materially, and with life-and-death consequences (that is, the wind that separated the Red Sea in Exod. 14:21 and 15:10). Elsewhere it is a breath, or an impersonal supernatural force, or a temporary or roving mood or disposition sent by God to occupy a person and influence her/his behavior (e.g., the "spirit of jealousy" in Num. 5:14, and the evil *ruach* from the Lord sent to torment Saul in 1 Sam. 16:14). *Ruach* may be the breath or animating life-force of all living things, usually but not always given and withdrawn by God (Gen. 7:22; Ps. 104:29, 30). As such its presence or absence determines life or death. The essential vivifying force or energy of a human being is *ruach*. ("Into your hand I commit my *ruach* in Ps. 31:5.) Most significant to us here, *ruach* may refer to the essential energy of God.[29] As such *ruach* "does not as a rule describe God's inner personality . . . [but rather] God's activity in relationship to the world."[30]

As a force that vivifies the human, *ruach* is the deepest self, the essential energies of the persons, the source of feeling, thinking, responding. (The *ruach* of Pharaoh was troubled Gen. 41:8.)[31] In this sense, *ruach* of a human and *ruach* of God are inseparably linked, sometimes in fact indistinguishable to the extent that the text is unclear whether the *ruach* of the person is given by God or is God within the person. When and where God's *ruach* is withdrawn, the human *ruach* too perishes and along with it life. The *ruach* of God gives life and is necessary for life to remain. "The *ruach* of God has made me" (Job 33:4). If he should take back his *ruach* to himself, "all flesh would perish together, and man would return to dust" (Job 34:14-15). The *ruach* as force of true life in the human being is utterly dependent upon the life-force of God extended to the human.

When giving God's *ruach* to the human creatures, God puts it "within" the individual (Ps. 51:10) or the people (Isa. 63:11), or "pours it out" on them. The psalmist implores: "Create in me a clean heart, O God, and put a new and right *ruach* within me. Cast me not away from thy presence, and take not thy holy *ruach* from me" (Ps. 51:10). God's *ruach* may be poured upon individuals, the people corporately, or "all flesh."[32] "I will pour out my *ruach* upon all flesh," declares God according to the book of Joel (2:28). In Isaiah, the people attest that God's "*ruach* is poured upon us from on high" (32:14-18), and God pledges, "I will pour my *ruach* upon your descendants" (44:3). God assures Ezekiel, "I will pour out my *ruach* within you" (36:24-38).

But, when poured out on people, what does God's *ruach* do that might enable people to live according to the ways of God? The Hebrew Bible suggests the following:

- God's Spirit instructs a people on how to live in times of great difficulty. God's Spirit "instructs" the Israelites in the wilderness (Neh. 9:20).
- Especially before the monarchy was established, Yahweh's *ruach* enables people to act as God would have them act (Gideon in Judg. 6:34, Samson in Judg. 14:6).
- Frequently, God's Spirit bestows on a person a particular attribute that usually is associated with wisdom. The gift may be wisdom itself (Gen. 41:38-39; Exod. 28:3; Deut. 34:9) or, the wisdom of God (Isa. 11:1-5). Or the gift may be ability, intelligence, knowledge, craftsmanship (Exod. 35:31), understanding, counsel and might, or fear of God. At least in the preexilic period, the Spirit's gift could be unusual physical strength (as with Samson in Judges 14:6, 19).
- God's Spirit may be given to human beings to arouse prophetic witness and vision. "Then the spirit of the Lord will possess you, and you will be in a prophetic frenzy" (1 Sam. 10:6). "I will pour out my *ruach* upon all flesh; your sons and your daughters shall prophecy, your old men shall dream dreams, and your young men shall see visions" (Joel 2:28-29). God's *ruach* may take possession of the prophet in order to denounce transgression of God's gift of laws for living rightly. "The spirit of God took possession of Zechariah; he stood above the people and said to them, 'Thus says God: Why do you transgress the commandments of the Lord, so that you cannot prosper? Because you have forsaken the Lord, he has also forsaken you'" (2 Chron. 24:20). Receiving the *ruach* for prophetic witness was often dangerous. The people "conspired against him and, by command of the king they stoned him to death" (2 Chron. 24:21).
- The Spirit brings justice and peace. "I have put my Spirit upon him; he will bring forth justice to the nations" (Isa. 42:1). When Isaiah

declares that the "Spirit of the Lord shall rest upon him" (Isa. 11:2), the result is the splendid reign of justice, righteousness, and peace foretold in Isaiah 11.

- After times of devastation, especially devastation that has befallen as a result of unfaithfulness or departure from life as God would have it, God's Spirit restores both life and right relationships (righteousness). *Ruach* brings life, flourishing, and righteousness out of social chaos, at times delivering people from collective self-destruction or folly. This may pertain to an individual, a people, or another living thing. In particular let us note that the Spirit restores justice, righteousness, peace, and secure dwelling, and makes "the wilderness a fruitful field" after disaster that struck as a result of leaving the hungry unsatisfied, depriving the thirsty of drink, and ruining the poor (Isa. 32:6-18).
- The *ruach* of God intertwines human well-being with the land's well-being. "Until a spirit from on high is poured out on us, and the wilderness becomes a fruitful field. . . . Then justice will dwell in the wilderness, and righteousness abide in the fruitful field" (Isa. 32:15-16). Elsewhere too the "pouring out" of God's Spirit or God "putting my spirit within you" links human flourishing with the land's flourishing (Isa. 44:3-4; Ezek. 36:26-36).

In short, in the Hebrew Bible, *ruach* when it refers to God's Spirit is a force emanating from God or the force of Godself that reaches into the depths of a people or a person and awakens agency (or *is* agency) for maintaining and restoring relationships that cohere with God's will for life. These relationships might be interpersonal, societal, between humans and the Earth, or between God and God's creation.

SECOND TESTAMENT

The Second Testament describes a presence and power of God reaching into Jesus' life, speaking to him, leading or driving him, filling him, and empowering him for his work. The writers of these texts called that power *Pneuma* or *Pneuma* of God. Where the Spirit comes upon, fills, speaks to, bids, drives, leads, or anoints Jesus, the result is tremendous power for remaining faithful to God in the face of temptation; for proclaiming the reign of God and the Jubilee message; and for liberating, healing, and giving sight. These acts lead some people to follow Jesus and others to become furious with him. That anger often is somewhat cloaked. It becomes dangerous and ultimately deadly for Jesus.

After Jesus' ascension the apostles—and people who repented and were baptized—received this Holy Spirit (Acts 2:38). Many of them experienced or witnessed a power of God reaching into their own or other people's lives, making things happen according to the ways of the God to whom Jesus pointed. This power touched both individuals and communities. These earliest believers apparently understood themselves, as individuals and as a body, to be filled with (Rom. 8:9) and led by the Holy Spirit, and empowered by gifts from that Spirit for doing the will of God. God's will, in their estimation, seemed to be that all would hear the "good news" and would fashion ways of life oriented around "all that [Jesus] has commanded," including the commandment to love one's neighbor as one's self. This power—like that which reached into Jesus' life—was called *Pneuma* and was understood to be the *Pneuma* of Jesus himself, the risen Christ. Latin translations rendered this *"Pneuma"* as *"Espiritu,"* which in turn became "Spirit" for English speakers.

Where the Spirit "comes upon" (Acts 19:6), "falls upon" (Acts 10:44), or "dwells within" (Acts 8:9) individuals or the believing community, the consequences are striking. The Spirit may instruct a person concerning what he or she is to do in a particular situation (as with Philip in Acts 8:29 and Peter in Acts 10:19; 11:12), empower a person to heed the instructions (Paul in Acts 20:22), or forewarn him or her about resulting persecutions (Paul in Acts 20:23). The Spirit also enables believers to communicate (Acts 21:4), discern what is good (Acts 15:28), belong to Christ (Rom. 8:9), claim that Jesus is Lord (1 Cor. 12:3), or "be [Jesus'] witnesses . . . to the ends of the Earth" (Acts 1:8).

The Spirit according to the Second Testament reveals Christ, sanctifies and justifies, gives life, sets people free from the law of sin and death, leads, prays on behalf of, renders people children of God, bears witness through the human spirit, intercedes within the children of God when they know not how to pray as they ought, enables people to live according to or in the spirit rather than the *sarx* (flesh), and allots or activates particular fruit or gifts. These gifts include strength, courage to proclaim Jesus as Lord in the face of other gods, prophecy, speaking in tongues, discernment, intercessory prayer, generosity, faith, love, and healing. Many of these gifts are useful for neighbor-love. Indeed Paul admonishes that these gifts are given "for the common good" (1 Cor. 12:7), not for the elevation of the individual.

The Spirit was understood to live within the people. This is variously expressed as "being in Christ," God's love being "poured into our hearts through the Holy Spirit" (Rom. 5:5), "Christ dwelling within," and "the Spirit of God dwell[ing] in you" (Rom. 8:9). In the words of Finnish theologian Veli-

Matti Kärkkäinen, the coming of the Spirit is the coming of God's power and presence to "dwell in and among the people."[33]

In heeding the direction of the Spirit and using the gifts of the Spirit, the early Christians seem—according to the biblical texts—to manifest a paradox. They tend to gain and use power for doing whatever the Spirit bids them do. Yet, they do so with mistakes, misjudgments, and other manifestations of their human fallibility. The Spirit does not enable perfection in living according to God's bidding. At times heeding the Spirit's bidding—especially if it means claiming Jesus as Lord—is dangerous.

In the Second Testament, the Holy Spirit is the face of God that leads people to walk according to the ways of life set out by God through the Torah, the Hebrew Prophets, and Jesus of Nazareth. These ways of life are centered in God's command to love neighbor as self, and love extends beyond the boundaries of interpersonal relationships.

Much is *not* clear. The implications of these findings for how contemporary people are to live and respond to the economic and ecological violence inherent in our lives are up for interpretation. It depends, of course, upon how one understands "life according to the reign of God," or "ways of life oriented around all that Jesus has commanded" or what it means to "love neighbor as self."

Nevertheless, a few things pertaining to moral agency for the work of neighbor-love in contexts of systemic evil may be said with some surety. The texts of the Second Testament, held together, testify that:

- The power and presence of God is immanent, dwelling within human communities, as well as transcendent.
- The Holy Spirit that is within communities and individuals is the same power and presence that animated Jesus (Rom. 8:11).
- This Spirit dwelling within communities and individuals brings moral power for neighbor-love.
- That love will be lived out and will be lived out with many mistakes, shortcomings, and other realities of human fallibility and finitude.
- The presence of this Spirit at times has a transformative impact.

Examining the Spirit—in both Hebrew scriptures and the Second Testament—yields disconcerting truth. Heeding the Spirit's bidding to follow God's ways may be dangerous. History confirms that following paths of neighbor-love, especially amidst forces of systemic domination, often has been dangerous. It requires courage.

Herein may lie a key to the Spirit's power. The Holy Spirit renders courage. According to Martin Luther, the most powerful courage known to humankind is generated by the Spirit living in the faithful. In a sermon, he speaks of the power, strength, and courage that may be imparted to the faithful by the indwelling presence of the Holy Spirit.[34] The Spirit brings into its human abode "true courage—boldness of heart." "The Hebrew word for spirit," Luther preaches, "might well be rendered 'bold, undaunted courage.'"[35] That "bold, dauntless courage . . . will not be terrified by poverty, shame, sin, the devil, or death, but is confident that nothing can harm us and we will never be in need."[36] This empowering courage is, according to Luther, greater and more powerful than any human on Earth. With courage comes hope.

HORIZON OF HOPE

"For I am convinced that neither death, nor life, nor angels, nor rulers, nor things present, nor things to come, nor powers, nor height, nor depth, nor anything else in all creation, will be able to separate us from the love of God in Christ Jesus our Lord" (Rom. 8:35-39).

Christian teachings, at their best, are in the service of hope and life. According to one understanding of Christianity, the destiny of creation is abundant life for all. This is the promise toward which all else points. The God who called this world into being loves it with a love beyond human imagining that will never die. That love cannot be taken from us by any force in heaven or Earth. Nor will that love desist in bringing the entire world into its destiny of life according to God's reign of love. While the forces of evil are fierce and virulent, the force of good—known in Christian tradition as divine love—ultimately will triumph.

The fullness of this promise is neither fathomable nor fully describable. It is articulated with images varied and verdant: paradise, the reign of God, the city of God, the Garden of Eden, the great shalom, heaven, the blessed community, the arc of the universe toward justice. This destiny is glimpsed in human love and in Earth's splendor, and has been the hope of peoples for millennia. For readers who embrace this promise and for those who find it untenable, may this brief sketch uncover some of its nuance and perplexing twists.

Puzzling paradoxes of Christian faith are located in this horizon of hope. One is the strange conviction that while this reality of pure love governing life *appears* only to be in the future, it also exists already in the present; it is "already and not yet." That is, eternal life does not begin after death; eternal life begins in the here and now. It is life in connection with the Spirit of God. God's call to us to love is a call to live according to that destined reality. In doing so, we serve God's purposes of bringing that reality into being, and of healing the world. By embodying God's love—even in our desperately imperfect and limited ways—we witness to its presence in the world and God's fierce intention to liberate and heal the world from all that thwarts the reign of that love. In other words, the future salvation of the world is in some sense already present. (One of the great self-betrayals of Christian faith by the tradition itself is the teaching that God's intended reign—traditionally referred to as heaven—is for life after death only; life on Earth does not really matter, for our reward and hope are found after death in heaven. This teaching was used for centuries to subdue peoples into accepting their own oppression and domination. It betrays the promise that God's gift of eternal life begins on Earth and that God intends creation to flourish.)

Another seemingly absurd paradox of hope, related to the first, is the promise that evil will be overcome. Despite all evidence to the contrary—and that evidence is overwhelming given the twentieth century's descent into two world wars, holocaust, and nuclear weaponry and the twenty-first century's trajectory of climate destruction—God's promise is that evil ultimately is overcome by the power of God's love. Perhaps the most powerful symbol of this hope in the face of evil's apparent triumph is the cross and resurrection of Jesus Christ.

For many people, as noted previously, moral inertia in the face of ecological and economic violence is born not of failure to see it, but lack of hope that it can change. The forces of wrong seem too powerful for human beings to impact. Resistance and work toward alternatives appear futile. Despair is sown by a deep sense that things will continue as they are in this world.

The cross and resurrection promise otherwise. They testify that in the face of death and destruction, God's life-bringing power prevails. Soul-searing, life-shattering destruction and death are not the last word. In some way that we do not grasp, the last word is life raised up out of brutal death. God "will not allow our complicity in . . . evil to defeat God's being for us and for the good of all creation."[37]

I have experienced that paradoxical and life-saving hope. In my time of youthful despair about systemic injustice, I needed to talk with a person who recognized the horror of structural sin and yet maintained hope and a sense of deep joy. The late Jon Nelson proved to be that person. After hearing my desperation, he responded with words that flooded my being with hope. "I have hope and joy," he calmly expressed, "because in all of my struggles for justice and peace, I know the end of the story." By this he meant the promise that, regardless of compelling indications otherwise, all forms of death and destruction that humankind and this earth may experience are overcome by resurrection.

This message of hope also bears danger. It may lead people to abdicate responsibility for public morality, leaving it in "God's hands." This would betray another central Christian claim—that God works through and with creation, and in a particular way, through human creatures.

Here appears a third paradox of hope central to Christian tradition. It is the strange dialectic between absolute trust in God's power to bring about the liberation and healing of the world on the one hand, and on the other hand the conviction that human beings—while unable to bring about the reign of God through human effort alone—are called to dedicate our lives to that very endeavor. God, not humans, can and will save the world. Yet, we are to live our lives toward that end, devoting our gifts and resources to it.

Dietrich Bonhoeffer expressed this startling dialectic between ultimate trust in God, and the necessity of human engagement through his unwavering critique of liberal Christianity's notion that God can be called upon like a kind of fix-it machine to solve life's problems while we just sit and wait. His ethic of responsible action to disclose and confront evil is grounded in absolute dependence on God and trust in God. "I believe that God can and will bring good out of evil," he writes, "even out of the greatest evil."[38] Yet Bonhoeffer denounces religion's proclivity for replacing human responsibility with appeals to God to act. He insists that God's power on behalf of the world is in God's embodied presence in and with responsible actions by human beings. To "bring good out of evil," he insists, "[God] needs [people]."[39]

All this is to name a simple faith claim and then to admit the profound complexities within it. The world is in God's hands and is/will be saved. Despite sin's pernicious presence, especially manifest in structural evil, we are called by God to live toward that "already but not yet" accomplished salvation. We do so by trusting God's justice-making love completely and embodying it in the world fallibly. This is, I believe, an inexhaustible source of hope. What embodying that love means is the material of the remaining chapters.

THEOLOGICAL SEEDS OF HOPE AND MORAL-SPIRITUAL POWER

Acknowledging the structural evil that taints our lives may tempt one toward denial or plunge one into hopelessness. Both thwart moral vision and power. Christian traditions offer theological resources countering denial and hopelessness. These resources are elements of what I have called "mystical vision," the companion to critical vision. These theological seeds of hope reveal a basic Christian promise—the great Spirit loves this world with a liberating love that cannot be dimmed and is dwelling within this world, luring it to choose life rather than death. Moreover, the Spirit empowers human communities to embody this love. The remaining chapters explore practicing this love as neighbor-love. The following story portrays one community seeking the meaning of God's call to love neighbor as self in the context of structural violence.

****

A LIFE STORY REVISITED

REVISITING EXPLOITATION OF WORKERS IN THE UNITED STATES

This story in chapter 4 saw Robin homeless after having lost her job at Walmart. The narrator was enjoying inexpensive Walmart products and a growing mutual fund invested in that company.

I've been putting my Walmart purchases to good use recently, and it's a relief that my mutual fund is finally doing a little better. My guilty conscience from encountering Robin Martin, the ex-Walmart employee living in a shelter, has been assuaged ever since I made the donation to a homeless shelter. But imagine if instead of passing by Robin on the street I ended up in a café with her, listening to her story. What would happen if I began to fully grasp the magnitude of her situation and how she arrived there? What if I realized that my Walmart purchase and the disheveled woman sitting in front of me were all connected?

Imagine that this realization—the connection between our consumer behaviors and conditions of low-wage workers—had captivated the hearts of a midsized mainstream church somewhere in America. Suppose that this church congregation, we'll call it Church of Grace, had recently restructured their outreach efforts, and as a result decided to embrace a commitment to addressing homelessness and poverty in their city. Church of Grace is now exploring what this commitment means and what it would look like for the church to engage these issues. I decided to attend their first meeting.

"Is everyone here?" Ruth asked, looking around at the handful of folks gathered together for the first Church of Grace Homelessness & Poverty Advocacy Committee meeting. We were seated together around folding

tables in the fellowship hall, sipping coffee. I imagined that the people present, like me, were wondering how on earth to begin to tackle these monumental issues.

"I think we should start by making sure we understand the issues. Ann, can you share what you've learned with us?"

A young woman sitting next to Ruth flipped through some sheets of paper. "I volunteered to do a bit of research for our meeting today," she said, looking up at us. "It turns out that homelessness is on the rise in our city. With the recent budget cuts, even more shelters are losing state and federal funds and will need to close their doors this year. At the same time, low-cost housing is being eaten up by high-end condo developments. Unemployment is still high in this area, but many homeless people are actually employed full time but earning minimum wage, which it turns out sometimes isn't enough to support one's housing, food, and health needs." Ann shared some statistics on wages, employment, and cost of living with the group, much of which was startling news to me. "It's all really depressing," she added at the end. "I don't know where to start."

"With all these factors affecting the homeless and poor in this area," a tanned man named Scott stated, "there's so much to consider. I mean we could try to tackle the lack of quality education that makes it hard for people to get relevant job skills, or public health concerns that keep people from being able to work. We could provide childcare here in the church so that working parents can actually get to work. Or we could join that campaign that recently started to protect low-cost apartments from developers."

"That's way too much for us to handle," a bearded man named Justin interjected. "It's not like we can actually solve the problem of poverty and homelessness in this city."

"Now wait a moment," said Ruth. "We're not asked to solve this problem right here in this room today by ourselves, but aren't we a community committed to discipleship in the spirit of Jesus through service to the poor and seeking justice? Didn't pastor Phelps preach just this last Sunday on that verse from Matthew, 'You shall love your neighbor as yourself'? Well I've been asking myself all week, what does that passage mean for our lives? If I love these folks out on the street without shelter or their own food to eat, then I've got to do something. And I'll be much more effective acting alongside the folks in this church than all by myself."

"Justin has a point," said Rachel, a young woman who didn't stop knitting as she spoke. "We can't tackle all these issues. It seems to me that much of the causes of poverty and homelessness lie in jobs and working conditions. What if we just focused on that?"

I joined several others nodding in agreement. Robin, after all, was in the situation she was in primarily because of substandard working conditions. "I came across some interesting information on wages in my research," interjected Ann. "Have you all heard of a living wage?" Ann went on to describe the concept of a living wage—an attempt to address the shortcomings of poverty indicators based on the minimum wage established by the U.S. government. "Living wage refers to the minimum hourly wage necessary for an individual to meet his or her basic needs, including housing, nutrition, transportation, healthcare, clothing, and recreation," she explained. It's different from a minimum wage that may or may not meet the requirements of a living wage."

"A lot of organizations are working on this issue," said Horace, a thoughtful man in the back who had been silent until now. What if we threw our weight behind the Let Justice Roll Living Wage Campaign?" He looked at the blank faces around him. "It's a coalition of business, labor, faith, and community organizations committed to raising the minimum wage to a living wage at both the state and the federal level. This might be perfect for us because," he said, looking at Justin, "it's working for policy reform and could have a greater impact than just our church working on issues here in this city."

Several people seemed interested in this. "But somehow, that doesn't feel like enough," argued Scott. "I definitely think we should work on reforming the laws in this state and country, but I keep thinking about what Rachel was saying—how our consumer practices really do connect us to the workers who make or sell all that cheap stuff. Did any of you see that documentary a few years back about Walmart?"

Scott described the film "The High Cost of Low Prices" and shared with the group some harsh realities about the challenging fight for economic justice within Walmart. For example, Walmart's CEO makes 2,500 times what an entry-level associate makes in a year. The company cracks down hard on unions, issuing a document called "Manager's Toolbox to Remaining Union Free" and shuts down stores where unions form.

"So you think we should all boycott Walmart?" asked Justin.

"We certainly could," replied Scott. "Boycotts can be really effective. We could also check out organizations like the Walmart Worker's Association and Wake Up Walmart. They provide resources for employees on campaigns and actions around changing Walmart. We could encourage this church to "adopt-a-Walmart" nearby to work for reforms. We could plan a movie screening and educate the congregation. We could write letters to the editor about this . . . there's really a lot that we could do."

"Religious leaders are involved too," added Ruth. "The group Wake Up Walmart announced a campaign by thirteen religious leaders from Texas, Georgia, Tennessee, Kentucky, Colorado, and Oklahoma to urge Walmart to adopt labor reforms."[40] *Eager to help, I used my iPhone to find an online version of the interfaith letter to Walmart CEO Lee Scott, and passed it around the circle. "Listen to this section," said Ruth, reading out loud.* "Walmart's values are not Christian values, nor do they reflect the values of any of our faiths. As people of faith, it is our duty, it is our moral obligation, to write to you and ask Walmart to reverse its anti-family policies. Walmart's anti-family policies are immoral, unjust, and a direct affront to the teachings of our faith. I bet our congregation would be willing to sign that."

We paused to gather our thoughts. Finally I decided to speak up. "You know, another option does come to mind. We keep talking about Walmart and these big box stores with their unjust worker policies, but there are other options for us as consumers: local, small businesses that care about their workers." I was thinking about how it seems like independent local businesses are springing back to life across the country. Ann was nodding her head. She shared the story of her college roommate who lives in Bellingham, Washington. In Bellingham six hundred local businesses formed "Sustainable Connections"—an alliance that creates what they call a "relationship economy" instead of a "one-night stand" economy.[41]

The group paused again to ponder all this information. Then Scott spoke up. "How do we know what legislation is out there that we could support? I'd like to talk to my elected officials about this, but I don't know what there is that I could encourage them to vote on." "How about the Faith Action Network?" Rachel responded. "They have an e-newsletter that alerts people to current legislation on a number of issues: hunger, homelessness, housing, healthcare, environment education, etc."

Justin sighed. "You know, we came up with a lot of options tonight. How do we decide what to do?" "But it's like Ruth said," Rachel responded. "We're not here to do it all, or do anything by ourselves. We're here to discern what steps we can take, as a community, here and now. And we're not acting alone." Horace chuckled, "Some people in this church are not going to like these suggestions." "Yeah," Ruth replied, "but what better place to talk about tough moral issues than in a church?"

The group continued discussing options, possible solutions, ways to engage and ways to educate their congregation. We debated how effective different measures would be, and continued long past the allotted meeting time. The array of possibilities for changing my relationship with people like Robin Martin are greater than I realized. We left the fellowship hall with a plan for several important first steps that we could take to do something about poverty in our city and the unjust working conditions that cause it.

★★★★★★★★★★★★★★★★★★★★★★★★★★★★★★★★★★

Notes

1. Union of Concerned Scientists, *World Scientists' Warning to Humanity*, 1992.

2. Found at http://fore.research.yale.edu/publications/statements/joint_appeal.html.

3. Irenaeus of Lyons, *Against Heresies*, 3.17.3.

4. The Beguines, as most movements undermining systems of domination, are riddled with paradox in their relationship to those systems, in some senses undermining but in others underwriting them. Excellent secondary sources include Emilie Zum Brunn and Georgette Epiney-Burgard, *Women Mystics in Medieval Europe* (Chicago and London: University of Chicago Press, 1989); John Milhaven, *Hadewijch and Her Sisters* (Albany: State University of New York Press, 1993); and various works by Carolyn Walker Bynum. Two primary sources for Beguine writings are: Hadewijch of Antwerp, *Hadewijch: The Complete Works*, trans. Mother Columba Hart (Mahwah, NJ: Paulist, 1980), and Marguerite Porete, *The Mirror of Simple Souls*, trans. Ellen L. Babinsky (New York and Mahwah, NJ: Paulist, 1993).

5. *Hadewijch: Complete Works*, "Letters," 1.

6. Ibid., 18.

7. Ibid., "Verses," 3.

8. Luther, "That These Words of Christ, 'This Is My Body,' Still Stand Firm against the Fanatics," *Luther's Works* 37:57.

9. Luther, "The Sacrament of the Body and Blood of Christ—Against the Fanatics," in Timothy Lull, ed., *Martin Luther's Basic Theological Works* (Minneapolis: Fortress Press, 1989), 321.

10. Leonardo Boff, *Cry of the Earth, Cry of the Poor* (Maryknoll, NY: Orbis, 1997), 153.

11. Mark Wallace, *Finding God in the Singing River: Christianity, Spirit, Nature* (Minneapolis: Fortress Press, 2005) and other works; John Hart, *Sacramental Commons: Christian Ecological Ethics* (Lanham, MD: Rowman & Littlefield, 2006).

12. Wallace, *Finding God in the Singing River*, 128.

13. Hart, *Sacramental Commons: Christian Ecological Ethics*, 3.

14. Philip Clayton, "The Panentheistic Turn in Christian Theology," *Dialog* 38 (1999): 289–93.

15. John J. Thatamanil, *The Immanent Divine* (Minneapolis: Fortress Press, 2006), 6.

16. G. W. H. Lampe traces controversies in concepts of God's immanence as they developed in patristic thought. G. W. H. Lampe, *God as Spirit* (Oxford: Clarendon, 1977). The trend in modernity has shifted. Theological liberalism emphasized God's immanence. Neo-orthodoxy critiqued this emphasis and emphasized God's transcendence. More contemporary theologies, especially some feminist and eco-feminist theologies, have reclaimed the legacy of an immanent God.

17. Nancie Erhard, *Moral Habitat: Ethos and Agency for the Sake of Earth* (Albany: State University of New York Press, 2007), 50.

18. Ibid., 55.

19. Ibid., 4.

20. Martin Luther, Luther's Works, 26, as cited by Larry Rasmussen, "Luther and a Gospel of Earth," *Union Seminary Quarterly Review* 51, no. 1–2 (1997): 22.

21. Theologies vary on who and what is situated in this rather incomprehensible paradox. Some hold that it pertains singularly to followers of Jesus; some see it as the condition of all people; others see the entire cosmos located in the "already and not yet" reign of God. My stance is that no humans, this side of death, can know the parameters of the reality. But I do know that to err on the including side is far more true to the God revealed in Jesus than to err on the excluding side. Thus I rest my hat on understanding that the entire creation is within the fold of God's "already and not yet" reign.

22. For Bonhoeffer, conformation with the form of Christ implies refusing conformation with ways of life that betray Christ. His use of *gestaltung* for "conformation" is a play on the word used by Hitler to mean conforming to fascism. Conformation with the form of Christ crucified, for Bonhoeffer—in response to his context—came to mean both standing on behalf of the persecuted, and assuming the guilt of the Western world. This convergence of two meanings assumes very personal meaning for Bonhoeffer. He lived them both: he was imprisoned and executed for an assassination plot that was, in significant part, a defense of (standing on behalf of) those persecuted by the Nazi regime. At the same time, in *Letters and Papers from Prison*, he refers often to his role as the guilty, assuming the guilt of Germany and of the Western world. In this sense, Bonhoeffer's understanding of the cross bridges the gap between theologies of the cross that see Christ atoning for human sin and theologies of the cross that see Christ executed by imperial power for his allegiance to the compassionate and justice-making reign of God. The cross for Bonhoeffer was both.

23. He writes: "The relation between the divine love and human love is wrongly understood if we say that the divine love [is] . . . solely for the purpose of setting human love in motion. . . . On the contrary . . . the love with which [humans] love God and neighbor is the love of God and no other. . . [T]here is no love which is free or independent from the love of God." Dietrich Bonhoeffer, *Ethics*, ed. Eberhard Bethge (New York: Simon & Schuster, 1995), 55–56.

24. Yves Congar, *The Holy Spirit in the Economy*, vol. 1, of *I Believe in the Holy Spirit* (London: Geoffrey Chapman/New York: Seabury, 1983), 4.

25. In addition to works cited, this section draws upon Michael Welker, *God the Spirit*, trans. John Hoffmeyer (Minneapolis: Fortress Press, 1994); Mark Wallace, *Fragments of the Spirit* (New York: Continuum, 1996); Jürgen Moltmann, *God in Creation: A New Theology of Creation and the Spirit of God*, trans. Margaret Kohl (San Francisco: Harper & Row, 1985).

26. *Ruach* is used 378 times in the Hebrew Bible (Congar, *The Holy Spirit in the Economy* 3), 264 of which are translated in the Septuagint as *pneuma* (Veli-Matti Kärkkäinen, *Pneumatology* (Grand Rapids: Baker Academic, 2002), 25. *Ruach* appears only three times as "holy" *ruach* (Isa.

63:10, 11; Ps. 51:11). *Neshamah* also is rendered "spirit" or "breath" in English." However, where the Spirit is that of Yahweh, it is *ruach*.

27. Alasdair Heron, *The Holy Spirit* (Louisville: Westminster John Knox, 1983), 3–4.

28. Helen Schüngel-Straumann, "Ruah (Geist-, Lebenskraft) im Alten Testament" in Maria Kassel, ed., *Feministische Theologie: Perspektiven zur Orientierung*, 2nd ed. (Stuttgart: Kreuz-Verlage, 1988), 61, cited in Moltmann, 40, 318n4.

29. The porous nature of boundaries among these is clear in the varied translations of a single text. Genesis 1:2 is translated variously as "a wind from God swept over the waters," the "spirit of God," or "a mighty wind." Psalm 51:12 is translated "uphold me [with thy] free spirit" in *Young's Analytical Concordance*, and as "sustain in me a willing spirit" in NRSV. The *ruach* of God, of humans, and as an elemental force is not always clearly distinguishable.

30. Heron, *The Holy Spirit*, 8.

31. The power of life in a more impersonal sense, as in lifeblood, is more often denoted by *nephesh*.

32. "All flesh" in the Hebrew Bible at times refers to human beings, at others to all flying creatures and creatures of the land including humans, and at times to all living beings. Often the referent is unclear and scholars debate it.

33. Kärkkäinen, *Pneumatology*, 34.

34. Martin Luther in *Sermons of Martin Luther*, ed. John Nicholas Lenker (Grand Rapids: Baker, 1992), 8:277.

35. Ibid., 8:275.

36. Ibid., 8:275–76.

37. Christopher Morse, *Not Every Spirit: A Dogmatics of Christian Disbelief* (Valley Forge, PA: Trinity Press International, 1994), 249.

38. Dietrich Bonhoeffer and Eberhard Bethge, *Letters and Papers from Prison* (London: SCM, 1967), 361.

39. Ibid., 361.

40. www.wal-martwatch.org.

41. Businesses such as carpentry, manufacturing, restaurants, tourism, and retail invest in each other. The unemployment rate for Bellingham is lower than elsewhere in Washington State, and in 2011 it was ranked second in the United States for vitality of independent businesses.

7

Love: Mystery and Practical Reality

"Radical acts of love—expressing solidarity and bringing mutual
relationships to life—are the central virtues of the Christian moral life."
                                            Beverly Wildung Harrison

◆

"Love . . . changes form and brings new forms into being . . . the forms of
love's expression cannot be identified with only one pattern or motif . . .
God in his creativity and freedom reforms the modes of love's expression."
                                            Daniel Day Williams[1]

This is the breathtaking claim of Christian faith: that the Light of life, the Sacred Source within all and beyond all is at play in the world, breathing life into it. We are beckoned to join with this Spirit of justice-making, Earth-relishing Love in its creating, liberating, healing work to bring fullness of life to all. We are to receive this Love, trust it, and then embody it into the world. We are to "love as God loves."

What love is and requires is the great moral question permeating Christian history. In each time and place Jesus' voice resounds: "You shall love your neighbor as yourself." The human response rings throughout the ages: "What does it mean to love neighbor as self in our day and place?"

What would be the shape of neighbor-love for a people who saw themselves as an integral and utterly dependent species in a tapestry of life—a planetary community of creatures and elements through which coursed the sacred energy of life itself? How would loving neighbor look if these people also were progressively destroying the conditions for life on Earth? What are practical implications of love embedded in the overarching determining realities of the early twenty-first century—the neoliberal global economy, and ecological devastation? How does the "thief" love the victim?

Bear in mind the ambiguity that attends human efforts to act according to love or the good. What course of action will embody justice-making love is frequently not clear. Ambiguity marks the path, including moral ambiguity. What serves the good in the short run may yield long-term damage. What may be just for one group may be unjust for another. One person's understanding of what constitutes a loving response to any situation may differ radically from another's. An action motivated by love may have unintended negative consequences.

Two claims emphasized by my own tradition, a Lutheran form of Christianity, help to explain this ambiguity. One is the acknowledgment that—in things human—good and evil are intertwined. The other is similar: human finitude renders our actions toward the good, including our acts of love and justice, imperfect. However, despite our imperfection and the intermingling of evil with good, we are called to move forward in justice-making love to the best of our ability.

We begin this chapter with Jesus' call to love, and then note the complexity and conundrums coloring any attempt to discern what love is and requires. Next, we sketch features of neighbor-love as a norm grounded in Christian theology and scripture.

COMMANDMENT, DECLARATION, PROMISE

"You shall love the Lord your God with all your heart and with all your soul and with all your mind. This is the first and the greatest commandment. And second is like it. You shall love your neighbor as yourself" (Matt. 22:37-39).[2] Jesus is calling upon God's commandment expressed in the Hebrew scriptures, to "love your neighbor as yourself. I am the Lord" (Lev. 19:18). According to Jesus, "all the law and the prophets hang on" the commandments to love (Matt. 22:40). Likewise Paul cites the Leviticus text in Gal. 5:14: "For the whole law is fulfilled in one word, 'you shall love your neighbor as yourself.'"[3] Indeed, it is the biblical view that to participate in what God is doing in this world is before all else, to live love into it.[4]

Jesus is not only instructing people in what they *should* do. He also is declaring what they *will* do. The verb, *agapao*, is in the future indicative. This is the case in all three synoptic gospels (Matt. 22:37-39; Mark 12:38-34; Luke 10:25-28). Likewise in the Pauline epistles, "you shall love" is expressing, in the words of New Testament scholar Matthew Whitlock, "assurance in the fulfillment" of this declaration.[5] This assurance is profoundly hope-giving, particularly as heard by contemporary people caught up in webs of structural injustice from which it is hard to imagine escape.

From a biblical perspective, love is the primary moral norm for human life. Loving neighbor as self—or loving neighbor as God loves—along with loving God, commonly is seen as the essence of morality. "[T]he whole thrust of biblical religion is toward the recovery of the broken human capacity to love," asserts Daniel Maguire.[6] These claims are widely held in Christian academic and ecclesial circles. "Our responsibility as Christians," insists Martin Luther King Jr., "is to discover the meaning of this command and seek passionately to live it out in our daily lives."[7]

COMPLEXITY AND CONUNDRUMS

Exploring the call to love is fraught with complexity and problems. Ignoring them is perilous. Any normative theology of love must at least acknowledge the problems entailed in arriving at it. Here, consider a few.

- The word "love" is used to signify many different things even by a single person. When I say, "I love to eat butterscotch," I mean something very different, for example, from when I declare, "God is love." "Love" is used for romantic love, personal preferences, divine love, friendship, familial love, love as a biblically based norm, and more. We limit this inquiry to the last of these.
- The word "love" is used to translate more than one word in the Hebrew Bible. The word most frequently translated into English as "love" is *aheb*. It is used to designate love for neighbor (Lev. 19:18), for God (Deut. 6:5), and God's love for God's people (Deut. 5:10; Hos. 3:1). *Aheb* is rich, vast, and hardly captured by its English translation. The English "love" occasionally is a translation of the Hebrew Bible's *hesed*—"steadfast love." *Hesed* bears similar but not the same connotations as *aheb*.
- Three different words of New Testament Greek are translated into English as "love": *agape, eros*, and *philio*. Most frequently used is *agape*, which is the word nearly always translating *aheb* and *hesed* in the Septuagint.[8] *Agape* is the Greek word used in Jesus' injunctions to "love neighbor as self," as recorded in the synoptic gospels. However, Jesus, as far as we know, may not have used the word "*agape*," because he spoke primarily Aramaic and not Greek. "Love," then, is a translation of a translation.[9] In this book, our inquiry into Jesus' call to love neighbor as self pertains primarily to *agape* (and, therefore,

also to the Hebrew words *aheb* and *hesed*). However, I make no firm or impermeable boundaries between *agape* and either *eros* or *philio*.

- In reading the word "love" in biblical texts, people make assumptions about what it means. Our unconscious inclination is to understand "love" in the biblical texts according to our existing understanding of the English term. Consequently, preconceived notions of love shape our understanding of Jesus and of what it means to heed his call to love. These assumed meanings may have little to do with love as a biblical norm, and they tend to limit our understanding of God's love and neighbor-love to our own socially constructed notions of love. This limitation is immense. It diminishes and compromises our sense of divine love and the call to embody it.

These problems are partially addressed by focusing on *agape*. Yet, other problems persist. The word's meanings shift over time and context, both canonical and historical. Moreover, different scholars and other interpreters over the centuries have held differing accounts of *agape*, depending on theological stands, social location, worldviews, faith community, and political and cultural context. The differences are consequential; the loci of conflict over what "love" means are also the loci of love's ethical implications. From a perspective that honors marginalized voices, recognizing that theologies of neighbor-love are contextual is crucial. Failure to do so threatens to obscure the understanding of love generated by subordinate voices.

This diversity presents yet another challenge. It is not possible in the context of one chapter to survey the vast corpus of writings within Christian and Jewish traditions on love. Which sources does one select? The ancients? Historical figures widely recognized as central in Christian theology? Theologians and ethicists for whom one holds particular respect?

Choosing which historical and contemporary voices to survey shapes one's interpretations. Drawing upon other scholars' interpretations means mine is subject to their biases and perspectives. The problem thickens because the available interpretations—until the dawn of feminist, liberationist, and other critical theologies—represent the dominant tradition, the scholarship of educated European or Euro-American men. While their social location does not invalidate their theologies, it renders them limited and perspectival, as do all social locations. Given my conviction that perspectives from marginalized positions are crucial, privileging dominant perspectives would be suspect. Reading this dominant body of knowledge (diverse in itself) is valuable *if* one does so while giving equal weight to figures who expose its limitations. For my account of *agape* as a biblical norm, I draw primarily upon two main streams of thought, the boundaries of which are not always clearly distinguishable. They are the accumulated teaching of dominant traditions in Christian theology and ethics, and feminist theological voices who hold this body of knowledge in a critical light.[10]

FEATURES OF LOVE AS A BIBLICAL AND THEOLOGICAL NORM

The nature of neighbor-love grounded in divine love is beyond full comprehension. As "God is love," and as God is both intimately knowable and infinitely beyond our knowing, so too is love. This inquiry will only glimpse the depth and breadth of the love given by and through the "I Am Who I Am," revealed in Jesus. To claim full or infallible knowledge of what love is or does would be theologically absurd.

Yet to relinquish the effort would be to reject a significant dimension of relationship with the Living God. Responding to God's call to love calls for a working understanding of what it means. Shying away from the quest to grasp implications of this word would mean abandoning it to the meanings it has held for previous contexts. This would avoid hearing what God is calling to us today.

Neighbor-love, in the form of Jesus, is contextual. He bids us ask, "What does it mean *here and now* to love neighbor as God loves us?" This is fitting, for the Holy One revealed in Jesus is a living God, dynamically and actively engaged in the world. She is an incarnate God, a God embodied in life's extravagant complexity and variation, not a God of timeless concrete rules implemented in the same way for all people in every situation. Thus, the "modes of love's expression" change throughout time, both biblical time and subsequent eras. "Context" has many facets. They include exegetical context, theological context, discursive context, political-economic context, geographic context, and ideological context, as well as the interpreters' social location.

What then, are features of love as a biblically grounded norm that are relevant across contexts, while playing out differently within them?

First, God's love is the foundation or the root of human love for God, self, others, and Earth. "From an Old Testament point of view," writes Hebrew Bible Scholar Katherine Dobb Sakenfeld, "any human loyalty, kindness, love or mercy is rooted ultimately in the loyalty, kindness, love and mercy of God."[11] This conclusion is widely held. However, *how* God's love roots human love remains a matter of inquiry and debate. Are human beings called to "love *as* God loves," or *because* God loves, or in grateful *response* to God's love, or with the actual love of God *indwelling*, or according to some other form of rootedness in God's love?

I recognize all of these "roots." The call to love *as* God loves means that God's love, in Christ, becomes the model for human neighbor-love. The obvious yet audacious question then becomes "What is the love of God like? What does it look like? What does it do?" The question permeates Christian history, human history, and this text.

The indwelling love of God as an actual presence abiding within us, being lived into the world by us, implies a boundless power to love. The apostle Paul, the author of the Gospel according to John, Martin Luther, Dietrich Bonhoeffer, Dorothy Day, and Martin Luther King Jr. all insisted that God's love not only inspires human love but also abides within human beings or human communities. "[Those] who [abide] in love [abide] in God, and God abides in [them]" (1 John 4:16).

The conviction that God's love is not only *for* us but also works *within* us for the sake of the world, takes on yet more force when accompanied by the claim that love is the most powerful force in all of creation. "Love," writes Martin Luther King, "is the most durable power in the world. This creative force, so beautifully exemplified in the life of our Christ, is the most potent instrument available in mankind's quest for peace and security."[12]

I, too, understand human love to be—in some way not humanly fathomable—the love of God dwelling within and among human beings and communities.[13] This love is at play there, on behalf of its human abode and on behalf of the world. This indwelling presence is pure gift from God. It is given freely, not bought by human goodness. God's indwelling love may be called the Spirit of God or the indwelling Christ. Love is the presence of God active in history (not only human history but cosmic history). That this Spirit also indwells other-than-human parts of creation is highly significant.

While these claims say a great deal, they also produce yet more unknowns. While the love of God may dwell within us, we humans do not necessarily love with it, or let it flow out. What enables it to flow, and what blocks it? This too is a core question of Christian life.

A *second* mark of neighbor-love pertains to its transformative power. Christians throughout the ages have claimed that *the love of God, including its embodiment in humans as neighbor-love, "proclaims and creates a new world situation."*[14] Recognizing love as transformative power becomes especially important in light of the historic tendency within Christianity to associate love with abnegation of power. Voiced strongly in feminist theology, the insistence on linking love with power found earlier expression in Martin Luther King. "Power, properly understood," he writes in response to the Black Power movement, "is the ability to achieve purpose. It is the strength required to bring about social, political, or economic changes. In this sense power is not only desirable but necessary in order to implement the demands of love and justice. One of the greatest problems of history is that the concepts of love and power are usually contrasted as polar opposites. Love is identified with a resignation of power and power with a denial of love. . . . What is needed is a realization that power without love is reckless and abusive and that love without power is sentimental and anemic. Power at its best is love implementing the demands of justice. Justice at its best is love correcting everything that stands against love."[15]

Third, neighbor-love actively serves the well-being of whomever is loved. It is a steadfast commitment to seek the good of whom or what is loved. Gene Outka refers to this as the "normative content most often ascribed to love. Agape is . . . an active concern for the neighbor's well-being."[16] Erich Fromm, in his classic text, *The Art of Loving*, concludes that love is the active concern for the life and the growth of that which we love.[17]

Neighbor-love, thus, is a matter of action, not of emotion alone. The Jesus who reveals God's love and pulls humankind into it, reveals God's love in actions. "We must remember that love reveals itself not by words or phrases, but by action and experience," cautioned Bernard of Clairvaux.[18] Centuries later, Martin Luther King insisted that "agape . . . is love in action."[19] More recently, Daniel Maguire echoes: "[L]ove is an energy that must be incarnated in action."[20] These figures base their assessment in the biblical witness.

"Serving the well-being of" is a slippery notion. It invites the patronizing sensibility of being "the helper," or the "giver" to the needy one. We address this danger presently in the discussion of mutuality.

However, love as a theological and biblical vocation is not reducible to action. Love acting toward well-being entails something beyond both action and emotion. It seems that the love to which Jesus calls us emerges from a way of perceiving the world and of being in it, as well as a way of acting and feeling in response to it. It is a perception that the neighbor bears infinite worth and is irrevocably beloved by God; she or he is, before all else, a creature beloved by God. Moreover, the neighbor is no less beloved and no less imbued with inherent worth than am I or my people. The action of love not only is grounded in this perception, but also nurtures it. Perhaps this way of perceiving is a glimpse of reality through the eyes of God. It is a mode of perception that clings to the created goodness of each person and seeks to actualize that goodness and belovedness. In the words of Paul Tillich, "*Agape* sees [the other] as God sees him [or her]."[21] In this sense, love is a *disposition, the fourth defining feature.*

Disposition, in the Aristotelian sense is nurtured by and nourishes action and emotion, but is distinct from them. It is a whole way of living, a state of being in the world developed and learned by exercising that very state of being. A disposition is an embodied attitude of the heart and mind that is formed by the practice of it and commitment to it. Disposition, used in this way, is not "natural," as in the temperament with which one is born or that comes naturally to one; rather, a disposition is chosen and cultivated.

This aspect of love draws us further into mystery, raising once again the questions: "From whence comes this love? How do people 'get' it? What brings it forth?" We harken here to two clues held paradoxically together. Neighbor-love, *as God's indwelling presence*, is pure unwarranted and unconditional gift from the Lover of all. Yet, *as disposition*, neighbor-love is cultivated by one's practices (choices, priorities, decisions, and actions), the ethos of society, and the communities with which one identifies.

The relationship of love as indwelling presence and love as cultivated disposition is the relationship between gift and human response. This relationship has provoked controversy for centuries. I am not suggesting that practicing love is a means of gaining God's love. One cannot do anything to earn or gain God's love. It is given unconditionally. "Practicing love" is a *response* to the already freely given gift of God's love. The salient point is this: love given by God to dwell within us may, then, be nurtured as a disposition. Through the practice of it, we grow in our tendency and ability to receive that love and live it into the world as neighbor-love.

Questions of moral formation spring to the fore. What factors or circumstances form us to perceive the gift of God's love and respond to it? What practices cultivate the disposition of love? Few questions are more important for opening the doors to more just and sustainable societies. While for Aristotle, a disposition is *intentionally* cultivated through practice, theories of social construction recognize the formative influence of *unintended*, even unconscious processes of socialization. We are socialized into practices that form disposition without our being aware of it. For example, our practice of consumerism forms a disposition toward consumerism. To form a disposition toward love in a society forming the disposition of consumerism demands intentionality.

Next, loving in the biblical sense seems to be even more important for the well-being of the one who loves than for the beloved. "He who does not love abides in death" (1 John 3:14). Not to follow the call to love then is, in some way, deadly. Likewise in Deuteronomy, God forewarns the people that choosing not to follow God's commandments, laws in which neighbor-love is central, would be "to perish," to choose "death and adversity" and "curses." Following these commandments, in contrast, would bring "life" and "blessings" for the people and for their descendants (Deut. 30:15-20). Elsewhere, according to the Deuteronomistic historian, God declares that these commandments are given by God to the people "for your own well-being" (Deut. 10:13). Love for God and for neighbor is the heart of God's commandments.

The next attribute of neighbor-love—and this is the *sixth*—pertains to self-love. *Agape weds other-love with self-love*. Until the rise of feminist critique, agape was understood as "other regard" *to the exclusion of self-regard*.[22] Moreover, *agape* as "other regard," according to dominant interpretations, reached its pinnacle in self-sacrifice. Sacrifice as the quintessence of *agape* is attributed most notably to Anders Nygren. Nygren's account of *agape*, in his 1923 *Agape and Eros*, holds self-sacrifice as the pinnacle of Christian love and explicitly negates self-love. "Christianity does not recognize self-love as a legitimate form of love," he writes. "Christian love moves in two directions: toward God and toward its neighbor, and in self-love it finds its chief adversary which must be fought and conquered."[23]

Here is the greatest departure between inherited tradition regarding *agape* and feminist reinterpretations beginning in the early 1960s. A feminist stance staunchly critiques this notion. Feminist theologians have disclosed the call to sacrifice throughout Christian history for what it often has been—theological justification for exploitation, abuse, and servitude of women and especially women of color.[24] Love as self-sacrifice and as antithesis to self-love has been used to justify centuries of sacrifice by women for the benefit of those who hold power over them or who are privileged by their self-sacrifice. I refute theologies of love that may perpetuate the subjugation of women, servitude, or the sacrifice of selfhood. As a feminist theologian, my reading of the Gospels finds self-love inherent in the commandment to love neighbor as self.

At the same time, as a theologian shaped by Central American Christians who were willing to sacrifice their lives to stand with impoverished and oppressed people in their struggles for justice, I understand that self-sacrifice may be an expression of profound love. This is the case when self-sacrifice is chosen, not forced or manipulated, and when it is in service of life, rather than being for the sake of self-sacrifice as a good in itself.

Can love's unbreakable commitment to the well-being of the neighbor coexist with feminist and womanist imperatives of self-love? Yes, it must. A theology of love is valid only if it upholds both self-love and other-love. In fact the biblical command of neighbor-love is constructed brilliantly to presuppose the normativity of self-love: "you shall love your neighbor as yourself."[25] The commitment to uphold the dignity and worth of the other, and to act toward the other's well-being is accompanied by the same commitment to self.

Seventh, human love is never perfect. Love is subject to the brokenness that pervades human history. We are human creatures, not God. The imperfection of neighbor-love does not negate it, nor its power for social transformation.

Feminist theology has established *mutuality as a normative condition of love from a Christian ethical perspective*, by virtue of the *imago dei*. This is an *eighth* quality of love as a biblical norm. The triune God is ontologically a relationship of mutual love moving between/within the three "persons" of God.[26] As beings created in the image of God, humans are created also in the image of mutual love; it is the true self toward which we are destined through God's saving grace.

Feminist theologian Dawn Nothwehr offers a definition of mutuality based on her detailed analysis of feminist theology and antecedents to feminist ideas of mutuality in the work of Thomas Aquinas, Martin Buber, John Duns Scotus, and H. Richard Niebuhr: "Mutuality is the sharing of 'power-with' by and among all parties in a relationship in a way that recognizes the wholeness and particular experience of each participant toward the end of optimum flourishing of all."[27] As it pertains to society, mutuality refers to "the sharing of 'power-with' by and among members of a society in a way that recognizes the fundamental dignity of each and the obligation to attain and maintain for each what is necessary to sustain that dignity." Mutuality as a feature of neighbor-love, then, calls for power shared with relative equity. In contexts of massively unbalanced power, love seeks dispersed and accountable power. Mutuality recognizes common power to give to, receive from, learn from, and challenge. And it aims at common well-being.

In seeking to understand the implications of mutuality as normative for neighbor-love, I initially was unsettled and disturbed. This norm challenged my central claim that neighbor-love pertains to people who are connected by the global economy, but who live thousands of miles apart and will never know each other. Our relationships with millions of distant "neighbors" whose lives are impacted by ours through economic systems and climate change cannot be relationships of mutuality, I began to think. To illustrate: If I exercise neighbor-love for the person in India whose life is threatened by global warming, by helping to transform Seattle into a low-carbon city, I cannot expect mutuality with that person in India. If neighbor-love is mutual, then perhaps it is not a norm for economic and ecological dimensions of life in the global economy, I thought. Perhaps my neighbor is not, as I have asserted, the people throughout the globe whose lives I touch through economic, political, social systems.

Such a conclusion would be based upon an individualized sense of mutuality that no longer holds. It reflects the anthropology characteristic of modernity—human beings as fundamentally autonomous individuals. The previous chapter acknowledged a potent shift in that anthropology. Theology and many natural sciences have recognized that we are, by our very nature, first and foremost beings-in-relationship. For beings who are ontologically relational in vast and overlapping webs of relationship that span both time and space, mutuality is much broader than interpersonal relationships of individuals. The mutuality of one's relationships is not a function of one's personal actions alone, but also of the "me" that is at the same time a "we." "I" may both give and receive from people and movements the world over by virtue of that collective "I" and a collective "you" or "they." Said differently, the norm of mutuality in neighbor-love may be manifest in collective as well as individual relationality.

As God's love lures people and all of creation toward union and communion with God and hence union and communion among the creatures and elements, so too agape *generates and nurtures community.* This is the *ninth* quality of neighbor-love. Voices in the church since at least the second century have held that God is "reaching from creation to consummation, in which God and all creatures are destined to live together in the mystery of love and communion."[28] Jesus in his ministry was incessantly creating community. The Hebrew Bible attests to a God who is seeking to build a community of God's people. Both Testaments indicate that community shaped by this God may take surprising new forms. Always it is community that serves life, and is informed by love.[29] King expounded on "*agape* [as] love seeking to preserve and create community. . . . In the final analysis, agape means a recognition of the fact that all life is interrelated."[30]

Finally, *love is subject to forces that work against it or that diminish, block, or distort it.* They are known as sin. A theology of love must contend with sin's power to sabotage it. As discussed in chapter 2, sin is manifest both in individuals and as structural sin. Neighbor-love is blocked in particular by love for wealth and prestige. According to nineteenth-century theologian Gerhard Kittel, "Two forces particularly are mentioned by Jesus as forces which man must renounce and fight against if he is to love God, namely mammon and vainglory." By "vainglory," the author means "love of prestige." He continues, "The love of prestige is incompatible with the love of God."[31] The monumental pull of sin, especially on a macro level, means that an adequate ethic of neighbor-love will account for the pervasive and pernicious presence of sin, especially at the societal level.

We have noted ten features of neighbor-love as a biblical and theological norm. A remaining few pertain to the identity of the neighbor and to the relationship between love and justice.

WHO IS MY NEIGHBOR?

The next feature of love concerns whom or what is my neighbor, the one whom I am called to love. Questions erupt. Four are particularly significant.

- Does "neighbor" refer only to people who are "my own people," or more broadly to all people?
- Does neighbor apply only to people whom I actually encounter in close proximity, or to those who are geographically distant?
- Is my neighbor an individual, or can "neighbor" also refer to people collectively?
- Does neighbor extend to the other-than-human parts of creation?

The last of these we address in the following chapter. The first three we consider jointly here.

Love is commonly understood as an interpersonal vocation. God's call to love neighbor as self is commonly seen as a call to love the people whom our lives touch personally. This may include family and friends, colleagues, acquaintances, and even utter strangers whom we pass on the street.

The idea that love pertains only to the interpersonal realm of life gained credence in the influential work of Reinhold Niebuhr. He concluded that love is possible only in the world of private relationships. In the public realm, while love remains the ideal to which we are called, it is an "impossible possibility," best approximated by "justice."

Key biblical texts could be interpreted as supporting this conclusion. The Levitical injunction to Israel to love the stranger and the foreigner *in their midst* (Lev. 19:34, italics mine) could be heard as a call to love only those who are proximate, people whom I might encounter personally. Likewise, the Levitical directive to "'not seek revenge or bear a grudge against *one of your people*, but love your neighbor as yourself" (Lev. 19:18, italics mine) may suggest that love pertains to one's own people, but not necessarily beyond. Jesus' calls to "honor your father and mother," to "love your neighbor as yourself" (Matt. 19:19), and to "love one another" (John 13:34) could be read as strictly interpersonal norms.

However, many scholars and people who have sought to practice neighbor-love have understood it quite differently. While love pertains to the interpersonal and intimate realm of life, it pertains also to social structural relationships. Martin Luther King, one of history's most highly respected interpreters of neighbor-love, was adamant that it is a call to love *all* people.[32] Feminist scholars have demonstrated the fallacy in Niehbuhr's private/public dualism overlaid with a love/justice dualism; they insist that public and private are not necessarily distinct, and that love's relevance extends far beyond the interpersonal to the social structural.

Jesus' injunctions to neighbor-love go beyond the boundaries of "our people." As Pheme Perkins writes, the parable of the Good Samaritan describes a love that "ignores social boundaries."[33] The neighbor who served the wounded person in that story is an "outsider," a Samaritan and thus not a member of the community. Jesus' call to "love your enemy" makes very clear that the love to which we are called extends beyond the boundaries of "my people." Moreover, Jesus' call to love the enemy, in his context, extends beyond the physically proximate and interpersonal. The first-century hearers of the Jesus stories—as people occupied, exploited, and threatened by imperial Rome—had distinct collective political enemies. Finally, the Levitical texts that could be interpreted as limiting love to the proximate are in fact equally well understood as all-inclusive.

My conclusion (and the *eleventh* attribute of neighbor-love noted herein) is that neighbor-love, as seen in Jesus' life and teaching, *pertains to whomever one's life in some way impacts or whose life impacts one's own.* Jesus' actions demonstrate the infinite value of loving care between known individuals. At the same time, given the current realities of globalization and climate change, North Americans' lives impact people around the world. The call to love pertains also to relationship with these distant neighbors. In stark terms, if I am proximate enough to join in taking another person's land, water, or livelihood (through collective actions), I am proximate enough to be neighbor. Anyone from whom we can steal is sufficiently connected to be "neighbor."[34]

★★★★★★★★★★★★★★★★★★★★★★★★★★★★★★★★★★★★

"I am one of those millions of children who are suffering in Pakistan thorough bonded labor and child labor, but I am lucky that due to the efforts of Bonded Labor Liberation Front (BLLF), I go out in freedom and am standing in front of you here today. . . . Unfortunately, the owner of the business tells us that it is America which asks us to enslave the children here because the carpets, the rugs, and the towels that we make are for America. People like it that way . . . so they want that to go on. I appeal to you that you stop people from using children as bonded labor because the children need a pen rather than instruments of child labor."[35]

The speaker is Iqbal Masih, a Pakistani boy who worked as a "bonded laborer" from ages four to ten in a Pakistani hand-loomed carpet business. Shackled to a loom, his growth was stunted. After gaining freedom through the work of the Bonded Labor Liberation Front of India, he went on to campaign against child labor. In an interview published in 1996, he is yet more pointed: "In my country, children think that America is to blame for our exploitation because most of the things we make are exported to the United States." Iqbal was murdered in Pakistan months after delivering the speech.

****

NEIGHBOR-LOVE SEEKS JUSTICE

"Justice," writes Daniel Maguire, "is the love language of the Bible."[36] Scholars throughout Christian history have argued that the biblical and theological norm of love is related in some way to the norm of justice. However, the nature of that relationship is widely disputed. In sweeping terms, constructions of the relationship between love and justice fit into three broad categories: (1) love and justice are contrasted, (2) love and justice are distinct but complementary,[37] or (3) love entails justice.

I land firmly in the third. My stance is grounded in many of the features of love discussed thus far, in particular that love seeks the well-being of whatever or whomever is loved. Where systemic injustice damages well-being and causes suffering, seeking the well-being or good of those who suffer—actively loving—entails challenging that injustice. Dietrich Bonhoeffer called this "putting a spoke in the wheel" of unjust power structures.[38] This challenge includes *seeing* systemic evil for what it is and acknowledging it, *resisting* it, and creating more just alternatives. Thus, where the neighbor suffers because of injustice, love will not simply bind up the wounds of the suffering. Love will seek to undo the injustice. The response of neighbor-love to slavery was not just to bring relief to individual enslaved people; it was to abolish slavery. In short, *the norm of neighbor-love includes the norm of justice.* This, then, is yet another mark of neighbor-love, the twelfth noted herein. This makes sense. Jesus was deeply rooted in the historical trajectory of the Hebrew prophets before him, from whom he often draws in his teaching. These prophets were among history's sharpest critics of injustice perpetrated by those in positions of privilege and power.

JUSTICE AND ITS MEANINGS

With justice (as with love), conceptual chaos reigns.[39] Many parts of the church speak of justice frequently and sincerely. It has become almost commonplace, bearing a sense of certainty and rightness. Justice, however, is a multilayered and complex term with multiple formal meanings and myriad connotations. Usually what is meant by the word is not stated. The word "justice" cries out for explication. What does this term mean and how might it deepen the understanding of love?

The idea of "justice" has a millennia-long and contested history. Its meanings shift and evolve. New meanings often are grounded in critique of established and assumed meanings. Here, we highlight only dimensions of the term that are useful for discerning what it means to seek justice as love's demand. Classical and modern Western notions of justice, more recent criticisms of them, and theological and biblical notions of justice inform this brief inquiry.

Justice is a central moral norm in Western thought, and is theorized in philosophical ethics, political theory, Christian ethics, and other dimensions of Christian theology. In its most ancient sense, justice referred to a power that maintained right relationship in the cosmos, including but not limited to human life. As ancient Greek society and philosophy developed, justice pertained more specifically to the human world. Conceived as a virtue of society, it consisted of institutions structured to promote virtue, social harmony, and happiness. Aristotle distinguished three broad categories of justice: [40]

- commutative justice focusing on transactions between individuals, both voluntary (that is, the exchange of goods and services) and involuntary (that is, theft);
- distributive justice assuring the fair distribution of a society's or community's benefits (goods, rights) and burdens (responsibilities);
- legal justice pertaining to individuals' obligations to society.

Modern thought maintains these three categories and adds others, including retributive justice, restitutional justice, restorative justice, and social justice. Retributive justice focuses on just punishment. Restitutional and restorative justice seek amends through reparation to victims of injustice. They focus more on the well-being of the victim than the punishment of the perpetrator. Where I refer to "justice," I am referring to "social justice." It is the form most closely related to justice as a biblically informed norm and to the biblical norm of neighbor-love.

JUSTICE AS SOCIAL JUSTICE

Social justice, notes theologian Richard McBrien, "is dedicated to the reordering of society, to the changing of institutions, systems, and patterns of behavior which deny people their basic human rights and which thereby destabilize society."[41] "Social justice . . . aims at correcting any oppressive and alienating trends within the community."[42]

While theological grounding for the Christian norm of social justice is present in earlier theology, it appears explicitly with the emergence of structural change as a concept and a political aim. With Pope Leo XIII's landmark encyclical, "The Condition of Labor" (*Rerum Novarum*) in 1891 and subsequent Catholic social teaching, "social justice"—as concern for the common good and for the well-being of economically poor people—enters the discourse."

Later Catholic social teaching identifies justice as a demand of love. According to these teachings, where exploitation and oppression exist, love requires action to replace structures of injustice with structures of justice. Vatican II (1962–65) and later the Latin American Conferences of Bishops (1968 and 1979) taught that God's justice is *not* impartial. It leans toward the needs and plight of the poor, and calls people of relative privilege to identify with those who are marginalized, dehumanized, or otherwise oppressed. This assertion, termed "preferential option for the poor," is grounded in Jesus' identification with marginalized people.[43]

Within Protestantism, the Social Gospel movement (late nineteenth through early twentieth centuries) elevated social justice to a central feature of the reign of God toward which society should aim. While Social Gospel theologians varied greatly, they shared the sense that spiritual growth included recognizing "the need to address social problems by systemic means as well as by individual conversion."[44] For them, personal piety was inseparable from work to build a more just and compassionate society.[45] They held that social justice required structural change, particularly change in or away from capitalism. Unbridled capitalism, they averred, was untenable from the perspective of social justice. (Many, at the same time, rejected socialism as an alternative.)

In the early 1970s, moral philosopher John Rawls theorized justice as the impartial assignment of duties and benefits to members of a society. The stress was on fairness and impartiality, and not on a human right to certain goods and rights. Rawls's notion of justice assumed a society in which people have the capacity to participate equally. That assumption is false in the current context.

Liberation theologies took up the cry for social justice. While having evolved into highly divergent forms, most are rooted in Latin American liberation theologies that developed in the 1960s in conjunction with Vatican II (and its ensuing teachings), and in the rising critique of American imperialism. Social justice in liberation theologies calls for dismantling structures of oppression that are damaging people in a given context, heeding the voices of oppressed sectors, and beginning theological reflection and social analysis from their perspective.

Classical and modern notions of justice and the presuppositions undergirding them came under strong critique in the last four decades, especially from feminist voices in theology, philosophy, and political theory. Those criticisms yielded numerous shifts in understandings of justice, relevant to our inquiry. One shift identifies the error in assuming that members of a society are equal in resources and opportunity to participate in shaping it. The second moves from justice applied impartially without consideration for power differentials and historical factors to a sense that justice may have different demands depending on what side of power one is located. Third is a shift in distributive justice to include not only distribution of goods, responsibilities, and burdens, but also distribution of power.[46] Fourth, what constitutes justice is best known through the experience of injustice or through struggles to overcome it.[47] The fifth shift counters the Niebuhrian claim that justice pertains to "public" life, while love is the norm for "private" life. A more recent development concerns the scope of justice. Historically pertaining to human relations, justice increasingly is seen as relevant to Earth's entire web of life.

The norm of justice in theological discourse is rooted in the Hebrew scriptures, and taken up directly and indirectly in the Second Testament. The Hebrew words *zedaqah* (justice, righteousness) and *mispat* (just, right) held together best approximate the moral implications of justice. Both are rich and textured terms; neither is adequately translated by any single English word. *Zedaqah* refers to right relationships between God and God's people, between persons, and between groups. Right relations are those that allow the needs of all to be met in a way in which relationships can flourish and community can be preserved. *Mispat* has judicial implications and also "has a broader meaning dealing with the rights due to every individual in the community, and the upholding of those rights."[48]

Justice as a norm grounded in the Hebrew scriptures:

- is "a chief attribute of God's activity in the world";
- when applied to humans, is based on and corresponds to the justice of God that is seen as liberating the oppressed, identifying with the vulnerable and upholding their rights, judgment, and mercy;

- is integral to love of neighbor, but not synonymous with it;
- is a foundation of the "already but not yet" reign of God;
- implies compassion and redistribution, with special attention to the needs of the marginalized;
- aims at freeing the oppressed, sharing food with the hungry, and housing the homeless;
- aims also at dismantling the sources of oppression and the political, cultural, and economic arrangements that contribute to hunger, poverty, and homelessness;
- is understood to be both demand of God and gift from God;
- is not, at least in the prophets, understood as a utopian impossibility, but as realizable.

Social justice, as informed by all of these sources, is a grounding orientation for all relationships. "This basic orientation is reflected in a continual probing that asks of any situation, What's wrong with this picture? What is unjust or unfair in how relationships are ordered in it? What stirs up indignation, anger, or even rage? What cries out for change?"[49] Who has power and who does not? Who benefits and who does not from "the way things are"? Whose voices are heard and whose are ignored? Who counts in decision making and who does not? Justice manifests "right relationship" with the God, self, others, and the Earth.

These observations about social justice give content to the norm of love.

PROBLEMATIC CONSTRUCTIONS OF THE LOVE-JUSTICE RELATIONSHIP

We began by identifying three constructions of the relationship between love and justice, and my stance that love as a biblically based norm entails justice understood as social justice. The other two constructions—that love and justice are opposed or are distinct and complementary—dangerously domesticate the norm of love. That is, they detract from its power as a norm for public life. What remains then is to signal the distinct problems in the logic of these two perspectives.

Anders Nygren is the modern theologian most notable for contrasting love and justice. But he assumes a meaning for justice that is *not* the meaning of "social justice." "Justice," for Nygren means that each person is due what she/he deserves. This is not "social justice." The fact that "to each his due" conflicts with love as a biblical norm does not mean that "social justice" conflicts with love as a biblical norm.

The remaining construction holds justice and love as complementary norms, distinct but not opposed. The connection is theorized in varied ways. My concern is where love is characterized primarily as the more affective partner to justice. "Love," according to this understanding, is an emotion that motivates justice. For Reinhold Niebuhr, love is the fundamental norm of Christian life and "is the primary law of [human] nature."[50] Yet love pertains only to the private arenas of life, not governments, states, or large institutions. For them, justice is the face of love.

This Niebuhrian theory requires clear demarcation between public and private. While that separation is problematic, it is not our primary concern here. The concern here is the characterization of love as the emotional corollary of justice. This invites the reduction of love to sentiment, even though that may not be the intent. Thomas Schubeck also describes love as the more affective complement to justice. "As for love," he writes, "we may associate it with acceptance, expressed by words of affection and affirmation as well as by kind deeds. Love elicits reasons of the heart."[51] "[E]xpressions of love—awakening, feeling compassion for, and forgiving others—affirm the goodness in others and in oneself."[52] Here a necessary feature of love is the positive emotions commonly associated with it. The problem is that love—understood in this way—entails a feeling that most people do not have for all others on broad societal or global levels.

Love, as the more affective or interpersonal counterpart to justice, becomes either emotionalized or spiritualized. The tendency to spiritualize and emotionalize love is theologically and biblically unsound. It truncates the meanings of *aheb* and *agape*. Biblical texts affirm that while love may involve emotion—and perhaps, at its best, does—emotion is not a *necessary* characteristic of love as a biblical norm. God's call to love the stranger and foreigner cannot depend upon one's feelings for them.

Limiting love to justice's emotional or spiritual counterpart is dangerous because if love's power *depends* upon emotional investment, love as a force for steadfast commitment to justice is effectively disarmed. Thus, systems of oppression are reinforced by the spiritualizing or emotionalizing of love. That reduction is common.

An example is the recent and important work of political theorists Antonio Negri and Michael Hardt on war and democracy. They explicitly call for "a political conception of love," writing, "[p]eople today, seem unable to understand love as a political concept, but a [political] concept of love is just what we need. . . . We need to recuperate the public and political conception of love common to pre-modern traditions. Christianity and Judaism, for example, both conceive love as a political act."[53]

Thus far, I agree. Yet they are mistaken in their understanding of *how* love is political. Theirs is the primary and dangerous mistake made in common discourse where the political implications of love are raised. For Hardt and Negri, "love as a political concept" means that the love you have "for your spouse, your mother, and your child . . . does not end there. . . . [It] serves as the basis for our political projects in common and the construction of a new society. Without this love, we are nothing."[54] This is a love profoundly dependent on emotion.

An adequate theology of love as a political vocation (and as an economic-ecological vocation), I contend, means quite the opposite. It means that the emotional love one has for one's loved ones does *not* need to be the basis for our political projects in common. Rather, love as a political virtue ensures that even where this intimate and emotional love is *not* the defining force in one's relationships with the body politic (as is humanly the case most of the time), society is structured such that the ends of love (the well-being of all with emphasis on the most vulnerable) are served. This is key. Love must seek structures of justice precisely because it usually is *not* the primary virtue motivating social relations with the impersonal many. As a political vocation then, love cannot depend upon emotions. A society cannot depend for justice upon voluntary feelings of goodwill that may come and go.

This does not contradict my previous assertion that agape love may include emotion and is all the richer for it. My point here is that neighbor-love does not *require* the loving emotions often linked with it. Nor may neighbor-love be reduced to the emotive source behind action for justice. Paul Tillich says as much in his treatise on love and justice: "All problems concerning the relation of love to power and justice, individually as well as socially, become insoluble if love is understood basically as an emotion. Love would be a sentimental addition to power and justice . . . unable to change either the laws of justice or the structures of power. Most of the pitfalls in social ethics, political theory, and education are due to a misunderstanding of the ontological character of love."[55]

I suspect that translations of the Hebrew *zedaqah* (justice) and *aheb* (love) into Greek, Latin, and English bear some of the fault for this emotionalizing and spiritualizing of love. *Aheb*, which, as we have seen, meant far more than charity, was translated into Latin as "*caritas.*" *Caritas*, also implying *more* than charity, is often translated into English as only that, charity. Justice, like love, easily becomes spiritualized and domesticated. The apostle Paul translated *zedaqah* into Greek as *dikaiosyne*, which often is rendered as "righteousness" in English. "Righteousness"—as commonly understood—does not bear the societal implications inherent in *zedaqah*.

NEIGHBOR-LOVE: POLITICAL AND DANGEROUS

Because it seeks justice, *love is a political as well as interpersonal vocation.* This is yet another feature of neighbor-love. If theft is done through political-economic systems, then love, as response, also works through political-economic systems. Here we use "political" not in its more common meaning—pertaining to government, formal interest groups, party politics, and so on—but rather in its classical or Aristotelian sense. In this sense "political" refers to the processes through which people deliberate and determine the terms of their life in common.

Christian ethics inherently recognizes this political nature of neighbor-love. Christian ethics begins with the recognition that how people treat each other is determined not only by interpersonal relationships but also by social structures.[56] Therefore, Jesus' teachings regarding how individuals are to treat each other apply to social structural spheres of life—political, economic, cultural systems.

The final feature of neighbor-love emerges from its justice-making, political, and broad-scoped nature. *Neighbor-love may be dangerous.* Jesus did not die to sacrifice himself in payment or expiation for human sins. Jesus was executed on a stake—the form of execution reserved by the Roman empire for rebels—because he was a threat to its hegemonic power. "His death was the price he paid for refusing to abandon the radical activity of love—of expressing solidarity and reciprocity with the excluded ones of his community."[57] As Jesuit priest Philip Berrigan once quipped, "If you want to follow Jesus, you had better look good on wood."

CONFOUNDING QUESTIONS

A host of unavoidable questions regarding moral responsibility and moral accountability leap forth. Does love prioritize the well-being of neighbor over well-being of self? Where the well-being of neighbors conflicts, which neighbor does one prioritize? Are there limits to what one is to give in terms of time, energy, and other resources? Shall I do so even at great cost to myself or at great cost to others whom I also love?

And what of human finitude? If my neighbor is whomever my life touches and, if my life touches enormous quantities of people the world over, I cannot possibly serve the well-being of all my neighbors. My time, energy, knowledge, and other resources are limited. Limited too is the scope of my influence. The people of industrialized nations are creating deadly climate change for neighbors. That relatedness renders us morally accountable. However, limitations on my influence create limitations on my moral responsibility.

For what are we morally responsible given that our agency is limited? Am I accountable for that which is beyond my control? On the other hand, this question in itself assumes the individualized sense of moral being and doing called into question in the previous two chapters. What routes to agency might unfold within a more interrelated and ecocentric worldview?

In pursuing these questions, Gene Outka concludes that the concept of agape allows only one restriction in its scope. That is human finitude. The human person "loving" "simply is incapable of enhancing the welfare of every neighbor with whom he has to do."[58] I agree. And I recognize the danger of allowing acknowledgment of finitude to slip into absolution from any responsibility for social structural evil. The limitations of human finitude are a given. Yet the possibilities of moral action (and hence moral accountability) burst their boundaries within a worldview that expands agency beyond the individual. These questions, valid throughout time, are particularly confounding today, given the exponential increase in human connectedness, collective power for destruction, and potential for collective moral agency.

NEIGHBOR-LOVE AS A BIBLICAL AND THEOLOGICAL NORM IN SUM

Human beings cannot know fully and definitively what it means to heed Jesus' call to love neighbor as self. Inquiry into love is inquiry into the Mystery of God with, within, and for the world.

We can say that neighbor-love, in the form of Jesus of Nazareth, is contextual. What it entails depends partly on the needs and circumstances at hand. Yet, as a norm applicable across time and place, it also bears characteristics that transcend context. We have noted such features of neighbor-love. It:

1. is grounded in God's love
2. embodies God's work to create a new world situation, is transformative
3. actively serves the well-being of those who are loved
4. is a disposition to be practiced
5. may be more important for the well-being of the one who loves than for the one who is loved
6. entails self-love
7. is not perfect
8. is mutual
9. builds community
10. is subject to sin, and is especially blocked by the love of wealth and prestige
11. pertains to whomever my life touches directly or through social or ecological systems

12. seeks justice
13. is political
14. may be dangerous

Along these lines unfolds the meaning of neighbor-love as a biblical and theological norm meant to guide our lives today in the midst of economic and ecological violence. To be guided by the call to love is to accept the tempestuous waves of moral ambiguity and paradox. What justice-making love calls for in a given situation is often unclear. Yet, despite pervasive moral ambiguity, limitations, and mistakes, we are called nevertheless to live in the shape of this love. The faultiness of our efforts to serve a God of love is no excuse to abandon them.

Moving On

The reality of love flows beyond the reach of human knowing and imagination. Love is the Mystery at the heart and source of life itself. Love creates us and the cosmos; love gives breath and awakens our being. "Love," as a word, is but a pale reflection of the Mystery that it bespeaks.

The features of love uncovered herein play out in the next chapter as it suggests the contours and content of neighbor-love for us, the world's high consumers. Before moving on, notice how the features of love might play out in the story of Ravi and the seeds.

****

A Life Story

Seeds

Ravi Chandekar's back is against the wall. Like many of his fellow cotton farmers in the Indian province of Vidarbha, Ravi has faced years of declining cotton harvests. He took out bank loans to buy hybrid seeds long ago, and then more loans to buy the necessary fertilizers and pesticides to support the genetically modified seed. Finally, he started taking out loans to pay back previous loans. Now he is left with failing crops, yet again, and huge debt. He cannot provide food for his wife and two daughters. One daughter is prepared to marry, but a dowry is unthinkable. His other daughter is chronically ill, and there is no money for medicine or doctor's fees. The shame of Ravi's insurmountable debt, his failure to provide for his family, and the bleak hopelessness of the future all weigh on him so heavily that there appears to be only one possible way out of it all.

Ravi's ancestors farmed this land for thousands of years. Long before the British arrived, the province of Vidarbha produced varieties of long cotton, carefully irrigated just so, spun on a charkha loom, and sold in the local market to support the farmers and their families. Seeds and organic fertilizers were either produced on the farm itself, or were affordable to buy, and most farmers made enough money to provide food, clothing, and shelter for themselves and their families. With colonization came railways, farm machinery, factory cotton mills, and a thriving export-oriented cotton industry centered in Bombay (Mumbai).

Droughts in the late 1960s spurred the Indian government to support struggling farmers by providing a "safety net" in the form of genetically modified seeds and petroleum-based chemical inputs. These so-called improvements were heavily marketed to them and supplied by the U.S.-based multinational agribusiness corporation Monsanto, as well as Archer Daniels Midland, Cargill, and others. Farmers were told through billboard and poster advertisements that they would benefit tremendously from using the genetically modified seeds. One of the most controversial was Bt cotton, a hybrid cottonseed from the United States that arrived in Vidarbha in 1977.

Like many farmers, Ravi was heavily courted by big agribusiness to buy their products. Farmers were shown on posters as having obtained high yields—twenty quintals per acre, when the reality was more like five quintals per acre. Monsanto has also been accused of placing a network of informal agents in villages: "farmers who earn a commission on sales that they bring about by promoting Bt seeds to their fellow farmers."[59]

The new seeds demanded large quantities of petroleum-based fertilizers, at costs far beyond what small-scale farmers could afford. Pests became resistant to the expensive pesticides marketed to farmers. And every year, the Indian government marketed new hybrid seeds from the United States and elsewhere, plastering large billboards with advertisements. Meanwhile interest rates on loans rose and debts accrued.

In the 1980s and 1990s, transnational corporations, along with governments of many industrialized nations, successfully shifted the global economy into a model of global trade and investment that highly favors the wealthier countries and their corporations as well as elite sectors in *impoverished nations, over the vast majority of impoverished people. Known in the United States as "free trade," and in Latin America, Africa, and Asia as neoliberalism, this model has forced Ravi and other formerly isolated, subsistence farmers to compete in a global market with relatively little chance of making it.*

Ravi took his own life out of desperation and utter hopelessness.

Nearly two hundred thousand farmers in India have committed suicide since 1997. In the eight years between 1997 and 2005, a farmer in India committed suicide every thirty-two minutes. Farmer suicides numbered 17,368 in 2009 alone; in some districts the rate is six to eight per day.[60] Although some farmers hang or drown themselves, most commit suicide by ingesting the chemical pesticides destined for their failing cotton crops.

The consequences for families left behind are severe. John Haide Manukonda, a graduate student from a region hard hit by farmer suicides, describes the "suicide widows," claiming that they are the first victims of farmer suicides. "If a man dies the whole family is helpless and hapless and his wife and children will fall on the road," he writes.[61] These widows take on responsibility for their late husbands' debts and work obligations. Ravi's wife took her two daughters, one still chronically ill, the other now without any hope of marriage, and moved to the nearby city to find work. She landed in a corporate factory, earning not enough to feed herself and her daughters, and vulnerable to sexual, physical, and verbal abuse.

But are we—the overconsumers of the United States—actually connected to these farmers? Are they our neighbors? Let us look more closely.

Monsanto and other U.S.-based multinational corporations urged the Indian government to heavily market the high-yielding GM seeds to farmers because Monsanto profited considerably from the increased sale in fertilizers and other chemical inputs. Monsanto charges heavy royalty for its GM seeds, and requires farmers to comply with Monsanto's herbicide and pesticide management regime—an arrangement that further benefits Monsanto.

"Monsanto's $11.7 billion of annual sales comes from seeds, increasingly of genetically modified varieties and from licensing genetic traits."[62] Together with four other—Advanta, DuPont, Syngenta, and

Bayer—Monsanto makes up 66 percent of the world pesticide market and controls a quarter of the world seed market.

We, the American people have allowed our government to acquiesce to corporate pressure for so-called "free trade" agreements that give multinational corporations unprecedented power. We have agreed to cotton and other agricultural subsidies that benefit primarily large-scale agribusiness in the United States. Our government heavily subsidizes American cotton. In 2005 the value of all cotton produced in the United States was $3.9 billion; the value of the cotton subsidy was $4.7 billion. This subsidy destroys cotton economies in other countries by artificially lowering cotton prices and allowing the United States to capture world markets that used to be accessible to poorer countries. P. Sainath, award-winning journalist for The Hindu, *states that U.S. subsidies are killing Indian people. Some of the top owners of Monsanto's large public stock holdings include retirement portfolios held by thousands of U.S. citizens such as TIAA-CREF and Oppenheimer Funds, thereby linking our privilege to the misery of poor farmers on the other side of the world.*[63]

✶✶✶✶✶✶✶✶✶✶✶✶✶✶✶✶✶✶✶✶✶✶✶✶✶✶✶✶✶✶✶✶✶✶✶✶✶

SEEDS REVISITED

Sarah and Stu pulled out of the long driveway, past the hand-painted "Griffington Farm" sign and back onto the Minnesota highway. They were both subdued, having just spent the evening with old friends whose family farm was on the brink of bankruptcy. The Griffingtons were struggling to compete with the enormous commercial agriculture industry that had replaced most small-scale farms in the past few decades. Sarah and Stu had listened as the Griffingtons described government subsidies that promote overproduction and drive down prices to the point that family farms cannot survive. They expressed reluctance to invest in large combines, petroleum-based fertilizers, and industrial machinery because they knew that the Earth, specifically the depleted soil, would pay the price. Moreover, with such investments the specter of debt hovered, ready to descend whenever a bad season or erratic weather patterns brought poor crops. But most of all, they were concerned that pollen from the neighboring commercial farm's genetically modified corn crop was blowing into their fields, contaminating their own corn and drawing attention from the Monsanto Corporation.

Two representatives from Monsanto had shown up at the farm, threatening to sue the Griffingtons for growing Monsanto's copyrighted corn without compensating the company. "We're enslaved by Monsanto," Joshua Griffington explained, "and it seems like folks out there just don't understand how dangerous they are." Sarah and Stu sympathized deeply with their old friends as they drove past miles of unchanging corn fields as far as the eye could see.

Sarah decided to listen to some news radio and flipped through several stations that their rental car's radio offered. They settled into an episode of "Democracy Now," which neither of them had heard of before. "We turn to the issue of farmer suicides in India, where a quarter of a million farmers have committed suicide in the last sixteen years. On average, that figure suggests one farmer commits suicide every thirty minutes." Sarah and Stu looked at each other, appalled. "Have you heard of this before?" Sarah asked her husband. He shook his head and they listened further. "The agricultural sector in India has become more vulnerable to global markets as a result of economic liberalization. Reforms in the country have included the removal of agricultural subsidies and the opening of Indian agriculture to the global market. These reforms have led to increased costs, while reducing yields and profits for many farmers. As a result, small farmers are often trapped in a cycle of insurmountable debt, leading many to take their lives out of sheer desperation." They listened as the show's guest, the faculty director from the Center for Human Rights and Global Justice at New York University, described Monsanto's heavy marketing of Bt cotton seed to Indian farmers, seeds that require much more water than regular cottonseed to produce high yields.[64] "Do you think the Griffingtons know about this connection they have to Indian farmers through Monsanto?" Stu asked Sarah. "I don't think any of my friends know about this," Sarah replied. "No news source I've heard has covered it."

The couple listened to the end of the program, and then Stu pulled out an iPad that his son had given him for Christmas and found the website for Democracy Now. He read aloud to Sarah, citing facts and linking to other webpages that offered more information. By the time their car crossed the border into Wisconsin they knew a great deal more about Indian farmers and cotton seeds, agricultural policy, biopiracy (the "theft" of indigenous knowledge and biodiversity through patents), and the control of seeds by a few major companies. Tapping into a fierce concern for people who they considered to be their global neighbors, both were ready to do something about it.

Stu and Sarah began by addressing the baffling fact that they had heard nothing of these Indian farmer suicides in mainstream media sources—not the evening news, not the local paper or radio, not the books or magazines that were easily accessible. Their friends were equally oblivious, even those who had traveled to India recently. They learned that almost all news outlets in America are controlled by five corporations, who effectively dictate what the American population would "know" about the world.[65] *The mainstream media's silence on this was unacceptable, and after letting their local television station and newspaper know how they felt, the couple began to seek out alternative news sources such as Democracy Now,* The Nation, *and websites of Public Citizen and Oxfam. While looking for a good documentary film, they found "Nero's Guests"—a presentation of India's agrarian crisis through the eyes of P. Sainath, the Rural Affairs editor of* The Hindu *newspaper—and they decided to organize a screening in their local community center.*

The connections between Indian cotton farmers and North American overconsumers are real, although not direct, the couple began to realize. The situation in India is part of a broader life-and-death question of who has the right to control the seeds from which food crops and other essentials spring. Stu and Sarah knew that the issue went well beyond India and cotton, and as their self-education continued, they began to think not just about the media's shortcomings in informing the public, but the couple's financial investments, and their country's public policy.

One night Stu and Sarah sat down to dinner with another recently retired couple and the subject of finances arose.

"My partner and I realized recently," their friend Erik explained, "that we've spent most of our lives investing in mutual funds that include all kinds of companies that profit greatly from corporate agricultural subsidies and other policies hurting poor farmers." "And it seems as though our mutual funds also have made a lot of money in corporations that impose horrible working conditions in the factories that those farmers and their kids have to work in after they lose their farms!" his wife cried. "I told him 'that's enough of that!' and we pulled out last month."

"Mind you," Erik said, "I'm grateful for all the wonderful things in our lives that we've been able to afford. We've been blessed with a nice

house and we entered retirement comfortably, so I'm not ungrateful. But," he mused, "Hilary and I are becoming a bit uneasy with this idea of blessings. I'm beginning to wonder if what we call blessings are really blessings at all if they are financed by investments in other people's misery."

Sarah and Stu were troubled by the conversation. In the following days, they took a serious look at their stock portfolio, and learned about Socially Responsible Investing (SRI) and triple bottom line companies. According to The Economist, *measuring a company's triple bottom line matters because "what you measure is what you get . . . what you measure is what you are likely to pay attention to. Only when companies measure their social and environmental impact will we have socially and environmentally responsible organizations."[66] Stu came across a number of "socially responsible investment" funds that weigh factors beyond profit in their investment decisions. He and Sarah sought out an investor who specialized in SRI.*

Next, Stu and Sarah sought out opportunities to support farmers whose plants and seeds are "hijacked" by corporate patents, and who were forced to use GMO seeds on their land. Oxfam has worked for several years to address the problematic federal subsidies that United States farmers receive for producing cotton, which encourages overproduction. The surplus cotton enters the international market and drives down prices, undercutting livelihoods of poor farmers in many impoverished nations. As part of their "Trade Campaign," Oxfam urges a complete removal of U.S. cotton subsidies. Oxfam argues that the world price of cotton would increase by 6–14 percent, aiding poor cotton farmers in West Africa and elsewhere.[67]

Later a friend at church told them about the Ecumenical Advocacy Network's Food for Life Campaign. Sarah, Stu, and several members of the congregation used these as alternative sources of information on food policy and hunger issues. They signed up for action alerts, and acted upon the periodic emails that arrived in their inboxes, requesting various kinds of action. The couple understood now some of the ways in which their lives, the land, the Griffington farm in Minnesota, the Indian farmers, and poor farmers worldwide were connected—and that the plight of each mattered to the rest.

****

Notes

1. Daniel Day Williams, *The Spirit and the Forms of Love* (New York: Harper, 1968), 4–5, 9.

2. See also Mark 12:38-34 and Luke 10:25-28.

3. See also Rom. 13:10.

4. The Second Testament iterates the command to love neighbor as self in Matt. 19:19; 22:39; Mark 12:31-33; Luke 10:27; Rom. 13:9; Gal. 5:14; James 2:8.

5. Matthew Whitlock, in conversation. Whitlock goes on to explain that Paul, in Gal. 5:14, sees Lev. 19:18 as a promise fulfilled in Christ and in the church.

6. Daniel Maguire, *The Moral Core of Judaism and Christianity* (Minneapolis: Fortress Press, 1993), 208.

7. Martin Luther King Jr., "Strength to Love," in *A Testament of Hope: The Essential Writings and Speeches of M. L. King Jr.* (San Francisco: Harper, 1991), 48. Here, King is speaking specifically of the commandment to love enemies.

8. Gerhard Kittel, ed., *Theological Dictionary of the New Testament*, vol. 1 (Grand Rapids: Eerdmans, 1964), 39, and Bernard V. Brady, *Christian Love* (Washington, DC: Georgetown University Press, 2003), 53.

9. The meaning of *agape* shifts from prebiblical philosophical literature into the extrabiblical literature of Hellenistic Judaism and into the life of Jesus, the apostolic period, and the early church.

10. For the former, I depend especially upon Gene Outka's *Agape: An Ethical Analysis* (New Haven: Yale University Press, 1972). It is useful in that his intent is to "identify the normative content most often ascribed to agape" (261) by "a representative group of thinkers, both Protestant and Roman Catholic" (2) commonly understood to be the most influential, important, and cogent voices" from roughly 1930 to the time of his writing in 1972.

11. Katherin Dobb Sakenfeld, "Love: Old Testament," in *Anchor Bible Dictionary*, ed. David Freedman (New York: Doubleday, 1992), 4:337.

12. King, *Testament of Hope*, 55.

13. See Cynthia Moe-Lobeda, *Healing a Broken World: Globalization and God* (Minneapolis: Fortress Press, 2009), chs. 4 and 5.

14. Kittel, *Theological Dictionary of the New Testament*, 47.

15. King, *Testament of Hope*, 577–78.

16. Outka, *Agape*, 260.

17. Erich Fromm, *The Art of Loving* (New York: Harper, 1956), 27.

18. Bernard of Clairvaux, Sermon 70:1, quoted by Bernard V. Brady, *Christian Love* (Washington, DC: Georgetown University Press, 2003), 275.

19. Martin Luther King Jr., "An Experiment in Love," in *A Testament of Hope*, 20.

20. Maguire, *Moral Core*, 220.

21. Paul Tillich, *Love, Power and Justice* (New York: Oxford University Press, 1954), 117.

22. A seminal work is Barbara Hilkert Andolsen's "Agape in Feminist Ethics," *Journal of Religious Ethics* 9, no. 1 (Spring 1981): 69–83.

23. Anders Nygren, *Agape and Eros* (New York: Harper, 1969), 217.

24. Valerie Saiving Goldstein first made this case systematically and in published form in "The Human Situation: A Feminine View," *Journal of Religion* (April 1960): 109. Her critique was deepened by Andolsen in "Agape in Feminist Ethics," 74.

25. Commonly held child development theory confirms that humans become able to love by being loved, and that healthy self-love is a requisite of mature capacity to love others.

26. See Catherine Mowry LaCugna, in *God for Us: The Trinity and Christian Life* (San Francisco: HarperSanFrancisco, 1992).

27. Dawn Nothwehr, *Mutuality: A Formal Norm or Christian Social Ethics* (Eugene, OR: Wipf & Stock, 1998), 96.

28. LaCugna, *God for Us*, 223.

29. Williams, *The Spirit and the Forms of Love*, 11.

30. King, "An Experiment in Love," 20.

31. Kittel, *Theological Dictionary of the New Testament*, 45.

32. King, "An Experiment in Love," 19.

33. Cited in Brady, *Christian Love*, 59.

34. Luther says as much. In his explication of the seventh commandment—you shall not steal—he theologically denounces the "liberal market" (the newly emerging capitalist economy) for stealing from the poor. See Martin Luther, "Large Catechism."

35. Iqbal Masih, "Acceptance Speech," and Blair Underwood, "Presentation to Iqbal Masih, Age 12: Reebok Youth in Action Award" (Reebok Human Rights Award, Boston, Massachusetts, 7 December 1994).

36. Maguire, *Moral Core*, 211.

37. How love and justice are complementary is in itself theorized in different ways. For elaboration and assessment see Outka, *Agape*, 78–85.

38. Dietrich Bonhoeffer, "The Church and the Jewish Question," in Geoffrey Kelly and Burton Nelson, eds., *A Testament to Freedom: The Essential Writings of Dietrich Bonhoeffer* (New York: HarperOne, 1990).

39. This subsection and the next are taken largely from Moe-Lobeda, *Public Church: For the Life of the World* (Minneapolis: Fortress Press, 2004).

40. More precisely, he distinguished two broad categories: particular or legal justice and general justice. The latter consisted of both commutative and distributive justice.

41. Richard B. McBrien, "Social Justice: It's in Our Bones," unpublished address cited by Ann Patrick, *Liberating Conscience* (New York: Continuum, 1997), 99.

42. Russell B. Connors and Patrick T. McCormick, *Character, Choices, and Community: The Three Faces of Christian Ethics* (Mahwah, NJ: Paulist, 1998), 66–67.

43. The term "preferential option for the poor" has additional implications. The most central is that God reveals Godself in the poor and their struggles for justice.

44. Douglas Strong, *They Walked in the Spirit: Personal Faith and Social Action in America* (Louisville: Westminster John Knox), 2.

45. Strong gives an excellent account of connections between personal piety and justice-making in the social gospel movement.

46. See Iris Marion Young, *Justice and the Politics of Difference* (Princeton: Princeton University Press, 1990), 33–40.

47. See, for example, Karen Lebacqz, *Justice in an Unjust World: Foundations for a Christian Approach to Justice* (Minneapolis: Augsburg, 1987).

48. Bruce C. Birch, *Let Justice Roll Down: The Old Testament, Ethics, and Christian Life* (Louisville: Westminster John Knox, 1991), 154.

49. Karen Bloomquist, "Seeking Justice," *Between Vision and Reality: Lutheran Churches in Transition*, LWF Documentation 47 (Geneva: LWF, 2001), 253.

50. Reinhold Niebuhr, *The Nature and Destiny of Man*, vol. 2 (New York: Charles Scribner, 1941), 244.

51. Thomas Louis Schubeck, *Love That Does Justice* (Maryknoll, NY: Orbis, 2007), 5, 2.

52. Ibid., 201.

53. Michael Hardt and Antonio Negri, *Multitude: War and Democracy in the Age of Empire* (New York: Penguin, 2005), 351.

54. Ibid.

55. Tillich, *Love, Power and Justice*, 24.

56. Paraphrase of Gary Dorrien, unpublished presentation at Society of Christian Ethics (New Orleans), 2011.

57. Beverly Wildung Harrison, "The Power of Anger in the Work of Love: Christian Ethics for Women and Other Strangers," *Union Seminary Quarterly Review* 36 (1981): 52.

58. Gene H. Outka, *Agape: An Ethical Analysis* (New Haven: Yale University Press, 1972).

59. Kravitha Kruganti's report, "The Marketing of Bt Cotton in India—Aggressive, Unscrupulous, and False" (February 2008), explores Monsanto's false advertising in India.

60. *Nero's Guests*, film, directed by P. Sainath, 2009.

61. John Haide Manukonda. "Ethical Reflections on the Farmers' Suicide in Andhra Pradesh and Its Implications for the Mission of the Church." An unpublished B.D. thesis submitted to the Gurukul Lutheran Theological College and Research Institute, Chennai, India, 2011, 9–10. Female farmers in this region also commit suicide, although at lower rates than men. Their death as suicide is often not listed on official records.

62. Max Frisch, "Monsanto Seeds - For Good or Evil?" *Business Standard*, August 7, 2010.

63. As listed in the Monsanto Ownership Profile online under "Top Owners": http://www.monsanto.com/investors/stock_performance/ownership_profile.asp.

64. *Democracy Now* broadcast with Amy Goodman and Juan González, "Every 30 Minutes: Crushed by Debt and Neoliberal Reforms, Indian Farmers Commit Suicide at Staggering Rate," Wednesday May 11, 2011.

65. See product webpage.

66. "Triple Bottom Line," *The Economist*, Nov. 17, 2009. http://www.economist.com/node/14301663.

67. "Burkina Faso: Cotton Story," *Oxfam International* website: http://www.oxfam.org/en/campaigns/trade/real_lives/burkina_faso.

8

Love: Ecological and Economic Vocation

"We cannot love neighbor without reducing our consumption."

Sallie McFague

How do the features of neighbor-love play out for "us," given the economic and ecological violence in which we are complicit? When mainstays of my life (automobiles, air travel, agribusiness, plastics, and more) depend upon damaging Earth's life-systems and exploiting neighbors, what does love require? What is neighbor-love toward the woman who lost home and fishing livelihood to the construction of the hotel from which I enjoy the beach view?

I make no claim to a comprehensive response. My intent is more humble. It is to identify initial components for an ethic of neighbor-love capable of responding seriously to questions like these, and to proffer partial responses. This means fleshing out the implications of neighbor-love for twenty-first-century earthlings who live as beneficiaries of systemic economic and ecological violence.

This chapter sketches three initial components of such an ethic. They are:

- A moral anthropology: What love means depends upon who we are.
- The scope of neighbor-love: Neighbor-love extends beyond the human.
- Principles of love as an ecological-economic vocation: Ecological sustainability, environmental equity, economic equity, and economic democracy.

The subsequent chapter identifies other key elements of this moral framework.

The biblical injunction to neighbor-love is also vital to aspects of life that are not the focus of these pages. They include life's interpersonal and

197

intrapersonal arenas. Both intertwine with and overlap the economic-ecological, but are not the primary concern of this inquiry. The focus here is a particular underrecognized dimension of neighbor-love, the dimension that emerges at the juncture of economic and ecological life.

What Love Means Depends on Who We Are

"At the heart of the pathology of the environmental crisis is the refusal of humans to see themselves as creatures contingently embedded in networks of relationships with other creatures, and with the Creator. This refusal is the quintessential root of what theologians call sin."[1]

Neighbor-love, we have seen, is contextual. Central to context is who we believe we are. Who are these human creatures, these beings called and created to love? What love means depends upon who we are. The "we," here, has double meaning: we as humans and we as the world's high-consuming beneficiaries of empire.

Chapter 5 argued that forging sustainable Earth-human relations marked by social justice will require a tectonic shift in moral consciousness. This entails a radically reoriented understanding of human being and purpose. "Who we are" is not "who we have assumed we are" in modern and postmodern Western societies. Modernity's glorious myth is that we are the benevolent masters of Isaac Newton's mechanized world ordained by God to have dominion over it. This myth has proven deadly. The more recent story—we the unique stewards of the Earth placed into it as caretakers—is biologically false. The Earth, arguably, has no need for us. Far from being the creature upon whom Earth depends for care, humankind is utterly dependent upon otherkind. They (for example, the microbes cleaning our skin, the trees giving us breath, the plankton of the sea creating food) are taking care of us.

Who then are we? Relational theologies of the last two decades convincingly have established the ontologically relational nature of human being. We are created to be in relationship with others. Increasingly acknowledged is the political nature of that relationality. The Bible attests that the relationality into which we are created and called is not only interpersonal. It is communal relationality, social structural relationality. We are called to receive the love of God and live it into the world, not only in interpersonal relationships, but also in shaping our life in common. The processes for shaping the terms of social life are, by definition, political. Hence humans are, both ontologically and normatively, political creatures. Being political is a reflection of our createdness as beings-in-relationship.[2]

We are not only relational and political creatures, but also earth creatures. In the words of a second-century theological guide, Irenaeus of Lyons, we are "mud creatures"—in Hebrew, *ha adam*—crafted from *adamah* ("dust of the earth, topsoil"). Humans are made from *humus*. That is, we are made of the very elements that existed with the big bang some 13.7 billion years ago and that comprise the soil. We are not above and outside of nature. We are of the animal kingdom, the phylum *chordata*, the genus *homo*, and the species *homo sapiens*. As mud creatures, our God-given task in relationship to the rest of nature at this point in history may be to re-see and re-situate ourselves *within* rather than *above* Earth's web of life.

As relational beings, political beings, and earthlings, we are also inherently economic beings. That is, our life together requires the use of material things and thus their distribution among us.

An ethic of love in the contemporary context must be adequate for human creatures who are by nature not only relational and and political beings, but also economic and ecological beings. From a theological and biological perspective, such an ethic of love holds that we:

- are "mud creatures," made of soil that is made of "star dust";
- are an integral and utterly dependent species in Earth's tapestry of life;
- share origins, body matter, and ultimate salvation with the Earth community;
- live within a *polis* and *economia* that are planetary if not cosmic;[3]
- need, in order to survive, the material goods that other humans and other-than-human parts of the planetary *polis* also require and, thus, must, in some way, distribute those goods;
- are charged with seeking the widespread good, not merely the good of ourselves and our own;
- are embedded in systemic evil that is enormously adept at parading as good, inevitable, natural, fate, or social necessity;
- are beloved by a love that will not cease to love us, is more powerful than any force on Earth or beyond, and loves also the entirety of creation;
- are bearers of that divine and indomitable love;
- are players in a story of hope;
- may be part of a vast global body of people committed to forging more just and sustainable ways of being human on Earth.

These are the creatures called to love neighbor as self. Any theology and ethic of neighbor-love will be tested by its power to move these "mud creatures" toward lives that serve the widespread good. I contend that we, the uncreators, will live that love into the world to the extent that we reconceptualize the Christian moral norm of "neighbor-love" from being primarily an interpersonal vocation to being also an economic-ecological vocation.

NEIGHBOR-LOVE IN AND FOR THE HOUSEHOLD OF EARTH

The God revealed in Jesus is a living God, engaged with the creatures and elements of Earth. The expression of God's engagement, divine love, responds to the realities of history. That love is not stagnant or heedless of the dynamic evolving nature of life's needs. God's love re-forms human love in response to where and how the world hungers for love's healing and liberating hand. The escalating destruction of Earth's life-systems in our day and the resulting human suffering cry out for new forms of love's expression. We are called to love (that is, serve the well-being of) the other-than-human parts of God's beloved creation, as well as the human.

This expanded scope of neighbor-love is not new with eco-theology and ecological ethics. Three decades before eco-theology emerged, H. Richard Niebuhr queried: "Who finally is my neighbor, the companion whom I have been commanded to love as myself?" "My neighbor," he responds, is "animal and inorganic being . . . all that participates in being."[4] *Hesed*, argues Bernard Brady in discussing love in the Hebrew Bible, is not limited to people.[5]

Extending the boundaries of neighbor-love beyond the human opens potholes the size of caverns. In what ways and to what extent does "neighbor-love" apply beyond humankind to the rest of nature? How? As object of love? As agent of love? As vessel of divine love? Biblical texts, read with ecological lenses, intimate all of these.

And what of justice? If neighbor-love demands justice, then to rethink the former is to rethink the latter. Feminist liberationist theories of justice insist that theories of justice start with injustice as described by those experiencing it. If the *polis* is planetary, how do we begin to consider the notion that we must hear voices of the Earth if we wish to understand more fully the injustices it suffers? How are we to perceive the cries and constructive proposals of waters, winds, and critters whose languages we do not yet know? The mode of knowing in modernity, reason, has proven inadequate. The mode of knowing in Western premodernity, revelation uncritically appropriated, proved deadly. Epistemology for the ecological era will incorporate and go beyond both; we will "learn to learn from" other-than-human parts of creation. We will seek to glimpse reality as experienced by otherkind.

The leap of expanding neighbor-love and justice beyond the human is not so vast where Earth's well-being is understood as a requirement for human well-being. But the implications of neighbor-love for the other-than-human are murkier when that move is grounded in the *intrinsic* worth of the other-than-human, rather than solely in its *utilitarian* worth to humankind. Questions of relative worth emerge, as do questions of what criteria determine where love is due. If all is neighbor, and if intrinsic moral worth abides in the other-than-human, how do we measure and compare moral worth? Moral obligations to a dog may be relatively easy to consider. But how, short of arbitrary opinion, do we distinguish between the moral claims of a dog and a fly? What moral constraints ought to be placed on human beings in light of our dependence upon and kinship with otherkind? On what grounds do specific moral values and obligations apply differently to human neighbors than to other-than-human neighbors? More perplexing is the question raised earlier of whether moral agency extends beyond the human to members of other biotic communities. Are we the only ethical species?[6]

And what of predation and plant life? We cannot eat without killing other life forms and destroying habitats of still others. Moreover, we are creatures in a chain of life that by nature includes not only predation but predation that causes suffering.[7] The call to expand the scope of neighbor-love beyond the human is not a call to see the rest of nature as a model of morality.

Nor can love for nature be based on anthropomorphic ideas. Lisa Sideris points out the problem of ecological ethics that call for loving nature in the same way that we love human beings. Loving human beings includes valuing and protecting the life of each individual, including the vulnerable on which other people might prey. Yet, basic biological sciences reveal the danger to ecosystems and therefore their living creatures, if humans were to protect most undomesticated animals from their predators.[8]

Neighbor-love as an interpersonal and economic norm has two faces: compassion and justice. Neighbor-love as an ecological norm adds a third: Earth's well-being. We have only begun to uncover the conundrums inherent this third face of love in love. The challenge of retheorizing love as an ecological vocation is a weighty and morally compelling challenge for religion of the early twenty-first century.

Neighbor-Love Reconstructs Economic life

An unquestioning society-wide commitment to economic growth at almost any cost; enormous investment in technologies designed with little regard for the environment; powerful corporate interests whose overriding objective is to grow by generating profit, including profit from avoiding the environmental costs they create; markets that systematically fail to recognize environmental costs unless corrected by government; government that is subservient to corporate interests and the growth imperative; rampant consumerism spurred by a worshipping of novelty and by sophisticated advertising; economic activity so large in scale that its impacts alter the fundamental biophysical operations of the planet—all combine to deliver an ever-growing world economy that is undermining the planet's ability to sustain life.

Gus Speth[9]

The difficulty lies, not in the new ideas, but in escaping from the ones, which ramify . . . into every corner of our minds.

John Maynard Keynes[10]

Economies—local, national, and global—are not given by fate. They are constructed by human decisions and actions. Said differently, the form of global economy that now shapes the conditions of life on Earth is not inevitable. We human beings can change it toward relative equity and ecological health. Many forms of action are cultivating that change. We will view them, in story and as parts of an ethical framework, as the remainder of this book unfolds. Believing that change is possible is the crucial first step toward realizing it.

But, tearing down "what is" will not build more just and sustainable economic ways. We also must develop new economic practices, policies, norms, and expectations. Different economic structures have different long-term consequences for human and ecological well-being. Given the tremendous role of economic relations in determining well-being—even life and death—for humans and for all of Earth's creatures and life-systems, one question becomes inescapable: What does loving neighbor as self mean for economic life? If neighbor-love directs us toward ways of living that enable all people to have the necessities for life with dignity and that nurture sustainable Earth-human relations, what is required of our economic lives?

Imagining and choosing economic structures that serve the well-being of all is a central moral and political task before our nation and our world. It is laden with ambiguity and moral conundrums. What is just is not always clear. Nor is it readily apparent what policies and practices will "serve the well-being of all." Action aimed at the good may have unforeseen and unintended damaging consequences.

How then are we to know, or to gain at least provisional knowing? One tool for perceiving the shape of neighbor-love in economic life is a moral vision for economic life. Here we sketch the contours of a vision for a moral economy by examining its four constituent principles: ecologically sustainable, environmentally equitable, economically equitable, and democratic. The remainder of this chapter examines these four defining features of an economy coherent with neighbor-love. The food we eat and how we get it is the illustrative lens.

This appeal to guiding principles is not a suggestion that these ideals will be *fully* reached in society. However, it is a firm proposal that we structure economic policies and practices at all levels—from household to international—to cohere with these principles. By so doing we move toward their realization.

One further point is necessary concerning the role of a religious norm such as neighbor-love in public life. Moral values must be brought to bear in determining the ongoing shape of society if that society is to be moral. For many people, moral values are grounded in religious belief. Religion, therefore, inherently comes into play. However, religious claims cannot determine public policy unless those claims also find warrants in nonreligious discourse and value systems. The four guiding principles suggested herein pass that test; while grounded firmly in Christian theology, they may be grounded equally well in secular political discourse. This is crucial.

ECOLOGICAL SUSTAINABILITY:
SITUATE HUMAN ECONOMIES WITHIN EARTH'S ECONOMY

Ecological economist Herman Daly has asserted since the early 1970s that human economies are, in fact, embedded in Earth's natural economy and must be recognized as such in economic theory if economic theory is to reflect reality.[11] Thomas Berry, cultural historian and Passionist priest, averred as much with his renowned assertion that humankind must situate our human economies within Earth's "great economy."[12] Daly's seminal insight has been iterated and expanded by eco-theologians and environmental ethicists. An elegant international appeal to situate human activity—including economic activity—within the limits of nature was crafted by the United Nations in 1982 in its "World Charter for Nature."[13]

To the contrary, however, classical and neoclassical economic theory and the capitalist economies they rationalize have treated human economies as entirely *separate from* Earth's economy. So doing portrays the world falsely and promotes the widely held false assumption that human economic activity is not contingent upon the Earth's physical limits. Chapter 4's discussion of the "economic growth myth" made this point. In short, the bottom line in corporate activity does not account for much of the ecological and social costs of that activity. Those costs are "externalized"; they are not paid by the corporation that creates the degradation and benefits financially. The costs are left to be paid by society or by future generations, or are borne by the people suffering from the degradation. The horrendous ecological and social costs of mountaintop-removal coal mining in Appalachia (poisoned rivers, toxic drinking and bathing water, loss of homes, valleys filled with dumped rock and waste, deforestation, flooding) illustrate.

For the Global North, achieving sustainable[14] economies entails the shift from fossil fuel–based economies to economies fueled primarily by renewable and nontoxic sources of energy. "Recent data confirms that consumption of fossil fuels accounts for the majority of global anthropogenic GHG [greenhouse gas] emissions."[15] Both global warming and ocean acidification mandate dramatic reduction in carbon dioxide (CO_2) levels in the Earth's atmosphere. This means reducing the parts per million (ppm) of atmospheric carbon dioxide.[16] Until the industrial revolution, human history transpired in an atmosphere of approximately 275 parts per million. "By the end of 2010 . . . CO_2 concentrations had increased to over 390 ppm."[17] Currently the levels are rising by 2 parts per million annually. That rise, unchecked, would be disastrous. As noted by one of the first scientists to raise the alert about global warming, James Hansen of NASA, "If humanity wishes to preserve a planet similar to that on which civilization developed and to which life on Earth is adapted, paleoclimate evidence and ongoing climate change suggest that CO_2 will need to be reduced from its current 385 ppm to at most 350 ppm."[18]

Three means of reducing atmospheric carbon dioxide levels are necessary and work in concert. One is technological solutions. They will help, but bear grave problems—technical solutions alone are not capable of resolving the issue, and the belief that they are seriously obstructs movement in other methods of reducing CO_2 levels. A second method is the switch to renewable energy sources. This too is crucial. Yet, alone, it also is an inadequate response because a significant amount of fossil fuel uses cannot be replaced by renewable sources.[19] Moreover, arguably, the rapidly increasing demand for energy caused by increasing growth cannot be met by renewable fuels in time. Therefore, a third method also is necessary. It is decreasing consumption of energy through efficiency and decreased demand for energy.[20] Note that in all three methods, the common person has much power for generating change.

The last of these—decreased energy consumption—calls for discarding growth (as measured by GDP) as the primary measure of economic well-being. This does not preclude all economic growth as a good. However, it cautions that growth as a measure of economic well-being must be accompanied by other measures and, as indicated previously, must be qualified. That is, growth-producing policies and practices must: (1) be ecologically sustainable; (2) reduce the wealth gap; (3) produce long-term, adequately compensated jobs open to unionization; and (4) bolster rather than undermine local communities and cultures."[21]

This principle—human economies situated within Earth's economy—and the requisite move from fossil fuel dependence call for more than individual commitment and technological innovation. Change in individual lifestyles joins forces with change in corporations, institutions of civil society, and governmental policy and practice. While structural change in corporate policy and practice may seem beyond the realm of the possible, it is not. Concerned citizens work through various gateways to achieve corporate change. Those gateways are the focus of chapter 10. Here we note three overarching reorientations for corporate policy:

1. replacing the financial bottom line with a triple bottom line of ecological sustainability, financial viability, and social impact;
2. internalizing social and ecological costs that currently are externalized;[22]
3. measuring profit and loss not only by the quarter, but by the long-term future.

Steps toward economies based on renewable energy sources are being debated and enacted in varied venues. These changes will occur on a widespread basis only when mandated by public policy and promoted by a degree of public will. Therefore, political will and moral courage may be the most crucial ingredients of all. The political nature of love appears yet again.

Situating human economies within Earth's economy of life entails shifts in values. For example: The high value of overconsumption will shift to the values of sufficiency or frugality. The value of globally traded food products will convert to valuing local and regionally produced and traded goods. Disposable goods will give way to enduring, repaired, and reused goods. Long-distance travel will dim in value.

What might it look like to live as if human economies were situated within and dependent upon Earth's economy of life?[23] What would it mean to live in a low carbon–producing society in which individuals, corporations, other institutions, and governments all contributed to that end? The question need not be hypothetical, for that change is being made by many people in the United States and the world over. And it is being made at the individual, corporate, other institutional, and governance levels. Let us take a look through the window of what we eat and how we procure it. Note how the choices and actions of individuals, institutions, corporations, and public policy shape each other.

****

THE PRINCIPLE ILLUSTRATED

It is said that a forkful of produce travels an average of 1300 to 2000 miles to reach an American plate.[24] According to Anna Lappé in Diet for a Hot Planet, *food transport and food production both contribute significantly to the emission of carbon dioxide and other gases that cause global warming. This includes everything from emissions related to transferring food from farm to store, to emissions from transporting inputs to our food (feed from Brazil or ammonia from Morocco).[25] A study comparing foods that are imported into California with foods produced there revealed a forty-five-fold increase in emissions from the imported foods, and five hundred times more emissions for those foods brought in through air freight.[26] The amount of fuel required to transport one year's worth of tomatoes to the state of New Jersey would power an eighteen-wheeler to drive around the globe 249 times.[27]*

We could, as a society and as households, choose a low-carbon diet, meaning a diet that requires fewer fossil fuels to arrive on our plates, and therefore produces fewer greenhouse gases. Many people are making this choice. They are eating less meat. They choose fresh foods that avoid the emissions associated with manufacturing, freezing, canning, drying, and packaging processed foods. They select food with little or no packaging, recognizing the problematic impact of individually wrapped food items, boxes within boxes, layers of plastic, paper, and cardboard that surround much of our food. According to the US-EPA, containers and packaging account of 30 percent of municipal solid waste in America.[28] Many people are limiting themselves primarily to foods harvested from within a short radius.

Community-supported agriculture (CSA), a rapidly growing industry in the United States that supplies weekly local and/or organic produce boxes to households and institutions from area farms, allows members to pay for a portion of a farm's operating expenses and receive a portion of the produce in return. The movement gains power as institutions join individuals and households in buying locally. In 2007 in Washington State, a coalition of children's health advocates, environmentalists, anti-poverty activists, farmers, and parents joined together in the "Local Farms-Healthy Kids" campaign. They passed the "Local Farms-Healthy Kids Act," groundbreaking legislation that establishes a Farm-to-School program within the Washington State Department of Agriculture, connecting schools to local farmers and stocking school cafeterias with fresh local produce. A low-carbon diet is also an economic justice diet. Purchasing from small local farmers enables them to thrive and resist takeover by agribusiness.

Lifestyle change itself will not produce a low-carbon food system nationwide. Many people go beyond the shift in what they eat to become advocates on the public policy level for low-carbon food and food justice. Organizations like Food Democracy Now, Food First, and the U.S. Food Sovereignty Alliance are but a few of the many groups working for broad-scale food justice.

And what of change at the corporate level? What if American citizens pressed the corporate world, through consumer pressure and legislation, to take initial steps in the corporate changes noted above (adopting a "triple bottom line," internalizing social and environmental costs of business, and measuring profit by the long-term rather than by the quarter)? Imagine the reduction in carbon emissions if, for example, large-scale agribusiness were taxed for its carbon emissions, or if General Mills or Kellogg measured not only its financial bottom line, but its ecological and social bottom lines?

One compelling example of a company's move to situate its economy within Earth's economy is Interface, Inc., the world's largest commercial carpet manufacturer. Ray Anderson, the company's longtime CEO, explained that for twenty years, he never gave a thought to the company's impact on its workers or the environment in the making of their products. But starting in 1994, customers began asking questions, like "What's *your company doing for the environment?" Anderson admits that the answer then was "not much," and this disturbed the customers. Anderson convened a taskforce of Interface leaders from around the world to assess the company's environmental position, to provide answers to those persistent customers. The taskforce asked Anderson to open the conference with his environmental vision. Desperate for something to say, he read Paul Hawken's book* The Ecology of Commerce. *He encountered E. O. Wilson's phrase "the death of birth" in reference to species extinction, and experienced an epiphany. Anderson felt, from that moment on, that if they could not manufacture carpets sustainably, then perhaps carpets didn't have a place in our world. "One day early in this journey, it dawned on me," says Anderson, "that the way I'd been running Interface, is the way of the plunderer, plundering something that's not mine, something that belongs to every creature on earth. And I said to myself, 'My goodness, the day must come when this is illegal . . . some day people like me will end up in jail."*[29]

Anderson challenged the company to adopt a bold vision, one that would require a completely new way of thinking. Their goals include 100 percent energy from renewable sources by 2020, becoming completely carbon neutral, and broadening their definition of waste to consider the entire supply chain.[30]

Some countries, especially in Europe, have placed "triple bottom line" laws into the books. France, for example, has its nouvelles régulations économiques—*"new economic regulations," in which businesses that are publicly traded on the French market must issue annual performance reports explaining their social and environmental impacts.*[31] *Denmark's "Green Accounts Act" stipulates that businesses in highly polluting industries must submit annual environmental performance reports including a director's report written for nonexperts and detailed data on resource consumption and emission of polluting substances.*[32]

This brief glance at "eating" and a carpet company illustrates not only what is possible, but what actually is happening to bring human economies in line with Earth's economy of life. Similar changes and movements are flourishing in the areas of housing, transportation, recreation, electronics, and clothing.

****

ENVIRONMENTAL EQUITY:
REVERSE ENVIRONMENTAL SPACE "INVASION"

Two thousand years ago, the geographic scope of an ordinary person's impact was much smaller. Given the reigning form of global economy, that scope has exploded; it is planetary. My life impacts the communities from whose land comes the oil to fuel my car, produce my plastic products, and fly my food from other continents. My life impacts countless Indian people who no longer have water because the Coca-Cola plant that feeds my desires has taken or poisoned their water. My greenhouse gas emissions impact the lives of the millions of environmental refugees surviving the effect of climate change.

What form then does neighbor-love take? Two suggestions challenge the Global North to acknowledge and account for "ecological debt" and overuse of "environmental space."[33]

ECOLOGICAL DEBT

"As human impacts to the environment accelerate, disparities in the distribution of damages between rich and poor nations mount."[34] So concludes a study led by University of California scientists "assessing the impacts of agricultural intensification and expansion, deforestation, overfishing, loss of mangrove swamps and forests, ozone depletion and climate change during a forty-year period, from 1961 to 2000." This unprecedented study, published in the *Proceedings of the National Academy of Sciences*, found that: "Climate change and ozone depletion impacts predicted for low-income nations have been overwhelmingly driven by emissions from [high-income and middle-income nations], a pattern also observed for overfishing damages indirectly driven by the consumption of fishery products. Indeed, through disproportionate emissions of greenhouse gases alone, the rich group may have imposed climate damages on the poor group greater than the latter's current foreign debt."[35] "At least to some extent, the rich nations have developed at the expense of the poor and, in effect, there is a debt to the poor," said coauthor Richard B. Norgaard, an ecological economist and UC-Berkeley professor of energy and resources. "That, perhaps, is one reason that they are poor. You don't see it until you do the kind of accounting that we do here."[36]

Do overconsuming countries of the Global North and the overconsuming elite in other countries owe an "ecological debt"[37] to those who are suffering most from ecological degradation but contribute least to it? Are reparations or compensation called for? "Yes," argue an increasing number of activists and others. Acción Ecológica, a civil society organization of Ecuador, defines ecological debt as: "the debt accumulated by Northern, industrial countries toward Third-World countries on account of resource plundering, environmental damages and the free occupation of environmental space, to deposit wastes, such as greenhouse gases, from the industrial countries."

Ecological debt has three aspects. The first refers to the "debt" owed by countries of the Global North to people of the Global South as a result of disproportionate greenhouse gas emissions and toxic waste dumping, other forms ecological damage, and five hundred years of resource plundering that have brought riches to the North at the expense of the South.

The term refers in another sense to the debt owed by current generations to future generations due to our excessive use of the nonrenewable resources and the resulting atmospheric damage. Climate change, ocean acidification, loss of biodiversity, endocrine-disrupting chemicals, and nuclear waste are examples of the impact that our overconsumption will have on future generations. Do we owe to them an "ecological debt"? What form of moral obligations do we have to our children and grandchildren?

Some theorists use "ecological debt" in a third sense, the debt owed by humankind to otherkind for the ecological damage we have wrought. Raised here is the question of whether and in what sense humans have moral obligations to other-than-human parts of creation.

Ecological debt, in the first of these forms, reflects the reality that the wealth of the Global North has been built on disproportionate use of the world's natural goods, and especially of the minerals, oil, and other goods extracted from lands of the Global South. It reflects too the ongoing displacement of people in the Global South by corporate activity that takes over their land, water, and forests. The World Council of Churches (WCC) and a number of secular civil society organizations connect "ecological debt" with the "external debt" charged to many impoverished nations by the industrialized world. They advocate cancelation of that external debt as one form of payment for the ecological debt.[38] This could be one way of addressing the moral dilemma raised in the story of the Mozambican bishop who identifies himself as a "debt warrior" and attributes poverty in Africa to the external debt.

The moral issues are not simple. At the least they call for *recognition* of ecological debt, and serious consideration of responsibility and obligation to stop contributing to it and to design some degree of compensation. In 2010 the Lutheran World Federation (LWF) and WCC wrote: "The call for eco-justice and the recognition of ecological debt are part of the church's witness for the care of creation. The formulation of demands to repair and repay the climate debt to the poorest, the most vulnerable, future generations and the Earth itself has become the prophetic stance of the churches as it confronts the most serious of ecological crises, the ethical and moral crisis of climate change."[39]

The notion that the wealthy owe a "debt" to the poor for having taken what is rightfully theirs is longstanding in Christian history. Fourth-century theologian Ambrose wrote: "You are not making a gift of your possessions to the poor person. You are handing over to him what belongs to him." Nine centuries later, Thomas Aquinas, one of history's most influential theologians said as much: "The superfluous goods that a few persons possess belong by natural right to the sustenance of the poor."

The United Nations Framework Convention on Climate Change (UNFCCC) suggests a broad guideline for response to climate debt. The "Parties [nations signing the Convention] should protect the climate system for the benefit of present and future generations of humankind, *on the basis of equity and in accordance with their common but differentiated responsibilities and respective capabilities* (italics mine). Accordingly, the developed country Parties should take the lead in combating climate change and the adverse effects thereof."[40] The Greenhouse Development Rights Framework, citing this standard, argues that "while people remain poor, it is unacceptable and unrealistic to expect them to focus their valuable resources on the climate change crisis." It "draws the necessary conclusion—that others who are wealthier and have enjoyed higher levels of emissions already, must take on their fair share of the effort. This does not mean that the countries in which poor people live are not required to cut their emissions, but rather that the global consuming class—both within these countries and especially in the industrialized countries—are the ones who must pay."[41]

Various means of honoring the ecological debt owed by the industrialized wealthy nations have been proposed. They include the aforementioned move to cancel the external debt of impoverished nations, paying the "cash value" of our debt for use in protections from climate-related disaster, transferring green technologies to the Global South at no cost, and paying other costs entailed in curtailing current emissions levels.[42] None is valid unless accompanied by a radical reduction in greenhouse gas emissions by countries of the Global North.

ENVIRONMENTAL SPACE AND ENVIRONMENTAL FOOTPRINT

Other activists and scholars, especially in Europe, advocate consideration of "environmental space,"[43] a rights-based and equity-based tool for measuring and comparing different populations' environmental impact. This policy tool, developed in 1982 by German economist Horst Siebert, was popularized in Europe in the early 1990s. It was promoted by Friends of the Earth Netherlands as part of its *Sustainable Netherlands Action Plan* and by Friends of the Earth Europe's *Sustainable Europe Campaign*. The tool has influenced national policy in the Netherlands, Norway, and Denmark. Environmental space conceptualizes eco-justice in terms of "equal rights to resource consumption for all peoples of the world within the carrying capacity of the planet."[44] The Earth's total "environmental space is the total amount of pollution, non-renewable resources, agricultural land and forests that can be used globally without impinging on the access by future generation[s] to the same resources."[45] The *Sustainable Netherlands Action Plan* "argues that each country has a right to the same amount of environmental space per capita." Environmental space implies eliminating at least international inequities in aggregate resource consumption and in CO_2 emissions. "Environmental space targets" are the "fair share" of resource use and CO_2 production to which any given country or person is entitled.

The complexities involved in approximating environmental space use and targets are staggering. Precision is not the aim; it is impossible to calculate precisely the global availability of any given resource, and its use by a particular population. What constitutes a "fair share" or an equitable distribution is equally controversial.[46] However, the concept is invaluable as a comparative measure and for its implications. As noted by New Zealand-based environmental scientist T. Buhrs, "[I]t recasts the notion of [planetary] limits in a form that highlights distributional and equity issues."[47] From a moral perspective, this recasting renders inadequate the goal of reducing carbon emissions; the moral goal is to reduce them in a *relatively equitable* manner. The implications play out at both societal and individual levels.

The most widely recognized tool for estimating the environmental space occupied by any given population is the "environmental footprint."[48] Environmental footprint "measures how much [biologically productive] land and water area a particular human population requires to produce the resource it consumes and to absorb its wastes," including CO_2. The tool converts that amount into a measurement called a "footprint." The footprint may be used to estimate the ecological costs of a nation, the world population, an individual, a city or region, a particular industry, or a product. Methods of measurement vary and are under rapid development in academic settings.[49] Where like methods are used, they are invaluable tools for comparative analysis, policy planning, and individual choices. Their value does not depend upon precision.

These tools imply that reduction of greenhouse gas emissions is a human right, and they suggest equal right worldwide to the use of the atmosphere. The idea that greenhouse gas reduction by countries overtaxing the atmosphere is a human right of people in countries suffering from that imbalance is a matter of debate. It is far from widely accepted. In human rights theory, the claim is grounded in the right to life, as well as the rights to food, water, and shelter guaranteed in the UN Declaration of Human Rights.

Theological and biblical grounding too is strong. Fundamental to Catholic social teaching is the notion of the "universal destination of goods," the principle that God intends the goods of the earth to be for all; all people should have access to the goods necessary for their full human development. This principle calls for economic orders that enable universal access to the necessities for life with dignity. Taken seriously, it would mandate radical change in the practices and policies that create global warming that deprives countless people of those necessities. The biblical notions of the Jubilee and the Sabbath are integrally connected with the teachings of Jeremiah, Amos, Hosea, and other Hebrew prophets who denounce the rich for building their luxurious lives on goods stolen from the poor.

Ambrose extends the biblical voices and foreshadows the "universal destination of goods." "How far, o rich, do you extend your senseless avarice?" he demands. "Do you intend to be the sole inhabitants of the earth? Why do you drive out the fellow sharers of nature, and claim it all for yourselves? The earth was made for all, rich and poor, in common. Why do you rich claim it as your exclusive right? The soil was given to the rich and poor in common. Wherefore, o ye rich, do you unjustly claim it for yourselves alone? Nature gave all things in common for the use of all."

The ground of these theological stands is God's love for the world and God's call to human beings to live according to that love. Foreswearing our environmental "space invasion,"—or vastly reducing it—would realize many of the features of love uncovered in chapter 7.

The obvious difficulty in calculating just distribution of emission rights is no reason to abandon the moral need to move in that direction. Moral questions of enormous import arise. They call for public and interpersonal moral deliberation regarding limits to the "right to do what I wish with my material wealth," the meaning of freedom, and the weight of the right to food and water versus the right to maximize profit.

****

THE PRINCIPLE ILLUSTRATED

Ashton Hayes is a small town in Cheshire, England. In 2009 it set out to become the first carbon-neutral town in England, an effort that other communities are watching, and some are emulating. Ashton Hayes has installed solar panels and wind turbines throughout the town, built footpaths to the school and local rail station to facilitate walking and bicycling, planted trees, and changed light bulbs. The county council erected demonstration turbines and solar thermal panels. The first turbine was built at the local primary school and provides all its power. I realized that the little things—switching off lights, turning down your thermostat—that sort of thing, could make a big change overall if you did it at a community level," says Gary Charnock, one of the project organizers.[50]

The town of Rock Port, Missouri is powered entirely by wind energy. Four large turbines outside of town power every light, every computer, and every appliance in the 1,300-person town. Landowners are paid between $3,000 and $5,000 per year to host the forty-foot-tall windmills. The turbines produce almost four times as much energy as the town needs, so the power company is able to sell the energy to neighboring towns.[51]

Not only small towns but large cities and even states are developing public policy that vastly reduces their contribution to the ecological debt and their use of environmental space. They work hand-in-hand with businesses making the same commitment. In 2004, the Portland city council passed a resolution known as the "diggable city initiative" to inventory vacant, publicly owned land throughout the city for its agricultural potential. Kansas City's "Climate Protection Plan" created by the Kansas City Office of Environmental Quality establishes a fund to convert contaminated lands to safe urban farms. Centers for resale of used building and remodeling materials are springing up in cities around the country, enabling reuse of doors, floor paneling, hardware, lumber, tiles, sinks, and other materials that otherwise would end up in a landfill.

In 2000, Seattle created the first carbon neutral electric utility, and in 2010, Seattle's city council established "carbon neutrality" as one of its sixteen priorities. As a result, Seattle's public transportation system includes electric buses ("virtually carbon neutral" and "twice as energy efficient as diesel buses"[52]) and much of its public fleet operates on alternative fuels.

Carbon neutrality requires rethinking food systems. The carbon-neutral town movement envisions a living space in which residents can walk or bike to their food seller's shops, and where much of the available food is produced locally, and secondarily, regionally, with the exception of a few international products such as coffee, tea, and chocolate. Many residents grow food on whatever space they have, including rooftops and the strip of land between houses and the road. Many forego beef and eat locally raised chicken on special occasions only. Small local food production companies replace huge global corporations. Many towns and cities have local ice cream shops, providing an alternative to the emissions-heavy global brands such as Nestlé, Magnum, and Häagen-Dazs. Local beer breweries are cropping up, offering alternatives to the environmental-space munching Miller-Coors, Sam Adams, and Budweiser. The question of "rights" emerges. As a society, our normative assumptions include the right to eat as much beef as we want, food shipped from a distance at any time of year, and highly packaged food, regardless of how much environmental space these habits consume.

Housing is responsible for about a third of the average American's environmental footprint. It includes home energy and water use, construction materials, spatial area of land that the housing occupies, and the amount of ocean area needed to absorb the carbon emissions resulting from home construction and maintenance. Goods and services are another major portion of our environmental footprint, including all the stuff we buy, as well as the impact of any services to which we subscribe. If all people on Earth lived the way the average American lives, we would need 5.3 planets to sustain our lifestyles.[53]

Many faith leaders are increasingly concerned with matters of environmental space and ecological debt. In 2010 a group of Anglican leaders from South and North America gathered in the Dominican Republic to reflect on climate justice and ecological debt. "We heard powerful witnesses to climate injustice and creative responses by dioceses, communities, and individuals," one participant reports.[54] Several concrete commitments emerged. The group committed to developing a mechanism, such as a "carbon tithe" or energy fund, to promote reductions of carbon emissions by affluent populations and to offer assistance in ways identified *by vulnerable communities. The group decided to recruit a core of "reverse missionaries," individuals from the Global South to come to the United States "in a ministry of accompaniment and consciousness-raising about the effects of climate change."*[55]

★★★★★★★★★★★★★★★★★★★★★★★★★★★★★★★★★★★

ECONOMIC EQUITY:
PRIORITIZE MEETING HUMAN NEED OVER PROFIT MAXIMIZATION

The economic inequity witnessed in the vignettes has many roots. Significant among them is the assumption that economic activity ought to maximize profit. This value is institutionalized and legalized in the structure of the business corporation as it exists today. Four features of the corporate charter work in concert to promote and enable profit maximization over most other concerns.

One is the rights of personhood granted to corporations in 1886 when the Supreme Court ruled that corporations are persons under the law and have all the legal rights of a person, including protection by the First, Fourth, Fifth, and Fourteenth Amendments. Two hundred and thirty state laws regulating corporations were ruled to be violations of the human right to due process. Exercising the legal rights of a human being dramatically enhances corporate power to increase profit at great cost to society and ecosystems. When states or cities try to curb corporate power through regulatory legislation, courts tend to invalidate the legislation. In the last three decades this aspect of corporate structure has been joined by the fierce deregulation movement.

A striking example involves the Monsanto corporation. In 1994 the Vermont legislature, responding to citizens' concerns about the safety of Monsanto's bovine growth hormone (Bovine somatotropin: rBST or rBGH), passed a law requiring products made with the synthetic hormone to be labeled.[56] Dairy and food-processing corporations, working through nonprofits created and funded by them, sued the state of Vermont. Monsanto supported the trade associations as a "friend of the court." The courts effectively struck down the labeling law on the grounds that it *violated the corporation's first amendment right to remain silent.*[57]

The problem with granting corporations the civil rights of persons is that a corporation is *not* a person. It therefore has neither the moral consciousness of a person nor the social responsibilities accompanying personhood.

A second feature of corporate legal structure is the "best interest of the corporation" principle. It mandates that directors and executives of a corporation act in its best interests, which means shareholder wealth maximization. "Corporations are created by law and imbued with purpose by law . . . it compels executives to prioritize the interests of their companies and shareholders above all others."[58] "In North America," says corporate legal scholar Dr. Janis Sarra, "courts usually only consider shareholder wealth maximization as the benchmark of whether the directors and officers are acting in the best interests of the corporation."[59] Profit becomes top priority.

Third is accountability only for the financial bottom line rather than accountability also for the social and ecological "bottom lines." This allows the corporation to ignore social and ecological costs. Society at large pays these costs, largely through the taxpayers or future generations. "The company's balance sheet has no way to recognize costs that are not its own, no reason or method to calculate future liabilities it causes but that someone else will have to pay. The incentives, in fact, run in the opposite direction. The firm will be rewarded with greater returns and higher stock prices if it manages to 'externalize' its true operating costs. It does this by pushing the negative consequences off on someone else: the neighbors who live downstream from a factory's industrial pollution or its own workers who lose job security and pension rights, or the community left with an empty factory, shattered lives, a ruined environment."[60] The fourth feature is limited liability.

These four factors magnify corporate power to do what it will in its quest for profit. When maximizing profit calls for speculating at the expense of countless small investors, Goldman Sachs and other investment firms do so. When public policy and cultural values allow General Electric to increase profit by closing plants in the United States and moving them to Mexico where labor is cheaper and unorganized and environmental protection unenforced, the company relocates the plants, sometimes demanding that its vendors do the same. "Ideally, you'd have every plant you own on a barge," declared GE's then CEO, Jack Welch.[61] The devastated lives and communities of laid-off workers in the United States, it seems, do not matter as much as does the increased profit.

In India, Coca-Cola makes more money by despoiling the land and water supply that have supported small farmers for centuries and by displacing these people into the city. An urban factory can then make more profit by hiring those same people—now urban refugees—at a less-than-living wage and dangerous working conditions. If, after a few years, the workers organize and call for higher wages and safety protections, then the plant can relocate to another country in which labor has not been allowed to organize. These moves serve the corporate mandate to maximize profit. And no local or international political entity—local, state, national governance—maintains the firm legal right to intercede.

If a company is bound by cultural norms and legal sanctions to maximize profit, then it may build a resort on coastal lands, destroying the fishing livelihood and food staple that had sustained the area's longtime inhabitants, rendering them homeless, jobless, and stranded on street corners begging. When the powdered milk industry in the United States can profit by "dumping" powdered milk at very low prices on Jamaica, it does so in spite of devastating the Jamaican dairy industry. It cannot compete with U.S. milk prices, which are enabled by a 137 percent federal subsidy to undercut Jamaican prices.[62]

The culprit is not just the corporations. The culprit also is our society that has legally and culturally sanctioned this systematic valuation of profit maximization over the needs of human and other life. Profit maximization has a corollary in individuals' "consumer life." It is the tacit assumption that we *should* get things at the lowest price; getting a "good buy" is a kind of virtue. On yet a subtler level, it is perceived as a right; we *deserve* the lowest prices. Thomas Prince notes, "When President Bush reneged in early 2001 on his campaign promise to reduce carbon emissions as called for in the Kyoto Protocol, the second reason [he gave] . . . was that reducing emissions would raise consumer prices."[63] Mass production of chickens in inhuman conditions is justified by the need to keep prices low. Having that low-cost chicken is an assumed right.

The cultural norm of profit maximization and the corporate charter mandating it help to explain a puzzling and gruesome contradiction. Many corporate leaders responsible for these decisions and actions are good people in their private lives. They may treat the people around them with care and respect, and may contribute substantially to charities, even to services for the very people damaged by their corporate actions.

The crucial point is that *these profit-maximizing moves are the result of human decisions and actions and thus can be changed by human decisions and actions.* Changes in values, public policy, and everyday practices can discourage and prohibit the corporate practice of profit maximization where the social and ecological costs are too great. Illustrations of these changes appear in this and the final chapter.

The biology, physics, and chemistry of the Earth render it impossible for future economies to continue obligating or encouraging profit maximization where so doing continues to unravel the life-systems within which human life unfolds. Said differently, *that* the norm of profit maximization at all costs will cease is a given; Earth will end this norm if human societies do not. However, the physical limits of the planet do not determine the nature and form of that change. Citizens do.

Human values, decisions, and actions will determine the shape of this transition. Toward what purpose and for whose benefit is a crucial moral question. One possibility would be to constrain the standard of profit maximization by ecological criteria alone, ignoring social equity. That is, we could seek to maintain the Earth's life-systems to the extent necessary to provide comfortable life for those who can pay for it. Such a move, of course, would diametrically contradict the norm of neighbor-love.

Neighbor-love, along with much political-economic theory, suggests a different path. It is the societal decision that profit maximization and wealth accumulation will take a backseat to ecological sustainability and human need. A second step on that path would be to value corporate policies and actions that diminish the gap between the wealthy and the impoverished, rather than increase it. The priority of human need over profit is solidly rooted in human rights discourse and Christian tradition.

A quick review of love's features highlighted in chapter 7 shows many of them at play in the principle of relative economic equity. One is the recognition that "neighbor-love is blocked by love for wealth and prestige." Christian history—from the time of Jesus through today—is replete with theological challenges to wealth accumulation, finding it antithetical to following Jesus and to life according to the reign of God. Jesus' challenge to a "wealthy young man" led St. Francis, John Wesley, and countless others to renounce their wealth. That challenge is reflected two thousand years later by the WCC in a study on poverty and wealth. "Excessive wealth," it states, "is contrary to gospel teachings. It cannot be separated from poverty. They have common causes. . . . Worse still, excessive wealth is itself [a] cause of poverty. The drive to create a rising tide of wealth and become rich does not benefit the poor and the rich alike. It does not bring an end to poverty but often exacerbates it."[64]

These theories and theologies do not stand apart from their concrete realization. The number and energy of organizations and movements throughout the United States and the world pushing for this shift from profit maximization to meeting life's needs is vast. Here again, change at different levels—individual, institutional, corporate, and governance—shape each other.

****

THE PRINCIPLE ILLUSTRATED

How might the principle of "meeting human needs over maximizing profit" reshape, say, my lunch? Perhaps I would reconsider the people behind the ingredients in my lunch bag. The people of Plachimada in the state of Kerala, India, initially welcomed the news of a Coca-Cola bottling plant with open arms. They were promised employment and improved education, but what they got was, as one resident described it, "worse than in the British days." The Coca-Cola plant drilled six large-bore wells and began extracting half a million liters of water per day. No laws were in place to prevent this. Between 1999 and 2006, the water level of the underground aquifer dropped by twenty-six feet, the farming community transformed into a desert. What water could be extracted was saline, hard, and foul smelling. Local residents claimed that waste from the bottling plant was disposed of at night onto their agricultural fields, and then later justified as "bio-fertilizer."[65]

"Three communities in India—Plachimada in Kerala, Wada in Maharashtra, and Mehdiganj in Uttar Pradesh—are experiencing severe water shortages as a result of Coca-Cola's mining of the majority of the common groundwater resources."[66] In January 2004, over five hundred protesters marched and rallied in Plachimada to condemn the Coca-Cola company. They demanded the closure of the plant and began a boycott of Coke products. Later in Mehdiganj, community leaders began a hunger strike to demand the closure of the Coca-Cola bottling plant. Kerala officials shut down the Coke plant in 2004, and later the entire state of Kerala banned Coke and Coke products.

The Coca-Cola company has been accused of transgressions on multiple fronts. High concentrations of pesticide and insecticide residue (including DDT, malathion, lindane, and chlorpyrifos—all known carcinogens) were found in Indian Coke bottles. Tests showed toxins at more than thirty times the standard allowed by the European Union.[67] Members of a labor union at a Coca-Cola plant in Colombia were intimidated, tortured, and killed by paramilitary groups affiliated with the plant managers and the government. The United Steelworkers union and a U.S. labor rights group filed a suit in 2001 charging Coca-Cola with hiring a right-wing paramilitary group to assassinate labor organizers, an accusation that the soft drink company denies. Coke's plastic and aluminum containers pose a serious environmental threat. In 2000, Coca-Cola paid $192 million to settle a class action racial discrimination lawsuit, and vowed to improve its treatment of minority employees in the United States.

It is one thing for people in India or Colombia to fight the Coca-Cola corporation's profit-maximizing practices, but how can consumers in America help? How, that is, can we move from benefiting from injustice (through products made inexpensive by exploiting people and lands) to supporting justice? What forms can transnational solidarity take?

We can make it our business to learn about and from the struggles of people who suffer the consequences of corporate profit maximization, so that we might transform our collective relationships with these neighbors. Becoming informed about justice struggles at home and globally is a powerful move against corporate dominance and is essential to "critical moral vision." Becoming informed means changing ingrained habits of information gathering. The following chapter suggests paths for that move.

Informed people become invaluable "allies" to movements struggling for human rights. According to Green America, "Coke's bottled water operations have made it the focus of at least two international water rights campaigns, as the company continues high-volume pumping in areas where extreme shortages of potable water are already a problem."[68] Boycotts in India spread to the rest of the world. In 2006 the University of Michigan—spurred on by student organizers—suspended all sales of Coca-Cola products on its three campuses, in response to allegations of human rights and environmental abuses overseas.[69] Church groups too fight for social change in Coca-Cola. Representatives of the Presbyterian Church USA spoke out at a Coca-Cola shareholders' meeting in 2006, citing the 475,000 shares of Coca-Cola held by the church and expressing deep concern over Coke's anti-union activities.

So what might I drink instead of Coke to satisfy my desire for a cool, fizzy, caffeinated drink with my lunch? Many local soft drink companies produce alternatives. Among them are Jones soda, Avery Sodas, Moxie, Cheerwine, Minnesoda, Foxon Park, and Seymour Beverages.

Generating a cultural shift toward prioritizing human and ecological well-being over maximizing profit entails reshaping what people expect of business, being willing to pay more for some products, and re-forming habits. One could avoid foods manufactured by corporate food villains such as Kraft, the company behind "Back to Nature" breakfast foods and the Ritz crackers, Oreo cookies, canned fruit, and Capri-Sun drinks found in countless lunch bags. Transnational food processors such as Kraft, Procter & Gamble, and Nestlé exemplify the concentration of power into *the hands of a few who then exert tremendous influence over food and agriculture policies to the detriment of small farmers, small suppliers, overseas workers, consumers, and the environment. In 2003 the California legislation considered a bill that would establish nutrition standards on foods sold outside the school lunch program, including vending machines. Eighty organizations supported the bill, including the California Teacher's Association and the American Academy of Pediatrics. Staunchly opposed was the Grocery Manufacturer's Association (GMA), whose 120 members, including Kraft, PepsiCo, and Mars, make over $680 billion in U.S. sales each year. Through a series of scare tactics and the manipulation of a "front" lobbying group, the bill was defeated.[70]*

People around the globe are awakening to the harsh effects of corporate profit maximization and are seeking alternatives through conscientious shopping and boycotts, shareholder action, education, protest, legislative advocacy, and more. In each case, the change begins with recognizing what is going on—critical vision.

****

ECONOMIC DEMOCRACY:
DISTRIBUTED AND ACCOUNTABLE ECONOMIC POWER

Corporations have been enthroned. . . . An era of corruption in high places will follow and the money power will endeavor to prolong its reign . . . until wealth is aggregated in a few hands . . . and the Republic is destroyed.

Abraham Lincoln[71]

♦

You can have wealth concentrated in the hands of a few, or democracy. But you cannot have both.

Louis Brandeis[72]

♦

[Americans] must forswear that conception of the acquisition of wealth which, through excessive profits, creates undue private power.

Franklin D. Roosevelt

The word "democracy" bears myriad, shifting, and often unexamined connotations. To use it meaningfully calls for sifting through its varied undertones. We do so here, before examining the principle of economic democracy.

****

EXCURSUS

DEMOCRACY: A CLOSER LOOK AT MEANING

In modernity, democracy "has been variously construed as a distinctive set of political institutions and practices, a particular body of rights, a social and economic order . . . or a unique process of making collective and binding decisions."[73] *Democracy may refer to an ideal or to an actuality, and misleads when the former is mistaken for the latter. The connotations of the term have developed over more than two millennia in diverse contexts, and stem from varied sources. "Greek, Roman, medieval, and Renaissance notions intermingle with those of later centuries to produce a jumble of theory and practices that are often deeply inconsistent."*[74]

In addition to arguably valid uses, "democracy" has been misused to justify military intervention, revolution, and dictatorship. The term has been distorted to connote free markets, capitalism, anything but communism, and development. It is a handy rhetorical tool for buying public approval in electoral campaigns.

Democracy often is reduced to the right to vote; if the right to vote (together with the formal freedoms of speech, press, and religion) exists, then democracy is present, and a political system is morally approved. However, the vote, while crucial to democracy, is not sufficient. Choosing between options that one has little power to establish does not necessarily imply voice and power in decisions shaping the common life. Feminist theorists have explored ways in which women have gained the right to vote without gaining equal political influence.[75] *Furthermore, democracy as the right to vote is a moot point when the right food, water, and other necessities are denied.*

With these complexities identified, we turn to a working understanding of democracy for the contemporary context of unprecedented corporate and financial power. "Democracy," joining the Greek demos *(the people) with* kratia *(rule, power, authority), implies rule by the many rather than by the few. Democracy exists where people have power—in terms of resources and institutions—to participate with relative equality and liberty in governance.*

Democracy, then, implies that political power is exercised by or accountable *to those who must live with the consequences of its exercise, and in which political power is* distributed with relative equity. *Because economic power converts to political power, where democracy is valued, publicly unaccountable or concentrated economic power is suspect. That is, democracy implies that the norms of accountability and equitable distribution apply also to economic power. Democracy, then, is relative, and the more accountability and equity in economic and political power that pertains among different social sectors, the more democratic the situation. To the extent that significant decisions about the shape of current and future life are removed from public deliberation and influence into the realm of an elite few to which the public has no significant access, democracy is undermined.*

This concept of democracy makes a claim regarding economic power in the current context, in which many corporations represent larger economies than do many nations. The claim is this: The democratic nature of a society is compromised if economic power is exempt from the norms of democracy, or if the right to economic freedom is upheld uncritically where it generates extreme economic inequality.[76]

This claim is situated in four historical debates. They expose contradictions between democracy and property rights, between democratic theory and neoclassical economic theory, between classical democratic theory and classical liberal theory,[77] and between democracy and capitalism.[78] We consider here the first two of them.

Exploring the historical conflict in the United States between democracy and property rights, Robert Dahl argues that, "From the beginning of our nation's existence, and indeed earlier, the question of the relative priority of democracy and property has received two fundamentally conflicting answers. . . . On the one side, supporters of property held that political equality must finally yield to property rights. . . . Those who supported the goal of democracy insisted, on the contrary, that a person's right to self government, and thus to political equality, was more fundamental than the right to property."[79] He suggests that modern democracy has done relatively well in terms of political liberty, yet not so in terms of political equality, a shortfall attributable in part to the ideology of economic freedom.[80]

Dahl also summarizes the conflict between democratic theory and neoclassical economic theory. Democratic theory and neoclassical economic theory have opposing accounts of the human, of freedom, and of power, he explains. Democratic theory sees the human as citizen, whereas in neoclassical economic theory, the human is primarily homo economicus *(a rational consumer, basing decisions singularly on maximizing gain). Democratic theory considers freedom as the freedom of "citizens entitled to participate as political equals in making the laws and rules under which they will live together."*[81] *Freedom, in neoclassical economic theory is, above all, the freedom of choice in the marketplace.*

From related angles, these contradictions suggest that where democracy is valued, unrestrained economic freedom is suspect. Economic freedom from political accountability and regulation and for unconstrained wealth concentration works against the democratic norms of accountable and distributed power. This emerging account of democracy harkens back to concepts of democracy obscured by the ideological fusion of democracy with capitalism and liberalism. Reclaiming and adapting this account of democracy, in the current context, challenges economic arrangements in which a few control the resources necessary for survival and well-being. In sum, where economic power is concentrated in the hands of a few, democracy is subverted.[82] *Where democracy is strong, unaccountable economic power is subverted.*

****

This glimpse at the meaning of "democracy" illumines its relevance for an emerging vision of a moral economy. The point is *not* that all corporations do wrong or that they do no good. Neither is true. The point is that no entities should be granted the legal sanction and tools to exercise such far-reaching and life-determining power for structural violence, while remaining publicly unaccountable.

Sin, as discussed above and in chapter 3, lures people to serve self-interest even at great expense to others. Where economic power becomes concentrated in a few hands, unaccountable to larger communities, so too does the capacity of those holding that power to serve self-interest regardless of the consequences to others or the Earth. (This holds true whether the economic system is state socialism or capitalism as we have known them. Both have concentrated economic power in unaccountable institutions.) Concentrated unaccountable economic power threatens the common good. The economic crisis culminating in 2009 is a prime example. Economic power was amassed in the hands of a very few: the high-level management of enormous finance and banking corporations.

A sequence of historic developments has rendered economic power in the United States progressively more exempt from democratic accountability. They began with the aforementioned 1886 Supreme Court decision that corporations are legally persons and have the legal rights of persons. The ruling enables corporations to strike down regulatory attempts by cities and states, by claiming that those regulations are violations of the corporation's human rights. Most recently the corporate front group Citizens United won a lawsuit against campaign finance laws, dismantling campaign finance regulation at the federal level. This "freed" corporations for unlimited spending to influence elections. Corporate personhood shifts the balance in power from the (real) people through their governments to economic entities bent on profit that may in fact damage "the people," their businesses, and their environments.

The second development was the gradual uprooting of corporations and financial institutions in the United States in the twentieth century. This entailed a shift from local operations to regional, then national, then international, and finally transnational operations. Links of accountability to local communities were severed. New Deal legislation, intended to keep banks servicing and accountable to their own communities, was defeated in this shift.

Next was the gradual wearing down of state charter restrictions and federal regulations regarding corporate operations. Eroded too was the enforcement of those restrictions, standards, and regulations. Corporations exist only as chartered by states. Centuries ago, state charters contained substantial restrictions aimed in part at holding the corporation accountable to the public good. Corporations throughout the decades have whittled away at these until little remains and what does is largely ineffective. Because state and federal political figures are often financially beholden to corporations, they are reluctant to sanction them.

Fourth was the progressive deregulation and "reregulation"[83] of banking and other financial services, largely achieved by the 1980s, either by law or by creative corporate arrangements such as holding companies and mergers. The result was financial services institutions operating not only across geographic boundaries, but also across service and institutional boundaries. One company, operating around the globe, could provide multiple financial services. Undone here was New Deal legislation intended to prevent the domination of financial markets by single institutions, and to prevent commercial banks from risking investors' money in the stock market. In a word, a constellation of legislation "freed" finance markets, including banking, from accountability for anything other than maximizing profits. As noted in chapter 2, this development, referred to as "financialization," is a central feature of neoliberal economic globalization.[84]

A Canadian documentary film, *The Corporation*, argues that the large business corporation, assessed as a "person" (that legally it is), behaves like a psychopath. "To assess the 'personality' of the corporate 'person,' a checklist was employed, using diagnostic criteria of the World Health Organization. . . . The operational principles of the corporation give it a highly anti-social 'personality': it is self-interested, inherently amoral, callous and deceitful; it breaches social and legal standards to get its way; it does not suffer from guilt, yet it can mimic the human qualities of empathy, caring and altruism."[85] The study delivered a disturbing diagnosis: the institutional embodiment of laissez-faire capitalism fully meets the diagnostic criteria of a "psychopath."

The problem of concentrated corporate power explodes with significance in the context of the neoliberal global economy. One of its defining features is the accumulation of wealth in the hands of a minute and publicly unaccountable portion of the world's people. They are the high-level management of large multinational business corporations. Three decades of highly effective corporate-driven effort to deregulate have shifted power from local, state, and national governments to corporations. Power to make decisions regarding water, food, forests, mineral resources, food-producing lands, and more is increasingly in the hands of a few people who are accountable to no one except corporate shareholders. That is, they are accountable only to the people who stand to gain if the decisions prioritize profit over all else. Yet, their decisions determine life or death for many people. This process subordinates *demo-cracy* (rule by the people) to "rule by the corporation."

Neighbor-love, taken seriously as the norm for human relations, is suspicious of movements toward concentrated unaccountable economic power. Neighbor-love favors policies and practices that guard against unchecked concentration of economic power.

But does limiting economic power "fit" in a democratic nation? The question calls for a look at the development of democracy in the United States. The Constitution sought to provide *kratia* (rule, power, authority) of the *demos* (people)—*democratia*—in the political realm. The motivating concern was to prevent tyrannical power from dominating the people. The Constitution guards against concentrated political power through the right to vote, the right of impeachment, a tripartite governmental structure, and the Bill of Rights. These protections were designed in a context in which the threat of tyrannical political power loomed in the public consciousness.

In the world of corporate- and-finance-driven global capitalism, not only political power looms tyrannical. So too does economic power. Arguably, therefore, the protection against concentration of *political* power ought to extend to *economic* power. Classical liberalism, to the contrary, has limited democracy to the political sphere, understood as the legal and administrative functions of the state. Classical liberalism assumed that where market forces did not serve the common good, they would be constrained by political forces. Limiting the scope of democratic accountability to exclude the economic sphere, however, has left its power for domination and exploitation insufficiently checked. Systems have been set up to accentuate the rights of the corporate power over the rights of *demos* power (governance).[86] Political democracy without economic democracy is limited by its vulnerability to the sway of economic power. This subordination of governance to powerful economic players, by definition, flies in the face of democracy. The remedy, asserts a growing body of people in the United States and elsewhere, is to *extend the principle of "rule by the people" to the economic realm.*

The idea smacks of impossibility. Enter here the crucial nature of "critical vision," and especially seeing "what could be." To believe that alternatives are possible, we must envision them. The most fruitful source of this vision is the strong efforts underway—some longstanding—to challenge economic power's concentration and to work toward more distributed and accountable economic power. These efforts go largely beneath the radar screen of public discourse in the United States, but they are robust both here and worldwide. They comprise movement toward "democratizing the economy."

DEMOCRATIZING ECONOMIC LIFE

As used herein, "economic democracy" is the term most suitable to the theological norm of shared power in the economic realm. "Economic democracy" has various referents. Often it is used in a more specific sense than I use it here. In that more narrower it refers to one or more theories of economy structured around social ownership of productive resources and banks rather than around private ownership. (Social ownership might be by workers, communities, regions, states, provinces, or nations.)

I use the term more broadly to signify diverse forms of relatively distributed and publicly accountable economic power at both micro and macro levels.[87] In either the more specific or the more general sense, "economic democracy" contrasts with the power-centralizing dynamics inherent in both capitalism and state-centered socialism. Economic democracy would preclude the recent power plays that enabled a few economic players to manipulate the global economy for their own benefit while devastating millions of people.

The term "economic democracy" refers less to an endpoint than to a process of piece-by-piece conversion from centralized economic power to more shared and publicly accountable economic institutions and practices, and the values and public policies that support them. In different terms, economic democracy describes situations in which people and communities have a role in the economic decisions that shape their lives. A variety of undertakings move toward economic democracy. They include:

- popular movements and projects to build more democratic economic alternatives from the ground up;
- public policy change toward economic democracy;
- legal and constitutional changes in the rights of the corporation; and
- changes in values, especially regarding the purpose and role of economic activity.

Popular movements and projects to build economic alternatives include consumer cooperatives, worker-owned or -managed businesses, producer-consumer co-ops, publicly accountable local or regional banks, fair trade, community-supported small-scale farms, publicly owned energy companies, community-based land trusts, and more. They serve as experimental workshops and leaven for a more just economy. The "Local Living Economies" network demonstrates the creativity and potential in this grassroots movement. The consistent factor is some form of business governance and ownership that involves a broader spectrum of stakeholders, rather than a small group of corporate executives and major shareholders.

A prominent example of wide-reaching *public policy change toward economic democracy* is the movement to curtail "free trade agreements" such as NAFTA, FTAA, and CAFTA.[88] Another example is popular protest against Memorandums of Agreement or Memorandums of Understanding between governments and global corporations. These are agreements giving the latter the right to the lands, seed supplies, and other resources of impoverished people in host countries.

Legal and constitutional changes in the rights of the limited-liability corporation are a third piece in the puzzle of the emerging impulse toward economic democracy. Earlier we noted four features of corporate structure that enable profit maximization over all other concerns. These features also grant the corporation freedom from accountability to the broader society. These factors are joined by another—the corporate lobby—that consolidates corporate power over democratic governance at local, state, or national levels.[89]

Legal and constitutional changes to strengthen democracy relative to the corporation include:

- rescinding corporate personhood and the rights of the person that accompany it.
- mandating accountability for social and ecological bottom line as well as financial bottom line.
- limiting corporate campaign funding and corporate lobbying.[90]
- rescinding the legal requirement that the corporation pursue its self-interest and maximum profit for shareholders above all other concerns.[91]

Efforts are underway in all of these directions.[92] These moves would radically alter who has the power to make many of society's life-shaping decisions, including decisions influencing whether or not people will lose homes and jobs, and who has access to water and food. In a democracy, such things must not be determined by a few very wealthy people who will not experience the long-term consequences of their decisions.

"Economic democracy" has a rich history "extending back to the cooperative and guild socialist movements of the nineteenth and early twentieth century" in Europe.[93] In the United States, the impetus toward more democratic forms of economy has a solid history in Christian ethics from its inception as a discipline in the early twentieth century. Various voices in the Social Gospel espoused democratization of the economy in different forms. All were rooted in the conviction that unfettered capitalism—because of its inevitable inequality and exploitation—is contrary to the way of Jesus and the reign of God. By mid-twentieth century, Christian theological and ethical appeals to democratization of economic life waned, only to appear again in German political theology, Latin American liberation theology, and many subsequent forms of liberation theology.

The future of economic democracy is "yet to be written."[94] That future will take forms distinct from its historical precedents, and holds possibilities heretofore nonexistent precisely because the context is unprecedented. Never before has this set of conditions pertained: (1) Earth's limits require limits to growth; (2) humankind has the technological and material resources to end abject poverty; (3) economic wealth and power are so keenly concentrated; and

4) a worldwide multifaceted movement against concentrated economic power exists.

This principle is not illustrated as were the first three, because chapter 10 in its entirety illustrates this principle.

NEIGHBOR-LOVE RECONSTRUCTS ECONOMIC LIFE IN SUM

Neighbor-love makes demands on economic life because economic practices and policies profoundly impact the well-being of neighbors around the globe. Where that impact is damaging, especially on a large scale, we are called to change it. This change requires a vision of "what could be," the vision of a moral economy. We have considered such a vision by viewing its four constituent principles. Economic life will:

- operate within Earth's economy (ecologically sustainable);
- heed environmental space and ecological debt (environmentally equitable);
- prioritize meeting human needs and Earth's needs over maximizing profit and accumulating wealth (economically equitable);
- challenge concentrated economic power and seek distributed and accountable economic power (democratic).

Economic life guided by the norm of neighbor-love would bear these four features. Together they challenge lynchpins of economic life as we know it—the right to accumulate as much as possible within legal constraints, the value of doing so, and the right to do what I wish with what I own. The "I" here is both the individual and the corporation.

In concert, these four principles for a moral economy change the assumed purpose of an economy. According to classical economic theory (the philosophy originally undergirding capitalism) the purpose of the economy was to maximize the production of goods and services. In advanced global capitalism, arguably the purpose is to maximize wealth accumulation, under the claim that the wealth generated will trickle down. The economy for a sustainable and more just society will have a different purpose. It is the threefold agenda of production, relatively equitable distribution of goods and their costs, and ecological regenerativity.[95]

Love as an Economic-Ecological Vocation

We, the world's high consumers, will embody neighbor-love in the world to the extent that we understand it as an economic-ecological vocation, as well as an interpersonal one. This chapter sketched three initial components of such an ethic of neighbor-love:

- A moral anthropology: What love is depends upon who we are.
- The scope of neighbor-love: Neighbor-love extends beyond the human.
- Four principles of love as an ecological-economic vocation.

The four principles comprise what the next chapter will refer to as a vision of a moral economy.

Human beings will not realize these ideals *fully* in human society. However, that is no reason not to structure society and our lives *in these directions* rather than in the direction we now are headed. For years, I taught my students that "moral agency" is the power to move from "the way things are" to "the way things should be." Life has taught me the danger of that maxim. Much of what we strive to realize in society will not be fully realized in our lifetimes. Moral agency, I now teach, is not the power to move *to*, but rather the power to move *toward* a more just, sustainable, and compassionate world. It remains now to sketch a moral framework for doing so. To that we turn in chapter 9.

Notes

1. Michael Northcott, *A Moral Climate: The Ethics of Global Warming* (Maryknoll, NY: Orbis, 2007), 16.

2. The relationship of the individual to the political has been understood variously. Perspectives range from the notion that humans are political by nature (Aristotle), to the political is a divine remedy for sinfulness (Augustine), to society is the realm of individuals' actions upon which political institutions intrude (classical liberalism).

3. In political terminology, the *polis* (which in Aristotle's world was the city-state and in modernity the nation-state) has become the planetary island we call Earth, if not the cosmos itself.

4. As cited in Larry Rasmussen, "Green Discipleship," *Reflections Yale Divinity School* (Spring 2007): 69.

5. Bernard V. Brady, *Christian Love* (Washington, DC: Georgetown University Press, 2003).

6. Christian Smith, *Moral, Believing Animals: Human Personhood and Culture* (New York: Oxford University Press, 2003).

7. For predation/evolutionary theory in an environmental ethic, see Lisa Sideris, *Environmental Ethics, Ecological Theology, and Natural Selection* (New York: Columbia University Press, 2003).

8. Ibid. Sideris values the processes over the products of the natural world.

9. James Gustave Speth, *The Bridge at the End of the World* (New Haven: Yale University Press, 2008), 7.

10. John Maynard Keynes, cited in Willem Hoogendijk, *The Economic Revolution: Toward a Sustainable Future by Freeing the Economy from Money-Making* (Amsterdam: International, 1991), 17.

11. See references to Daly in chapter 4, note 40. Daly is recognized as a seminal thinker in the field of ecological economics, which has emerged as a crucial theoretical and institutional alternative to growth-based economics.

12. Thomas Berry, *The Great Work* (New York: Harmony/Bell Tower, 2000).

13. The Charter was approved by the General Assembly. One hundred eleven nations approved it. One, the United States, voted against.

14. The term "sustainability" bears some problems. It has been co-opted as a marketing tool by many ecologically unsustainable corporations. It may be inadequate; given the extent of ecological damage already done, "regenerativity" may be the more adequate norm. Often used to modify "development," sustainability suggests that development as economic growth can proceed if it meets environmental criteria. However, the usefulness of the term outweighs these problems.

15. IPCC, *Special Report on Renewable Energy Sources and Climate Change Mitigation* (Cambridge: Cambridge University Press, 2011), 3. GHG has two major forms: increases in carbon dioxide, due primarily to fossil fuel use, and increases of methane and nitrous oxide due primarily to agriculture.

16. "Parts per million" is the measure of CO_2 levels in the atmosphere.

17. CO2now.org. Data posted by the National Oceanic and Atmospheric Administration in the United States. The report continues: "For the past decade (2001–2010) the average annual increase is 2.04 ppm per year."

18. Cited by Bill McKibben, in web article posted on 8/31/10.

19. Kenneth Sayre in *Unearthed: The Economic Roots of Our Environmental Crisis* (Notre Dame: University of Notre Dame Press, 2010), 152–55 provides percentages of fuel use that is replaceable by nonfossil fuel.

20. Sayre notes additional reasons for this third measure. One is the ecological problems initiated by clean energy use; ibid., 161–64.

21. Cynthia Moe-Lobeda and Daniel Spencer, "Free Trade Agreements and the Neo-Liberal Economic Paradigm," *Journal of Political Theology* 10, no. 4 (2009): 685–716.

22. For example, a factory would factor into the bottom line the cost of keeping water clean, replacing cropland, maintaining carbon neutrality, and so on.

23. John Cobb and Herman Daly provide an early and excellent blueprint for economies situated within Earth's economy. They base it on their detailed account of the disastrous consequences of growth-oriented economies. See John B. Cobb Jr. and Herman E. Daly, *For the Common Good: Redirecting the Economy Toward Community, the Environment, and a Sustainable Future* (Boston: Beacon, 1989).

24. *National Sustainable Agriculture Information Service website "Reducing Food Miles."*

25. Anna Lappé, *Diet for a Hot Planet: The Climate Crisis at the End of Your Fork and What You Can Do about It* (New York: Bloomsbury, 2010), 220.

26. Ibid., n32.

27. Ibid., n82.

28. Municipal Solid Waste Generation, Recycling, and Disposal in the United States: Facts and Figures for 2005.

29. *The Corporation*, documentary film, interview with Ray Anderson, 10.53.50.

30. See http://www.interfaceglobal.com/Sustainability/Our-Progress/Waste.aspx.

31. "CSR and the Triple Bottom Line," http://www.zipcon.net/~laura/laws.htm.

32. Ibid.

33. For concise accounts of "ecological debt" and "environmental space," see Karen Mickelson, "Leading toward a Level Playing Field, Repaying Ecological Debt, or Making Environmental Space," *Osgoode Hall Law Journal* 43, no. 1/2 (2005): 138–70; and Duncan McLaren, "Environmental Space, Equity and the Ecological Debt," in Julian Agyeman, Robert Bullard, and Bob Evans, eds., *Just Sustainabilities: Development in an Unequal World* (Cambridge, MA: MIT Press, 2003), 19–37.

34. Press release from the University of California: "Rich Nations' Environmental Footprint Falls on Poor," January 22, 2008.

35. U. Thara Srinivasan et al., "The debt of nations and the distribution of ecological impacts from human activities," *Proceedings of the National Academy of Science* 105, no. 5 (February 5, 2008): 1763–73.

36. UC Press Release (see n50).

37. The concept of "ecological debt" entered the international discourse with the 1992 United Nations Conference at Rio de Janeiro, where it was introduced by Latin American NGOs. For more on "ecological debt, see websites of: Southern People's Ecological Debt Creditor Alliance (SPEDCA), European Network for the Recognition of Ecological Debt (ENRED), Ecuador's *Acción Ecológica*, England's Christian Aid, Friends of the Earth International, and WCC. See also Athena K. Peralta, ed., *Ecological Debt: The Peoples of the South Are Creditors: Cases from Ecuador, Mozambique, Brazil and India* (Quezon City, Philippines: WCC, 2004); WCC Central Committee, "Statement on ecological justice and ecological debt," 2009; Andrew Simms, *Ecological Debt: The Health of the Planet and the Wealth of Nations* (London: Pluto Press, 2005); and ecologicaldebt.org.

38. Three such organizations are SPEDCA, ENRED, and *Acción Ecológica*.

39. LWF and WCC delegations to COP16 in Cancun, "Why Are the Churches at the UN Conference on Climate Change in Cancun?," December 13, 2010. COP refers to Conference of Parties (nations) signing the UN Framework Convention on Climate Change (UNFCCC).

40. UNFCCC, Article 3.1.

41. Tom Athanasiou, Paul Baer, Sivan Kartha, and Eric Kemp-Benedict, "The Greenhouse Development Rights Framework: The Right to Development in a Climate-Constrained World" (Christian Aid, the Heinrich Böll Foundation, EcoEquity, and the Stockholm Environment, 2008), 6.

42. Obvious complexities include the difficulty of quantifying ecological debt.

43. The term "environmental space" comes from the Dutch *milieugebruiks—ruimte* (literally *environmental utilization space*)." Julian Agyeman, "Fair Shares in Environmental Space?" in *Just Sustainabilities*.

44. Friends of the Earth International website.

45. *Sustainable Netherlands Action Plan*.

46. See Carol Robb, *Wind, Sun, Soil, and Spirit: Biblical Ethics and Climate Change* (Minneapolis: Fortress Press, 2010), 28–43, for excellent discussion of theories of justice and equity vis-à-vis greenhouse gas emissions, in particular the conflicts between the Global South and Global North about equitable distribution.

47. T. Buhrs, "Sharing Environmental Space: The Role of Law, Economics, and Politics," *Journal of Environmental Planning and Management* 47, no. 3 (May 2004): 429–47.

48. The tool was developed in a doctoral dissertation at the University of British Columbia in the early 1990s and published subsequently in Mathis Wackernagel and William E. Rees, *Our Ecological Footprint: Reducing Human Impact on the Earth* (Gabriola Island, BC: New Society, 1996).

49. Developments in accounting methods are described in World Wildlife Fund's *The Living Planet Report* and the Global Footprint Network's annual "National Accounts."

50. Sarah Mukherjee, "Village Aims to Kick Carbon Habit," *BBC News*, July 15, 2009.

51. Barbara Pinto, "Inside the First Wind-Powered City in America," *ABC World News, Technology*, May 19, 2008.

52. www.seattle.gov/transportation/transit

53. Bridget Bentz Sizer, "How to Shrink Your Ecological Footprint," *Washington Post*, March 12, 2006.

54. Frederica Helmiere, in conversation.

55. From a statement issued by Bishop Marc, Diocese of California in December 2010.

56. A number of studies had found that the hormone increased risks of cancer in humans and had harmful effects on cows.

57. Richard Grossman and Community Environmental Legal Defense Fund, *The Daniel Penncock Democracy School Curriculum* (Chambersburg, PA: CELDF, 2009), 243–45.

58. Joel Bakan, *The Corporation: The Pathological Pursuit of Profit and Power* (New York: Free Press, 2004), 36–37.

59. Dr. Janis Sarra in an interview with Joel Baken, cited by him, ibid., 176–77. She goes on to say, "The way in which corporate law is currently structured requires directors and officers to justify any socially responsible actions under the guise of, or the aim of, either short-term or long-term shareholder wealth maximization."

60. William Greider, *The Soul of Capitalism* (New York: Simon & Schuster, 2003), 39.

61. Jeff Crosby, President of IUE Local 201 in Lynn, MA, in "Our Developing World's Voices" 6, no. 1 (Winter 2000): 1, 4.

62. For impact of U.S.-based corporations and economic policy on Jamaica: *Life and Debt*, film produced by Stephanie Black, 2001.

63. Thomas Prince, "Consumer Sovereignty, Heroic Sacrifice," in *The Environmental Politics of Sacrifice*, Michael Maniates and John M. Meyer, eds. (Cambridge, MA: MIT Press, 2010), 151.

64. Michael Taylor, "Christianity, Poverty, and Wealth: The Findings, 'Project 21'" (Geneva: WCC, 2003), 1, cited in WCC, *AGAPE.*

65. "Kaippuneeru" (The Bitter Drink), film by Third Eye Communications, directed by P. Baburaj and C. Saratchandran, 2003.

66. http://www.killercoke.org/crimes_india.php.

67. http://www.killercoke.org/crimes_india.php.

68. Green America's *Responsible Shopper* page," Coca-Cola." http://www.greenamerica.org/programs/responsibleshopper/company.cfm?id=204.

69. AP news, "University of Michigan Suspends Coca-Cola Sales," January 2, 2006. Cited by *CorpWatch: Holding Corporations Accountable.*

70. Michele Simon, "Can Food Companies Be Trusted to Self-Regulate: An Analysis of Corporate Lobbying and Deception to Undermine Children's Health," *Loyola Law Review* 39, no 1 (2006): 169.

71. Cited in Harvey Wasserman, *America Born and Reborn* (New York: Collier, 1983), 89–90.

72. Cited in Chuck Collins and Felice Yeskel, *Economic Apartheid in America: A Primer on Economic Inequality and Insecurity* (New York: New Press, 2000), 13.

73. Robert Dahl, *Democracy and Its Critics* (New Haven: Yale University Press, 1989), 5.

74. Ibid., 2.

75. See, for example, Anne Phillips, "Public Spaces, Private Lives," ch. in *Engendering Democracy* (University Park: Pennsylvania State University Press, 1991), 92–119, and Carol Pateman, *Participation and Democratic Theory* (Cambridge and Melbourne: Cambridge University Press, 1970).

76. Many feminist and radical democratic theorists also make this point. See, for example, Pateman; Phillips; Dahl; Ellen Meiksins Wood, *Democracy against Capitalism: Renewing Historical Materialism* (Cambridge: Cambridge University Press, 1995); Harry Ward, *Democracy and Social Change* (New York: Modern Age, 1940); and Samuel Bowles and Herbert Gintis, "The Economy Produces People," in *Religion and Economic Justice*, ed. Michael Zweig (Philadelphia: Temple University Press, 1991).

77. Western liberal societies tend to conflate democratic theory with liberal theory despite their fundamental distinctions. In their early modern forms, liberal theory and democratic theory were opposed in this sense: Locke's theory of liberalism held that humanity's original state of nature included the natural rights to life, liberty, and property. In contrast, Rousseau, founder of modern democratic theory, held that in humanity's original state there was no private property, and that only in staking out private property did humans develop inequality, domination, and the need for politically organized community. Liberal theory defended the natural right to private property while democratic theory saw it as source of inequality and domination requiring the constraint of political community.

78. The theory that capitalism and democracy are antagonistic: The capitalist norm of wealth concentration works against the democratic norm of relatively equal political power, and the capitalist principle of excluding economic power from democratic accountability works against the democratic norm of accountable power. This argument is articulated by Harry Ward, and by Eileen Meiksins Wood. She argues that the notion of capitalist democracy that developed in the United States gave formal political powers (eventually) to all, but retained the power of control through capital in the hands of the propertied elite. Thus, formal democracy could coexist with power inequality intact.

79. Dahl, *Democracy*, 65–66.

80. Ibid., 52–83.

81. The quotations in this paragraph are from Dahl, *Democracy*, 324–26.

82. Wood, in *Democracy against Capitalism*, contends that defendants of the capitalism-democracy inseparability argue the opposite. "The characteristic way that capitalist democracy deals with [the economic] sphere of power is not to check it but to liberate it . . . in fact not recognizing it as a sphere of power . . . at all. This is, of course, especially true of the market, which is . . . conceived of as a sphere of freedom" (234). See Rose and Milton Friedman, *The Right to Choose* (New York: Avon, 1979), xvii. They state that, "The free market provides an offset to whatever concentration of political power may arise." See also Milton Friedman, *Capitalism and Freedom* (Chicago: University of Chicago Press, 1962), 16. Occupied with the threat of concentrated state power, this argument ignores the threat of concentrated economic power.

83. Tayyab Mahmud, "Is It Greek or Deja Vu All Over Again? Neoliberalism and Winners and Losers of International Debt Crises," *Loyola University of Chicago Law Journal* 42, no. 4 (2011): 668–83.

84. See Supplement to chapter 2 on the book's webpage.

85. www.thecorporation.com.

86. These include the aforementioned corporate rights of the person and limited liability, as well as clauses in "free trade" agreements that give corporations the right to sue governments directly, free trade zones in which many labor and environmental protections are suspended, and use of the United States Constitution's Contracts and Commerce clauses to give preferential rights to corporations over rights of municipalities.

87. See Allen L. White, "Transforming the Corporation," GTI Paper Series 1: *Frontiers of a Great Transition*" (Boston: Tellus Institute, 2006), 16–20, for an example of three quite diverse forms of economy all characterized as "economic democracy."

88. North American Free Trade Agreement, Free Trade Area of the Americas, and Central America Free Trade Agreement.

89. Another enhancer of corporate power over local government is the section of the commerce clause in the constitution that enables corporations to encourage state and federal governments to preempt municipalities that pass laws limiting corporate exploitation of their people and land.

90. Based on data from the Senate Office of Public Records, the Center for Responsive Politics reports that $3.5 billion was spent in corporate lobbying in 2010. The top spenders were the U.S. Chamber of Commerce and General Electric. William Dumhoff argues that "[t]he corporate community's ability to transform its economic power into policy influence and political

access, along with its capacity to enter into coalition with middle-class social and religious conservatives, makes it the most important influence in the federal government." William Dumhoff, *Who Rules America: Power, Politics, and Social Change*, 5th ed. (New York: McGraw-Hill, 2006), xiii.

91. At least seven states have passed laws creating an alternative corporate structure that enables a company to include social and environmental efforts in its mission along with profit.

92. See chapter 10.

93. Gary J. Dorrien, *Economy, Difference, Empire: Social Ethics for Social Justice* (New York: Columbia University Press, 2010), 168.

94. Dorrien, *Economy*, 142.

95. Rasmussen, "Green Discipleship."

9

Love's Moral Framework

"Where there is no vision, the people perish."

Proverbs 29:18

♦

"While it is true that without vision the people perish, it is doubly true that without action the people and their vision perish as well."

Johnnetta Cole[1]

If we, the world's overconsumers:

- acknowledge that advanced global capitalism cannot go on as it has (because Earth cannot sustain it) and that the direction of the change will be determined in part by human decisions;
- recognize that our ways of life endanger Earth's regenerative capacities;
- admit that millions of people the world over suffer as a result of how we live;
- in some part of our souls, hunger to love neighbor, self, Earth, and God; and
- cling to hope despite evidence to the contrary . . .

. . . then we will move toward reshaping our society along the lines of ecological sustainability, environmental equity, economic equity, and distributed power. These are the terms of an ethic of neighbor-love as an ecological-economic calling. They transgress the logic of advanced global capitalism and call us to set our intelligence, our creativity, and our life-force against bondage to its sugar-coated mandates.

The maddening questions loom: What does this commitment imply for what we are to *do*? What are the practical implications of this realignment?

What would it look like to defy the logic of neoliberal globalization, and forge life-serving alternatives to it?

Valid responses are diverse, multilayered, and constantly emerging. The challenge is to navigate this complexity with creativity and tenacity. How do we swim into these waters while attending to the demands of everyday life and relishing its joys? These questions lie before us in this chapter and the next.

A Framework Introduced

To call for a radical change at individual and societal levels borders on the absurd if not accompanied by some kind of framework for unraveling what that conversion entails and some practical illustrations of it. Here I propose such a framework. The final chapter illustrates how it might play out. It may be seen as a framework for expressing neighbor-love as an ecological-economic vocation, or as a framework for translating neighbor-love into secular terms and public life. It also is a framework for confronting "hidden" structural violence or structural evil.

A basic theme of this book arrives here: Central to moral agency in the face of social structures that appear insurmountable is the recognition that they were constructed by human beings and therefore can be changed by them. The neoliberal global economy—including its manifestation in national economies—was constructed by people. It can therefore be replaced. This form of economy was put into place by overturning certain public policies and establishing others. Milton Friedman, one of the chief and early architects of what was to become neoliberalism, declared precisely that point: "[A]ctions that are taken depend upon the ideas that are lying around. That, I believe, is our basic function: to develop alternatives to existing policies, to keep them alive and available until the politically impossible becomes politically inevitable."[2] With this conviction, he helped destroy much public policy that had been established in the New Deal to restrain the greed of powerful people seeking to concentrate wealth in a few hands. This conviction—that ideas expressed in public policies can accomplish the apparently impossible—helped to build today's neoliberal global economy. In like manner, this conviction can help to reverse it and build more just alternatives to it.

However, the path from longing for social change to achieving it seems to travel through a thick and swirling fog. The complexity and vastness of the possibilities are confounding. Daunting obstacles jut across the path, as does awareness that the changes necessary are far beyond whatever "I" can do on my own. That fog needs illumination, a lantern to reveal pathways. A theoretical framework—in this case a moral framework—serves as one such lantern. Its elements are tools for making sense of apparently impenetrable complexity.

My intention is to sketch key components of a moral framework for reorienting our economy and our lives around the principles of ecological sustainability, environmental equity, economic equity, and distributed power. The proposed framework is not comprehensive. Rather it develops a few crucial components that often receive inadequate attention in ethical analysis, but that are essential to morality in the face of systemic evil. The point is to take the seemingly impossible and render it possible by opening it up to see its various parts and how they are at work bringing what may appear impossible into being. The framework pulls together ideas and methods developed earlier in the volume, and adds to them.

Imagine the elements of a framework for morality in the face of systemic evil as an initial and roughly hewn map charting a course into a more equitable and sustainable world. Readers traveling this course have passed through the first two stations on their journey, identified in chapter 8 as components of an ethic of neighbor-love. They are a moral anthropology (an understanding of who and what the human as a moral being is) and the scope of neighbor-love.[3]

Our trekkers will move along two intersecting streams, "resistance and rebuilding." The travelers begin with traditional sources of moral knowing, and soon add another. The path leads them through arenas of life in which change takes place. Next, it ascends through successive levels, moving from a moral vision of the future to the practices that realize it. The trail concludes with moral formation.

These, then, are key components of a moral framework for forging more equitable, sustainable, and democratic economic structures and practices:

- A radically reoriented moral anthropology
- A scope of neighbor-love that extends beyond the human
- Complementary streams of change: resistance and rebuilding
- Sources of moral knowing
- Agents of change and arenas of life in which change takes place
- A path from vision to practice:
  - Vision of a moral economy
  - Principles of the vision
  - Goals for moving toward those principles
  - Policies for realizing those goals
  - Practices that flow from and contribute to those policies
- Moral formation (including practices of worship)

These components do not function in a linear fashion. The travelers wind through them moving back and forward, understanding each in light of the others. The remainder of this chapter fleshes out these elements, while the subsequent chapter illustrates the most concrete of them—practice and policies.

Two Streams: Resistance and Rebuilding

Resistance and rebuilding are two independent streams (or arms) of action for social change. Gandhi knew these two streams as "two strings [in the] nonviolent bow" of *satyagraha*.[4] They were:

- *noncooperation with evil*—the refusal to obey pass laws, travel restrictions, and other unjust measures (sometimes the word *satyagraha* is used to refer only to this string); and
- *cooperation with good* in forms such as education and political empowerment in Indian communities, community living, locality-based farming, simplicity, the elimination of untouchability, boycotting foreign cloth, uplifting women, and more.[5] All were located within the principle of *svadeshi* or localism.

Resistance and rebuilding are two sides of the same coin. One alone cannot begin to free us from our bondage to economic and ecological violence. "Resistance" means refusing to participate in some aspects of an economic system that is fast destroying earth's atmosphere and countless livelihoods, communities, and lives. "Rebuilding" signifies supporting more socially just and ecologically healthy alternatives that are accountable to a "triple bottom line" (social, ecological, and financial). Many of these alternatives will be small-scale regional business and agriculture. "Resisting and rebuilding" are anchored in Christian theology as *denouncing* that which thwarts the in-breaking reign of God and *announcing* that which furthers it.

The "stories revisited" spread throughout this book provide many examples of both resistance and rebuilding. Another illustration may be helpful. To withdraw one's money from the megabanks and investment firms that turn money into a commodity aimed at amassing great wealth for a very few people is to resist. To then conduct banking in a community-based bank and invest in a community redevelopment fund is to rebuild.

The reader will quickly note that doing such things will not, alone, change the economic order on a societal scale. Yet, at the same time these actions are crucial. Without ordinary people taking action, the societal changes will not happen; our actions are the seeds of societal change. Chapter 3 introduced this contradiction. It is further elaborated later in the current chapter as the "paradox of practice."

SOURCES OF MORAL KNOWING

Moral agency in the face of systemic evil depends upon people's capacity to imagine and live toward freedom from it. That imagination and movement depends upon what we know. What we know, we draw—consciously and not—from various sources of moral knowing that inform our lives. In Christian ethics the sources traditionally are understood as four: *Scripture, the tradition of the church throughout the ages, experience, and other bodies of human knowledge.*[6] According to the moral consciousness sketched in chapter 8, this configuration of sources is dangerously flawed. As traditionally used, it perpetuates an anthropocentric and winner-centered moral consciousness. Our travelers moving toward a world shaped along the lines of social justice and ecological well-being will need to adjust where and how they gain moral wisdom. Without such change, they may flounder and flail in "the way things are."

Two modifications of this centuries-old set of sources are requisite. Both appeared in chapter 5. They herald an epistemological realignment from modernity's assumptions regarding knowledge.

One modification is to add a fifth source: *other-than-human voices of the Earth.* As noted previously, the Earth crisis casts unfamiliar meaning onto the ethical principle of seeking moral wisdom from the underside of power and privilege. Earth's waters, soil, air, fauna, foliage, and biosphere have joined that underside. Human creatures are invited to learn, from the other-than-human parts of creation that now groan under our weight, wisdom for living in sync with Earth's well-being. Moral knowing informed by Earth is uncharted epistemological terrain. Learning to negotiate it is an intriguing step for the "uncreators" seeking paths to becoming tillers and keepers of God's glorious garden.[7]

The other alteration is to place a modifier on the four traditional sources. We, the uncreators, will seek to "read" scripture, tradition, experience, and other bodies of human knowledge from *standpoints of people who are on the losing side of the global economy and more specifically, people whose lives are damaged or threatened by ours.* We will "learn from people whose different stories reveal [our] participation in" structures of injustice.[8] "Experience" no longer will refer primarily to *my* experience or the experience of people "like me." To learn from experience will mean to learn also from the experiences of people who suffer because of the systems that bring our material excess and who are proposing alternatives. And it will mean to learn from the experience of "the Earth."

The idea of "learning from people on the margins of power and privilege" has become standard in the rhetoric of Christian ethics. *Not* yet standard is acknowledging the enormous obstacles to it and suggesting how to go about such an epistemological revolution. How might we operationalize the epistemological privilege of those who are, in George Zachariah's terms, "uprooted from life"?[9] How am I to learn from people whose lives are threatened by mine when I do not even know who most of them are? How do I "learn from" people without repeating the colonizing assumption that "I" have the right to possess what is theirs, in this case knowledge? These are the questions of economic–ecological literacy raised earlier.

This shift in the grounds of knowledge does not come easily. Pathways for making it are not clear. Therefore, here we explore a few practical steps toward hearing and privileging perspectives of people on the losing end of the economic and ecological violence that buys our wealth. These steps are illustrative, meant to engender awareness of others.

"Mercy," I asked her, "what would you advise U.S. citizens to do to support your struggles for justice?" My companion was Mercy Kappen, a highly accomplished feminist leader in India's people's movements. I had listened to her or her colleague for two days. They talked of their struggles on behalf of children, women, workers, and others. "U.S. citizens," she responded, "who want to support our struggles for justice should get to know us and our social movements."

Her statement was wise. Few things have more power to spawn moral agency than witnessing the courage and fierce tenacity of people's resistance to structural violence. Mercy's suggestion—getting to know people on the underside of the global economy and their social movements toward justice—is a step into the mutuality discussed in chapter 7 as a "feature of love."

How, short of international travel, are we to connect with social movements toward justice in other lands? The best answers will come from the readers. I offer two.

One is to uncover and build on connections that already exist, that may be unknown to us or untapped. Transnational civil society has strengthened greatly in recent decades in the traditional realms of religious, labor, and other activist communities and through web-based connections between social movements. For instance, what if Lutherans in the United States were to listen regularly to Lutherans of the continent to our south? We might hear the "Declaration on the Foreign Debt, Neoliberalism, and Globalization," written by the conference of Bishops, Presidents, and President Pastors of the Latin American Lutheran Churches declaring the "foreign debt of the third world . . . [to be] illegitimate," and calling for its cancelation.[10] Rev. Angel Furlan, one of the declaration's authors, describes its content: "As Lutheran bishops of Latin America, we denounce the economic and financial powers and the transnational companies that have imposed at a global level a model that has only produced poverty and exclusion. In this document we also say that the external debt, one of the tools of this model, has become a weapon that destroys the lives of millions."[11]

Existing connections to social movements for justice may be religious, labor-related, professional, artistic, agricultural, interest-based, ethnic, or other. Recognizing and following up on them may lead to relationships and to learning from those movements. Their perspectives are varied and fallible, as are all human perspectives. But reflective respectful engagement with them will crack open our awareness, strengthen the muscles of critical vision, and plant seeds of moral agency.

Choosing alternative sources of news and information is another related means of learning from people on the underside of our consumer privilege and ecological debt. The way in which we perceive the world depends upon who we stand beside as we see it, and whose interpretation we ingest. Most United States citizens understand what is happening in this country and the world through the voice of United States mainstream media. Our view is as narrow as a crack in the wall. We might, instead or in addition, develop the practice of hearing from alternative news and information sources, as a *regular diet*, not merely an add-on. Our children will know a different world if they are raised assuming that everyday life includes alternative as well as mainstream news sources.

Alternative sources take many forms. Beginning to locate them requires only a thoughtful search on the web. The following list is a sampling, like viewing a few flowers in an expansive and expanding meadow. These examples are selected for their relevance to the vignettes in this volume.

- Websites of networks struggling for rights to food, water, land, homes, fair wages, community, environmental safety, or for Earth's well-being[12]
- Online newspapers or journals from other continents
- Action alerts, news feeds, Facebook pages, or tweets from groups such as the Fair Trade Federation, Ecumenical Advocacy Network, United for a Fair Economy, World Council of Churches, Friends

Committee on National Legislation, Green America, World Social Forum, local or regional advocacy networks, and so on
- Organizations that offer models for economic and financial reform[13]
- Documentaries

Where we turn for moral knowing is a key component of the emerging moral framework. Morality in our context calls for dramatic alterations in the traditional sources of moral knowing. The standard four "sources" in ethical deliberation welcome a fifth; it is other-than-human voices. And people in sites of privilege will begin learning to "read" the standard sources from perspectives of people on the losing side of our privilege.[14] Our travelers, forging a path toward the world we seek, will dare to embrace knowing in these ways.

Four Change Agents and Arenas of Change

A degree of power for resisting what we deplore and rebuilding ethical alternatives emerges simply by recognizing different categories of change agents or "actors." The agents of change may be categorized variously. I find it helpful to view them as:

- individuals and households,
- organizations of civil society,[15]
- corporations and other business and,
- governments and public policy (local, state, national).

The actions of each reinforce the work of the others.

These change agents may seek change in various arenas of society including: individuals and households, organizations of civil society, corporations and other business, and governments/public policy. To illustrate:

- As an individual, I work for change in my own household and in the university where I work, in corporations, and in public policy.
- The Seattle city government works for change in how individual Seattleites live (recycling and composting), in business (environmental regulations and zoning laws), and in federal policy.
- Faith communities work toward change in individuals' lives, in public policy (through advocacy efforts), and in corporate practices (moral persuasion, shareholder action, boycotts).

These arenas of change shape each other, often in unrecognized ways. Change in one arena opens doors to change in the others. In this knowledge, a seed of hope resides; our efforts extend further than we may know. The story of

"Free Trade and Sweat Shops Revisited" demonstrates the interaction. Students against Sweatshops (an organization of civil society as agent) acted for change in all four arenas: in what *individuals* purchase, in how *corporations* treat workers, in universities' (*civil society*) purchasing policies, and in *governmental* policy regarding international trade. Change in any of these arenas made change in the others more viable.

A Path from Vision to Enactment

The next five elements of the moral framework work as a unit. It reveals a path from moral vision to its enactment. It begins with a *moral vision* for economic life and moves progressively through that vision's: *constituent principles*; *goals* for realizing those principles; *public policies* moving toward those goals; and, finally, the most concrete level, *practices* of everyday life that flow from and contribute to these policies and goals.

Vision of a Moral Economy

"Moral vision is the vision of the good we hold . . . it is the socialized (or internalized) reflection of the communities we move among."[16] In general, we assume moral vision unconsciously; we are not necessarily aware of it. It is shaped by the values, norms, and practices of the society and significant groups in which our lives unfold. It is taught by the narratives of history, advertising, cultural "heroes," religious traditions, news media, and social structures assumed to be normal. A moral vision—conscious or not—tells us what is good, right, and true. By "*economic* moral vision," I refer to the vision of what would be good, right, and true for economic life.

Moral vision shapes how people live. An economic moral vision in which people are affirmed or rewarded for accumulating wealth to the extent that they are able within the boundaries of legality, encourages people to do so. If, in contrast, according to the prevailing moral vision, wealth accumulation beyond a certain point was considered morally repugnant, people would be far less likely to pursue it.

Larry Rasmussen and Bruce Birch (discussing not economic moral vision but moral vision in a general sense) note that a changed moral vision affects all elements of the moral life. When what is considered in a particular society to be moral becomes seen as immoral, human behaviors, policies, and institutions change. Institutionalized race-based segregation moved from being considered moral to immoral in the span of a few decades. It was a shift in moral vision resulting in changed behavior, public policies, institutions, and norms for marriage and other human relationships.

As with an overall moral vision, so too with the vision of a moral economy: with a changed economic moral vision come changed behaviors, public policies, institutions, cultural norms, standards of achievement, goals, and more. The film "I Am" includes a brief provocative animation. The character inhabits a world in which it is considered insane to accumulate more than what is needed for a healthy happy life. The animation—only moments long—swept across my mind with the power of the boy who revealed that "the emperor has no clothes." It disclosed our accumulation and consumption-based economic vision as the social construct that it is.[17]

When moral vision changes, what is perceived as *possible* also changes. A few centuries ago in many Western societies the legal equality of women and their legal right to freedom from nonconsensual sex would not have been seen as possible. The moral vision shifted and with it the seemingly impossible became possible.

It is wise to be aware of what economic moral vision is guiding a society, an individual life, a family, or other group. With an economic moral vision come life decisions. My students who understand that their families will be proud of them and consider them "good" people if they make a lot of money, buy a luxurious house, and drive a sophisticated car, tend to make certain choices during their college years. (According to many student accounts, these may not be the choices that they wish to make.) Students who sense that their parents envision for them a life of artistic production or service to society and who might be a bit chagrined by the large house or other conspicuous signs of wealth, tend in other directions. The two sets of students are responding to differing economic moral visions.

An account of a young Cherokee boy growing up in the early twentieth century described the hunting philosophy of the boy's people. As the boy's grandfather explained, they were to hunt only the animals that they needed for food. He was describing a lived economic vision. It contrasted starkly with the prevailing economic vision of his day, and it shaped a way of living.

The advocates of a particular economic moral vision had best be clear about what is at stake in it. For an economy as powerful as that of the United States, moral vision can determine life or death for millions. The economic moral vision suggested herein is of economies in which all people have the necessities required for a healthy life, Earth's life-systems are sustained and regenerated, and none accumulate vast wealth at the cost of impoverishing others or Earth's life-support systems.

DEFINING PRINCIPLES

It is one thing to envision such an economy. It is another thing to move in that direction. A step toward doing so is to identify defining features or principles of this economic vision. We have done so. They are ecological sustainability, environmental equity, economic equity, and democracy where democracy implies relatively distributed and accountable economic power.

As we have seen, these principles cannot be approximated within the current form of global economy, neoliberal capitalism. It would be absurd not to acknowledge the daunting reality that emerges from the contradiction between the proposed economic moral vision and neoliberalism. It is this: The forces and interests lined up to perpetuate the concentration of financial capital and other wealth—and hence of power—in the hands of the most wealthy are monumental and formidable. The recent and, for many people, continuing global economic meltdown is evidence. The raw power of unregulated finance capital motivated to maximize profit regardless of the cost to others cast countless people into misery and managed to remain unaccountable to the "demos" (the body politic). Movement toward distributed accountable power, equity, and ecological sustainability (the principles of a moral economy) directly counters that concentration of power.

No less significant is the fact that courageous people around the globe already have lost their lives in struggles for economic and ecological justice. My point is not that privileged United States citizens are likely to be killed in the quest for a more just and sustainable economic order. Rather, my point is to face the reality of "what is." Some people will go to any length to maintain their power and wealth. Without the sustaining power of community and resources for hope and courage, the challenge might be insurmountable.

One test of a moral vision and its defining principles is whether one can construct practical steps toward realizing them. Those steps include mid-way goals and the policies and practices for reaching those goals.

GOALS TO REALIZE THE PRINCIPLES

A cavernous gap separates these four principles or features of a moral economy from "the way things are." Mid-way goals—in ethics known as "middle axioms"—are a tool for bridging that gap. Said differently, to realize principles of moral economic life, goals along the way help. They provide some sensibilities regarding how to get there. They serve as directives and criteria for whether a particular policy or practice accords with the moral vision. Mid-way goals are more specific than are the four overarching principles, yet not as specific as the actual public policies and practices that move toward reaching the goals.

Goals along the way to a more sustainable, environmentally and economically equitable, and democratic economic order include the following. They pertain to the high-consuming world. I am not proposing goals for the Global South. This account is *illustrative* rather than comprehensive.

- Vastly reduced energy use through energy efficiency and reduced consumption, especially consumption that degrades people or environments.
- Conversion to renewable nonpolluting energy for that portion of current fossil fuel use that can be converted. (This may be expressed as a shift from a carbon-based economy to renewable energy economy.)
- Far higher percentage of businesses being locally owned, accountable to stakeholders, and not "too big to fail."
- Far higher percentage of businesses—including large corporate business—operating with a triple bottom line.
- Primarily (but not exclusively) local and regional food production and consumption loops; prioritizing agriculture for local and regional consumption.
- Primarily small-holder agriculture.
- Agriculture that prioritizes long-term sustainability of the soil and is in line with the ecosystems of bioregions, rather than use of agro-chemicals and monocropping.
- Reduced influence of wealth in legislative and electoral processes, international trade treaty formulation, and other public policy–related mechanisms.
- Control and regulation of global financial markets.[18] (That is, constrained speculative investment and constrained international mobility of finance capital.)
- Increased citizen control (public accountability) over what is now the limited liability, publicly traded global corporation.
- International trade agreements and trade relations that favor "fair" over "free" trade.[19]
- Cancelation of the debt of the highly indebted and highly impoverished nations; responsible and accountable lending.
- Taxation that favors wealth distribution over wealth concentration.[20]
- Some form of accountability for the "ecological debt."

These goals counter the power imbalances at the heart of structural violence. With significant movement toward these goals, the world's trade in seeds would not be controlled by a few mega-corporations. The children of indebted poor countries would not see their food and healthcare disappear down the drain of insurmountable and illegitimate debt payments. Robin and others like her would not be forced into homelessness while working for people receiving 400 times what she makes. We would not fill our plates consistently with food that is trucked to us over hundreds of miles by carbon-spewing vehicles, and that is grown on land desperately needed by impoverished people to produce their own food. Our clothing would not be produced in sweatshops. Nor would hundreds of thousands of Americans lose their savings and livelihoods to speculative investors.

The crucial point, the transformative reality, is this: While for many of these goals, fulfillment is a long a way down the road, they are attainable. These goals may be achieved through the commitments, decisions, and actions of human beings working together. Moreover, people around the globe are working avidly toward each one of them.

POLICIES AND PRACTICES TO REALIZE THE GOALS

A moral vision and the goals for reaching it ultimately depend upon people putting them into practice. Vision, principles, and goals must be lived. The next steps in a moral framework leading from an economic moral vision toward its realization are public policies consistent with the goals, and then "practices" related to those policies.

By "practices" I mean what individuals, organizations, corporations, governing bodies, and other units of society *do* on an ongoing basis. They are the actions or behaviors that give shape to life in the home, workplace, school, place of worship, and the other venues in which daily life unfolds. "Practices" may be intentional or they may be rote.

"Public policy" refers to laws and regulations established by people through their governing bodies, be they local, state, provincial, or national. Public policies shape practices. The opposite also is true; practices influence the formation of public policy. Moreover, individuals' practices influence a society's practices and policies. So too, of course, the policies and practices of a society influence the practices of individuals. Thus the morality of a society and the morality of individuals are mutually informing.

FORMS OF PRACTICES

Actions to build economies—local, national, and global—marked by ecological sustainability, economic and ecological equity, and relatively shared power take countless forms. In discerning one's place in the movement toward a more just and sustainable world, it is useful to view the range of actions. Here then, is a typology. Its categories are neither rigid nor mutually exclusive. The value is not in establishing a particular set of categories. Rather, the value is in revealing the multiple forms of practices and how they enable each other and contribute to reaching the goals identified above.

The practices in this schema stand in three kinds of relationship to the identified goals. Some practices contribute *directly* to one or more of the goals. Supporting economic alternatives such as independent local businesses is an example. Other practices—such as legislative advocacy—aim at *changes in public policy that lead toward* one or more of the goals. Still other practices contribute to the goals by *forming people* capable of making choices in their direction. Earth-honoring worship exemplifies this kind of relationship. The forms of action apparent in this book's "Life Stories Revisited" appear here.[21]

- Lifestyle changes

  - Housing, transportation, eating, consumption levels, travel and recreation

- Economic advocacy

  - Boycotts, shareholder advocacy,[22] socially/ecologically responsible buying, socially and ecologically responsible investing

- Legislative advocacy and electoral advocacy[23]

  - Local, state, national

- Community organizing campaigns

  - Examples noted in this text include the Immokalee tomato growers, Jubilee Campaign to cancel the debt, living wage campaigns, and more

- Education and consciousness-raising

  - Alternative sources of news and information
  - Regularly seeing the "total cost" of a product rather than only the monetary price to be paid for it
  - Public art, including theatre, for social justice
  - Resisting the lure of advertising and corporate PR

- Public witness

    - Public protest and demonstrations
    - Public art, including theatre, for social change
    - Civil disobedience

- Economic alternatives

    - Co-ops
    - Worker-owned business
    - Municipality owned services such as cable, telephone, and internet services
    - Local or regional banks
    - Community-supported agriculture and farmers' markets

- Direct service to people in need and monetary contributions
- Worship and prayer

    - Earth-honoring liturgy, hymnody, biblical hermeneutics, and art
    - Public lament
    - Celebrating religious heritage of resistance
    - Prayers of repentance and for courage and wisdom
    - Eco-hermeneutics

- Transgressing the boundaries of our privilege to have a foot in a world on the margins

    - Building coalitions across "class lines" and national borders
    - Listening to and "companioning" movements domestically or in the Global South that are resisting exploitative enterprises
    - Learning from social movements of people flung from their homes, lands, livelihoods, or lives by the economic systems that put food on our tables and money in our pockets
    - Finding ways to disavow some of the unwarranted "advantages" that come with privilege based on class, race/ethnicity, gender, or caste.[24]

These are practical forms of "loving neighbor as self" in our context. They are steps toward the aforementioned goals. As such, these practices are means of resisting economic and ecological violence and rebuilding more equitable, sustainable, and democratic economic life.

A sharp tension accompanies any honest look at the practices entailed in movement toward economic lives that do not exploit and endanger neighbors and Earth. On the one hand is the magnitude of the changes necessary and the shortness of time (in light of climate change). On the other is the fact that we also are responsible for the realities of everyday life and relationships: getting to work or school on time, acquiring and cooking food, bringing attention and joy to family and friends, washing our hair and the dishes, studying, clothing ourselves and family, taking out the garbage, caring for friends or family who are sick or suffering, earning a living, fixing broken cars and worn-down houses. Many of us do not have time to add more "things to do." This reality is most fierce for households in which the adult or adults work full time (or more than full time) at low-paying jobs, and no extended family is available to care for children or other dependent members of the household.

This tension points to the burning need for the structural changes that this book and its vision of a moral economy seek. Over time, the aim of the aforementioned goals is to rearrange systems of transportation, food production, housing construction, and so on so that our daily activities are in themselves practices that contribute to healthy ecosystems and socially just human relations.

I do not propose to resolve the tension here. The resolution clearly varies depending upon circumstance. A family in my neighborhood offered one piece of a fruitful response. This family fits the above description of two working adults with dependents needing special care and having relatively low income. In moving toward a more just and sustainable lifestyle, they have not added more things to do, but rather have changed the way they do things. Each month, this household makes one change that moves it into the trajectory of justice and Earth-care. One month they began washing clothes only on the "short wash" setting of their laundry machine, noticing that clothes came out just as clean while using less water and energy. The parents instilled in their daughters the preciousness of water. At another point they began hanging out laundry to dry rather than using the energy-intensive dryer: "We actually hung our cloth diapers to dry," recalled, Karen, the mother in the family. Packaged food soon disappeared from the kitchen, replaced by food bought in bulk from the local co-op, and plastic products and containers were largely replaced by glass, metal, bamboo, or other alternatives. "When changes are taken one step at a time, it's not that big a deal," Karen explained. "If you try to do it all at once it's self-defeating." Both parents now bike to work; one is able to show up in bike clothes a bit sweaty and the other changes clothes at work. "We don't frame it as a sacrifice, biking to work or taking the bus," Karen explained. "It enriches our lives. We get exercise while biking. We meet new people on the bus. It connects us to the community."[25]

Over the years, as these changes have accumulated, the family's daily activities have come to include practices from all of the categories noted in the typology above. One comes away from dinner in their home far more aware of legislation to support, products to boycott, and how to join a campaign to protect local business from global corporate enterprise. One also spends much time in laughter. These friends—and countless other people having made similar choices—are a beacon of hope, quietly shining on what is possible.

THE PARADOX OF PRACTICE

A tree grows near the street on which I live. One small strand of root pushing up against the asphalt and the concrete has no apparent impact. It is as inconsequential as my divestment in large-scale banking and investment firms. However, many strands of root woven together and persisting in their effort to nurture the life of that tree have pushed up large blocks of the concrete sidewalk and the asphalt street. Trucks driving over the ridges in the road rattle, so great is the disruption caused by those tenacious strands of root working together on behalf of life. If each strand of root opted out on the basis of its insignificance, the powerful force on behalf of life would go untapped.

A vexing paradox colors the commitment to take action toward social change. Depending on how it is perceived, this paradox may render moral defeatism in the quest for justice or moral tenacity for pursuing it. The stakes, then, in recognizing and interpreting the "paradox of practice" are high.

Few concepts are more important to moral agency than recognizing the constructive interplay between individuals' behavioral changes and social structural change. Many of my students argue that what individuals do in their everyday practices—riding bikes or buses instead of driving, giving up beef and packaged food, drinking fair trade coffee, boycotting Walmart, sending emails to legislators, shopping at co-ops and farmers' markets, and so on—are ineffectual and relatively insignificant. What is needed, they insist, is major public policy change, legal mandates, and large-scale institutional change.

Other students insist the opposite. Social structural change through public policy and legal mandates, they aver, will not occur to the extent that we need it. What is needed are individual people and households deciding to live in ways that are ecologically sound and economically nonexploitative and then doing so.

It is a delight to help them unearth the synergy between behavioral change and structural change at varied levels. Imagine city streets in the United States filled with bicycle riders, as are many streets of Amsterdam. How to get there? People are more likely to ride a bike to work (behavioral change) if city policy makes bike-riding safer and more convenient. (These policies would provide bike lanes on all arterials; create low-cost bike acquisition programs for low-income people; close many streets to all but bikes, scooters, and buses; and so on.) Such policies will come about because of individuals changing their outlook and behavior.

One's everyday practices in fossil fuel use, food-related decisions, and other consumer choices may seem inconsequential for change at the macro level. Yet, these practices are necessary and "effect"ive. Every "system of evil requires personal actions to make it work."[26] Thus every system of evil also requires people to resist their own and others' participation in it, even while acknowledging that their acts of resistance in themselves appear relatively ineffectual. Corporate power continues unfettered because "so many players, right down to individual human beings, facilitate its operation."[27] While individual acts will not in themselves change the course of social structures—including the global economy—they are necessary for that change to be achieved.

The paradox of practice invites two contrasting and morally weighted responses. One is the sense of powerlessness and hopelessness discussed in chapter 4. Its cost is astronomical—widespread failure to challenge the structural injustices that shape our lives.

A far more empowering response is recognizing that while structural injustice transcends individual agency, it does *not* transcend collective agency; collective agency can overcome structural injustice, and collective agency requires individual agency. As "I" becomes "we," individuals' practices bear rich fruit. The channels of impact are psychological, political, economic, and cultural:

- Practicing more just and ecologically sound alternatives is an example to others. People learn by modeling. A few years ago many students would arrive in my classes with purchased water. One woman, in striking contrast, consistently entered the room with her own water container full of tap water dangling from her backpack. At one point she spoke briefly about the devastating impact of bottled water, and the values of tap water. By the term's end a number of other students began appearing with their own containers of tap water.

- Individuals' actions influence the public moral climate, paving the way for policy change and institutional change. Not two years later, a student movement was afoot to ban the sale of bottled water on the Seattle University campus. It succeeded.
- Practicing justice-making and Earth-care actively counters powerlessness, denial, and despair for oneself and for others who see that practice. Citizens around the globe who took part in the Jubilee Campaign to cancel the debt of highly impoverished countries proved that people working together can influence some of the world's most powerful institutions in the name of justice.
- Individuals' practices reveal that opposition exists. The farm workers' union would not have made the gains it made for migrant laborers had not protesters and boycotters countrywide proved to exploitative employers that opposition was strong.
- Practicing alternatives reveals to the world that alternatives are possible. Taking one's money out of Bank of America opens that door for others who did not realize that alternative banking was alive and well.
- What people do influences policy. Civil rights legislation required a groundswell of people resisting segregation and practicing desegregation in their daily lifestyles.

The classic feminist adage, "the personal is political," rings true. Personal practices and public policy are inextricably related. Change in the one catalyzes change in the other. Choices in personal life have political impact.

The "forms of practice" appearing below illustrate many facets of the emerging moral framework.

****

A Life Story Revisited

Blood Minerals Revisited

The story of blood minerals in chapter 4 ended with the political, environmental, and human-rights implications of mining columbium-tantalum in the Congo.

I hear stories about atrocities and suffering in Africa a lot, and I usually just sigh and move on because I doubt there's anything I can do about it. But I could no longer deny that my electronic product purchases were connected to intense misery on the other side of the globe. I started to wonder: who do I think I am anyway . . . do I have the right to own and use all of this stuff if it causes so much suffering? I decided to do something. I started by taking a serious look at the electronics in my household and considered if any of them were redundant or just plain too indulgent. My friend and I discussed the possibility of sharing a video -game console and maybe some other electronics, and we think a sharing arrangement might work.

Next, I called my state senators and asked them to support the Conflict Materials Trade Act. It requires the commerce department to audit mineral mines and declare them conflict-free or not. Although it's not a ban on conflict minerals, it is a beginning.

After that I contacted Apple, and asked them to support the Conflict Minerals Pledge.[28] It is a pledge to stop using conflict minerals and allow independent supply-chain verification to that effect. I told them that I was committed to purchasing electronics only from firms that are abiding by the Conflict Minerals Pledge, and that I was going to tell my friends and family about the role of conflict minerals in the Congo.

Why on Earth did I not know about this problem, I wondered? How could a smart guy like me not realize what was going on behind my cell phone, iPod, and computer? What if other things that I buy or use also come at such a price? I've decided that I'm not going to spend the rest of my life not knowing. I'm going to organize for a speaker to come to my school—an expert, a witness, or survivor of the conflict, someone who will be able to reach the students on a deep level and spur them to take action. The simple fact that most people have no idea that their electronics are fueling such violence, I think, is the main reason more significant action isn't taken. And I decided to petition the organizer of our weekly campus film series to show "Blood in the Mobile," a film documenting how our cell-phone use finances the war in the Congo.[29] Next term, I think we'll petition the university administration to purchase only conflict-free electronics. I can just imagine being part of a nationwide movement of universities committed to blocking conflict minerals.

My theology prof said that I could get "service learning credit" for community organizing around a social justice issue. So this summer at home I plan to get the local religious community involved. I found out online that Jewish World Watch offers speakers and education for congregations who want to spread knowledge of genocides and mass atrocities. They could help convince my congregation to become a "conflict-free congregation."[30] *And once people's eyes are opened, I know they'll pass on the knowledge.*

I learned that other organizations are already working on this and that I could do more if I connected up with them. The Enough Project seems to know what they're doing, so I sent them a donation and now I follow their progress online. Finally, I started thinking about everyone else I know who isn't a part of my school or church. I decided to let them know—through email and Facebook—about an audit system the Enough Project has produced. It ranks electronic companies on their progress toward responsible sourcing of conflict minerals. I'll urge everyone to buy only conflict-free electronics, or, if that's not possible, to buy from the companies with the highest rankings. Well, I guess I'll also urge them—and myself—to buy less electronics altogether.

★★★★★★★★★★★★★★★★★★★★★★★★★★★★★★★★★★★★

MORAL FORMATION

Moral formation is the elephant in the room of social change. How do we become "the people that we need"? The question has been present, explicitly or implicitly, throughout these pages. What forms the economic moral vision of a people? What sculptors—generous and generative or confining and excluding—craft our vision of "what ought and could be" regarding the distribution of Earth's goods? What forms the moral-spiritual power to move toward "what ought be," especially if doing so entails transgressing cultural norms and the lifestyle habits solidified over a lifetime?

Commonly the field of ethics locates moral formation in values and the practice of them. Clearly, it is important to identify requisite shifts in values. Foremost among them are sufficiency over endless acquisition, economic justice over concentrated wealth, meeting needs over material accumulation, collaboration and community over privatized living, well-being over growth, service and empathy over blind pursuit of individual gain.[31] A theme emerges. It is the problem of valuing wealth too much. Kenneth Sayre puts it simply: "Return to environmental health requires diminishing society's high regard for wealth . . . this will involve curtailing both society's general endorsement of wealth as a personal goal and establishing countervailing values that forbid accumulation of excessive wealth . . . equity is a normative value that might be effective in this countervailing role."[32] Particularly toxic is the extraordinary valuation of wealth as criterion of success. Had ours been a society in which equity was highly valued, and excessive wealth accumulation was widely considered a vice, the world would be radically different.

However, I leave further thinking about specific values changes in the hands of others. We focus here on a different point about values and on a question that is infrequently posed.[33] Both concern moral formation.

The point is this: While indeed significant shifts in values are needed, many people already hold dear many of the values we need, and seek to practice them in interpersonal relationships, *but do not apply them to our lives as parts of social systems.* These are values such as compassion, justice, service, empathy, love, and sacrifice for the sake of life. The pivotal question becomes: How are we to become people who bring into *public* life the values we treasure in our interpersonal relationships? How do we form ourselves and others for practicing these values as members of social systems that have life-and-death impact on millions of people? Here we view clues emerging from the morally formative power of what people *do* (our practices), first considering practices in general and then practices of worship.

LIFE PRACTICES AS MORALLY FORMATIVE

I am reminded of a Cherokee tradition in which a wise elder narrates a story to the tribe's young people about a fierce battle between two wolves that live inside him. One wolf, clever and proud, is known for its greed, hate, envy, and violence. The other, strong and courageous, is known for its grace, love, peace, and humility. As the Cherokee elder describes the frequent and mounting tension between the two wolves, an excited boy implores him, "Please tell us which wolf will win!"

"The one who will win," the elder replies, "is the one I feed."[34]

This story holds rich truth. A principle of ethics is that we become what we do. What we "practice" shapes what we value, how we see the world, our sense of what is right and good. The habits of everyday life—one's "lifestyle"—over time "feed" one wolf or the other. The wolf that is nourished best is the one that grows. This pertains to both individuals and societies.

Yet, in the context of structural sin or structural violence, the story of the wolf also harbors a lie. A basic thrust of this book is that one might grow in moral goodness in personal life, while yet continuing in paths of structural evil *because one does not recognize that evil for what it is;* structural evil hides. Where hidden, it is not resisted. Compassion, generosity, and justice may be nurtured to reign strong in the personal lives of people who nevertheless are unknowingly killing others through economic and ecological violence.

Therefore, the "practice of moral goodness"—if it is to shape people for challenging the structural violence in which they swim—must be informed by critical awareness of that violence. Moral formation calls for "seeing" structural evil and its persistent ability to hide. Thus, critical vision is a central ingredient of moral formation for justice-making and earth-keeping in the context of structural evil. The tools for developing critical vision, discussed throughout the volume, take on added importance.

WORSHIP PRACTICES AS MORALLY FORMATIVE

"…join in the hymn of all creation."[35]

From its earliest years, the church has affirmed that the practice of worship—and particularly the sacraments of Eucharist and baptism—is morally formative. It influences how people act in the world.[36] As articulated by liturgical theologian Don Saliers, "there is an internal, conceptual link between liturgy and ethics. How we pray and worship is linked to how we live."[37]

Contemporary theorists in multiple disciplines argue that human identity, subjectivity, and action are shaped by the narratives that we experience and the rituals that reinforce them. Liturgical theology concurs. The practice of worship shapes people by enacting a vision of the world, and by telling an epic story in which the worshiping community is a player.[38] The vision and story teach the people how to live and empower them for that life. Martin Luther, speaking of the Eucharist, describes this influence: "The sacrament . . . so changes a person that he is made one with the others." "Thus by means of this sacrament, all self-seeking love is rooted out and gives place to that which seeks the common good of all."[39]

However, a troubling question hovers. How is it possible that Christian communities of the Global North worship and celebrate the Eucharist regularly and sincerely, and yet continue in patterns of life that damage Earth's life-systems and bring many neighbors suffering and destruction? We do not love neighbor by resisting economic arrangements that buy our luxury at the price of others' blood. Instead, we give of our wealth to help others, fail to ponder our wealth's connections to others' impoverishment or to Earth's distress, and carry on with life as usual. I, for instance, am sent forth by the Spirit from worship every Sabbath day to embody God's justice-making and Earth-honoring love.

In stark contrast, however, I go forth from worship to produce, on that Sabbath day, outrageous amounts of greenhouse gases.

To speak of worship forming humans for the work of love appears as the height of theological hubris and self-deception, unless we acknowledge the overriding reality of our participation in structural sin. Sri Lankan theologian Tissa Balasuriya poses the contradiction starkly: "Why is it that in spite of hundreds of thousands of Eucharistic celebrations, Christians . . . who proclaim Eucharistic love and sharing deprive the poor people of the world of food, capital, employment, and even land . . . inequities grow . . . [and] the rich live like Dives in the Gospel story?"[40]

Theologians have grappled with the contradiction between the call to love experienced in worship, and people's apparent obliviousness to that call in lived life. The contradiction is expressed theologically and sociologically in multiple ways. Typically liturgical theology posits it as the "radical conflict"[41] between how we worship and how we live, or between "worship and social-ethical practice,"[42] or between "a purely believed"[43] faith and a faith embodied in society.

Our focus is on how it could be otherwise. How might worship help to shape the worshiping community for neighbor-love that is relevant and empowering in the face of massive *structural* sin and our participation in it? Three pointers lie in the "story" told in worship, communal lament, and worship as a "school for seeing."

WHAT VIEW OF THE WORLD . . . WHAT STORY TOLD?

If indeed the moral life of worshipers is formed by liturgical enactment of a "vision of the world," then the "vision of the world" chosen and enacted *matters*, and it matters much. Perhaps worship will better form the people for love as an economic-ecological calling if worship enacts an alternative "vision of the world" in which humans are creatures with all the other creatures, dependent, for example, upon millions of microbes inhabiting our bodies enabling us to sing and taste the bread and wine. Or what if the alternative vision of the world enacted in worship portrayed water, trees, and bodies—rather than buildings—as sacred abode of God? What if the vision enacted in worship portrayed not only all people with enough, but the overconsumers no longer having too much? What if the vision foretold the "uncreators" forsaking the curse of uncreating, and instead honoring the original charge given to us by God, to "keep and till" God's garden Earth? Where would worship enacting such "visions of the world" take place? What would it look like?

The questions thickens. Whose "vision of the world" is to be told? Is it "ours"? Or is it an alternative vision of the world as told, for example, by indigenous Americans whose great grandparents were pushed out of their homes, cultures, and livelihoods by the descendants of the tribes of Europe? Whose interpretation of scripture and of God will ground the vision of the world enacted in "our" worship?

If the moral life of worshipers is formed also by an epic story told through the process of worship, then what epic story is "told" matters. What if the story told in the sermon, songs, chanting, sacraments, and art highlighted the Christian heritage of resistance to systemic domination? What if the practice of worship taught our children that they stand in a long line of courageous resisters who stood up against structural evil even at cost of life: the daring midwives who rescued Moses from the Pharaoh's deadly hand, Jesus who refused to comply with the ways of empire, the early martyrs who resisted imperial demands, the abolitionists, the "righteous gentiles" who defied Hitler's death machine, the Huguenots in the village of Le Chambon-sur-Lignon whose quiet resistance saved four thousand Jews even while occupied by fascist forces? What if our children frequently heard sermons such as that preached by one of my pastors: "I could empathize with Paul in prison," she declared, "because last time I was in prison, I too was in solitary confinement." She had been jailed many times for protesting the Trident nuclear submarines stationed near Seattle. What if our congregations were morally formed to see themselves as walking in the footsteps of fiercely loving resisters? What if the story told, including us as characters, truly honored our rich heritage of resistance to dominant powers where they demanded that people transgress God's commandment to love? Telling this story would not be too strange, for that heritage is at the heart of Christian and Hebrew scriptures. Were the story told in worship, might we be more fertile ground for love that defies economic and ecological violence?

COMMUNAL LAMENT

In a powerful sermon on the book of Joel, Christian womanist ethicist Emilie Townes claims that, for people living in covenant relationship with God, social healing begins with communal lament. Lament was integral to the ancient Hebrews' covenant relationship with God, suggests Townes, drawing on the work of Walter Brueggemann. A loss of lament meant "also a loss of genuine covenant interaction with God."[44] Where the assembly praises God but does not lament, "covenant is a practice of denial and pretense."[45]

Communal lament, as Townes explains it, is the assembly crying out in distress to the God in whom it trusts. It is a cry of sorrow by the people gathered, a cry of grief and repentance and a plea for help in the midst of social affliction. Deep and sincere "communal lament . . . names problems, seeks justice, and hopes for God's deliverance." Lament, as seen in the book of Joel, she says, forms people; it requires them to give name and words to suffering. "[W]hen Israel used lament as rite and worship on a regular basis, it kept the question of justice visible and legitimate."[46]

Perhaps for us too, lament is integral to social restoration. Could it be that worship that empowers the people of God for social and ecological healing will include profound lament for the ways in which our lives unwittingly endanger Earth's life-systems and vulnerable neighbors far and near? Imagine churches offering space for "public lament" about the fact that we have allowed hundreds of thousands of children, women, and men to go homeless in our land.

Worship may remind the people why they can lament without drowning in despair. Sacred Power for healing this beautiful and broken world is present with, among, and within the stuff of Earth. That saving presence flows instinctively to life's broken places. There it nurtures power for love, including the love that reforms society.

SCHOOL FOR SEEING

According to a longstanding Christian claim, God comes to and within the worshiping community through the sacraments. The Latin, "sacramentum," was used in early Christianity to translate the Greek, "mysterion." The mysterion of God, at least in the apostle Paul's work, "are the ways of God in getting through to us, in opening our eyes to face reality, in bringing us faith, hope and love."[47] The sacraments then are God's ways of getting through to us in at least two ways. They open our eyes to reality, even when reality may seem too painful to face. And they bring us faith, hope, and love, the ingredients of agency for responding to reality in ways that reflect God's healing and liberating presence.

Since at least the third century, the Eucharist has been known by some as a school for seeing.[48] Cyril of Jerusalem, in his teaching on the Eucharist, admonishes participants to "hallow your eyes by the touch of the sacred Body, and then partake. . . . After partaking of the Body of Christ [and] . . . receiving also the Blood of Christ . . . while It is still warm upon your lips, moisten your fingers with It and so sanctify your eyes, your forehead and other organs of sense."[49] Thirteen centuries later, Martin Luther insisted that vision of how we are to live in accord with faith is obscured when sacramental practice is ignored or distorted.[50] In a contemporary Lutheran baptismal rite drawing upon this heritage, the cross is traced on the eyes with the words "receive the cross on your eyes that you may see the light of Christ, illumination for your way."[51]

To what reality will the sacraments open our eyes if, through them, God is enabling Her people to see differently so that we may live more fully the love for which we are created? What will the sacraments reveal if they are to evoke wisdom and courage for the work of justice-making and Earth-healing? The elements of "critical mystical vision" suggest that the sacraments ought to help us to perceive:

- "what is" happening on this fragile planet,
- "what could be" (understood as just and ecologically sound ways of living), and
- God's power and presence coursing through all of creation.

How, then, will the church practice worship in a manner that opens our eyes to see what is, what could be, and God's power flowing through us and the world, unleashing moral-spiritual power for reshaping society toward justice, compassion, and Earth-care?

As long as people who "benefit" materially from structural injustice develop and practice liturgy through the perceptual filters of privilege, our vision of God and of how we ought to live will be dim and distorted. Our vision will tilt toward reinforcing the injustices that benefit us. The Jesus Christ whom we encounter in worship will continue to be colored by our vested interests in existing social arrangements. Worship—shaped and experienced through lenses of privilege—inadvertently and despite our best intentions may reinforce that privilege.

Consider the extent to which worship formulated over the centuries by Euro-Western mindsets reinforces white privilege even for white people who in their conscious minds abhor racism:

- The portrayals of Jesus in many sanctuaries would have a newcomer assume that Jesus came from some village in Norway. If a black Christ, an indigenous Christ, or an Asian or Latino Christ appears, he is identified as "black" or by his ethnicity, while his brother the white Christ is never called "the white Christ."
- And what of God, the first person of the Trinity? Until literacy became prevalent in Europe, art was a powerful medium of teaching about God. A walk through Florentine museums displaying two millennia of Christian art proclaims without words the whiteness of God. And Mary, the epitome of the holy and of proximity to God, is overwhelmingly pale.

- A quick trip through the hymnal and use of the words "white" and "black" in the church reveals a veritable indoctrination in the goodness of white and the evil of black.
- To what extent do our joyful claims that we are "one in the Spirit" insulate dominant-culture Christians from the lived reality of disunity in a world that privileges and universalizes their expressions of Christianity?[52] I will never forget a representative of the Sami people at the Lutheran World Federation General Assembly in Winnipeg. "Our legacy with the church," he declared, "has been one of having to adopt the ways of the colonizers. . . . They consider their ways as universal. Therefore we have often experienced how dangerous it can be to welcome a well-intentioned invitation by the majority to 'celebrate' our unity. We have experienced so many times that this meant to enter the fellowship on the premises of the majority. We had to leave ourselves behind."[53]

In a similar vein, worship held constantly in walled spaces in which the only nonhumanly constructed things are domesticated and formally arranged flowers tends to reinforce anthropocentric assumptions about what is sacred. If trees and soil were as sacred as altars and chalices, why do we not see those things of Earth in worship?

If the practice of worship is to be socially transformative, then it must help worshiping communities see the eyes through which we view reality and, especially, to perceive from perspectives of people who are oppressed by our privilege and are struggling to overcome it. Worshiping communities will seek to bring those views to bear on liturgical reformation. And worship will guide us in the strange effort to perceive from perspectives of Earth. Socially transformative worship will evoke also the visions of more just and Earth-honoring social structures, and God's presence luring creation in their direction.

Imagine baptism in rivers where the baptizing community has been practicing river restoration. Or worship space designed to leave no carbon-footprint. How about liturgical blessing of congregations heading out to protest against wage theft, or blessing of youth "mission trips" to work on the "living wage" campaign?

Consider the "tree-planting Eucharist" developed by the African Earth-Keeping churches. And what of the water-conserving, food-growing rituals of the Georgetown Gospel Chapel in a low-income industrial area of Seattle? I recall vividly the simple outdoor worship space initiated by a rural and agricultural program of Tamilnadu Theological Seminary, a Christian seminary community dedicated to eco-justice in India's Tamilnadu province. The chancel has no walls and no roof. Vines growing from one side to the other provide a small bit of coverage from rain. The cross is honed from a nearby tree, and the altar and celebrant's chairs are large stones.

I think of the Dalit liberation liturgy celebrated by many Dalit communities in India.[54] Valley and Mountain Fellowship also comes to mind. This Christian community in Seattle includes acts of "creative liberation" as a form of worship. The community gathers alongside unions, community groups, environmental groups, and other faith communities for public witness supporting worker justice, environmental justice, immigrant rights, and more. Communities of "Green Sisters" are spread throughout the United States, Canada, the Netherlands, Nigeria, and the Philippines. "Green Sisters" refers to Catholic sisters dedicated to heeding the plight of the Earth, healing the Earth, and developing a religious culture that enables both. In their Earth literacy programs, they practice "Earth body prayer." Their "Earth meditation trails" invite people to meditate on Earth-human relations, celebrate the journey of the universe, and strengthen their connections with self, others, Earth, and God.[55] The Maryknoll Ecological Sanctuary in Baguio, Luzon, has created the Stations of the Cosmos instead of the Stations of the Cross, a nature walk of discovery into the earth's deep interconnectedness. Beyond this, I invite the reader to a growing body of creative faithful resources.[56]

The church claims that Christian worship forms and empowers believers to heed God's call to love neighbor as self. In contrast, the church of the Global North tends to comply with ways of life that accumulate and consume at terrible cost to others and to Earth's life-systems. The question here has been: "How can this be, and how might it be otherwise?" We have uncovered clues to Christian worship that nurtures the capacity to serve God's justice-making, Earth-tending work.

IN SUM

This chapter sketched key elements of a moral framework capable of enabling movement toward more equitable, sustainable, and democratic economic life. The framework begins with the moral anthropology and the understanding of neighbor-love's scope developed in the previous chapter. The framework entails both resistance and rebuilding, and depends upon substantive shifts in sources of moral knowledge. According to this moral framework, change agents include individuals, institutions, business, and government, and change happens in these same four arenas. This framework stems from a vision of a moral economy and its four constituent principles. It identifies goals for realizing those principles and then policies and practices of life that would enable these goals to be met. Finally, this framework acknowledges the role of moral formation in enabling social transformation.

In theological terms, this is a framework for expressing neighbor-love as an ecological-economic calling. It remains now to illustrate more fully the most concrete pieces of this framework—policies and practices. That is the intent of chapter 10.

Notes

1. Johnnetta B. Cole, *Conversations: Straight Talk with America's Sister President* (New York: Anchor, 1993), 75, cited in Patricia Hill Collins, *Fighting Words: Black Women and the Search for Justice* (Minneapolis: University of Minnesota Press, 1998), 188.

2. Milton Friedman, *Capitalism and Freedom* (Chicago: University of Chicago Press, 1962), xiv.

3. Any Christian ethical framework presupposes, and hence includes, a moral anthropology and a scope of love. While usually not made explicit, they ought be, for their impact on morality is immeasurable.

4. Gandhi lays out his full description of *Satyagraha* in his book *Non-Violent Resistance* (Satyagraha) (Mineola, NY: Dover, 2001).

5. Michael Nagler, *The Search for a Nonviolent Future* (Novato, CA: New World Library, 2010).

6. This fourth source has been understood differently in different Christian traditions. It is known in Catholic moral theology as "reason." It also has been defined as "philosophy" or "descriptive accounts of reality."

7. That we can learn from "nature" does not mean that the processes of nature are necessarily moral. Nature houses countless processes that we would not claim as moral for human behavior.

8. Gloria Albrecht, *The Character of Our Communities: Toward an Ethic of Liberation for the Church* (Nashville: Abingdon, 1995), 85.

9. George Zachariah, *Alternatives Unincorporated: Earth Ethics from the Grassroots* (London: Equinox, 2011), 1.

10. Conference of Bishops, Presidents, and President Pastors of the Latin American Lutheran Churches, "Declaration on the Foreign Debt, Neoliberalism, and Globalization," reprinted in René Krüger, ed., *Life in All Fullness: Latin American Protestant Churches Facing Neoliberal Globalization* (Buenos Aires: ISEDET, 2007).

11. Angel Furlan, "The Unbearable Weight of the Illegitimate Debt," address to the Norwegian Social Forum, Oslo, Oct. 29, 2003.

12. Imagine the insight to be had after a few weeks of engaging the website of any of the organizations noted in the stories herein.

13. For example: New Economics Foundation, Institute for Policy Studies' New Economy Working Group, or New Rules Project.

14. Excellent resources for reading the Bible "from the margins" include Peter Nash, *Reading Race, Reading the Bible* (Minneapolis: Fortress Press, 2003); Miguel de la Torre, *Reading the Bible from the Margins* (Maryknoll, NY: Orbis, 2002); Bob Ekblad, *Reading the Bible with the Damned* (Louisville: Westminster John Knox, 2005); many books in feminist hermeneutics.

15. Organizations of civil society include schools and universities, not-for-profit or nongovernmental organizations, clubs, public interest advocacy groups, synagogues, churches, mosques, temples, and so on.

16. Larry Rasmussen and Bruce Birch, *Bible and Ethics in the Christian Life*, rev. ed. (Minneapolis: Augsburg, 1989), 60.

17. Film *I Am*, directed by Tom Shadyac, Flying Eye Productions, 2011.

18. Due to the global financial crisis, voices calling for controls over transnational speculative finance now include mainstream economists. See, for example, David Felix, "Why International Capital Mobility Should Be Curbed and How It Could Be Done," in Gerald Epstein, *Financialization and the World Economy* (Cheltenham, UK: Edward Elgar, 2005), 384–408. See also Joseph Stiglitz, "Toward a New Global Economic Compact: Principles for Addressing the Current Global Financial Crisis and Beyond," delivered to Interactive Panel of the United Nations GA on the Global Financial Crisis, 30 October 2008, United Nations.

19. A more equitable alternative to "free trade" agreements are regional and subregional agreements that strengthen the capacity of impoverished countries to promote and protect their own interests and are not based on liberalization, deregulation, and privatization.

20. Proposals include taxes on speculative investment, carbon, and other pollution taxes on large companies, progressive income taxes, and so on. For multiple proposals, see Chuck Collins and Felice Yeskel, *Economic Apartheid in America: A Primer on Economic Inequality and Insecurity* (New York: New Press, 2000)

21. Collins and Yeskel, chapter 5, describes the second through fifth.

22. Shareholder activism "is a key tool for speaking out against rising CEO pay and harmful corporate practices. . . . In addition to legislation, it is one of the most powerful tools for advancing corporate reforms." United for a Fair Economy at http://faireconomy.org/issue/corporate-responsibility/about.

23. Legislative advocacy is simplified by subscribing to legislative alerts from advocacy organizations.

24. Excellent work exists on disavowing white privilege and male privilege. Similar work could be done regarding economic privilege.

25. Interview of Karen Snyder-Chinn by Freddie Helmiere on April 1, 2012.

26. James Poling, *Deliver Us from Evil* (Minneapolis: Fortress Press, 1996), 121.

27. Ibid.

28. Sponsored by the Enough Project, this pledge asks companies to trace the supply chain for tin, tantalum, tungsten, or gold in their products to verify their mines of origin, and conduct supply-chain audits to document the routes, intermediaries, and transactions made from mine to final product.

29. "Blood in the Mobile" won the 2011 Cinema for Peace Justice Award in Berlin.

30. Jewish World Watch offers a draft "Conflict-Free Congregation Resolution" for congregational use.

31. Kenneth Sayre, *Unearthed: The Economic Roots of Our Environmental Crisis* (Notre Dame: University of Notre Dame Press, 2010), 337.

32. Ibid.

33. See for example, Sayre, *Unearthed*, chapters 15, 16, 17, 18.

34. Patrick Howell, "Lent Challenges Us to Make Positive Choices," *Seattle Times*, March 14, 2009.

35. A chanted phrase in the liturgical practice of the Evangelical Lutheran Church in America.

36. Gordon W. Lathrop, *Holy People: A Liturgical Ecclesiology* (Minneapolis: Fortress Press, 1999), 227.

37. Don Saliers, "Liturgy and Ethics: Some New Beginnings," in *Liturgy and the Moral Self*, ed. E. Byron Anderson and Bruce T. Morrill (Collegeville, MN: Liturgical, 1998), 174.

38. Saliers, "Liturgy and Ethics: Some New Beginnings," *Journal of Religious Ethics* 7, no. 1 (Fall 1979): 16.

39. Martin Luther, "The Blessed Sacrament of the Holy and True Body and Blood of Christ, and the Brotherhoods," in *Theology of Martin Luther*, ed. Timothy Lull, 251, 260.

40. Tissa Balasuriya, *The Eucharist and Human Liberation* (Maryknoll, NY: Orbis, 1979), xi–xii.

41. Wayne Meeks in *The Origins of Christian Morality: The First Two Centuries* (New Haven: Yale University Press, 1993).

42. Bruce T. Morrill, *Anamnesis as Dangerous Memory: Political and Liturgical Theology in Dialogue* (Collegeville, MN: Liturgical, 2000), 64.

43. Johann Baptist Metz, in Morrill, *Anamnesis*.

44. Emilie M. Townes, *Breaking the Fine Rain of Death* (New York: Continuum, 2001), 24.

45. Ibid.

46. Ibid.

47. Christopher Morse, *Not Every Spirit: A Christian Dogmatics of Disbelief* (Valley Forge, PA: Trinity Press International, 1994.)

48. Timothy Gorringe, *The Education of Desire* (Valley Forge, PA: Trinity Press International, 2001), 104.

49. *The Works of Saint Cyril of Jerusalem*, vol. 2, *The Fathers of the Church*, trans. Leo P. McCauley, S.J. and Anthony A. Stephenson (Washington, DC: Catholic University of America Press, 1970), 203.

50. As Caryn Riswold points out, Luther condemned Rome's doctrine of the mass as sacrifice offered rather than gift received, because that doctrine "quench[ed] the power of baptism . . . in adults, so that now there are scarcely any who call to mind their own baptism . . . *so that they might know what manner of men they were and how Christians ought to live.*" Luther, "The Babylonian Captivity of the Church," Luther's Works 36:58.

51. *Holy Baptism and Related Rites*, in Renewing Worship series (Minneapolis: Augsburg Fortress, 2002), 27.

52. This question was catalyzed for me by Tracie West in *Disruptive Christian Ethics*.

53. Tore Johnsen, representing the Church of Norway in a statement at the LWF General Assembly 2003.

54. "Dalit" refers to the people formerly known as "untouchables."

55. Sarah McFarland Taylor, *Green Sisters: An Ecological Spirituality* (Cambridge, MA: Harvard University Press, 2007).

56. See, for starters, the resources offered at www.earthministry.org, www.webofcreation.org, nccecojustice.org, seasonofcreation.com.

10

Love in Action: Resistance and Rebuilding

"It is a complex journey from consciousness to the concrete politics of empowerment, and one which is, by definition, full of contradictions and detours. It is perhaps most important, individually and collectively, simply to stay on the right road."

Patricia Hill Collins[1]

♦

"I cannot do everything, but I can do something. And I will not let what I cannot do interfere with what I can."

Edward Everett Hale

We are not morally powerless in facing the economic and ecological violence that inundates our lives. To the contrary, as "I's" that are "we's" spanning the globe, and as "we's" attentive to the beckoning of God whose love will bring abundant life for all, we are replete with moral power. That divine love breathes in us, urging us to dedicate intelligence, creativity, energy, political savvy, skill, and the song or our souls toward a world in which all people and all of creation may flourish. That love beckons us to renounce economic and ecological violence and to craft more moral economic policies and practices.

We now step into a landscape of world-changing practices and public policies that already are resculpting our world. My aim is not to be exhaustive but to illustrate in such a way that the most important point emerges clearly. It is that we are not bound to "the way things are." We, ordinary people of the

Global North, can live toward justice and sustainability. We can resist being "uncreators" and exploiters.

Many of the goals suggested in chapter 9 may seem nearly impossible. One purpose of this book is to argue that they are not. Therefore, it behooves us to spend time with one goal that appears, in the public consciousness, to be far from the realm of the possible. It is the goal of *increased citizen control over large global business corporations.* In my years of teaching and public speaking, I have found a nearly ubiquitous assumption that transnational corporate power is beyond common citizens' power to rein in. To the contrary, as this chapter demonstrates, policies and practices aimed at increasing democratic power in relationship to global corporations are currently at work. They are playing out in households, civil society organizations, governments, and even some corporations.

Unaccountable corporate power plays a role in all of the "life stories" recounted herein. Significant movement toward this goal would help to transform each situation of economic and ecological violence portrayed in these stories. Moreover, making headway in increasing public power over the transnational corporation would open doors toward most of the other aforementioned goals.

CRUCIAL CLARIFICATION

I want to be clear. The point of this goal is *not* that all large corporations do flagrantly bad things (environmental destruction, child labor, inadequate wages, and so on). Nor is the point that large corporations are solely to blame for the environmental and social damage done by our economic practices. This is not true. The primary point of this goal is otherwise.

It is *to curtail the concentration of power in the hands of a tiny segment of humankind,* the high-level leadership of large corporations. The world economy—which can determine the fate of ecosystems and can determine who has and does not have access to water, seeds, food, jobs, and other means of survival—should not be so heavily influenced by so few people.

This goal serves an additional purpose. By lessening the control that the finance industry has over business, progress toward this goal would enable small and medium-size business to thrive without doing social and ecological damage. The demands of Wall Street limit the power of business leadership to choose moral options. In order to maintain a financially competitive edge and a standing in the stock market, business corporations must take actions that counter the aims of sustainability and justice, in the long-term if not the short.

From a moral perspective, finance should not have that degree of control over business.

Good and evil are always intertwined in human life. No person, group, or entity composed of human beings is singularly good or singularly evil. Moreover, as we have noted already, morality is often ambiguous. An uncompromisable guideline in the effort to discern what we, as people and societies, are to do and be is that no persons or groups may be demonized.

Six "Gateways" Introduced

Imagine a world in which global investment firms, mortgage markets, and other globally operating corporations do not have the "freedom" to pursue self-interest regardless of the cost to millions of human beings and their homes, jobs, health, food and water supplies, and communities. The goal of curtailing unaccountable corporate power intends to bring that image into the realm of the real. This goal has a companion goal among those noted in the previous chapter. It is to "control and regulate global financial markets." These two goals are the antithesis of advanced global capitalism. Its central tenet is the "freedom" of corporations and capital to pursue their interests unencumbered by public accountability.

A vibrant, vast, and highly diverse global movement is oriented around these goals. Active the world over, its composition spans the fields of human endeavor and expertise. This movement includes peasants and other farmers, scientists, lawyers, landless and homeless people, religious communities, small businesswomen/businessmen, artists, students, and others. They work not as autonomous individuals but as parts of networks.

These actors, while diverse in race/ethnicity, nationality, social class, caste, religion, gender, age, political stance, and more, share three conclusions. The first is that the drive to *maximize* profit (as opposed to simply make a profit) is the problem. It leads to exploitation of people and environmental devastation. Secondly, corporate and finance control of the global economy tends to hurt small farmers, low-level workers, indigenous peoples, impoverished people, women, and other sectors of society who tend to be marginalized. There are many exceptions to this rule in people who have benefited from the global economy as we know it. However, the damage to the many vastly outweighs the benefits to a relative few. Finally, "there are goals more important than efficiency, growth, and getting the cheapest goods to the consumer or the most profit to the seller."[2]

Here I offer a simple schema that should help ordinary people establish public policies and practices that rein in the power and negative impact of large corporations. Equally important, the examples herein should spur imagining other such policies and practices. The schema entails six "gateways" for redressing the power imbalance between global corporations on the one hand and people and their governments on the other.[3]

In the context of this book and its inquiry into the moral norm of neighbor-love, the reason for pursuing these goals takes theological form. "We," as all people, are called to love neighbor as self and to nurture Earth's well-being. Yet powerful corporate structures are shaping our relationships with neighbors around the globe and with the Earth. By participation in those structures (as consumers, employees, investors, voters or nonvoters, silent bystanders) we do great damage to people whom we are called to love. Christian traditions throughout history have claimed that where the "powers that be" require people to defy God's call, then allegiance to God takes precedence; we are to obey God rather than other powers. To do otherwise is to worship other gods.[4] The goal of curtailing unaccountable corporate power may be articulated theologically. It is to reduce the power of large global corporations and finance agencies to determine our relationship with neighbors and the Earth and, thereby, our allegiance to God.

Following are six "gateways" to gaining more public power in relationship to corporate power in order to protect workers, communities, and marginalized sectors in them, and ecosystems:

1. Small-scale business alternatives with emphasis on the local and regional, and on reducing consumption.
2. Moral culture within the business corporation.
3. Citizen action / consumer pressure to achieve "voluntary" constraints on corporate conduct.
4. Citizens using governments to achieve publicly mandated (regulatory or legislative) constraints on corporate conduct, and limitations on the privatization and marketing of some essential goods (for example, water, seeds, and HIV/AIDS drugs).
5. Citizen action to rescind corporate personhood and the first amendment rights of the "natural person" that personhood grants to the corporation.
6. Organizing to expel or prohibit the establishment of unwanted corporations.

These approaches are complementary. Each has strengths and weaknesses. None of these gateways is adequate without the others; they work in concert.

The first gateway is the turn to local and small- or medium-scale business and finance as an alternative to global corporate business and finance institutions. The second and third gateways—widely known as "corporate social responsibility" (CSR)—entail voluntary change in corporate behavior.[5] The next, in contrast, seeks legally mandated constraints and often is called "corporate social *accountability*," because it renders corporations accountable to laws and regulations. The fifth seeks constitutional change in the rights of the corporation, tackling the mechanisms that have enabled its accumulation of power. The final gateway prohibits corporate activity where the citizenry finds it destructive to human or environmental well-being.

We consider each in turn, pausing along the way to compare voluntary corporate change with legally mandated change. The intent is to illustrate: (1) the nature of each gateway, (2) its viability, (3) the interplay of different kinds of action within each gateway, and (4) the interchange between individual behavioral change and change at the macro level. The emerging picture should reveal possibilities for change that are not evident when only one or two forms of action are viewed apart from the others.

All six gateways are composed of both policies and practices. The proposed practices pertain to "us," overconsumers who also are U.S. citizens. The central message of this schema as a whole bears repeating: We, you and I, are not powerless. As parts of networks of committed people—including and informed by those who suffer the consequences of the systems that enable life as we live it—we can move mountains.

Before looking more closely at each of the six gateways, we pause for a sequel to the story of "International Hazardous Waste." In this story, the gateways to change in corporate power and behavior appear.

****

A Life Story Revisited

International Hazardous Waste Revisited

This story in chapter 2 left Alma Bandalan and her family immersed in highly toxic scrap waste, and left Jason enjoying a new iPod, unaware that his recycled iPod may have ended up in just such a toxic site.

A hemisphere away from the Bandalan family and the recycling plant on Mactan Island, Jason made his way to class. He drank a fruit smoothie concocted that morning in his new blender and strode to the beat of a favorite song playing from his new iPod. His first class was Environmental

Justice: Analysis of Contemporary Issues. Jason enjoyed this class. The professor was engaging, the assignments were usually a bit unorthodox, and several of his friends were taking the class.

True to form, Professor Robbins announced an interesting new assignment. "Each group will select a contemporary issue related to environmental justice and illustrate some current actions that address it. Your challenge is to demonstrate all six of the 'gateways' to curtailing the power of large business corporations and holding them accountable for their public impact, presented in last week's lecture."

Jason thought about some of the approaches that Dr. Robbins had presented earlier: changes in the moral culture of the corporation itself, voluntary constraints, small-scale or local alternatives, etc. Recalling his broken blender and iPod, and all the appliances his mom was currently discarding in her kitchen renovation, he knew of an idea to pitch to his group.

"Electronic waste, or hazardous waste," Jason stated in the study lounge that night. "We can use the six gateways to illustrate approaches to the problem of transferring all these electronic products into the developing world for 'recycling.'" No one objected, and before long textbooks, class notes and laptops were out as the four friends began searching for examples.

"Okay, here's a big one," said Yasmin, scanning her textbook. "The Basel Ban Amendment. It looks like there was a huge conference in 1995 around the transport, tracking, and minimization of hazardous waste in Basel, Switzerland. The attending countries were trying to address the movement of hazardous waste into developing countries, saying that it could only be imported with 'prior informed consent' by the receiving nation. But after the convention some countries and environmental groups said it didn't really go far enough and they proposed this Basil Ban Amendment."

"Yeah, it says here that Denmark and many nations of the Global North adopted this amendment," said Jordan, who had found the same page in the textbook and was reading ahead. "It bans the export of hazardous waste, including recycling, from OECD countries to developing countries. It was controversial, of course, and the vote seems to have been messy. It looks like it was technically blocked by some of the wealthier nations and industries, but it's still considered 'morally binding' by the signatories." Jordan was involved in several campus activism clubs and was more familiar with this terrain than the rest of the group.

"*But that didn't stop some countries from moving ahead,*" *said Jason, who was reading about the Basel Convention online.* "*Several EU countries have made this amendment legally binding under their own countries' laws, and called it the Waste Shipment Regulation (EWSR). Other countries launched more informal approaches to ensure the sound management of hazardous wastes when they are moved to developing countries. And also, several African nations made a treaty called the Bamako Convention that prohibits importing any hazardous waste.*"

"*So this would probably apply to gateways 3 and 4, right?*" *asked Cortney, a business major and good friend of Jason's.* "*In some cases there are mandatory legislative restraints imposed by the Basel Convention, and then the Amendment invites voluntary self-regulation, or country-specific laws.*" *The group agreed and kept searching.*

"*There seem to be a decent number of organizations working on the fourth gateway—publicly mandated limitations on corporate conduct,*" *said Jordan.* "*I keep coming across examples of activist groups across the globe working for national policy reform around transboundary dumping, trying to pass laws that ban e-waste from landfills, establishing recycling programs at home, and targeting the electronics industry itself.*" *He looked up.* "*This is probably the area in which citizens in industrialized nations can really join forces with people in poorer countries. We can support their protests to block transboundary dumping and pass legislation that changes corporate practices.*"

"*But on the other hand, businesses are more likely to respond to an economic incentive than a rule,*" *said Cortney.* "*I'm interested in the third gateway, the voluntary limitations on corporate conduct or self-regulation. Any ideas?*" *The other three scanned books and computer screens for a moment.*

"*Some electronics companies, such as Apple, Dell, and Sony have eliminated or at least reduced a carcinogenic flame-retardant chemical called PBDE,*" *said Jason.* "*And Apple will recycle your old laptop in the United States if you buy a new one through them. But that's not really ideal—it just perpetuates the consumer cycle.*" *He suddenly thought about the laptop he was currently using, the third one he had ever owned, and wondered where the old ones were at this moment.*

"*Well, since so many citizens in wealthier nations consume electronics, I think the primary responsibility lies here at the production and* consumption levels," Jordan explained. "Our recycling club here at school has been talking about all the computers that end up discarded on this campus and what we can do about it. They're thinking of partnering with the Grassroots Recycling Network and their 'computer take-back campaign'—it asks computer producers to claim responsibility for the products at the end of their lifespan." Jordan described the concept of "zero waste"—redesigning products so that every part can be reused or composted, and reclaiming the waste that's already out there.

"The fifth gateway is tricky," Cortney observed. "Getting rid of 'corporate personhood' and corporations' constitutional rights as 'persons' seems important, but hard to do."

"Well here's a group called Network of Spiritual Progressives that's organizing to do just that," offered Yasmin as she checked out the organization's website. "And here's another, Move to Amend. They have local groups all around the country. Hey, both of them are working on that Supreme Court decision that we discussed in class."

"What ruling?" Jordan asked. "Well if you came to class on time once in a while, you might know," quipped Cortney. "It's the ruling that corporations can spend as much as they want on federal elections because they're legally 'persons,' and in this country people have freedom of speech under the First Amendment," she explained. "Anyway, the Network of Spiritual Progressives really explains the need to reform corporations here on their website, and it totally relates to our project."

Yasmin paused. "For the first gateway," she mused, "I don't need the Internet. I can just use my cousin as an example. She and her family have a system in their neighborhood, like a little co-op, where they share household goods including electronics. They decided about a year ago that they didn't need all the gadgets and appliances that they have, and started sharing with their neighbors: DVD players, blenders, lawn mowers, etc. They all live on the same block so it's pretty convenient, and one guy is really handy with electronics, so he fixes things when they break. I don't think they've bought any new electronics this whole year. That's definitely one way to address the issue—stop hazardous waste at the source. If we don't buy as many electronics, there's less waste to deal with at the end."

"Here's an example of gateway six, prohibiting the establishment of unwanted corporations or expelling them," said Jordan. He read from the class textbook. 'Citizens in Malaysia protested so vehemently to the *construction of a massive e-waste processing plant by Citiraya Industries Inc. that the State rejected the proposal, even though their own Department of the Environment approved the Environmental Impact Assessment.' And get this," he read on, "it pertains to us: 'Environmental Justice activists from several nations helped to locate resource persons to provide expert input on the environmental impact statement and provided comments on the reality of the dirty technology.'⁶ I sure hope some of those groups were from the United States." "Well, doing something like that would be a great senior project for environmental science majors," Jason noted, looking at Yasmin, a junior who was majoring in just that.*

"We haven't found many specifics for the second gateway," observed Jason.

"I can think of one," said Cortney suddenly. "Me."

"Huh?" puzzled Jordan.

"Well," said Cortney, "right here in the business school, one of my professors, Dr. Amity, has convinced me that business has a responsibility for its environmental and social impacts, as well as its financial viability. It's called the 'triple bottom line.' And she's been teaching us about this thing called 'cradle-to-cradle,' the idea that production processes can be efficient and waste free—like the way nature cycles nutrients. For example, we read about some companies that offer electronics take-back programs, where the producer takes back the product at the end of its life and reuses as many parts as possible. It's not perfect but it helps, and often makes good business sense as well. After studying with Dr. Amity and taking this class, I can tell you that when I'm in management, I'm definitely not going to be exporting dangerous materials regardless of how much money it could save my company! People are talking this way more and more in my business classes. It makes me feel hopeful about the future."

The four students began to consolidate the information they had gathered and type up a formal presentation, eager to share their knowledge with the rest of the class.

****

Gateway 1: Small-Scale Local and Regional Alternatives

It may be difficult to imagine a world in which globe-spanning investment firms, banks, and other corporations do not shape our lives. However, alternative forms of banking, saving, credit, production, and other business are operating and have been for decades. Two long-term advocates of "the new economy," John Cavanaugh and Jerry Mander, write:

> Transition to more economically democratic structures becomes easier to visualize once we recognize that many human-scale, locally-owned enterprises already exist . . .
>
> There are very few of our daily needs that cannot be met by small and medium-sized enterprises operating within a market economy of a kind—but one that is characterized by a multitude of small players rather than a handful of giant, absentee owners. And all of them would operate without the benefits of stock market investing, limited liability, or corporate personhood, so crucial to large corporations.
>
> From the point of view of sustainability and democracy, there is no reason why giant transnational corporations are needed to run hamburger stands, produce clothing and toys, publish books and magazines, grow and process and distribute food, make the goods we need, or provide most of the things that contribute to a satisfying existence.[7]

Many people counter corporate power by withdrawing their economic activity as much as possible from enormous corporations and, instead, doing business with small-scale local or regional business. Likewise they shift their banking and investing from global financial corporations to community-based banks and finance. This is the epitome of "resistance and rebuilding," the two streams of action toward social change.

This trajectory has a long and rich history, especially in Europe.[8] In the United States, the last decade and a half has seen this movement flourish.[9] Many people involved in it refer to these small and medium-scale business alternatives and the values they demonstrate as the "new economy." Others use the terms "economic democracy," "localizing the economy," or "alternative economy." It is far more than a shift in size of business. It also is a shift in purpose of economic life, a move from profit alone to also building community and community well-being.

Much has been written about the "new economy."[10] What follows is a glimpse adequate to demonstrate the crucial role of alternative economic endeavors and their widespread and vibrant nature. Noted too are two problems that could inhibit the movement's growth.

The vignettes throughout this book illustrate many streams of this movement. They include coalitions of small independent business, community-supported agriculture, fair trade/alternative-trade networks, consumer and producer cooperatives, community land trusts, partnerships, community-based banking, and local credit unions. Among these are both new and longstanding endeavors. New initiatives are sprouting up constantly and jubilantly, with astounding confidence in their ability to bear the fruits of equity, participatory power, and ecological sustainability.

One prime and broad-based example is BALLE, the Business Alliance for Local Living Economies. This network of socially responsible businesses is committed to building bottom-up, community-oriented "local living economies" in which "economic power resides locally to the greatest extent possible, sustaining vibrant, livable communities and healthy ecosystems in the process."[11] BALLE assembles coalitions of community leaders and government officials, social innovators, local and independent business leaders, and economic development professionals who work together to build these "local living economies." Employers and profit-makers are first and foremost neighbors and community-builders. This kind of economy serves as a powerful challenge to overly concentrated power. It is a significant step toward economic democracy.[12]

The new economy includes locally owned banks that emphasize the triple bottom line—financial, social, and environmental goals. Local deposits tend to support businesses and projects in the community, including such things as renewable energy, low-income housing, and green building. Most community banks shun the speculative investment that is so central to the banking industry as we know it.

The Fair Trade movement, one aspect of "the new economy," aims at supporting small-scale producers, and ensuring fair wages and working conditions. Initially known as "Alternative Trade Organizations," these networks emerged first in Europe in the 1960s, and spread to the United States within a decade, becoming more commonly known as fair trade. The rapidly growing movement now boasts federations or networks in many countries.

What qualifies a business as "alternative" or as part of the "new economy movement"? The response must be contextual, varied by industry and locale as well as by mindset and theoretical stance. There is no normative prototype and the movement is marked by diversity and creativity, but across the board there seems to be a general consensus that size, ownership/control, and accountability are primary factors.

"Size" refers to small-scale (or small- and medium-scale), but what constitutes small or medium is understood variously. The European Commission defines "small and medium business" as "those with less than 250 employees, annual sales under $35 million, and total assets under $24 million. Even this may seem too large for some, but not by the standards of mega-corporations; total sales of the Forbes Global 500 list of companies for 2002 ranges from a low of $4.9 billion to Citigroup's $1,051 billion in assets. Still, the category of small and medium can include substantial enough enterprises to be able to produce most essential goods and services efficiently."[13] To others, "small scale" is much smaller.[14] Most proponents, I believe, would agree that small scale means not large enough to monopolize the market, determine consumer choice on a widespread basis, shape political agendas or international treaties, displace smaller thriving businesses, or "manipulate the symbols of personal identity through mass advertising."[15]

Community-based ownership and control is another key standard. Like size, its interpretations are many, and a variety of ownership and control structures mark the movement.[16] Broadly speaking, in an alternative business, ownership is not in the hands of people thousands of miles away who are largely unaware of or unaffected by the harmful consequences of a company's actions (loss of water supplies, closure of plants, outsourcing, foreclosures, toxifying the environment, etc.). Rather, control is largely in the hands of or accountable to people who stand to bear the consequences of the company's decisions.[17] Control shifts from *shareholders* to *stakeholders* (of which shareholders may be one element).

The "new economy" and alternative business does not mean a full rejection of global business connections or corporations. That idea would be untenable. It does mean *prioritizing* local business and consumption, and turning to global business where the local or regional cannot suffice. Regarding banking and finance, German theologian Ulrich Duchrow attests, "[S]mall-scale alternatives are not in a position to be able to transform the entire financial system into a life-enhancing system, but they are starting the process of removing money from a cycle based on wealth accumulation."[18]

Some voices argue that practicing fair trade and small-scale or local business will not change the world. This effort, they aver, just leaves prevailing power structures in place. People therefore ought not waste time and energy on them but rather invest their energies in the other gateways that seek structural change or at least direct corporate change. Here emerges another version of the "paradox of practice." Indeed, practicing alternatives will not in itself bring about just and sustainable business as the norm. Yet, doing so is crucial. It moves us *toward* more viable, accountable, and ecologically healthy economies on a large scale. These alternatives signal that a different way is possible.

Claiming that developing small-scale or local alternatives is "the" singular solution to excessive corporate power is equally problematic. Where this notion leads people away from work for change on a larger scale, it too is a dangerous assumption. The other gateways are necessary complements to bring about structural change. Here again we see the necessary interplay between personal practices (in this case, supporting businesses in the "new economy") and public policy advocacy, community education, and other efforts to change structures of society.

Choosing small-scale, locally or regionally based alternatives to the corporate- and finance-driven economy is a vital gateway along the road to freedom from being forced by economic systems into exploitative relationships with Earth and with neighbors far and near. The power of this move is more than it seems. Birthing and nurturing alternatives proves that they are possible. It shatters the façade of inevitability that enshrouds advanced global capitalism. This move spawns hope for a different future by breaking into it.

GATEWAY 2: MORAL CULTURE WITHIN

A second impetus for corporate constraints comes from within corporate leadership itself. In some cases the moral consciousness of corporate managers and executives leads to substantive action toward fair wages, safe working conditions, reduced carbon emissions, and other such steps toward ecological and economic justice. Ray Anderson, the CEO of Interface, Inc., discussed in chapter 7, is a prime example. I refer to this as the "moral culture within the corporation."

Enter here the role of society's morally formative influence. Business schools could play a decisive role in reshaping the forms and roles of business in the world. Imagine business schools teaching Paul Hawken's call for "a system of commerce and production where each and every act is ecologically sustainable and restorative."[19] Educators from preschool through graduate school, families, faith communities, and other mentors of the young may be the root of such decisions.

Not long ago, an Islamic student who was a graduating senior in my ethics course wrote his paper on a serious moral dilemma that he faced. His major was business and, as a very accomplished student, he had been offered more than one excellent well-paid position in banking. These positions would put him in line for significant advancement. His dilemma was this: according to his scripture, the Koran, charging interest is not acceptable. The student used his ethics paper to deliberate this decision. His conclusion was not to accept any of the banking positions offered to him. Granted, this decision did not change the banking industry, but I have little doubt that this young man—whether he enters some other aspect of the corporate world or not—will be capable of difficult moral decisions that could have sweeping significance. (I recently met this young man again, at a lunch with Cornel West and Tavis Smiley, held for leaders in anti-poverty work in the Seattle area. This former student has become a highly successful leader in the nonprofit world.)

Gateway 3: Voluntary Constraints: Corporate Social Responsibility

A third approach to limiting corporate power for the sake of the widespread good is widely applauded within the corporate world. In some cases this approach serves the ends of equity and sustainability. In many others it betrays those ends.

"Voluntary constraints" designates changes in corporate behavior that are not legislated and are monitored by the corporations or their designees. These changes may be initiated from within, but more commonly are achieved through citizen/consumer pressure. For at least four decades, concerned citizens of the Global North and South have engaged in national and transnational citizen action networks to constrain corporate practices considered detrimental to human or other well-being.[20] These citizen alliances catalyze public pressure by raising public awareness.[21] Consumer boycotts and shareholder actions are a primary tool. The international campaign against sweatshops is a recent example.

Historically, faith communities, working with other organizations of civil society, have played a leadership role. Foremost has been the World Council of Churches, one of the early voices to critique the dangers presented by what were then known as transnational corporations (TNCs) to workers and other vulnerable people of the Global South. The Sisters of Loretto, an order of Catholic women religious, are credited with beginning the movement of shareholder activism in the United States. In the 1960s they brought public attention to the environmental and labor problems with strip mining in Appalachia by initiating shareholder resolutions against the Blue Diamond Coal Company.

Citizen and consumer pressure for Corporate Social Responsibility (CSR) has born significant fruits. They include fair trade networks and companies, green buildings, more energy-efficient business operations, safer working conditions, environmentally friendly products, and much more. Consumer boycotts have improved worker conditions in Hanes factories of El Salvador and Guatemala, Gap factories in El Salvador, carpet production in South Asia, and Nike's child labor sites in Vietnam. Voluntary "codes of conduct" are proliferating.[22]

It is becoming normative for business corporations to claim "corporate social responsibility" grounded in moral consciousness, and to depict that responsibility through public relations. Their assertion is that with this kind of moral consciousness, mandatory regulation (accountability) is not necessary. "The growing popularity of these programs is undeniable," conclude Richard Morgenstern and William Pizer, in their study of corporate voluntary environmental programs.[23]

One burning question, of course, is whether voluntary self-regulation actually works. Are codes of conduct established, monitored, enforced, and assessed by the corporations themselves likely to have adequate impact? More pointedly, "can such programs serve as a substitute for mandatory requirements or should only modest gains be expected from these [voluntary] efforts?"[24] The question has led the CSR movement to experiment with varied certification and monitoring schemas aimed at external third-party certification by NGOs not affiliated with the company in question, to replace corporate self-monitoring. The question is hotly contested to say the least.[25]

The corporate world attests, "yes": If consumer initiative, through boycotts, shareholder action, and responsible purchasing, makes social or environmental responsibility good for the bottom line, then corporations will do so. Advocates assert that a public ethos is developing that encourages multiple forms of corporate social responsibility. The Motorola Company declares, "We're on the threshold of a new era in which all of us—corporations, individuals, government, and other organizations—can join together to cooperate on the healing of our earth. . . . Our challenge for the new millennium is to learn how to live in harmony with the earth."[26] McDonald's Social Responsibility Report for 2003 notes, "Social Responsibility . . . has always been a part of who we are and will continue to be the way McDonald's does business."[27] According to Ford Motor Company, "A great company . . . offers excellent products and services but also strives to make the world a better place."[28] The Kellogg company notes that "we hold ourselves accountable for our social responsibility."[29]

Not surprisingly, prominent leaders in corporate social responsibility among relatively smaller corporations express similar sentiments. Jeffrey Hollender, founder of the American Sustainable Business Council and member of the board of directors of Vermont Businesses for Social Responsibility, avers that CSR is "the future of business. It's what companies have to do to survive and prosper in a world where more and more of their behavior is under a microscope."[30]

Other analysts and concerned citizens argue that while voluntary self-regulation serves some good purposes, it cannot substitute for laws. History, these voices argue, illustrates the importance of law to constrain corporate practice on behalf of the common good. Starting in the late 1900s, the United States saw a trend of corporate mandatory regulation to protect against monopolies, price-fixing, child labor, and other labor abuses. The eight-hour work week and the right to unionize were established and child labor was banned. The mid-1960s saw further legislation to protect against occupational hazards, environmental dangers, unsafe consumer products, and so on. Legally mandated constraints are known in some circles as "corporate social *accountability*."

The deregulation agenda of the mid-1970s on, led by the U.S. but quickly spreading elsewhere, reversed that trend. The emphasis quickly shifted away from public legal accountability to self-regulation.[31] Within the United States, voluntary self-regulation or "corporate social responsibility" replaced the prior emphasis on external, legally binding regulation that ensured a degree of corporate accountability to the broader society.[32]

Danger looms where claims to corporate social responsibility mask the opposite. Illustrations abound. Some corporate signatories of the UN Global Compact (the voluntary code of conduct launched in 2000) turned the Compact into a public relations tool by reporting on and exhibiting their best practices while retaining largely socially and environmentally degrading practices.[33] The World Business Council on Sustainable Development issued a "manifesto" titled "From Challenge to Opportunity," promising to "seek greater synergy between our goals and those of the society we serve." This engaging document celebrates the "role of business" in addressing pressing social issues such as poverty and the environment. *Co-chaired by BP's Chief Executive for "Refining and Marketing,"* the document emphasizes the "imperative" that business "operate within the carrying capacity of the earth." *Among companies creating "the most strategic options" to "embrace a low-carbon world," the manifesto notes BP, Shell, and ChevronTexaco.* One marvels at the contradictions between this statement and BP's role in the Gulf oil spill or Shell's role in the Niger

Delta. Cargill Dow is credited for its "commitment to 'eco-efficiency.'" Not mentioned is the role of Cargill in hundreds of thousands of small farmers going out of business and losing their livelihood. (This, along with other mitigating economic conditions as a result of unfettered globalization, has driven thousands of farmers in India to suicide, as seen in chapter 7's story of Ravi.)

Advocates of mandatory constraints argue that voluntary self-regulation, though it may appear effective, is in fact sorely inadequate and, at times, dangerously deceptive. Their reasons are many.

- Self-monitoring or monitoring by third parties under contract with the company in question relies on the word of the companies involved. Why should that word be trusted?
- Even where monitoring and certification are by independent third parties with no vested interest in the company or the assessment's outcome, the process depends upon internal reporting. "Workers in most developing countries know that they are vulnerable to being fired without cause, and that legal redress, if it is available at all, may take years in the process. Rather than lose their jobs, most individual workers will exercise caution in criticizing their employer or airing their grievances."[34]
- Compliance tends to be measured by participation rather than by outcomes, and reporting mechanisms enable corporations to report positive compliance without revealing that it mitigates only a minute fraction of the company's negative social and environmental impact.
- The purpose of the "business corporation as currently structured severely limits its capacity to make regulations and apply penalties and fines that are against its own self-interest."[35] The corporation is mandated to serve the "best interests" (read: economic gain) of shareholders. Thus it is unlikely that the business corporation will take actions in the public interest that might significantly undermine profits. (The tobacco industry, to illustrate, was unlikely to print on cigarette packages the warning that "cigarette smoking may be hazardous to your health," unless mandated by law to do so.)
- The demands of Wall Street for short-term profits leave little option for voluntarily sacrificing maximum short-term gains in the name of social responsibility. (Thus, for example, a company would be discouraged from voluntarily internalizing the costs of displaced communities, destroyed rainforests, children poisoned by water, global warming, etc.)
- A company may put enormous amounts of creative and financial resources into public relations to construct a convincing socially

responsible public face regardless of how far it may be from the truth.[36]

- Highly publicized contributions to important causes such as fighting homelessness or AIDS, also labeled as "corporate social responsibility," may win a company a good reputation enabling it to escape public censure for its human rights or environmental violations.

A Brookings Institute study of "market forces that encourage and limit the practice of corporate social responsibility" concludes that although the CSR movement does "promote social and environmental innovation by business," the reality that it is voluntary and market-driven means that "companies will engage in CSR only to the extent that it makes business sense for them to do so. . . . Unlike government regulation, it [CSR] cannot force companies to make unprofitable but socially beneficial decisions," which limits CSR's functional agency.[37]

Another set of case studies on corporate voluntary environmental programs concludes that: "voluntary programs can affect behavior and offer environmental gains but in a limited way. . . . [N]one of the case study authors found truly convincing evidence of dramatic environmental improvements . . . we find it hard to argue for voluntary programs where there is a clear desire for major changes in behavior."[38] Yet the corporate world continues to promote the adequacy of self-regulation.

Questionable effectiveness is not the only problem. Another is the matter of power imbalance discussed throughout this text.[39] Economic and ecological violence are rooted in asymmetrical power relationships. Voluntary self-regulation *as a substitute for publicly mandated regulation* maintains power in the hands of an infinitesimally small elite subset, corporate management, and out of the hands of the *demos*. Power here is no small thing; we are talking about the ability to decide who will control and use the world's water, food supplies, and lands. These may be the means of survival of existing communities who stand to lose them for the sake of corporate profits. "A 1996 study of campaigns [for social responsibility] conducted by European NGOs on transnational corporations . . . cautioned: 'The system of voluntary codes of conduct needs to be questioned from a long-term perspective, since it gives in to the TNCs' strategy to keep control of TNCs out of public/governmental hands.'"[40] Voluntary self-monitored constraint on corporate behavior is a problem to the extent that it is seen as a *substitute* for democratic control aimed at protecting the widespread good or vulnerable populations through publicly mandated requirements.

Environmental leader Bill McKibben sums up well the dangers of limited effectiveness and asymmetrical power:

> Without public policy established by the people through their governance structures "Will business save the world?" turns out to be the wrong question. The right question is "How can we structure the world so that businesses play their part in saving it?" And the answer to that, inevitably, is politics. Some of it is the politics of public awareness. . . . But mostly we need politics of a more straightforward, and entirely unglamorous, variety. If you want energy companies to rearrange their portfolios so that way more money goes to renewables and way less to hydrocarbons, the best way forward is not to appeal to the CEO's conscience—it's to pass laws to push him in the right direction. This is what has happened in Europe, where regulators told car manufacturers . . . to cut vehicles' greenhouse emissions by 25 percent—or else.[41]

I tend to agree, and also see a place for voluntary corporate social responsibility *if the following conditions were upheld*: (1) compliance standards were established with valid participation of the more vulnerable stakeholders, (2) monitoring and certification were by a third party having no vested interests in the corporation or industry in question, (3) workers who testify against a company were in fact protected from repercussions, (4) rhetorical claims to mitigate climate change and other environmental damage were tested for veracity, and (5) the weaknesses and dangers of voluntary mechanisms noted above were born in mind.

Voluntary self-regulation is dangerous where it leads the public to believe that a company is having predominantly positive social and environmental impact when it is not. That is, the move to environmental or social responsibility may represent a tiny fraction of the company's activity, and may be outweighed heavily by the company's negative impacts. Yet the company's marketing may portray a singularly beneficial impact and distract public attention from the negative. Walmart's decision to sell organic produce, for example, is problematic to the extent that it leads people to assume that Walmart's impact is becoming largely positive and to overlook the facts that this organic produce represents a minute fraction of the company's products, the produce was shipped long distances and undercuts local organic producers, and the company's labor abuses may go on unchecked. I am reminded of a small group of activists in Delhi, India supporting tribal people's rights.

They quietly showed me the vibrantly green and ecologically progressive self-portrayal of a steel company on the company's web page. From there, the activists proceeded to document for me that company's extensive abuses of indigenous rights, displacement of tribal peoples and forest dwellers, and environmental devastation. The effectiveness of corporate social responsibility is compromised if it hides significant ongoing negative social and environmental impacts behind an image of CSR.

GATEWAY 4: PUBLICLY MANDATED CONSTRAINTS

Having considered voluntary corporate social responsibility and its relationship to publicly mandated constraints, we look now more closely at the latter. This gateway entails legally enforceable standards for corporate conduct, galvanized by citizen action or by policy makers at any level of governance: local, state, national, and international.

The following illustrations begin with the local level and move up to the national level. The first few are specific laws already proposed or passed. The remainder are *forms* of laws under consideration in various locations.[42]

- The living-wage movement has been described as "the most interesting (and underreported) grassroots enterprise to emerge since the civil rights movement."[43] As of 2004, "over 123 cities, counties, and universities have passed [a] living-wage ordinance,"[44] most requiring companies doing business with them to pay workers a living wage. Since 1996 the movement has been encouraged by a coalition of "Business Leaders and Investors for a Living Wage."
- In 1998, the citizens of Arcata, California passed a referendum requesting that the city government "ensure democratic control over corporations conducting business within the city, in whatever ways are necessary to ensure the health and well-being of our community and its environment." The group initiating the bill, "Citizens Concerned About Corporations (CCAC), reported that owners of the many locally owned businesses "were either supportive or neutral, and two businesses ended up publicly endorsing the initiative."[45]
- Rep. Cynthia McKinney (D-GA) introduced the Corporate Code of Conduct Act (H.R. 2782), a bill that would hold U.S.-based corporations accountable in this country and abroad. It requires adherence to certain standards regarding human rights, fair employment, and workplace safety. Among other things, the bill prohibits retaliation against whistleblowers and requires a living wage, the right to unionize, and safety protections.[46]

- The Income Equity Act, first proposed in 1993, has been reintroduced a number of times since. Its purpose is to discourage excessive wage gaps between a company's top executives and its low-paid workers. Currently in the House Ways and Means Committee, the act would "deny employers a tax deduction for payments of compensation . . . exceeding the greater of twenty-five times the lowest compensation paid to any other employee or $500,000."[47]

Moving from specific legislation to *forms* of legislation demonstrates the wide range of possibilities at the national level for shifting power from the large business corporation to the *demos*. The following examples are either proposed or under public discussion.

- Legislation banning trade in hazardous wastes, and pushing for international bans on the same.
- Legislation eliminating or limiting corporate subsidies.
- Legislation that prevents corporations from deducting CEO salaries from taxable corporate profits (such as the Income Equity Act noted above).[48]
- Legislation mandating internalizing the costs of environmental degradation including greenhouse gas emissions, and legislation mandating labeling the "greenhouse gas content" of products.
- Legislation that taxes carbon emissions and other forms of environmental destruction.
- Legislation creating some form of a "financial transaction tax" and calling upon the U.S. government to advocate for internationally established "financial transaction taxes" to curb speculative investment.[49]
- Fair trade bills[50] and international trade agreements that do not grant corporations power over governments; disadvantage poor countries and sectors; favor investors over wage-earners; allow significant displacement of people; or sacrifice long-term ecological sustainability.
- Campaign finance reform and other legislation to protect democratic processes from money's power.[51]
- Progressive taxation that discourages rather than encourages wealth inequity and income inequity.[52]
- Legislation mandating that corporations above a particular size account for a triple bottom line (economic and social as well as financial).

Equally important are moves at the international level toward legally mandated corporate constraints. Among possible implementing institutions are the United Nations through its various agencies, a reformed IMF and World Bank, and the International Criminal Court. Again, the illustrations below represent policy proposals already under discussion and having a substantive international movement behind them.

- A global legal framework which demands immediate emissions reductions by nations and by multinational corporations over a specified size. It could be enacted through the UN Framework Convention on Climate change (UNFCCC).[53]
- A global legal framework disallowing corporate relocating within certain time-frames to nations with lower environmental standards and labor standards.
- A "financial transaction tax" in order to minimize capital flight and discourage speculative investment. The idea has been discussed seriously at least since proposed by Nobel prize–winning economist James Tobin in 1972. Originally proposed as a tax on foreign exchange transactions, some versions now include speculative investment in food and other survival commodities. Some versions propose that revenue be used to finance sustainable development in the Global South, and some advocate this as partial payment for the ecological debt.[54]
- "Public mechanisms of price stabilization" to "eradicate speculation on [food] commodities."[55] (Incidentally, Martin Luther, half a millennium ago, theologically denounced speculation on food commodities on the same grounds for which they are opposed today: the danger they pose to impoverished people.)
- Cancelation of the illegitimate debt owed by highly impoverished nations to wealthy countries and their banks, and prohibition of predatory lending.
- Some advocates of legal constraints at the international level work from a different angle. It is to redefine certain essential goods as belonging to the "public commons" and as unavailable for full-fledged privatization and commodification. These include water, seeds, food staples, and some pharmaceuticals such as HIV/AIDs drugs. The rapidly growing "right to food" and "right to water" movements exemplify these efforts, as does the fierce opposition to Trade Related Intellectual Property Rights (TRIPs), one of the most intensely opposed aspects of the World Trade Organization.[56] These movements seek internationally established prohibitions on corporate ownership of goods redefined as belonging to the "public commons."

Publicly mandated corporate constraint is, then, a fourth gateway or approach to regaining a degree of democratic control over large corporations, and particularly to hold them accountable for their impacts on human beings, society as a whole, and Earth's life-systems.

Gateway 5: Rescind Corporate "Personhood"

In recent years another approach to reining in corporate power on behalf of human and ecological well-being has emerged. It is the movement to revoke "corporate personhood" and the constitutional rights of a person that personhood grants. Under the 1886 Supreme Court ruling that a corporation is legally a person, corporations are protected by the Bill of Rights and have the rights granted under the Constitution's Commerce Clause.

The latter enables corporations to block local and state legislation protecting lands and people. The demise of family farms in the United States, which has caused untold suffering, illustrates. Laws protecting family farms from corporate takeover have been undone by agricultural corporations. Citizens of Iowa, for example, seeking to protect family farms from large out-of-state meatpacking corporations passed a law "making it illegal for pork processing corporations to own and raise hogs in Iowa." Smithfield Foods Corporation together with Murphy Farms LLC and Prestage-Stoecker Farms, Inc. sued the state of Iowa and won. The Iowa law protecting family farms was nullified on the grounds that it violated corporate rights under the Constitution's Commerce Clause. This case is but one of many in which corporate personhood has enabled agricultural corporations to uproot family farming. Some communities have attempted counter-legislation.[57]

Corporations defend their right to unlimited spending on congressional lobbying, arguing that it is an expression of freedom of speech protected under the first amendment. In 2010, based on constitutional rights including free speech, the Supreme Court overturned congressionally established limits on corporate spending to influence federal elections. The ruling ignited widespread energy behind the movement to revoke corporate personhood. The Move to Amend campaign now has branches in cities and states across the country. It is one of many networks calling for a constitutional amendment to establish that the inalienable rights of human beings belong to people only.[58] The advocates argue, along with Supreme Court Justice Stevens in his dissent to the 2010 ruling, that "corporations have no consciences, no beliefs, no feelings, no thoughts, no desires. Corporations . . . are not themselves members of 'We the People' by whom and for whom our Constitution was established."

GATEWAY 6: EXPELLING OR PROHIBITING UNWANTED CORPORATIONS

Activists in many communities and countries have organized to expel corporations that are putting small local businesses out of business, displacing communities, usurping their water supplies, poisoning their air or water, or destroying their food supplies. Other threatened people have organized at an earlier phase to preclude a corporation from establishing itself in a community in the first place. These two recourses comprise the sixth gateway to constraining corporate power. It was seen in the story of Ravi and Monsanto in India and in the story of Robin and campaigns against Walmart. Many cities or towns in the United States have successfully prevented Walmart from locating in their areas.

In some parts of the world, the effort to expel or preclude a corporate presence is motivated by the near impossibility of holding global corporations accountable when human rights or other abuses occur. Essentially, the corporate entity can "get away with anything" because a nation's legal and governance systems cannot or will not prevent it. A 2011 report by the International Commission of Jurists notes: "The complex corporate structure of the multinational, with networks of subsidiaries and divisions, makes it exceedingly difficult or even impossible to pinpoint responsibility for the damage caused by the enterprise. . . . Persons harmed by the acts of a multinational corporation are not in a position to isolate which unit of the enterprise caused the harm."[59]

The moral framework developed in the previous chapter began by noting two streams of action toward social change: resistance and rebuilding. Preventing or curtailing corporate activity where the citizenry finds that such activity would damage the community's well-being is a form of resistance. In some, cases people resort to this form of resistance at grave risk to their safety or lives. The resistance to bauxite mining in India portrayed in chapter 2 illustrates both the action and the danger. So too does the Monsanto Quit India Campaign noted in the story of farmer suicides in India.

IN SUM

The previous chapter sketched a moral framework for movement toward a moral economy. It is an economy grounded in the principles of ecological sustainability, environmental equity, economic equity, and economic democracy. The framework included a set of midway goals that direct the way toward realizing these principles.

Our aim in this chapter was to illustrate the viability of these mid-way goals by examining one that seems least possible, and teasing out the kinds of public policies and practices that could achieve it. It is the goal of increased citizen control over transnational business corporations and finance institutions in order to protect workers, communities, marginalized sectors in them, ecosystems, and democracy. Among the many goals noted in chapter 9, I chose this one in order to challenge the widely held public assumption that it borders on impossible. Moreover, this goal addresses a theme running throughout the book. It is that too much power concentrated in too few hands, or too much power unaccountable to broader society, imperils the widespread good. A commitment to the widespread good calls for distributed and accountable power, that is, democracy.

We examined a tool for identifying public policies and practices that lead toward this goal of increased citizen power in relationship to corporate power. The tool entails six gateways to achieving this goal. By moving through these gateways we viewed a small sampling of the myriad practices and public policies already at work or proposed that lead toward the goal. The intent was to suggest an approach to a seemingly impossible situation (concentrated and unaccountable corporate power) that would crack open its façade of intractability and reveal it as a humanly constructed situation that is, therefore, subject to human actions.

An indispensable point emerged: All of these gateways to reining in corporate power rest ultimately on citizen action, be it direct action or action through governance. Tenacious informed people's action through organized public networks—transnational where appropriate—may be the most important factor in constraining socially and environmentally destructive corporate power. Judith Richter, following her extensive analysis of corporate social responsibility and accountability, concludes, "The most crucial ingredients in any attempt to curb corporate power . . . are lucid analysis, principled and concerted action, and the courage and stamina to continue raising controversial issues if the public interest so requires."[60] These are keys to achieving the moral vision of a more equitable, democratic, and sustainable world. Democracy—people power to shape the terms of their life together—requires citizen action. Morality in the context of economic and ecological violence requires citizen action. Neighbor-love toward people whose lives or livelihoods are being destroyed by corporations that provide our food, toys, metals, electronics, clothing, vacations, and household goods requires our action.

To be sure, we have illustrated only one of the nearly fifteen goals identified in the previous chapter. The transition to a more equitable, ecologically sustainable, and democratic society entails movement toward all of them. Some—such as "vastly reducing energy use" and "conversion to renewable nonpolluting energy"—are quite different from the one illustrated herein. All will require some degree of increased citizen power relative to corporate power. And all depend upon "tenacious informed people's action through organized public networks."

My hope is that conceptualizing these gateways to change and how they facilitate each other will generate faith that this goal and the others noted are far from impossible. Significant movement toward them is underway and clamors for the engagement of additional concerned, courageous, ordinary people. Glimpsing the practices and policies in this chapter also should catalyze the creative thinking needed to generate others. Efforts such as these, where aimed at claiming and creating ways of life that enable all people to have the necessities for life with dignity, and that enable Earth to flourish, enact neighbor-love as an ecological-economic vocation.

Notes

1. Patricia Hill Collins, *Fighting Words: Black Women and the Search for Justice* (Minneapolis: University of Minnesota Press, 1998), citing Barbara Ransby and Tracye Matthews, "Black Popular Culture and the Transcendence of Patriarchal Illusions," in *Race and Class* 35 (July 1993): 57–68.

2. Robin Broad, *Global Backlash: Citizen Initiatives for a Just World Economy* (Lanham, MD: Rowman & Littlefield, 2002), 17, 243.

3. Many proposals for limiting the power of global corporations focus on one or more of these "gateways" but do not use that term. For proposal, see James Gustave Speth, *The Bridge at the Edge of the World: Capitalism, the Environment, and Crossing from Crisis to Sustainability* (New Haven: Yale University Press, 2009); David Korton, *The Post-Corporate World: Life after Capitalism* (San Francisco: Berrett-Koehler, 1999); The New Economy Working Group at www.neweconomyworkinggroup.org; Allen L. White, "Transforming the Corporation," GTI Paper Series: *Frontiers of a Great Transition* (Boston: Tellus Institute, 2006); Broad, *Global Backlash*.

4. Even Martin Luther, renowned for his allegiance to civil authorities, insisted that where the civil authorities call for actions that disobey God, Christians are to obey God.

5. See Philip Kotler and Nancy Lee, *Corporate Social Responsibility: Doing the Most Good for Your Company and Your Cause* (Hoboken, NJ: Wiley, 2005), 3.

6. Sangaralingam, cited by David Pellow in *Resisting Global Toxics: Transnational Movements for Environmental Justice* (Cambridge, MA: MIT Press, 2007), 213–14.

7. John Cavanagh and Jerry Mander, eds., *Alternatives to Economic Globalization* (San Francisco: Berrett-Koehler, 2002), 144–45.

8. "By 1990, there were between 12,000 and 15,000 self-managed companies in Germany with around 1,000,000 workers." Ulrich Duchrow, *Alternatives to Global Capitalism* (Utrecht: International, 1995), 254.

9. The movement includes alternative schools of business, centers theorizing alternative economic models, organizing networks, and consumers as well as small-scale or local businesses. Helpful "centers" include the New Economics Foundation (London), New Economy Working

Group of the Institute for Policy Studies (Washington, DC), Institute for Local Self-Reliance, Rocky Mountain Institute, and E. F. Schumacher Society.

10. Bill McKibben's idea of the "new economy," described in *Deep Economy: The Wealth of Communities and the Durable Future* (New York: St. Martin's Griffin, 2008), calls for building local economies, which yield fewer goods but richer relationships. Ulrich Duchrow offers a theological vision for a new economy, economic theory to match it, and examples. Cavanaugh and Mander demonstrate the viability of small-scale alternatives for four key "economic operating systems": energy, agriculture, transportation, and manufacturing (151–207). They provide a general blueprint for a shift from "factory-farming" to "small-scale, diversified . . . agricultural systems" (172). Gary Dorrien provides a descriptive and normative account of economic democracy in *Economy, Difference, Empire* (New York: Columbia University Press, 2010), 168. Michael Shuman, in *The Small-Mart Revolution* (San Francisco: Berrett-Koehler, 2006), 9–10, and *Going Local* (New York: Free Press, 1998), articulates how localities may "reinvigorate their economies by 'going local.'" The "NGO Forum Treaty on Alternative Economic Models" produced by the NGO forum at the "Earth Summit" in Rio includes a set of principles elaborating a "vision of alternatives to the current economic models." Ekins and Max-Neef offer critique, theory, and practical examples of the "new economy."

11. See the BALLE website at: www.livingeconomies.org.

12. Localized democratically operated economic alternatives have flourished for decades: for example, Seikatsu Club Consumers' Co-operative Union (SCCU), a Japanese federation of twenty-nine consumer cooperatives; Mondragon cooperative system in the Basque region of Spain; Co-op Atlantic in Canada.

13. Cavanaugh and Mander, *Alternatives to Economic Globalization*, 146.

14. For some, the term "small-scale" refers less to size than to being locally owned.

15. Cavanaugh and Mander, *Alternatives to Economic Globalization*, 146.

16. See Dorrien and Duchrow.

17. "Fair share" is variously defined.

18. Duchrow, *Economy, Difference, Empire*, 264.

19. Paul Hawken, *Ecology of Commerce: A Declaration of Sustainability* (New York: Harper Business, 1993), xiv.

20. The movement arose in the 1970s largely in response to the rapidly expanding "global reach" of (what were then referred to as) transnational corporations (TNCs) into nations of Africa, Latin America, and Asia and TNCs' increasing influence over those nations' economies and governments.

21. In 1975 this movement pushed the UN to establish the UN Commission on Transnational Corporations (UNCTC). The agency's focus was on achieving a UN-based "code (or codes) of conduct." Free market forces under the Thatcher and Reagan administrations caused the closing of the UNCTC before UN-based code could be achieved.

22. One is the UN Global Compact (UNGC) launched in 2000 by then Secretary-General of the United Nations, Kofi Annan. It specifies ten principles of corporate social responsibility regarding human rights, labor, and environment. As we will see, it also epitomizes many shortcomings of voluntary self-regulated constraints.

23. Richard Morgenstern and William Pizer, *Reality Check: The Nature and Performance of Voluntary Environmental Programs in the United States, Europe, and Japan* (Washington, DC: Resources for the Future, 2007), 2.

24. Ibid., 1.

25. Judith Richter, *Holding Corporations Accountable* (London: Zed, 2001), 28–43, analyzes the debate.

26. Motorola's "Environmental Vision Statement" cited in Kolter and Lee, *Corporate Social Responsibility*, 207.

27. CSRwire, Oak Brook, "McDonald's Social Responsibility Report: One-Year Global Update" (2 May 2003). Cited in Kotler and Lee, *Corporate Social Responsibility*, 7.

28. Telephone interview with Andy Acho, worldwide director, Environmental Outreach & Strategy, Ford Motor Company, April 13, 2004. Cited in Kotler and Lee, *Corporate Social Responsibility*, 6.

29. Carlos M. Gutierrez, "Corporate Citizenship," Kellogg Company. Cited in ibid., 6.

30. Jeffrey Hollender and Stephen Fenichell, *What Matters Most: How a Small Group of Pioneers Is Teaching Social Responsibility to Big Business and Why Big Business Is Listening* (New York: Basic Books, 2004), dust jacket.

31. Richter writes: "Through the end of the 1960s corporate regulation was seen as a matter of democratic control over corporations . . . it was understood that firm rules were needed to ensure both optimal operation of markets and the prevention of . . . abuses of power and corporate neglect of responsibility" (17). See Richter (6–27) for a historical account of the regulation of transnational corporations and the ensuing deregulation movement. One of the most vociferous attacks on the idea of "regulation" was from the Chicago School of Economics.

32. Richter, *Holding Corporations Accountable*, 6–26.

33. Two were Nike and Rio Tinto.

34. Pharis Harvey, Terry Collingsworth, and Bama Athreya, "Developing Effective Mechanisms for Implementing Labor Rights in the Global Economy," in Lance Compa and Maria Cook, eds., *Workers in the Global Economy: Project Papers and Workshop Reports* (Cornell University, International Labor Rights Fund, Institute for Policy Studies, and Economic Policy Institute, January 2001), 42–49, cited in Broad, *Global Backlash*, 231.

35. Harris Gleckman and Riva Krut, *The Social Benefits of Regulating International Business* (Geneva: UNRISD, 1994), 8–9, cited in Richter, *Holding Corporations Accountable*, 41.

36. The process whereby toxic "sludge" was renamed "biosolid" and reassigned from "hazardous waste" status to "class A fertilizer" exemplifies the power of corporate PR to avoid regulation by manipulating public perception. In the early 1990s, the sewage industry, faced with limited locales for storing "sludge" contaminated by industrial waste, enlisted its PR organization to orchestrate a name change and pave the way for sludge to become a fertilizer. The Name Change Task Force landed on "biosolids," and the EPA modified its standards regulating the application of sludge to farm lands; "sludge" (biosolids) became a "Class A" fertilizer for use on food crops. The EPA enlisted a PF firm to educate the public regarding benefits of sludge as a fertilizer. It remained toxic. See John Stauber and Sheldon Rampton, "A R.O.S.E. by Any Other Name," *PR Watch* 2, no. 3 (Third Quarter 1995).

37. David Vogel, *The Market for Virtue* (Washington, DC: Brookings, 2005), 3, 4.

38. Morgenstern and Pizer, *Reality Check*, 184.

39. Richter says as much, arguing the need to "reassess the trend away from externally binding regulation" (5). While self-regulation and co-regulation are in some instances sufficient, she posits, the need is to "explore how balances of power can and should be shifted back in favor of such regulation" (5). Richter goes on to propose a number of "ways of limiting and offsetting the power of [transnational corporations]" (208–9).

40. M. Vander Stichele and P. Pennartz, *Making It Our Business: European NGO Campaigns on Transnational Corporations* (London: Catholic Institute for International Relations, 1996), 47, cited in Richter, 192.

41. Bill McKibben, "Hype vs. Hope: Is Corporate Do-Goodery for Real?" *Mother Jones*, November–December 2006, 52.

42. Chuck Collins and Felice Yeskel, *Economic Apartheid in America: A Primer on Economic Inequality and Insecurity* (New York: New Press, 2000), propose multiple legislative moves to rein in corporate power and decrease the income gap and wealth gap in America.

43. Robert Kuttner, editor of *The American Prospect*, cited in Collins and Yeskel, *Economic Apartheid in America*, 182.

44. Collins and Yeskel, *Economic Apartheid in America*, 189, using data from the Living Wage Resource Center.

45. Paul Cienfuegos, "The Arcata Initiative on Democracy and Corporations," *Synthesis/Regeneration* 17 (Fall 1998).

46. Introduced in 2001 and 2006, the bill was referred to committee and did not come to a vote.

47. Summary of bill at www.govtrack.us/congress/bill.xpd?bill=h112-382&tab=summary.

48. Collins and Yeskel, *Economic Apartheid in America*, 184–85.

49. See Robert Pollin, "Applying a Securities Transactions Tax to the United States: Design Issues, Market Impact, and Revenue Estimates," in Gerald Epstein, *Financialization and the World Economy* (Cheltenham, UK: Edward Elgar, 2005), 409–25 for a rather conservative proposal.

50. Numerous campaigns exist at state and national levels. See for example the New England Fair Trade Campaign.

51. Political theorist Robert Dahl suggests "campaign finance reform" as one of seven "reforms to increase political equality in the United States." Robert Dahl, *On Political Equality* (New Haven and London: Yale University Press, 2006), 100–103. Collins and Yeskel, in *Economic Apartheid in America*, propose fifteen "rule changes that would create a more equitable system of financing elections" (152–56).

52. See Collins and Yeskel, *Economic Apartheid in America*, 204–10.

53. Michael Northcott, *A Moral Climate* (Maryknoll, NY: Orbis, 2007), 284.

54. A Tobin-like tax is more widely discussed in Europe and Canada than the United States.

55. WCC testimony.

56. TRIPS agreements—pushed through largely by the United States and huge agribusiness corporations—allow seeds to be patented by companies, effectively denying peasant farmers the right to save seed for replanting. These agreements figured in the story of Ravi and cotton seeds in chapter 7.

57. In 2002, the township of Porter, Pennsylvania passed "the first ordinance in the nation declaring that corporations are not people." See "Township Ordinance Attracts National Attention," *Clarion News* (5 February 2003). Section 5 of the Ordinance states that "corporations shall not be considered to be 'persons' protected by the Constitution of the United States . . . within the township of Porter, Clarion County, Pennsylvania." Subsequently similar ordinances were passed in other municipalities. See Community Environmental Legal Defense fund and Richard Grossman, *The Daniel Penncock Democracy School Curriculum* (Chambersburg, PA: CELDF, 2009), 229–334.

58. They include: the Program on Corporations, Law, and Democracy (POCLAD), Network of Spiritual Progressives, Alliance for Democracy, Community Environmental Legal Defense Fund, Reclaimdemocracy.org, and the U.S. branch of the Women's International League for Peace and Freedom, among others.

59. Union of India v. Union Carbide, before the District Court, Bhopal, 6, cited in International Commission of Jurists, "Access to Justice: Human Rights Abuses Involving Corporations—India" (Geneva: International Commission of Jurists, 2011), 62.

60. Richter, *Holding Corporations Accountable*, 5.

11

Closing Words

The great Spirit, hovering over her creation, exclaims in delight and love, "Oh this is so very *tov*." It is good, a good that generates life. Planet Home brings forth life out of death.

There is hope for the "uncreators." We may accept resurrection from the death of "uncreating." Reborn we may be, reborn as "keepers and tillers" of this magnificent fecund garden, Earth. Created in the image of the God of love—created, that is, to be lovers—we may claim that destiny, seeking evermore fully to love God, self, and neighbor as self, especially neighbors far and near who now are damaged or destroyed by how live.

The reader has mustered moral courage. It is the courage to face squarely the structural evil that inhabits our lives, not because we intend it but because of the social structures—the policies, habits, assumptions, and institutions—that shape our lives. Faith in the God whom Jesus loved calls forth this courage, because to repent of such evil requires recognizing it. Doing so is dangerous. It can break one's heart. A student of mine once said that her education at Seattle University had broken her heart. I gasped. I did not want her to leave with a broken heart. "And," she went on, "my time here also put my heart back together again, much bigger, much stronger." While here, she explained, her eyes had been opened to the agonizing suffering wrought by economic injustice, ecological destruction and other forms of structural sin. Yet her eyes were opened also to the worldwide quest for justice and the power of the Sacred in it.

Daring—as an ongoing practice of morality—to see the devastating impact of economic life as we live it is far less perilous *if* simultaneously we use a second and a third form of vision. The second is seeing "what could and should be"—that is, more just, compassionate, and ecologically sound ways of living. The third kind of vision is seeing ever more fully the life-giving, life-saving Mystery that is God flowing and pouring through all of creation, and working there toward creation's flourishing. This, we have called "mystical seeing." It is down-to-earth, practical.

Christian ethics is charged with helping people meet the moral challenges of each new time and place, guided by the resources of Christian traditions in dialogue with many other bodies of human knowledge. In the case of this book the moral challenge at hand is a dramatic re-orientation, the likes of which the world has never before known: humankind's high-consuming people moving from an unsustainable relationship with planet Earth and exploitative relationships with huge sectors of the human family, to sustainable Earth-human relations marked by steadily diminishing levels of social injustice.

A moral framework emerged herein. The magnitude of the moral challenge we face may render it seemingly impossible. The beauty of a moral framework is its capacity to lay hold of a moral challenge that seems beyond the possible and reveal it as possible by shining a light into the foggy mess and discovering paths through it. The light illumines also where those paths intersect and where they already are being trod by people the world over. These people are at work bringing the seemingly impossible into being.

Christian ethics, I have claimed, is the art of coming to know ever more fully both God and the historical realities of life on Earth, and holding them in one breath, so that we may respond to the latter in light of the former. Where the forces that mask systemic injustice cloud our vision and knowledge of God or of life's realities, a task of Christian ethics is to enable seeing more clearly. My hope is that the journey of this book has, to some small degree, done just that.

The corporate-and-finance driven global economy will change. Earth no longer can support it, and the human urge toward compassion cannot tolerate it. In what direction it changes is up to human beings. God's ancient call to love neighbor as self may help us to direct that change toward social justice and Earth's well-being. Words from the opening serve well in parting: "This book is one tiny part of a much larger human endeavor, the seeming impossibility of which should dissuade no one from joining it. It is the reorienting of human life to render it both sustainable on this Planet Home and characterized by increasing degrees of social justice. In this re-orientation we are called by God and by life itself to celebrate, relish, and stand in awe of Earth's beauty, unfolding complexity, and life-generating goodness."

The test of a Christian ethic is fourfold:

- Does it speak truth about life on Earth, demystifying what is hidden from view by the blinders of power and privilege?
- Does it seek faithfully to know more fully the God revealed in—but not only in—Jesus Christ?

- Does it move people to align themselves with justice-seeking, Earth-honoring, self-respecting neighbor love?
- Does it wed moral vision with pragmatic steps toward that vision?

Whether or not the moral framework proposed herein passes that test remains for the future to tell.

Closing Words

The great Spirit, hovering over her creation, exclaims in delight and love, "Oh this is so very *tov.*" It is good, a good that generates life. Planet Home brings forth life out of death.

There is hope for the "uncreators." We may accept resurrection from the death of "uncreating." Reborn we may be, reborn as "keepers and tillers" of this magnificent fecund garden, Earth. Created in the image of the God of love—created, that is, to be lovers—we may claim that destiny, seeking ever more fully to love God, self, and neighbor, especially neighbors far and near who now are damaged or destroyed by how we live.

The reader has mustered moral courage. It is the courage to face squarely the structural evil that inhabits our lives, not because we intend it but because of the social structures (policies, habits, assumptions, and institutions) that shape our lives. Faith in the God whom Jesus loved calls forth this courage, because to repent of such evil requires recognizing it. Doing so is dangerous. It can break one's heart. A student of mine once said that her education at Seattle University had broken her heart. I gasped. I did not want her to leave with a broken heart. "And," she went on, "my time here also put my heart back together again, much bigger, much stronger." While here, she explained, her eyes had been opened to the agonizing suffering wrought by economic injustice, ecological destruction, and other forms of structural sin. Yet her eyes were opened also to the worldwide quest for justice and the power of the Sacred in it.

Daring—as an ongoing practice of morality—to see the devastating impact of economic life as we live it is far less perilous *if* simultaneously we use a second and a third form of vision. The second is seeing "what could and should be"—that is, more just, compassionate, and ecologically sound ways of living. The third kind of vision is seeing ever more fully the life-giving, life-saving Mystery that is God flowing and pouring through all of creation, and working there toward creation's flourishing. This, we have called "mystical seeing." It is down-to-earth, practical.

Christian ethics is charged with helping people meet the moral challenges of each new time and place, guided by the resources of Christian traditions in dialogue with other bodies of knowledge. In the case of this book the moral challenge at hand is a dramatic reorientation, the likes of which the world has never before known: high-consuming people moving from exploitative

305

relationships with Earth and with huge sectors of the human family, to sustainable Earth-human relations marked by steadily diminishing levels of social injustice.

A moral framework emerged herein. The beauty of a moral framework is its capacity to lay hold of a moral challenge that seems impossible and reveal it as possible by shining a light into the foggy mess and discovering paths through it. The light illumines also where those paths intersect and where they already are being trod by people the world over. These people are at work bringing the seemingly impossible into being.

Christian ethics, I have claimed, is the art of coming to know ever more fully both God and the historical realities of life on Earth, and holding them in one breath, so that we may respond to the latter in light of the former. Where the forces that mask systemic injustice cloud our vision of God or of life's realities, a task of Christian ethics is to enable seeing more clearly. My hope is that the journey of this book has, to some small degree, done just that.

The corporate- and finance-driven global economy will change. Earth no longer can support it, and the human urge toward compassion cannot tolerate it. In what direction it changes is up to human beings. God's ancient call to love neighbor as self may help us to direct that change toward social justice and Earth's well-being. Words from the opening serve well in parting: "This book is one tiny part of a much larger human endeavor, the seeming impossibility of which should dissuade no one from joining it. It is the reorienting of human life to render it both sustainable on this Planet Home and characterized by increasing degrees of social justice. In this reorientation we are called by God and by life itself to celebrate, relish, and stand in awe of Earth's beauty, unfolding complexity, and life-generating goodness."

The test of a Christian ethic is fourfold:

- Does it speak truth about life on Earth, demystifying what is hidden from view by the blinders of power and privilege?
- Does it seek faithfully to know more fully the God revealed in—but not only in—Jesus Christ?
- Does it move people to align themselves with justice-seeking, Earth-honoring, self-respecting neighbor love?
- Does it wed moral vision with pragmatic steps toward that vision?

Whether or not the moral framework proposed herein passes that test remains for the future to tell.

Index

350.org, 134

Acción Ecológica, 209, 234nn37–38
advertising, 99, 100–102, 187–88, 196, 202, 252, 282
advocacy: 127, 157, 246, 267n15, 270n23; bike, 134; economic, 253; legislative, 223, 252–53; public policy, 283; shareholder, 252
agape/agapao, 166–68, 171, 173, 175, 183–84, 186, 194n9
agriculture: adequate to feed world, 46n30; commercial, 188–93, 222; community-supported, 207, 253, 281; greenhouse gas emissions and, 129, 233n15; local and regional, 207, 242, 250, 295n10; small-scale, 242, 250, 297n10; sustainable, 233n24, 250
Agyeman, Julian, 38, 234n43
aheb, 167–68, 183–84
Albrecht, Gloria, 109n12, 269n8
Ambrose, 94–95, 211, 213
American Sustainable Business Council, 286
Amnesty International, 134, 136n36
Andolsen, Barbara Hilkert, 194n22, 194n24
Aquinas, Thomas, 174, 211

Balasuriya, Tissa, 262, 269n40
banks/banking, 45n9, 226–28, 242; local or community-based, 229, 233, 242, 257, 280–82
baptism, 20, 261, 264, 266, 270n50
Bartholomew, his Holiness Patriarch, 59
Basel Ban Amendment, 276

beef production, 69, 129; greenhouse gas and, 111n45, 129, 215; protein and, 129
beef, not eating, 215, 255
Beguines, 141–42, 161n4
Bernard of Clairvaux, 171
Bernays, Edward, 100, 110n34
Berry, Thomas, 135n16, 203, 233n12
Birch, Bruce, 195n48, 247, 268n16
Bitter Drink (film), 235
blood minerals, 83–86, 257–60
Blood in the Mobile (film), 258
Bloomquist, Karen, 195n49
Boff, Leonardo, 143, 161n10
Bonhoeffer, Dietrich, 49, 66–68, 78n1, 80n41, 93, 144, 147, 156, 162nn22–23, 163n38, 170, 178, 195n38
Borg, Marcus, 64
Boulding, Kenneth, 110n41
Bowles, Samuel, 235n76
boycott, 11, 117, 159–60, 220–22, 242, 246, 252, 255, 257, 284–85
Brandeis, Louis, 222
Bretton Woods, 110n39
Broad, Robin, 296nn2–3, 298n34
Brookfield, Stephen, 63, 88–89, 99, 105, 109n13, 109n17, 109n20, 111n44, 136n22
Brubaker, Pamela, xi, 34, 46nn25–26
Brueggemann, Walter, 87, 109nn9–10, 135n4, 263
Bt cotton, 188, 191
Buber, Martin, 174
Buhrs, T., 212
Bullard, Robert, 38, 47n38, 47n40
business: agribusiness, 69–70, 188–90, 197, 207, 299n56; local and regional,

CPSIA information can be obtained at www.ICGtesting.com
Printed in the USA
BVOW03s0845061114

373881BV00004B/67/P